# Research in Technical Communication

Contributors

**Dale-Marie Wilson, Aqueasha M. Martin et al.**

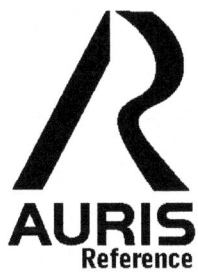

www.aurisreference.com

**Research in Technical Communication**

Contributors: Dale-Marie Wilson, Aqueasha M. Martin et al.

**Published by Auris Reference Limited**
www.aurisreference.com

United Kingdom

**Copyright 2016**

The information in this book has been obtained from highly regarded resources. The copyrights for individual articles remain with the authors, as indicated. All chapters are distributed under the terms of the Creative Commons Attribution License, which permit unrestricted use, distribution, and reproduction in any medium, provided the original author and source are credited.

**Notice**

Contributors, whose names have been given on the book cover, are not associated with the Publisher. The editors and the Publisher have attempted to trace the copyright holders of all material reproduced in this publication and apologise to copyright holders if permission has not been obtained. If any copyright holder has not been acknowledged, please write to us so we may rectify.

Reasonable efforts have been made to publish reliable data. The views articulated in the chapters are those of the individual contributors, and not necessarily those of the editors or the Publisher. Editors and/or the Publisher are not responsible for the accuracy of the information in the published chapters or consequences from their use. The Publisher accepts no responsibility for any damage or grievance to individual(s) or property arising out of the use of any material(s), instruction(s), methods or thoughts in the book.

**Research in Technical Communication**

ISBN: 978-1-78154-763-2

British Library Cataloguing in Publication Data
A CIP record for this book is available from the British Library

Printed in the United Kingdom

# Contents

*List of Abbreviations* .......................................................................... *vii*
*List of Contributors*............................................................................... *ix*
*Preface*.................................................................................................... *xi*

**Chapter 1**     **iTech: An Interactive Virtual Assistant for Technical Communication ... 1**
Dale-Marie Wilson, Aqueasha M. Martin and Juan E. Gilbert

**Chapter 2**     **Innovative Approaches to Teaching Technical Communication .......... 29**
Richard Selfe, Tracy Bridgeford and Karla Saari Kitalong

**Chapter 3**     **Contemporary Research Methodologies in Technical Communication ....................................................................................... 229**
Brian McNely, Clay Spinuzzi and Christa Teston

**Chapter 4**     **Near Field Communication: Technology and Market Trends ............ 249**
Gabriella Arcese , Giuseppe Campagna, Serena Flammini and Olimpia Martucci

**Chapter 5**     **A Survey on Communication Technologies and Requirements for Internet of Electric Vehicles ..... 277**
Islam Safak Bayram and Ioannis Papapanagiotou

           **Citations** ...................................................................................... **319**

           **Index**............................................................................................. **321**

# List of Abbreviations

| | |
|---|---|
| AMI | Advanced Metering Infrastructure |
| ASR | Automatic Speech Recognition |
| CSCW | Computer-Supported Cooperative Work |
| DSL | Digital Subscriber Lines |
| EMU | Energy Management Units |
| EV | Electric Vehicles |
| FAR | Faculty Activity Report |
| FIPSE | Fund for the Improvement of Post-Secondary Education |
| GIS | Geographic Information Systems |
| GSM | Group Special Mobile |
| GSMA | Group Special Mobile Association |
| GT | Grounded Theory |
| GUI | Graphical User Interface |
| HAN | Home Area Network |
| HCI | Human Computer Interaction |
| IEC | International Electrotechnical Commission |
| IOEV | Internet of Electric Vehicles |
| IP | Internet Protocol |
| ITV | Interactive Television |
| KR | Knowledge Repository |
| LTE | Long Term Evaluation |
| MNO | Mobile Network Operators |
| NFC | Near Field Communication |
| NIPP | National Infrastructure Protection Plan |
| NIST | National Institute of Standards and Technology |
| PLC | Power Line Communications |
| QRA | Question Resolution Algorithm |
| SAE | Society of Automotive Engineers |
| SALT | Speech Application Language Tags |
| SIM | Subscriber Identity Module |
| SP | Service Providers |
| STC | Scientific and Technical Communication |
| TTS | Text to Speech |
| TVC | Tourism Value Chain |
| UGS | Unsolicited Grant Service |
| UTEP | University of Texas at El Paso |
| VIN | Vehicle Identification Number |
| WER | Word Error Rate |
| WLAN | Wireless Local Area Network |
| WMN | Wireless Mesh Networks |
| WRAN | Wireless Regional Area Network |

# List of Contributors

**Dale-Marie Wilson**
University of North Carolina at Charlotte, USA

**Aqueasha M. Martin**
Clemson University USA

**Juan E. Gilbert**
Clemson University USA

**Richard Selfe**
Humanities department at Michigan Technological University

**Tracy Bridgeford**
Department of English at the University of Nebraska at Omaha

**Karla Saari Kitalong**
University of Central Florida in Orlando

**Brian McNely**
University of Kentucky

**Clay Spinuzzi**
University of Texas, Austin

**Christa Teston**
Ohio State University

**Gabriella Arcese**
Department of Business Studies, Roma Tre University, via Silvio D'Amico 77, 00145 Rome, Italy

**Giuseppe Campagna**
Department of Business Studies, Roma Tre University, via Silvio D'Amico 77, 00145 Rome, Italy

**Serena Flammini**
Department of Business Studies, Roma Tre University, via Silvio D'Amico 77, 00145 Rome, Italy

**Olimpia Martucci**
Department of Business Studies, Roma Tre University, via Silvio D'Amico 77, 00145 Rome, Italy

**Islam Safak Bayram**
Qatar Environment and Energy Research Institute, Qatar Foundation, Doha, Qatar

**Ioannis Papapanagiotou**
Computer and Information Technology, Purdue University, West Lafayette, IN 47907, USA.

# Preface

Technical communication is a means to convey scientific, engineering, or other technical information. Individuals in a variety of contexts and with varied professional credentials engage in technical communication. The text *Research in Technical Communication* presents the principles of data collection and interpretation or the methodological distinctions of a particular method appropriate to technical communication research. In first chapter, the motivation and design of iTech are discussed. Innovative approaches to teaching technical communication have been presented in second chapter. Contemporary research methodologies in technical communication have been focused in third chapter. The aim of fourth chapter is to provide a comprehensive review oriented to the analysis of the scientific contributions related to near field communication (NFC) technology, to deepen them through an analysis of its analyze the technical-economical elements. In last chapter, we provide a comprehensive survey on the communication requirements, the standards and the candidate technologies towards the Internet of electric vehicles (IoEV).

# Chapter 1

## ITECH: AN INTERACTIVE VIRTUAL ASSISTANT FOR TECHNICAL COMMUNICATION

Dale-Marie Wilson[1], Aqueasha M. Martin[2] and Juan E. Gilbert[2]
[1]University of North Carolina at Charlotte, USA
[2]Clemson University USA

## INTRODUCTION

A manual accompanies almost every product or device. Manuals are usually included with products or services to provide customer assistance and provide technical information to users. However, Thimbleby states, "User manuals are the scapegoat of bad system design." (Major, 1985; Thimbleby, 1996). Technical communications are provided through several mediums and manuals are one example of this. Other mediums range from interactive animation to virtual reality (Hailey, 2004), with each new medium attempting to improve upon the drawbacks of the previous one. The first medium introduced was the paper manual. However, issues with paper manuals have been widely documented, especially by technicians in the armed forces. Problems include lack of portability, inaccuracy, and increasing content and complexity (Ventura, 1988). To improve upon the drawbacks of paper manuals alternative mediums such as online manuals for technical communication emerged.

Although, alternative mediums have improved upon some of the drawbacks of paper manuals, traditional technical communication mediums still often entail a timely search through a large paper manual or rigorous cognitive processing to generate an appropriate query to search an online manual. As a result, consumers oftentimes spend much more time searching for an appropriate solution, have trouble finding an appropriate solution, or become frustrated and result to other means to find a solution. Research suggests that when choosing a technical communication medium one should consider the needs of the audience, the functionalities of the new information technology and how the functionalities are to be utilized, and the application of the new medium and if it will prove the concepts for introducing the new medium. Therefore, alternative mediums for technical communication should also be compared for their ability to communicate information to consumers effectively and with reduced frustration.

In this chapter, iTech is introduced. ITech is an interactive technical assistant that was designed to assist users in finding information about a product, in this case vi, a programming editor. In this paper, the motivation and design of iTech are discussed. Furthermore, the design and results of a research study conducted to examine the usability, effectiveness, and efficiency of iTech are presented.

# LITERATURE REVIEW

## Technical Communication

Technical communication refers to the process of delivering technical information to the user. Albing defines it as, "...the creation, control, delivery, and maintenance of distributed information across the enterprise and in a network that includes sources and users." (pp. 67) (Albing, 1996). An effective technical document is determined by the following factors (Zachary et al., 2001):

- Is the analysis of the communication problem complete?
- Is the goal/task to be explained clearly identified?
- Is the vocabulary used to explain the goal comprehensive and does it follow conventional guidelines?

These factors are used for evaluating all mediums of technical communications. However, as the need for manuals has grown, little investment has been placed in the development of these manuals. Paper manuals often need updates; therefore, become outdated quickly, are hard to understand, inaccessible, erroneous, and difficult to search if the index is not designed properly. On the other hand, while online manuals provide additional benefits such decreased search time, smaller documentation, and better search techniques (Barnett, 1998), they also require increased query pre-processing for either the user or the search engine. With the introduction of web-based mediums such as animations and virtual reality has also come the concern of available technologies, end user expectations, and usercentered design (Zachary et al., 2001). Therefore, this suggests that mediums that provide higher degrees of user satisfaction and ease of use may be important to delivering effective technical communication.

## Animated Agents and Interactive Assistants

Interactive assistants aim to aid users in managing their environment (Kirste & Rapp, 2001). Because computers are continually becoming more ubiquitous, permeating aspects of people's daily lives, there is a need for an efficient interface between users and computers. Interactive assistants address this need by providing natural, intuitive, and effective interaction between people and computers (Oviatt et al., 2000). Interactive assistants typically contain multimodal features including speech input and output, gesture and handwriting recognition, and animated agents or avatars. These features provide users with interaction choices that can circumvent personal and/or environmental limitations, require little or no training. They also have great potential to promote new forms of computing and expand the accessibility of computing to a diverse group of users ((Lester et al., 1997).

Interactive assistants have been used in various types of user help systems including training, education, and marketing [11, 12]. Additionally, research has been conducted on how the inclusion of such agents impacts user's interactions with the system. Some of the earlier agents were designed in the domain of education. Rosis et al. designed the XDMAgent, an animated character that aids in illustrating interface objects for software development in user-adapted interfaces and explain which tasks may be performed and how (Rosis et al., 1999). Steve an animated pedagogical agent was created to help students perform procedural tasks (Johnson & Rickel, 1997). Other early animated agents such as Adele, Herman the Bug, Cosmo and PPP-Persona were also introduced as providing user assistance (Johnson & Rickel, 1997).

However, with all the advances in animated agent help systems, research aimed at the usefulness of conversational interactive assistants for assisting users in searching technical communication in particular is limited. Additionally, minimal research has been conducted on how the introduction of such agents and their design impacts user's interactions with technical communication documentation. iTech is an interactive technical assistant that was designed and developed to address some of the limitations of current mediums for technical communication while improving user satisfaction and the user experience by taking advantage of the opportunities provided by interactive assistants.

# RESEARCH METHODOLOGY

## Design

iTech is an interactive virtual assistant that was designed and developed to address the limitations of the current mediums of technical communication including paper-based and online systems. More specifically, iTech was designed to address the limitations associated with current technical documentation including understandability, portability, accessibility, accuracy, search time, and the ability to make updates. Although these limitations do not apply to all mediums of technical communication, there is an application limitation for each medium. In the process of designing iTech several additional limitations associated with automatic speech recognition (ASR) engines were encountered, i.e. population of the question-database and conversational questioning answering. In the design of iTech, the goal was to provide iTech with the ability to understand natural language queries from a variety of speakers as is without any additional training. To do so, is was necessary to eliminate the preprocessing step that is associated with many other techniques. In addition, it was desirable to have iTech be able to effectively answer (return an appropriate answer) even if the question asked did not appear in the database.

The accuracy of automated speech recognition (ASR) engines for speaker-independent systems has a higher word error rate (WER) than those that are trained. The WER can be reduced by a limited grammar, but natural language questions necessitate a larger grammar to account for the questions that may be asked. To allow for a large grammar, the database used to generate the grammar must be populated with all relevant questions that a user may ask. Each answer must then be mapped to a relevant question. Additionally, each answer is not restricted to a specific question. Because of this the database must be populated with a massive amount data. Furthermore, current techniques for conversational question answering require pre-processing (parts-of-speech tagging, semantic interpretation) of queries before execution and removing what the authors argue to be relevant information.

iTech utilizes the Answers First (A1) approach for conversational question answering (Wilson et al., 2010). In A1, unlike many other information retrieval or natural language processing techniques, requires no language processing before the query is executed. The users query once recognized is sent to a server and decomposed into bigrams (word pairs). The bigrams are matched to a repository of questions using a question resolution algorithm and the question with the highest concentration of matched terms is returned. This process continues, prompting the user appropriately until an appropriate solution is found. iTech has a client-server architecture as shown in Figure 4.

iTech's Architecture. The user initiates the conversation with iTech by pressing a button to speak and ask a question. The built-in speech recognition engine, Microsoft English ASR Version 5 Engine, recognizes the user's question and passes the recognized speech to the browser environment of the page where the Speech Application Language Tags (SALT) are hosted (Cisco

Systems Inc. et al, 2002). Additional client-side scripts then manipulate the SALT elements. The resulting text of the recognized speech is then sent as a request to the server.

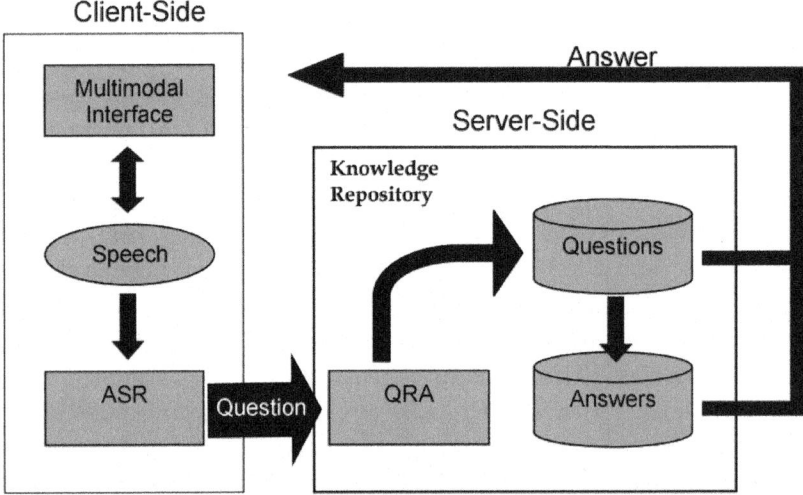

**Figure. 1.** iTech's architecture.

The server side consists of the Knowledge Repository (KR) that is populated with question answer pairs generated from the chosen manual (Wilson et al., 2010). The Question Resolution Algorithm (QRA) module resolves the recognized question with the KR, identifies the question-answer pair with the highest concentration of matched terms and retrieves the relevant answer (Wilson et al., 2010). The retrieved answer is then displayed to the user.

The system works in the following way. A user initiates the system by opening up the application's browser. Once loaded, iTech welcomes the user and tells them of his purpose and how to ask a question. The user presses the 'Push 2 Speak' button and asks their question. The browser interacts with the user and identifies the exact content of the question. The question is converted into text and sent to the QRA module (Wilson et al., 2010). The QRA module performs three tasks. First the users text is broken into bigrams or word pairs. Second, the QRA matches the question's terms against a corresponding table of word pairs residing in the KR. Third, the KR finds the question with the highest concentration of terms and the indexed answer to that question is returned to the iTech's interface with a link to the corresponding document. Finally, the answer is displayed for the user.

iTech's interface is multimodal and can be housed on any personal computing device with a microphone or the ability to add a microphone. The microphone is used to collect the user's speech. The graphical user interface (GUI) consists of two frames: the Navigation frame and the Content frame. The Navigation frame consists of an animated agent and the Speech Application Language Tags (SALT). The presence of a likeable animated pedagogical agent has been shown to improve student performance by enhancing the student's desire to learn (Baylor & Ryu, 2003). This desire is increased as the student forges a personal connection with the agent, thereby making the learning experience more enjoyable. However, the agent must possess certain characteristics for this to be effective. The agent must be engaging, person-like, and credible; promoting relationships with the learner requires the presence of these characteristics (Baylor & Ryu, 2003). iTech is male. This choice was deliberate and influenced because findings suggest that male pedagogical agents are perceived as more extraverted and agreeable resulting in a more satisfying experience by the learner (Baylor & Kim, 2003). The ethnicity of iTech was chosen as African-American. This choice was determined by study results that indicated AfricanAmericans were more inclined to choose an agent of the same ethnicity than Caucasians (Baylor et al., 2003). The agent was generated using SitePal and embedded into a HTML file (Oddcast Inc., 2008). The SitePal application allows for greater developer control over the appearance of iTech. To enable the agent's perceived participation in conversations, SALT and JavaScript were used.

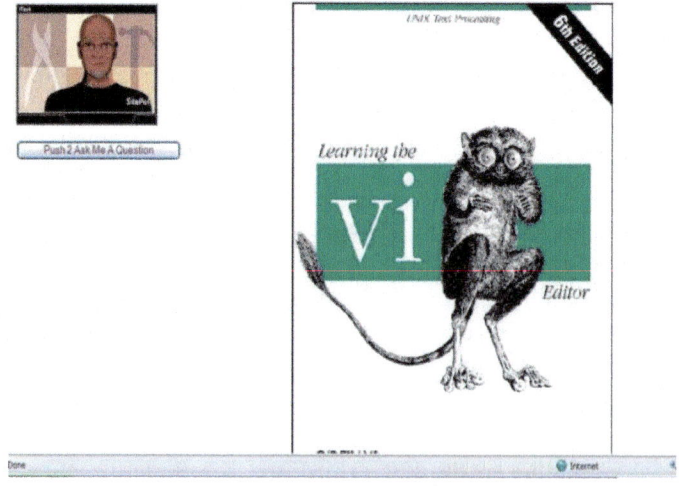

**iTech:** Hello, I am iTech ....
**iTech:** I am here to help you with the vi editor
**iTech:** When you need assistance. Just push the button to ask me a question

**Figure. 2.** iTech's welcome screen and welcome instructions.

JavaScript was used to provide text-to-speech (TTS) capabilities to the agent. SALT is then used to enable iTech's hearing. SALT is embedded in a compliant browser and using Microsoft's recognition engine allows iTech to listen to user's questions. Once the question is recognized, the question resolution algorithm is applied, an answer is identified and retrieved and is displayed in the Content Frame.

When iTech is loaded for the first time, the Content frame displays the cover of the vi manual (See Figure 2. iTech's welcome screen and welcome instructions). Once interaction begins, the Content frame dynamically displays the solutions retrieved by the question resolution algorithm (QRA. The QRA is initiated by a PHP script that connects to a MySQL database that houses the KR.

## Equipment

To test the iTech design, a usability study to measure performance and user satisfaction was conducted. The authors set out to answer three research questions related to search time and user satisfaction:

- Does iTech improve search time compared to other technical communication mediums, namely the book and online mediums?
- Does iTech improve task completion time compared to other technical communication mediums, namely the book and online mediums?
- Does the introduction of an interactive agent, increase user satisfaction compared to other technical communication mediums?

Search time refers to the amount of time the participant spent referencing their assigned medium before the correct solution was found. After finding the correct solution, the user had to read the solution. The task completion time was the amount of time the participant spent referencing their assigned medium before the participant read the correct solution. User satisfaction refers to the effectiveness, efficiency and user's overall experience with the system.

The experiment was setup in a private room furnished with one large table and five chairs. All testing was conducted on a Gateway 2000e CPU running the Windows XP operating system and equipped with a 17" Sony Monitor, a standard scroll mouse, and a Logitech USB headset. In addition, we downloaded Internet Explorer 6.x, the Microsoft Internet Speech Add-in 1.0., and the SecureCRT 4.07 software on the machine. All user interactions were recorded with a Sony 700x Digital Handy cam video recorder.

## Participants

Seventy-four college level students were recruited as participants. Institutional Review Board (IRB) approval was granted by Auburn University and all participants signed informed consent forms before participating in the study. Participants had little or no exposure with the vi editor before participating in the study. The vi editor is a short hand editor used on Unix and Linux operating systems. Computer programmers often used the vi editor on these systems because it provided an efficient editing tool at the Unix/Linux command line; however, the vi editor has a huge learning curve. The vi editor is not a WYSIWYG (What You See Is What You Get) editor. It requires the user to know several keyboard shortcuts before using vi. As such, the vi editor is very difficult to use without proper training. Today, most users of Unix/Linux systems prefer WYSIWYG editors like pico; therefore, very few college students are familiar with vi. Many participants in the study had some experience using either Microsoft Office Word or Corel Word Perfect. To ensure that all participants had similar experience using a personal computer and editing text documents, our recruitment was focused on student enrolled in at least one course from the College of Engineering.

## Experiment

The usability evaluation was designed as a controlled experiment. To reduce the casual effects of other factors, the following controls were applied:

- All participants sat in the same chair in the same room with the researcher.
- Each participant completed the same task in the same order. The only independent variable that changed was the medium of technical communication.
- Participants were randomly selected to use the book manual, online manual, or iTech.
- Participants who were assigned the iTech medium used the Logitech USB headset.
- The delay time before starting the survey was the same for each participant. The preexperiment survey was started when the participant arrived in the experiment room. The post-experiment survey was started immediately after the participant finished his or her task.
- Participants were asked not to discuss the experiment with others to ensure that all participants had equal knowledge of the experiment.

The experiment was conducted for three different mediums. Medium I was a book manual entitled Learning the vi Editor published by O'Reilly. Medium II was the combination of a search engine and the electronic PDF version of the book manual used for Medium I. The combination of a search engine and the PDF was used to ensure that each medium being tested had the same content. To generate this medium, each section of the PDF was separated and saved as an individual file. Once the electronic manual was decomposed into individual sections, Google Desktop (Google Inc., 2009) was installed on the experiment computer. The preferences for Google Desktop were set to search a specific folder on the experiment computer's hard drive. This was to once again insure that the content of Medium II was the same as that of Mediums I and III. Medium II could be accessed through a floating desktop bar that was positioned in the top right corner of the monitor. When a participant entered a search query a list of all relevant documents was returned. Medium III was iTech. iTech was populated with information from the book manual. The answers indexed in iTech were the same electronic copies of the individual sections of the manual used in the online medium (Medium II). Consistency in content was maintained across all three mediums to reduce the probability that any difference in search and/or task completion were not due to any variable other than medium.

Twenty participants were assigned Medium I, twenty-four participants Medium II, and thirty participants Medium III at random. At the beginning of each experiment each participant was asked to fill out a pre-experiment questionnaire. Participants were then given an information sheet explaining the experiment and an instruction sheet that included tasks that the participants were asked to complete. Participants were assigned a medium and it was explained to the participant that they would be using the medium in completing the task. If the participant was assigned Medium I, they were given the book Learning the vi Editor. If the participant was assigned Medium II, the participant was directed to the floating desktop bar in the right hand corner of the screen and was instructed that he or she would be using a search engine linked to an online manual to assist in completing the task. If Medium III was assigned, the participant was instructed to put on and adjust the Logitech headset and iTech was launched. The participant was then directed to the SecureCRT terminal containing a file named example.txt to be edited. The participant was informed that they would be accessing the vi editor and the file from the current terminal. Lastly, the video recorder was started and the participant began his or her task.

The tasks were selected from the Exploring Microsoft Office 2003 textbook (Grauer, 2003). Participants were asked to figure out how to open the specified file and edit it. Editing included deleting individual words, changing words, changing characters, deleting and inserting sentences, and deleting and inserting paragraphs. When the participants completed the assigned tasks, they were then asked to fill out a post-experiment survey.

## Data Collection

During the course of the experiment, several approaches were used to collect data including video recordings and surveys. Table 1. Experimental Instruments and Measures provides an overview of the experimental measures and instruments used. Pre-experiment surveys were used to gather demographic information about participants and to determine whether they met the criteria established for classification as a vi editor novice. In addition, questions were asked about the participant's familiarity with computers such as how long they had used a computer, how often they use a computer, computer programming experience, and experience with specific software applications like word processors.

Performance data was collected using a video camera. Recordings were used to measure search, reading, and task completion times. Characteristics of spoken queries such as the average number of spoken queries per search per user, the number of recognition errors, and the total number of spoken terms per query were also derived from the participants' utterances. Informal and formal user observations were also employed to gather performance data.

Post-experiment questionnaires were used to gather user satisfaction data. Two postexperiment questionnaires were designed for the experiment. One was administered to participants that used iTech and the other was administered to all other participants. Part I of the questionnaire was identical in both versions of the questionnaire. It gathered overall participant ratings using six bi-polar rating scales. Part II of the questionnaire included a series of Likert-like scales where participants were asked to rate their reactions to the system. This part of the questionnaire included statements concerning the medium's ease of use and intuitiveness. The version of the questionnaire designed for iTech included statements concerning participant's reactions to the agent. Lastly, each questionnaire included a section where participants could share suggestions or comments regarding the medium assigned.

**Table 1.** Experimental Instruments and Measures

| Instrument | Description |
|---|---|
| Pre-experiment Questionnaire | User background, demographics, computer literacy, etc. |
| Performance data | Time, QRA accuracy |
| User Observations | Qualitative and quantitative observations |
| Post-experiment Questionnaire | User satisfaction |

# RESULTS

For the purposes of this paper, the authors will focus on results related to search time, task completion time and user satisfaction. The Jmp Statistical Software package was used to analyze the data collected for each of these measures (SAS Institute, 1984).

## Participant Analysis

An analysis of participant data shows that participants' ages ranged from 18 to 27 years with a mean age of 20 years (See Table 2). Of these, 71% were male and 29% were female. Participant's average number of years of computer use was 12 and the minimum number of years of computer use was 8. Therefore, the majority of the participants were comfortable using a computer.

Table 2. Participant Background Data

| Measurement | Medium I N = 20 | Medium II N = 24 | Medium III N = 30 | Total |
|---|---|---|---|---|
| Average Age | 19.15 | 19.22 | 22 | 20 |
| % female | 20% | 37.5% | 23.33% | 26.67% |
| Avg. years of computer use | 8.3 | 16.0 | 11.53 | 11.94 |
| English as a 2nd Language | N/A | N/A | 6.67% | N/A |

## Performance results (search time and task completion)

To determine if iTech provided an improvement in search time compared to the book and online mediums, an analysis of the distribution of search times for each medium was performed. Additionally, the Shapiro-Wilk's test for normality was used for its resilience to the outliers present in the data. Table 3. Mean Search Time by Medium displays mean and standard deviation for each medium. This analysis suggests that Medium III (iTech) had the fastest average search time.

**Table 3.** Mean Search Times by Medium

| Measurement in secs | Book | Online | iTech |
|---|---|---|---|
| Mean | 119.55 | 176.49 | 38.13 |
| Standard Deviation | 145.66 | 235.43 | 74.2 |

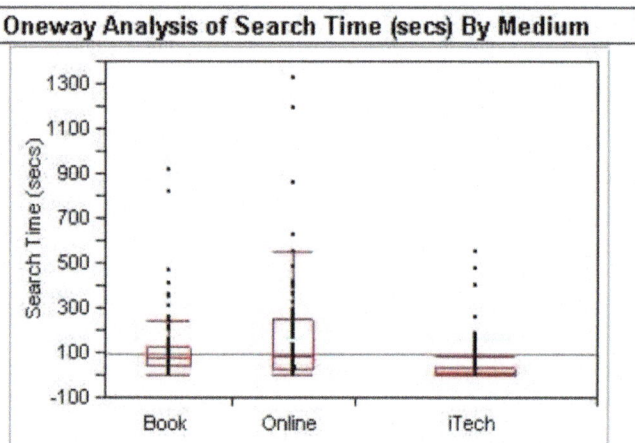

**Figure. 3.** Side-by-Side Box Plots of Medium Search Times.

The Shapiro-Wilk's test provided very strong evidence to reject the null hypothesis that states that the means are normally distributed. With $\alpha = 0.05$ the Book medium [W = 0.6195, p = 0.0000], Online medium [W = 0.6811, p = 0.0000] and iTech medium [W = 0.5174, p = 0.0000] all strongly support this deduction. Because of this finding, the Kruskal-Wallis or Wilcoxon test was used to check for statistical significance.

The Kruskal-Wallis nonparametric analysis of variance provides a method for coping with data that contain extreme outliers and that have more than 2 independent variables. It does this by replacing the observation values by their ranks in a single sample and applying a one-way analysis of the F-test on the rank-transformed data (NIST, 2003). The result of this test [$F(1,2) = 106.9946$, $p < .0001$] is a Kruskal-Wallis test statistic of 106.9946 with a p-value $< .0001$ from a chi-square distribution with 2 degrees of freedom. The null hypothesis for this test states that the search time means for the mediums are equal. The Kruskal-Wallis test provided strong evidence to reject this null hypothesis. Thereby, there is statistical significance that supports that the search time means are different. Thus, there is strong evidence to reject the null hypothesis that states that the means were equal. The KruskalWallis test allows for the comparison between three or more unpaired groups, however it does not allow for deductions between specific pairs or means. The resulting p-value, which is very small, indicates that the deduction can be made that the difference in the group means is not a coincidence. However, this does not mean that every group differs from every other group. The Kruskal-Wallis test only determines that at least one group differs from one of the others. Thus, a post-test was applied to determine which groups differed from the other groups.

The Tukey-Kramer test analyzes data of unequal sample sizes and determines whether the differences between all existing pairs are due to coincidence (NIST, 2003). The results of the Tukey-Kramer test provided very strong evidence that the differences in the pairs of means were statistically significant (See Table 4). The positive values between each pair of means indicate that their differences are significantly different. Thus, there is sufficient evidence to deduce that the independent variable of medium type had a statistically significant effect on the search times, with the search times for the iTech medium being the most expeditious. Next an analysis was performed to determine the effects of search time on task completion time.

**Table 4.** Tukey-Kramer Test Results

|  | Online | Book | iTech |
|---|---|---|---|
| Online | - | 3.368 | 91.582 |
| Book | 3.698 | - | 35.528 |
| iTech | 91.582 | 35.528 | - |

The same tests were applied to medium search times to task completion times. The mean task completion times are displayed in Table 5. Mean Task Completion Time by and the normality spreads are shown in Figure 4. Side-by-Side Box Plot of Medium Task Completion Time. Preliminary observations indicate that Medium I (Book medium) had the fastest average task completion time. The Shapiro-Wilk's test did not however provide sufficient evidence to either strongly reject or accept the null hypothesis that states that the means are normally distributed. With $\alpha = 0.05$ the Book medium [W = 0.9395, p = 0.229], Online medium [W = 0.9664, p = 0.582] and iTech medium [W = 0.9501, p = 0.199] all results recommend the failure to reject the null hypothesis, indicating that the distributions are fairly normal. As a result, the Kruskal-Wallis was used to check for statistical significance.

**Table 5.** Mean Task Completion Time by Medium

| Measurement | Book (secs) | Online (secs) | iTech (secs) |
|---|---|---|---|
| Mean | 1360.58 | 1666.63 | 1377.87 |
| Standard Deviation | 290.95 | 500.1 | 420.87 |

An application of the Kruskal-Wallis yielded no significant differences. The result of this test [$F(1,2) = 5.7065$, $p = 0.0577$] suggests a failure to reject the null hypothesis that states that the differences in the mean task completion times is due to coincidence. Therefore, there is no statistical significance that indicates the task completion time means are different. An investigation as to the cause of this effect, led to the effect of reading times. Reading time was recorded as the time the participant spent reading and understanding the solution once it was presented to the user by the respective medium. This recorded time represented the time from the appearance of the solution on the monitor to the time the participant touched the keyboard. Results are shown in Table 6. Mean Read Times by Medium and Figure 5. Sideby-Side Box Plots of Medium Read Times.

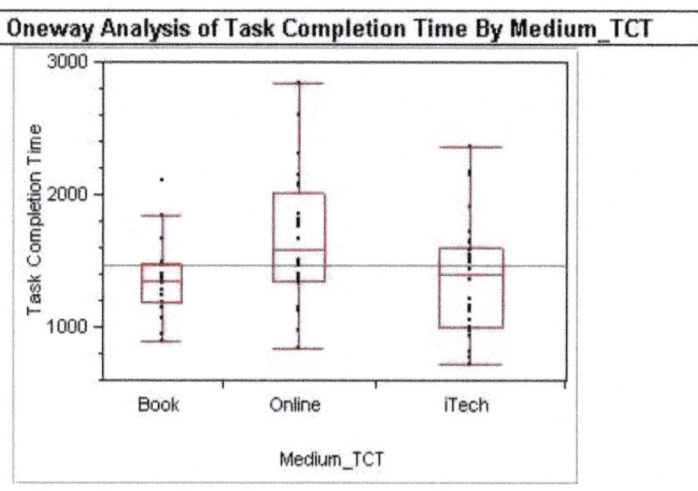

**Figure. 4.** Side-by-Side Box Plots of Medium Task Completion Time

**Table 6.** Mean Read Times by Medium

| Measurement | Book (secs) | Online (secs) | iTech (secs) |
|---|---|---|---|
| Mean | 42.36 | 33.09 | 47.77 |
| Standard Deviation | 38.34 | 33.08 | 45.34 |

Preliminary observations show that there is very little difference between the mean read times for the different mediums. Application of the Shapiro-Wilk's test for normality yielded these results; Medium I (book medium) [W=0.7854, p<.0000] and Medium III (iTech medium) [W = 0.7694, p < .0000] and provides strong evidence that the means are not normally distributed. As the Kruskal-Wallis test is just as effective on normal distributions and allows for consistency of applied tests, it was applied to the read time data. On application of the test, the result [F(1,2) = 9.1906, p = 0.0101] indicates that there is evidence that the difference between the means is statistically significant. However, further investigation as to which pairs were significantly different was required. The Tukey-Kramer test was applied and it demonstrated that only the difference between the online and iTech mediums was statistically significant. With respect to task completion time, it was observed that participants spent more time reading online than with the Book medium. When a solution was found, several participants' encountered difficulties understanding the text, therefore although iTech found solutions faster, participants read the solutions longer than with the Book medium. It should be noted that the solutions were all identical regardless of the medium used.

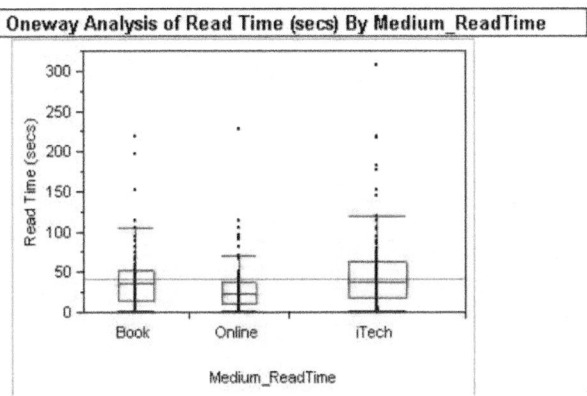

**Figure. 5.** Side-by-Side Box Plots of Medium Read Times.

Also, a significant proportion of participants did not read the solution carefully and as a result either had to return to the solution several times, or implemented an incorrect action that led them further away from the correct action. These results suggest improvements in the content and understandability of technical communications may increase the improvements in search time provided by the iTech medium. Lastly, performance analysis of task success showed that nearly all participants were able to successfully complete the assigned tasks. Task success was determined by comparing the file updated by each participant to a correct version of the updated file. 95% of all participants successfully completed the task using one of the three mediums provided.

## User Satisfaction

To get a better idea of users reactions to iTech compared to the book and online mediums a post-experiment questionnaire was used to collect data using two rating scales. The first rating scale included a five-point bi-polar scale. This scale presented several qualities that might influence usability. The rating means are shown in Table 7. Bi-polar Rating Scales assessing General Usability. For each of these scales a higher rating indicates a number closer to the positive side with the exception of the anchor usable to not usable. For this anchor a higher rating indicates a number closer to the negative side. A quick review suggests that the participants' reactions to iTech were generally more favorable than the other two mediums. However, investigation of just the means does not provide a complete picture of the users' evaluations. For example, although iTech's rating of the Terrible-Wonderful anchor is lower than the Online medium, iTech received 19 ratings at levels 4 - 5 while the Online medium received only 16. Therefore, an analysis of the entire distribution for each rating was conducted.

Table 7. Bi-polar Rating Scales Assessing General Usability

| Bi-Polar Scale Anchors | Book Ratings (Mean) | Online Ratings (Mean) | iTech Ratings (Mean) |
| --- | --- | --- | --- |
| Terrible - Wonderful | 3.17 | 3.55 | 3.29 |
| Frustrating - Satisfying | 3.23 | 2.90 | 3.0 |
| Dull - Stimulating | 2.93 | 3.62 | 3.79 |
| Usable - Not Usable | 2.4 | 2.31 | 2.57 |
| Boring - Fun | 2.9 | 3.38 | 3.64 |

Three scales were used to examine the usability of iTech: 1) terrible – wonderful, 2) dull – stimulating and 3) boring – fun. The five-point rating inherently assigns the score of 3 a neutral rating, with scores 1 and 2 being negative and scores 3 and 4 positive. For the book medium, 33.33% of the participants rated that medium with a score of 4 or higher on the terrible to wonderful scale. The online medium received 53.33% and iTech 65.52% for the same score values (See Figure 6. Terrible Wonderful Distributions).

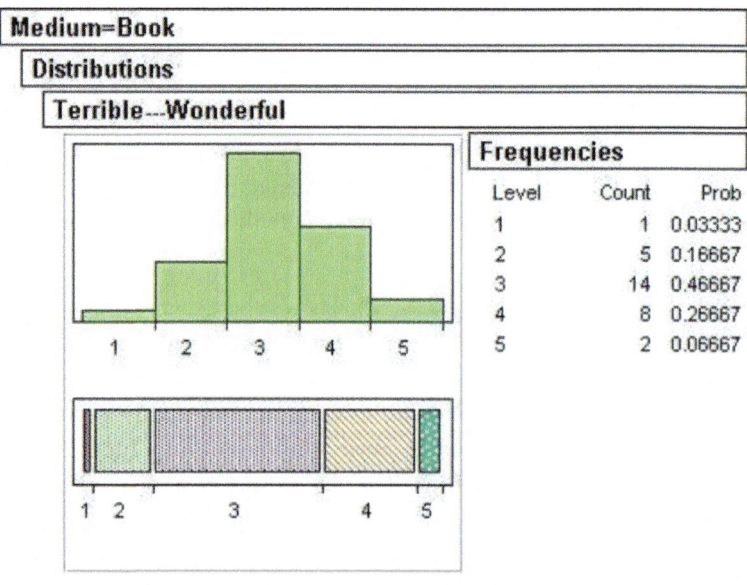

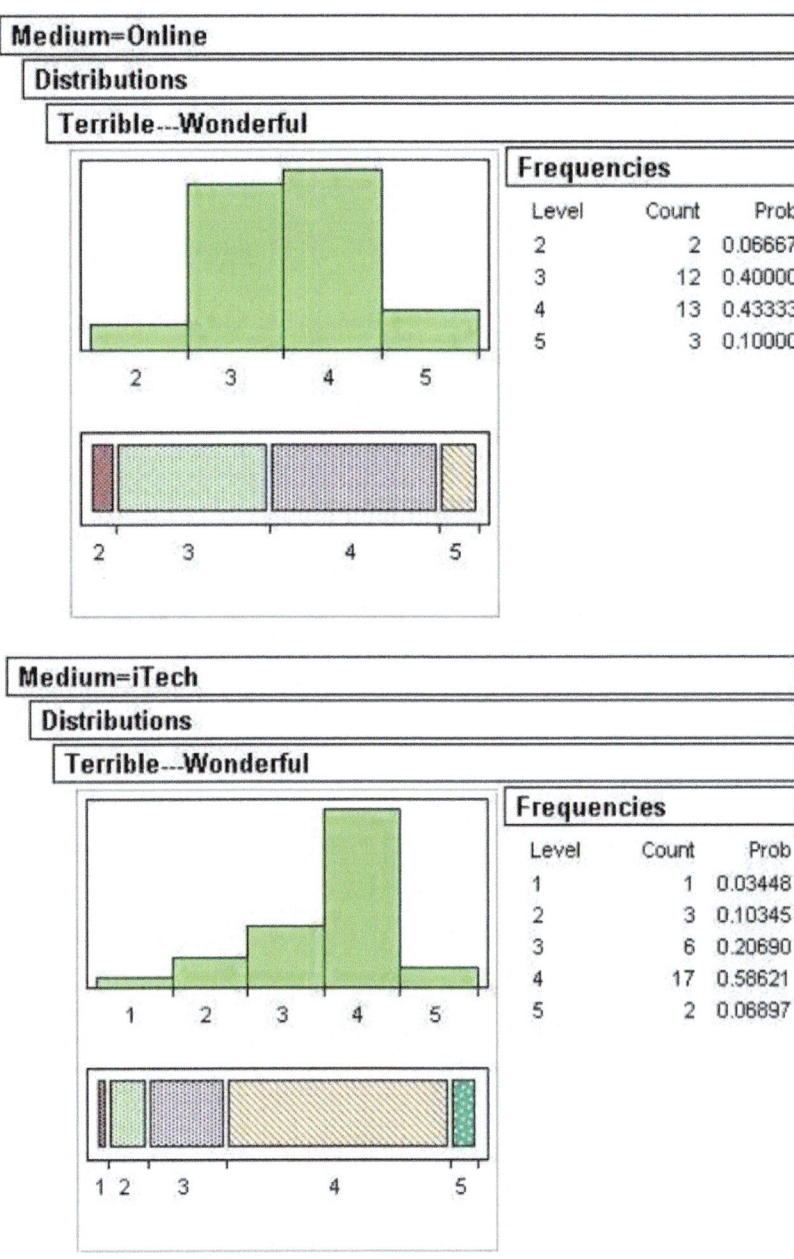

**Figure. 6**. Terrible - Wonderful Bi-polar Distribution.

On the scales of dull to stimulating and boring to fun, iTech received the highest scores with respect to the other two mediums. For these scales, a much larger disparity in the distribution of scores is observed with respect to the book medium versus the online and iTech mediums. (See Figure 7. Dull-Simulating Distributions Distribution and Figures 8. Boring-Fun Bi-polar Distributions)

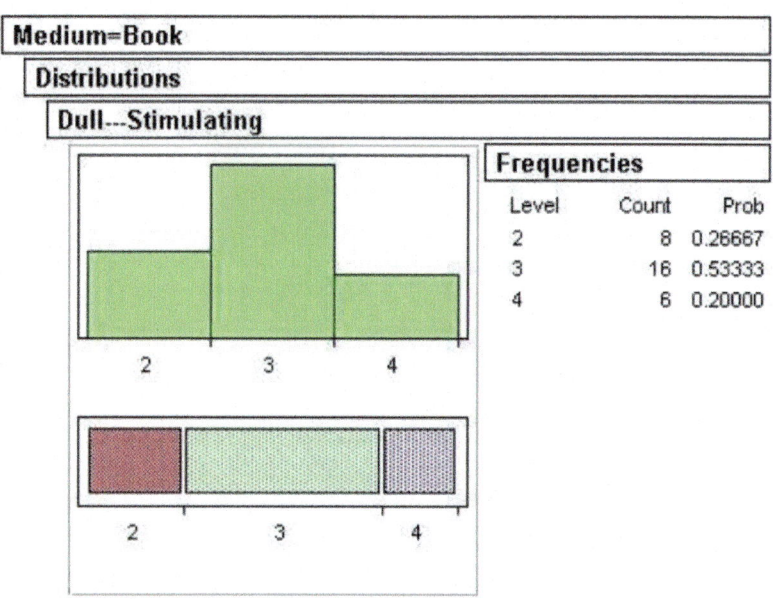

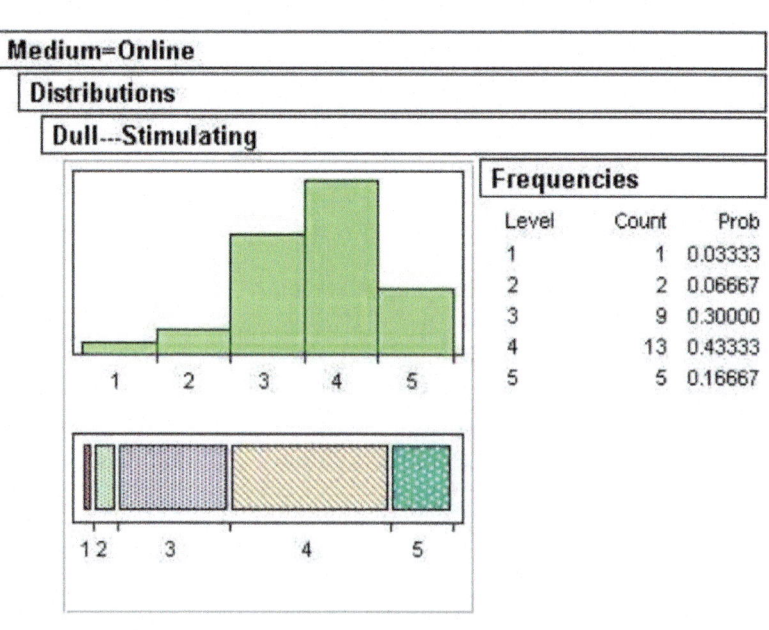

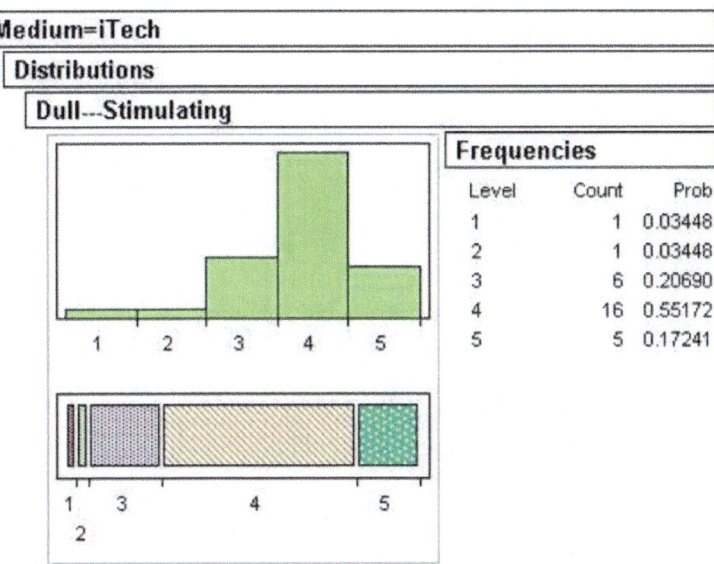

**Figure. 7.** Dull – Stimulating Bi-polar Distribution.

The second set of rating scales consisted of items designed to examine reactions to specific aspects of the participants' interaction experience. These scales each contained an assertion e.g. 'The medium was easy to use', to which the participants responded using a five-point scale. This scale contained the following ratings: Strongly Agree, Agree, Neutral, Disagree and Strongly Disagree. We assigned each rating a weight. This weight was used for statistical analysis. The Strongly Agree was assigned a rating of 5, Agree a rating of 4, Neutral a rating of 3, Disagree a rating of 2, and Strongly Disagree a rating of 1.

Version I of the post-experiment survey contained 10 Likert-like ratings and Version II of our post-experiment survey contained 22 ratings. The first 9 ratings for each questionnaire were identical and as a result were compared across all three mediums.

### Medium=Book

#### Distributions

##### Boring---Fun

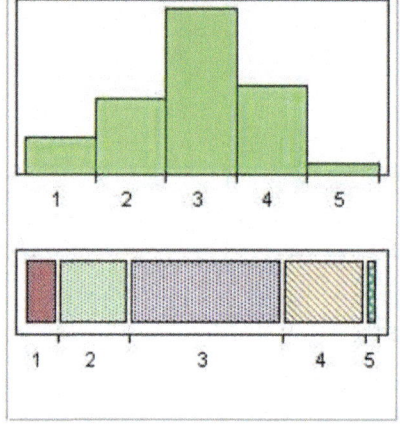

**Frequencies**

| Level | Count | Prob |
|---|---|---|
| 1 | 3 | 0.10000 |
| 2 | 6 | 0.20000 |
| 3 | 13 | 0.43333 |
| 4 | 7 | 0.23333 |
| 5 | 1 | 0.03333 |

### Medium=Online

#### Distributions

##### Boring---Fun

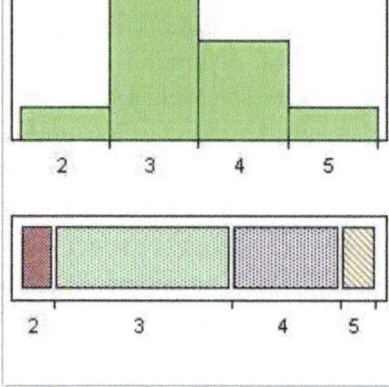

**Frequencies**

| Level | Count | Prob |
|---|---|---|
| 2 | 3 | 0.10000 |
| 3 | 15 | 0.50000 |
| 4 | 9 | 0.30000 |
| 5 | 3 | 0.10000 |

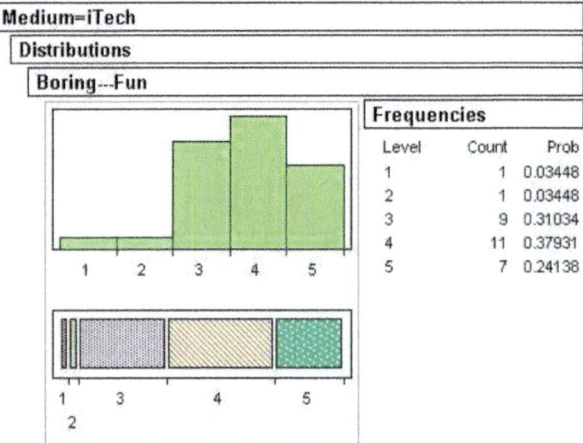

**Figure. 8.** Boring - Fun Bi-polar Distribution.

The first property analyzed was the affordance of the mediums. This property was derived from the question, "It was easy to get started". Results show that iTech received a score of 4 or higher from 60.7% of the participants, while the book and online mediums received 46.67% and 30.0% respectively (See Figure 9. Affordance Distributions). This data is in agreement with the trends found in the mediums' search times. The online medium had the worst average search time with iTech having the best, suggesting that an application's affordance is an important feature of the application's success.

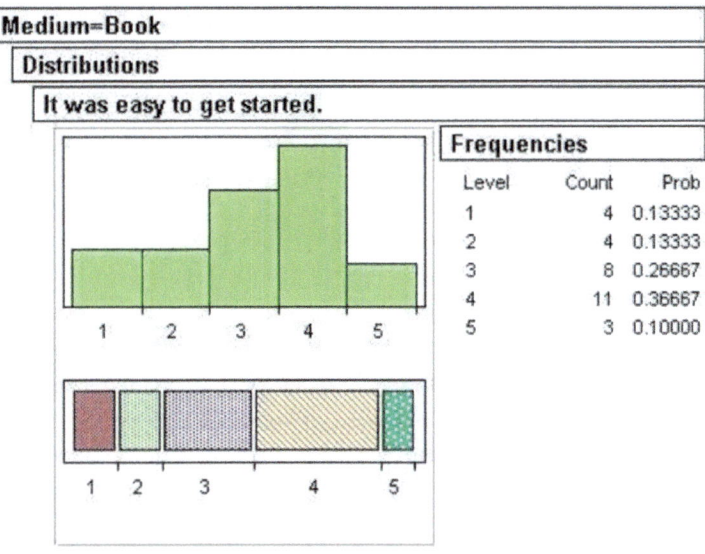

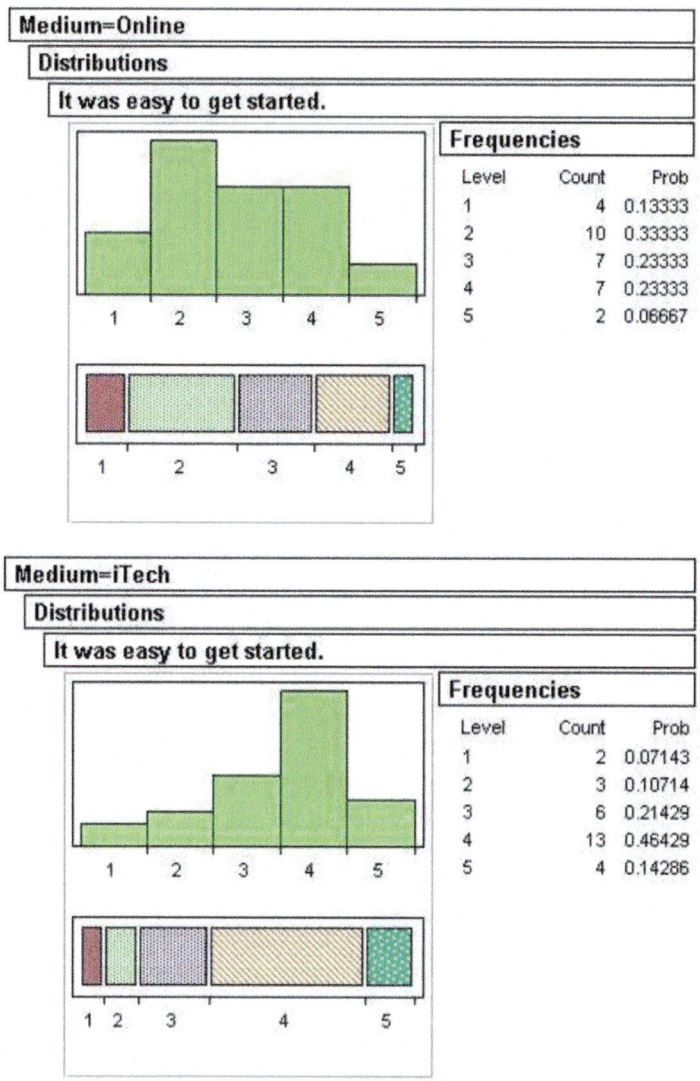

**Figure. 9.** Affordance Distributions.

The scores for "understanding document updates" were over 80.0% for all mediums suggesting that we selected tasks that needed little training to get started. The results for the property of 'ease of use' reflect the problems with speech recognition accuracy. There were problems with recognition accuracy due to heavy southern accents and incorrect usage of the recording box. Subsequently, though the range for the medium averages is small, the scores for the iTech medium are the lowest in response to the statement, "It

# iTech: An Interactive Virtual Assistant for Technical Communication 23

was easy retrieving an answer". The results are as follows: book medium – 63.3%, online medium – 50.0% and iTech medium – 48.27% for scores of 4 or higher. In spite of the recognition accuracy issues, iTech received the highest ratings with respect to knowing how to use the medium (See Figure 10. Getting Started Distributions). Next, we analyzed the user's reactions to the iTech medium.

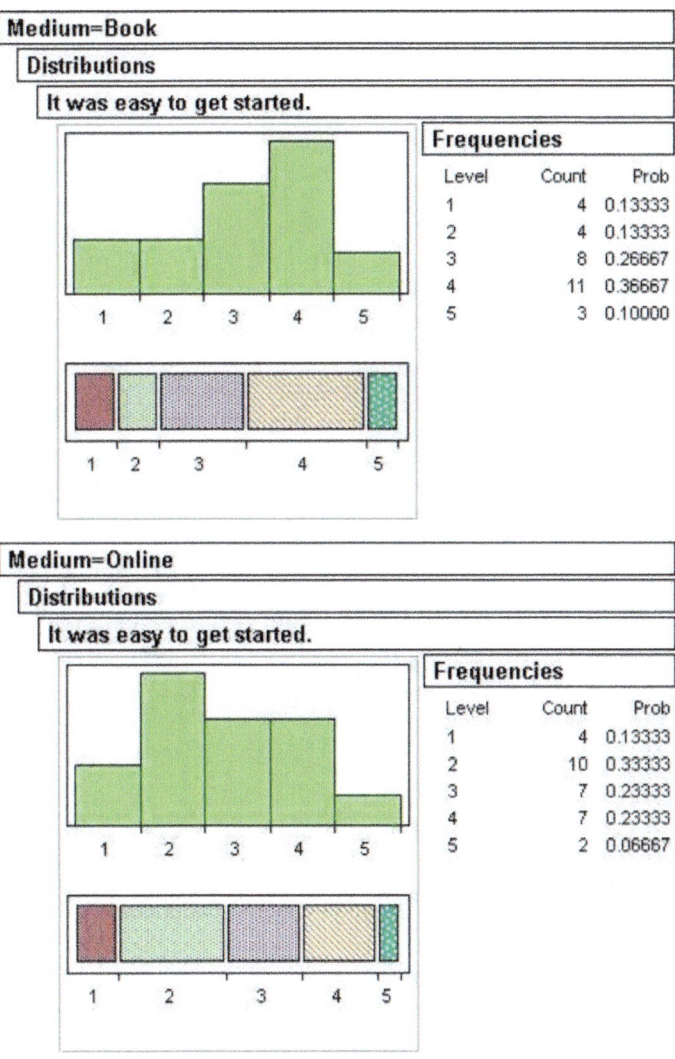

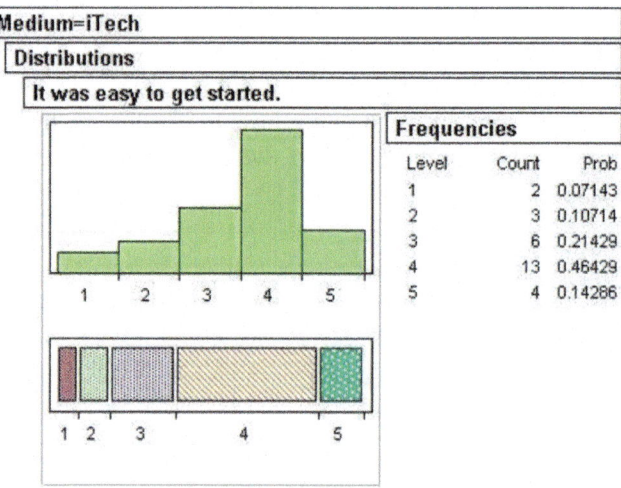

**Figure. 10.** Getting Started Distribution.

Before beginning the analysis of user's reactions to iTech, statements unique to iTech were placed into one of six possible categories. These categories represented the six factors investigated user's attitudes towards speech systems (Hone, 2003). Results are shown in Table 8. Participants liked the appearance of iTech and results suggest that they would reuse the application. Participants were able to understand iTech and thought that the application retrieved their answers in an expedient fashion. In addition, they agreed that computer novices would be able to use the application. The high user satisfaction ratings were solidified by additional comments.

"Worked greater than expectations based on previous speech help programs…"

"Pretty easy to use. User friendly"

"I really enjoyed iTech …the layout and technology used was great"

"It was overall very helpful and would be useful for people whom are computer literate".

**Table 8.** Analysis of User's Reactions to iTech

| Likert-like Scale Item | Mean | % with Score of 4 or higher |
|---|---|---|
| **Cognitive Modeling** | | |
| iTech worked as I expected it during the task. | 3.41 | 55.1 |
| I was confident that iTech would be able to help me. | 3.86 | 72.4 |
| **Perceived System Response Accuracy** | | |
| iTech gave me the correct answers. | 3.69 | 72.41 |
| iTech had problems understanding me. | 3.52 | 68.97 |
| **Cognitive Demand** | | |
| I had problems understanding iTech. | 2.32 | 71.14 |
| **Likeability** | | |
| I would use iTech again. | 3.82 | 78.57 |
| I liked the appearance of iTech. | 4.18 | 89.29 |
| I would have preferred a female technician. | 2.97 | 13.79 |
| I would have preferred iTech having no face, just a voice. | 2.10 | 7.9 |
| **Habitability** | | |
| iTech would be easy to use by people who don't know a lot about computers. | 3.62 | 75.86 |
| **Speed** | | |
| iTech was fast enough in response to my question. | 4.03 | 86.21 |

# DISCUSSION AND IMPLICATIONS

The results suggest that overall; iTech is a viable technology for use in the area of technical communications. The introduction of an animated agent that allows users to speak questions and return an appropriate solution through our research has been shown to decrease search time and task completion time, as well as overall user satisfaction compared to both book manuals and online searchable manuals. Therefore, such systems may provide some improvement over traditional technical communication mediums such as books and online search systems. More generally, because iTech is a speaker-independent system that employs conversational questioning answering techniques suggests additional advantages. Because iTech is speaker independent, there is no need for training. Additionally, because iTech allows users to answer spoken questions, query-preprocessing time is eliminated.

Another advantage of iTech like systems is that it improves on many of the limitations of online and paper manuals including portability and frequent updates. iTech is computerbased and therefore there is no need for a bulky paper manual, only a computer, cell-phone, or other Internet connected device is needed. Also, iTech transfers the search task from the user to the computer, removing the need for users to understand indexes. Because, iTech's content resides on a server in a database, the ability to make frequent updates is less time consuming and does not require an entire re-print and shipment of manuals to users. Users therefore will have access to the most recent version of the manual at all times. The study results present a new opportunity for professional communicators to incorporate the best of these two mediums, search engines and manuals. Furthermore, iTech has the potential to change the way technical information is communicated across numerous domains. For example, automobile manuals have significantly grown in size. At the same time, these manuals have found their way online in the form of Adobe Acrobat documents that can be easily searched by drivers. iTech has the potential to be integrated within the vehicle to provide instant access to manual information using the driver or passenger's voice. Another compelling domain is the military. When military personnel travel, they carry a great deal of equipment, including a laptop and manuals. iTech has the potential to consolidate their manuals into a single laptop with a natural language interface, e.g. typed or spoken text.

The need for effective technical communication to provide user assistance will continue to be an issue of importance as long as new products and devices are introduced into society. As these devices become more complex so will the documentation accompanying them. Therefore, usability and user satisfaction will continue to become an important factor in creating documentation that is among others easy to search, easy to understand, and easy to use. iTech addresses the limitations of paper and online manuals by providing technical communication through a personable virtual interactive technical assistant.

## CONCLUSIONS

The results of this study show that iTech yielded faster search times than its paper and online counterparts. In addition, iTech had favorable usability results. Overall, the use of iTech was favorable and provided evidence that such a tool would be a viable option for providing technical assistance. In addition positive user comments show that users of iTech were satisfied with their experience with the tool. In addition, this research suggests that the application of interactive virtual assistants to technical communication is a viable research area for increasing usability and user satisfaction.

## REFERENCES

1. Albing, B. (1996). Process constraints in the management of technical documentation, in Proceedings of the 14th Annual international Conference on Systems Documentation: Marshaling New Technological Forces: Building A Corporate, Academic, and User-Oriented Triangle (Research Triangle Park, North Carolina, United States, October 19 - 22, 1996). SIGDOC '96. ACM, New York, NY, 67-74, 2006, Available: DOI= http://doi.acm.org/10.1145/238215.238257.
2. Barnett, M. (1998). Testing a digital library of technical manuals.

Professional Communication, IEEE Transactions on, vol.41, no.2,1998, pp.116-122. Available: DOI: 10.1109/47.678553 URL: http://ieeexplore.ieee.org/stamp/stamp.jsp?tp=&arnumber=678553&isnumber=1 4943.

3. Baylor, A., & Ryu, J. (2003). The effect of image and animation in enhancing pedagogical agent persona. Journal of Educational Computing Research, 28(4), pp. 373-395.

4. Baylor, A. & Kim, Y. (2003). The Role of Gender and Ethnicity in Pedagogical Agent Perception. G. Richards (Ed.), Proceedings of World Conference on E-Learning in Corporate, Government, Healthcare, and Higher Education 2003. Chesapeake, VA: AACE, 2003, pp. 1503-1506.

5. Baylor, A., Shen, E. & Huang, X. (2003). Which Pedagogical Agent do Learners Choose? The Effects of Gender and Ethnicity. In G. Richards (Ed.), Proceedings of World Conference on E-Learning in Corporate, Government, Healthcare, and Higher Education 2003. Chesapeake, VA: AACE, 2003, pp. 1507-1510.

6. Cisco Systems Inc., Comverse Inc., Interl Corporation, Microsoft Corporation, Philips Electronics N.V., & Speech Works International Inc. (2002). SALT Speech Application Language Tags (SALT) 1.0 Specification. Google. (2009).

7. Google Desktop. [Online] Available: http://desktop.google.com/.

8. Grauer, R. (2003). Exploring MS Office XP and Exploring FrontPage 2003 plus the Train and Assess IT Generation, Prentice Hall Publishing Co. ISBN: 0-536-83155-6.

9. Hailey, D.E. (2004). A Next Generation of Digital Genres: Expanding Documentation into Animation and Virtual Reality. Proceedings of the 22nd Annual International Conference on Design of Communication, Memphis, TN, 2004, pp.19-26.

10. Hone, K.S. & Graham, R. (2001). Subjective Assessment of Speech-System Interface Usability. Eurospeech .

11. Johnson, W. L. & Rickel, J. (1997). Steve: an animated pedagogical agent for procedural training in virtual environments. SIGART Bull. 8, 1-4 (Dec. 1997), 16-21. DOI= http://doi.acm.org/10.1145/272874.272877.

12. Kirste, T., & Rapp, S. (2001). Architecture for Multimodal Interactive Assistant Systems. Statu- stagung der Leitprojekte "Mensch-Technik-Interaktion", Saarbrucken, Germany, 2001, pp. 1-5.

13. Lester, J. C., Converse, S. A., Kahler, S. E., Barlow, S. T., Stone, B. A., & Bhogal, R. S. (1997). The persona effect: affective impact of animated pedagogical agents. In Proceedings of the SIGCHI Conference on Human

Factors in Computing Systems (Atlanta, Georgia, United States, March 22 - 27, 1997).

14. S. Pemberton, Ed. CHI '97. ACM, New York, NY, 359-366. DOI= http://doi.acm.org/10.1145/258549.258797.

15. Major, J. H. (1985). Pulling it all together: a well-designed user's manual. Proceedings of the 13th Annual ACM SIGUCCS Conference on User services: pulling it all together, Toledo, OH, 1996, pp 69 -76.

16. NIST. (2003). NIST/SEMATECH e-Handbook of Statistical Methods, http://www.itl.nist.gov/div898/handbook/. Oddcast Inc. (2008). SitePal: Now you're talking business. [Online] Available: http://www.sitepal.com/.

17. Oviatt, S. L., Cohen, P., Vergo, J., Duncan, L., Suhn, B., Bers, J., Holzman, T., Winograd, T., Landay, J., Larson, J. & Ferro, D. (2000). Designing the User Interface for Multimodal Speech and Pen-based Gesture. Applications: State-of-the-Art Systems and Future Research Directions, Human Computer Interaction 15, 4, pp. 263-322.

18. Rosis, F., Carolis, B. & Pizzutilo, S. (1999). Software Documentation with Animated Agents. SAS Institute. (1989). JMP IN: Software for statistical visualization on the Apple Macintosh Cary, NC.

19. Thimbleby, H. (1996). Creating user manuals for using in collaborative design. Conference Companion on Human Factors in Computing Systems: Common Ground (Vancouver, British Columbia, Canada, April 13 - 18, 1996. M. J. Tauber, Ed. CHI '96. ACM Press, New York, NY, pp. 279-280.

20. Ventura, C. A. (1988). Why Switch from Paper to Electronic Manuals?. Proceedings of ACM Conference on Document Processing Systems, ACM, New York, Santa Fe, New Mexico, 1988, pp. 111-116.

21. Wilson, D.M., Martin, A. & Gilbert, J.E. (2010). 'How May I Help You'- Spoken Queries for Technical Assistance. ACM Southeast Conference, Oxford, MS, April 15-17, 2010.

22. Zachary, C., Cargile-Cook, K., Faber, B., & Zachary, M. (2001). The Changing Face of Technical Communication: New Directions for the Field in a New Millennium. Proceedings of the 19th Annual International Conference on Systems Documentation, 2001, pp. 248 – 260.

# Chapter 2

# INNOVATIVE APPROACHES TO TEACHING TECHNICAL COMMUNICATION

Richard Selfe[1], Tracy Bridgeford[2] and Karla Saari Kitalong[3]

[1] Humanities department at Michigan Technological University
[2] Department of English at the University of Nebraska at Omaha
[3] University of Central Florida in Orlando

## INTRODUCTION

The idea for this collection grew out of a discussion about humor in technical communication. Humor is usually proscribed in technical communication practice, both because it does not cross cultures well and because it may make complex and even dangerous technologies seem frivolous. When the three of us started paying attention to and collecting humor related to the technical communication field, we noticed that it is most often connected to Dilbert cartoons, the For Dummies genre of third-party software manuals, and Dave Barry–like rants about poorly written instructions. In short, the available humor about technical communication doesn't paint a pretty picture of our chosen profession.

Because we enjoy playful attitudes toward technical communication, we put aside the field's reservations about humor and began to ask ourselves how we might incorporate humor into our technical communication classrooms. Under what circumstances, we wondered, might humor be permissible or even desirable? How might it be used productively in the technical communication classroom?

In exploring that question, we concluded that perhaps what we were really talking about was how to demonstrate to technical communication students how creative the field could be. We were all teaching at Michigan Technological University at the time and had begun to notice that many students seemed disillusioned with the prospect of beginning their careers as traditional technical communicators. Writing instructional manuals for the computer industry or documenting ISO 9001 procedures for a government contractor seemed as dull as Dilbert's cubicle to them, especially when juxtaposed against the seemingly glamorous career prospects of Web or multimedia design. We didn't agree with them; in fact, our technical communication work as teachers, practitioners, and consultants has shown us its creative potential. For us and for the discipline at large, rendering complex information accessible and usable to an intended audience is interesting—even, at times, exhilarating. We wanted students to see that technical communication frequently involves creative effort, whether the project is a 500-page printed instruction manual or a digital media production. In other words, we were not willing to make the technocentric distinction many students seemed to be making between dull, document-based information and exciting, digital-media development. Naturally, our first inclination was to blame ourselves. Had something about our previous teaching practices predisposed students to make unwarranted distinctions between project types? We thought we had carefully crafted our technical communication course assignments to show that the skills needed to design an interactive multimedia kiosk (a task students valued highly) were equally applicable in assembling a high-quality, well-indexed, and smoothly cross- referenced documentation set (a task many dismissed as boring). But somehow, our convictions were not getting through to them; moreover, another important idea that we wanted to emphasize—that success in all types of technical communication work necessitates strong and versatile writing skills—was apparently also lost on some undergraduate students. Imagine our chagrin when a graduating senior stated the opinion to one of our colleagues that writing is retro!

To impress our values on students and to convince them of the innovative practices available to technical communication professionals, the three of us developed a special topics course—Innovative Approaches to Technical Communication—which we offered to undergraduate scientific and technical communication (STC) majors at Michigan Technological University during the winter quarter 1997–1998. Our syllabus characterized the course as a way to engage more fully with the profession of technical communication by "considering a variety of attitudes, approaches, and practices." In the course design, we shifted students' attention (and our own) toward a more inclusive and creative view of the profession of technical communication. Course units advocated and modeled approaches that might not ordinarily be considered in technical communication. Students wrote, of course, but they also composed in other modalities such as mapping, drawing, scripting, acting, pantomiming, and MOOing. They read a variety of texts, including challenging theoretical texts not commonly assigned to undergraduates: Marilyn Cooper's (1996) Technical Communication Quarterly article on postmodern operator's manuals, James Porter and Patricia Sullivan's (1996) work on postmodern mapping, David

Dobrin's (1989) "Armadillo Armor" article, and some articles on play theory (Huizinga 1990). To help students make the desired connections between their prior technical communication education and these new ideas, we assigned Janice Redish's (1988) "Reading to Learn to Do" article, Dorothy Nelkin's (1995) work on media representations of science and technology, and an excerpt from Robert Pirsig's (1974) Zen and the Art of Motorcycle Maintenance. To the stack of theoretical readings, we added newspaper editorials and articles about product assembly (Rooney 1997; Perelman 1976); cartoons from the Dilbert Zone (see www.dilbert.com); technology ads from popular magazines (Miller 1997) Will Weaver's short story titled "A Gravestone Made of Wheat" (1990); even some government documents—the Declaration of Independence and the Equal Rights Amendment.

The process of developing the reading list and the activities and techniques that went along with it ultimately reinforced our belief that the inspiration for our work as technical communication educators could come from almost anywhere, that our work could be as creative as we would allow it to be, and that we could approach the teaching and learning that goes on in technical communication courses in a variety of ways and from a variety of problem-solving perspectives. As we shared this discovery about teaching with students, they too came to realize that many theories, cultural artifacts, and issues could and should influence the work they do as technical communicators.

The learning that took place in the class does not represent a major paradigm shift in our students' thinking. But we are convinced that each student took away something profound. For example, one day, after reading a play theory essay and discussing the value of designing work spaces to facilitate playful interaction as well as serious labor, we each mapped our ideal work spaces. Michelle's included a desk for her best friend, collaborator, and longtime roommate, Jen, who had recently graduated and moved away. When Michelle shared the map with the rest of the class, she seemed a bit embarrassed by her dependence on her friend, and she hastily acknowledged the reality that she and Jen would never again work together. "Jen's desk" in a corner of Michelle's ideal work space stands as a metaphor for the lasting and palpable influence of a successful and pleasurable collaboration. Jen was not lost to Michelle: although she lived in another city and had chosen a technical communication career path that diverged from Michelle's, she would always be present in Michelle's work practices and habits of mind.

## Defining Terms and Assumptions

Program Names. Program naming conventions vary from institution to institution. Sometimes names signal the presence of deep and often contentious disciplinary boundaries. For instance, at some colleges, communication is a reserved title; its absence in English departments' course and program names may point to disciplinary turf wars. When we name our programs—technical and scientific communication, professional communication, professional or technical writing, business communication, and many others—we signal our institutional as well as our disciplinary allegiances. At base, though, the names are irrelevant. The editors of this collection are convinced that the techniques, approaches, technologies, and assignments suggested in this volume will transfer to programs across the disciplinary spectrum. Teachers in all these programs will find the materials described in this volume quite valuable.

That said, we assume that all teaching is highly contextualized and that the pedagogical explorations represented here will need to be adapted to the institutional, instructional, and material conditions that exist in each program and in each classroom. We hope that readers of this volume will not stop with the ideas and approaches presented herein, but will be inspired to continue to explore and test pedagogies from a variety of sources. One of the strengths of our diverse, but still related, disciplines is that we make it a point to attend carefully to the changing literacy practices that surround us, in academia and in society at large.

*Critical.* We use the term critical advisedly; the word and its seemingly commonsense derivations—critical reflection, critical pedagogy, critical thinking, critical approach—all carry a good deal of theoretical baggage and deserve to be, well, considered critically. However, we think that a critical approach to technical communication can yield quite practical results. In this volume we assume that critical approaches include any thoughtful, rhetorical, and culturally founded application of a technical communication process, practice, or approach to projects or documents (print and digital).

*Innovative.* Its prominence in the title of this collection makes innovative the term that most demands a common understanding. For us, to innovate means to introduce a new idea or to reintroduce an old idea, perhaps in a new way or in a new context. In this collection, then, an innovative approach is one that introduces, rearticulates, or creatively juxtaposes theories or practices, especially those not currently or commonly used within the context of technical communication teaching.

Some of the approaches described in this collection are unusual in technical communication pedagogy, curriculum development, or program design, even though they may be commonplace in other disciplines or contexts. Other approaches may be common in technical communication, but for some reason have not been published or otherwise officially entered into our professional discourse. The number of responses we received to our call for essays (almost three times as many as are included here) confirmed for us that innovative practices abound in technical communication classrooms, programs, and curricula.

To elicit the accounts of innovation we knew were "out there," we encouraged the authors to approach this collection as a way to share their most innovative instructional ideas, and we encourage readers to approach it as a catalyst for innovation in their work. We have asked authors to converse with their colleagues—the readers of this collection—by writing relatively short pieces that concisely but thoroughly describe their innovative activity or project in ways that allow readers to visualize implementation within a range of institutional contexts. We have also asked the authors to concentrate on the positive aspects of their approaches without sacrificing a critical discussion of problems posed by or reflected in their approaches, so that readers can more accurately project how approaches that appeal to them might fit into their institutional contexts.

## The Theoretical Need for Innovation

From plain style to instrumental discourse to social constructivism and rhetoric, theoretically informed pedagogical discussions in technical communication have consistently focused on how best to prepare students for work (see, for example, Harris 1982, 630). This collection is timely and necessary as we consider our pedagogical responsibilities for preparing students for work now—at the beginning of the twenty-first century. Our thinking about pedagogy and the need for innovation (and hence, the selection of chapters for this volume) grows out of our reading of Etienne Wenger's (1998) Communities of Practice; Mary Sue Garay and Stephen Bernhardt's (1998) Expanding Literacies: English Teaching and the New Workplace; and James Paul Gee, Glynda Hull, and Colin Lankshear's (1996) The New Work Order: Behind the Language of the New Capitalism. From different perspectives, each of these books emphasizes the important aspects of what work means, as well as what it means to prepare students for work in the twenty-first century.

Although the new work order does not excuse students from developing an understanding of the forms of technical communication and how to execute them, Gee, Hull, and Lankshear(1996) point out that in this emerging work landscape, much more extensive and intensive literacies are expected than ever before. In essence—and this belief is something the technical communication discipline has known and accepted for a while—students' success depends on a commitment not only to classroom learning but also to lifelong learning. Workers in many fields can no longer consider their education to be complete upon graduating from college; today's college students need to develop learning strategies they can draw on throughout their careers, especially if they work in intensive, high-technology fields. But, according to authors like Wenger, Garay and Bernhardt, and Gee, Hull, and Lankshear, a commitment to lifelong learning is just the tip of the proverbial iceberg. Students need, as well, to be able to respond quickly and effectively to continually changing local and global conditions and to rapid and unpredictable technological advancements. They need to develop and sustain a repertoire of learning and information management strategies and to reflect critically upon their choices and actions. In this environment, mastery of the forms and typical genres of technical communication is still necessary but is far from sufficient as a prerequisite for success in the new work order.

In short, as technical communication faculty, our charge to prepare students for work is complicated by the exigencies of the new work order. Our pedagogical practice is further complicated—and our job rendered perhaps even more important—in the wake of national and international events that swirl around us as this book goes to press. We are currently witnessing twin economic challenges—the volatility of high-tech industries and the upheaval of war and terrorism—that necessitate an attitude of innovation as an integral part of the technical communication teacher's toolkit for the classroom because it models the attitude of innovation that students need for their toolkits for the workplace. We think you'll see that the Innovative Approaches authors—each in his or her way—focus on issues such as lifelong learning, the need to build workplace communities, changing workplace conditions, the globalization of technical communication work, and the increasing literacy demands being placed on technical communication practitioners.

## About This Collection: Responding to the Need for Innovation

Innovative Approaches to Teaching Technical Communication grows, then, out of students' apprehensiveness about their career paths, our efforts to understand the vagaries of the twenty-first century workplace, and our observation that many theoretical and disciplinary perspectives can potentially inform technical communication teaching, program administration, and curriculum development. Given pervasive changes in technology, the workplace, and cultural attitudes, new, dynamic, and flexible pedagogies seem warranted. Innovative Approaches to Teaching Technical Communication begins to address this need by demonstrating for technical communication faculty, graduate students, and program administrators the value of interrogating and innovating classroom and programmatic practices. The chapters were selected to highlight activities, projects, and approaches that have not been documented extensively in publications about technical communication teaching, curriculum development, or program administration. This chapter, therefore, offers the discipline another opportunity to energize its pedagogy and to critically examine current teaching practices.

The approaches described in this collection are practical, readily adaptable to a range of technological and institutional contexts, theoretically grounded, and pedagogically sound. They bring together a variety of scholars/teachers who expand an existing canon of publications about teaching technical communication (Fearing and Sparrow 1989; Selber 1997; Staples and Ornatowski 1997). Three objectives helped structure this collection. We wanted to

- capture a range of pedagogical perspectives that can inspire and invigorate technical communication teaching,
- present a variety of inventive, critical pedagogical practices for the technical communication classroom, and
- emphasize an array of partnership possibilities in technical communication pedagogy.

Using this framework, we looked for essays that demonstrated innovation in pedagogical perspectives, practices, and partnerships. We see this collection as broadening and making publicly accessible conversations already occurring in hallways, in faculty lounges, on listservs, and at conferences, but—for one reason or another—have not yet been made public. We hope that you will find as much inspiration in reading the pages of this chapter as we did in compiling them.

This collection is framed by the need for innovative pedagogical and curricular approaches that consider new perspectives that describe new types of practices, and that exemplify new ways of establishing partnerships with industry. In each section, the authors think about and enact their pedagogical approaches by describing new ways of working and new strategies for adapting to changing workplace conditions.

## THE STATUS OF SERVICE IN LEARNING

During the last decade, a number of scholars/practitioners have explored the geographies of our fields, mapped the boundaries, and developed the landscape by building bridges (for example, Sullivan and Porter 1993; Blyler 1993; Forman 1993; and Allen 1992). One of the most important points in this discussion about identity has been the realization that to create a field of our own, we need to create our own major, one that will be independent and not subordinate. Sullivan and Porter (1993) explain that by *conceiving of writing as a major, professional writing breaks with the dominant service identity assigned to composition. The development of professional writing as an academic entity signals a key conceptual shift: from the traditional notion of writing as ancillary to some other subject matter (i.e., writing as service to some other set of concerns—whether business, engineering, literature, or rhetoric/composition) to a recognition of writing as a discipline in its own right (i.e., a view that sees writing itself as a specialty area and as a subject of study). (405–6)*

As they make a claim for professional writing's independence, Sullivan and Porter highlight service as one of the essential terms in the discussion. They link it to "the traditional notion of writing as ancillary to some other subject matter" and recognize that, for the most part, those of us who teach writing have been and continue to be marginalized (and to marginalize ourselves) because of connotations and history associated with service.

Yet, even as Sullivan and Porter (1993) long to break from that "dominant service identity" in order to get us to change our collective clothes, so to speak, and put on the mantle of respectability (which for them is associated with research), they recognize that what we do, at least to some extent, is indeed service. They explain that even with writing as a major, English departments "can continue their service functions and continue to be seen in that service role by some in the university" (406). Thus, despite their desire to cloak our "service identity," they do not dismiss it entirely. Service, deeply rooted in the spaces associated with writing, manages to maintain a presence in the landscape even as Sullivan and Porter work to re-map and re-present it.

In this chapter, my intention is not to argue with Sullivan and Porter's goal of achieving disciplinary status. I agree wholeheartedly that writing should be a discipline in its own right and a "subject of study." I disagree, however, that we need to break "with the dominant service identity" to accomplish those objectives. For that reason, I begin an inquiry into the concept of "service," a word many members of the profession of English language studies seem to want to keep hidden away like Rochester's wife in Jane Eyre. I examine some of the negative and positive connotations of the term when it is used as a modifier, such as those associated with being a "service discipline" and with the pedagogy of "service-learning," suggesting that we in the field of technical and scientific communication should bring service out of the attic, redefine it, and accept it as an integral component of our missions. In particular, I believe that service learning, when used fully and reflectively, has the potential to enable us to move beyond negative modifiers. By accepting service as essential to what we do, we redraw the lines of the discussion, make the definitions we want to advance explicit, and take an active role not only in creating a curricular geography but also in assigning ourselves a place on the academic map that best represents us. Such an active role might enable us to achieve parity with other disciplines within the institutions of higher learning and avoid the fates of the non-European countries represented by European mapmakers, who were often marginalized, regardless of their actual size or status (Barton and Barton 1993).1 More importantly, by accepting service as a key pedagogical goal, we revise our notion of scholarship and link practice and theory together in a manner reminiscent of classical Greece and Rome where rhetors worked to serve the public good.

## The Faces of Service

Use the term service, and you get many responses. On one hand, we have large, expansive definitions of service such as military service and service to country (the Kennedy inaugural speech or the 1993 National and Community Service Trust Act come to mind here), which are associated with volunteerism and duty. Linked to religious and social concepts, those who serve contribute to the public good and make their communities and country stronger (Bellah 1985; de Tocqueville 1974). On the other hand, there is a less expansive conception of service, the kind one expects while eating or shopping. Here, those who serve do so for pay or out of obligation or indenture, and there is little in the way of public advantage. The advantages are almost always private. In academe, the word service has a long history. Having just completed my annual , I'm well aware of the three criteria that others use to evaluate me: teaching, research, and service. And I know that at my school, a large, land-grant university, of the three criteria, service is the least valued. To use a common metaphor, academic work is seen as a stool with three legs. Unfortunately, in nearly every instance, service ends up being the shortest leg (Martin, 1977, vii; Mawby 1996, 49), and those who do more of it have less stable places to sit. The concept is accorded far less respect than its sister concepts of teaching and research (Boyer 1990).

Many members of the academy see service as subordinate to teaching and research, so that even if they acknowledge that a primary mission of higher education is to serve, they argue that teaching and research, as the means to the end, should receive the most weight. To give an example, what should count is the research that leads to the discovery of a blight-resistant strain of corn or the teaching of how to plant and tend it. The planting and tending, the labor of bringing that plant to bear fruit, have far less weight. In our discipline, the argument has long been that we don't have a subject of study. Our mission is not to discover new strains of corn or new processes for planting; our mission is to help those who do the discovering communicate their knowledge. Thus, most academics, including many of our colleagues in literature, justify their treatment of us because, for them, we exist in the less expansive mode. Our departments and courses exist because members of the university have a need for us. We are paid, so to speak, to provide others with services they need to do their work that will benefit the community. Returning to Sullivan and Porter's discussion, one can see that implicit in their desire to be rid of the term is the belief that when service is used as a modifier, what or who it modifies is second-rate (as in "Oh, they're a service discipline" or technical writing is "merely a service course"). Used in this manner, the term service falls into the second, less expansive mode; it is pejorative and condescending. Those involved in such work are more servants than equals, providing something necessary, yet something mechanical—a skill that other disciplines see as separate from their endeavors.

## Service as Conduct Becoming a Discipline

In the military where I spent fifteen years of my adult life, I learned that there are actions or conduct that "become" one. These acts represent what is best about one's profession; they exemplify it, and members are expected to enact them by living in accordance with a code of conduct. So it goes for other professions as well, including that of teaching writing. We must know what is expected of us and live up to those expectations. Clearly, one of those expectations for teachers of professional writing is to teach students how to write well. Doing so is central to our profession; to deny otherwise is to bury our heads in the sand. More important, doing so—teaching students how to write well—is no easy task. To teach students how to write well, we need to understand what we're doing; we need to study both the act of writing and the teaching of the act of writing. We also need to study the effects those acts of writing have on others and use that knowledge to improve our teaching. Our work is a circle involving experiential learning—one that might be best expressed by Kolb's (1984) Learning Cycle, which combines concrete experience, through a reflective stage, on to an analytical stage, to a testing step, ending where it began, back at experience. This work, which I've argued elsewhere is like a Möbius loop, is essential to our field (see Dubinsky 1998). We must involve the act and art of teaching writing in the discussion. The strategy, however, is to argue that what we do, our labor, is inseparable from our teaching and our research. Thus, our service is of a piece with our scholarship.

### *The Service Mission of Higher Education*

Rather than deny what has much truth (that we do, indeed, serve as Sullivan and Porter assert) or try to find a way to cloak or cover up that service with some "higher" calling such as study, we need to yoke the two concepts of service and study together. My first reason is that, as I've already stated, not all connotations of service are derogatory. Those that focus on "conduct tending to the welfare or advantage of another" (OED) are positive. These definitions seem in line not only with our field's historical role as the discipline responsible for literacy instruction but also with the mission of many institutions of higher learning, which is often associated with the concept of service.

Relying on historical arguments and mission statements from colleges and universities, some scholars have been working to revive the concept of service. In Scholarship Reconsidered, Boyer (1990) argues for a redefinition of scholarship (the term associated with research that led to the uneven stool and a denigration of the concept of service when the modern university system was instituted). He wants to see a broader definition of scholarship, one that encompasses what he calls the "scholarship of application" (16), a concept in which "service [is seen as] serious, demanding work requiring the rigor—and the accountability—traditionally associated with research" (22).

Along these same lines, a diverse group of educators has been working to create situations that require "reflection-in-action" (Schön 1983), involving a pedagogy that has come to be called service-learning, "an expanding . . . movement [that] educates students . . . for the benefit of society" (Henson and Sutliff 1998, 189). With this pedagogy, there is an emphasis on the scholarship associated with what Aristotle called productive knowledge (Miller 1984; Phelps 1991; Schön 1983), which links thought to action and theory to practice.

## Service-Learning: Key to Redefining Service

These goals of redefining service and yoking the words service and learning speak directly to the issue presented by Sullivan and Porter (1993). How can we argue for independence and disciplinarity when one of the most difficult tasks we face as writing teachers is that we are not teaching a "subject of study" only? In nearly every course in nearly every technical communication curriculum I've examined, there is a practical component associated with the subject of study. We don't teach just document design; we teach how to design documents. We don't teach just about desktop publishing; we teach how to publish using tools available on our desktops. Even when we teach "theory" courses, all too often the theory revolves around the acts of writing (our own or those whom we teach or advise). As a result, there is a tension between how much emphasis we place on that practical component and how much we place on the subject of study.

The question at this point is how to make the argument about service and disciplinarity without giving up or relinquishing the connections, both historical and practical, to the work of teaching writing. One means is to consider the pedagogy of service-learning, which connects service to learning and unites practice and theory. Service-learning is a pedagogy in process and one that hasn't yet stabilized, having, according to one scholar, 147 different definitions (Kendall 1990). Despite the many definitions, there is quite a bit of agreement about the essential dynamics of the pedagogy, much of it codified at a national conference sponsored by the National Society for Internships and Experiential Education in 1991 (Giles, Honnet, and Migliore). The term refers to activities that combine work in the community with education. The "service" component is activity intended to assist individuals, families, organizations, or communities in need. The "learning" involves structured academic efforts to promote the development (intellectual and social) of the student. It also involves testing and reflection (thus, the link to the Kolb cycle presented previously). Although there is still much research to be done, there is statistical evidence that demonstrates an improvement in students' learning and commitment to a concept of citizenship (Markus, Howard, and King 1993; Cohen and Kinsey 1994; Parker-Gwin and Mabry 1998).

The pedagogy of service-learning elevates service's status to that of an equal with learning, one that doesn't have to be hidden away. It yokes two terms (learning and service) together that many have seen as oppositional; learning, the goal of higher education—knowledge for knowledge's sake—is literally tied by the hyphen to service. I argue elsewhere for the essential nature of the hyphen, but suffice it to say that the hyphen introduces an element of reciprocity, which results in a leveling of the legs of the stool (see Dubinsky 2002). The hyphen brings together learning-by-doing and serving (applying what one learns to one's community/society). One cannot have service-learning without some action, some activity conducted by the learners for and with other human beings. Doing, however, is only part of the equation. There is an added dimension of ethical and social growth, fostered by reflection and conversation, designed to increase the students' investment in society. Consequently, the term service-learning implies both a type of program and a philosophy of learning (Anne Lewis, quoted in Kunin 1997, 155). What isn't readily apparent in the two words that compose the term is the key component of reflection, the glue that not only holds the two words together but also makes the whole far greater than the parts. Service-learning requires that students do more than just serve or learn; they must understand why and whom they serve and how that service fits into their learning (Bringle and Hatcher 1996; Sigmon 1994).

Service-learning, used fully and reflectively, helps students develop critical thinking skills; it also prepares students for the workplace in a more comprehensive way than many other pedagogical strategies because students apply what they've learned by working to develop reciprocal relationships with real audiences. These relationships, which are directed toward change not charity, enable students to meet their citizenship responsibilities (Dubinsky 2002). Service-learning pedagogy enables us to make our courses "a matter of conduct rather than of production" (Miller 1984, 23; Miller's emphasis). Students learn skills they'll use in the workplace, and they gain a practical wisdom (phronesis) that enables them to be critical citizens (Sullivan 1990).

## Technical Problem Solving or Service

To implement a pedagogy integral to creating an identity, one that creates relationships with people outside the academy and expands our classrooms beyond their traditional walls, we need to think about what we are doing and why. One of the key issues to resolve is whether we consider our work technical problem solving or service. Both have advantages, as outlined in a recent exchange between Johnson (1999) and Moore (1999), in which Moore is an advocate for "instrumental discourse," arguing that many technical communicators coming out of academic programs are held in low esteem because their communication skills are insufficiently developed, the same complaints made about the engineers in the early twentieth century (Kynell 1996). Moore's focus on instrumental skills, however, is the very focus that plays into the hands of those who want to belittle service.

If what we do is defined by the job market only, if our work is measured by comma splices and the ability to use certain desktop publishing programs, then we are defining ourselves narrowly and not acknowledging the scope of what we do. If, however, we construct a definition of service so that we not only produce graduates who can use their skills for business and industry but also produce graduates who desire sincerely to use those skills to meet the community's needs and who have a desire to "share the common experience of learning about humans as they wrestle with technology in everyday situations" (Johnson 223), we are then embracing a version of service expansive and beneficial to society. One key issue we need to consider concerns the attitudes we adopt and encourage students to adopt when we choose projects designed to help others. Although anxious to do good work, it is all too easy to adopt a charitable attitude that, while often well-intentioned, demonstrates that those doing the work feel superior because they have the answers to solve problems. Kahne and Westheimer (1996) describe this situation in terms of two competing models—charity and change—arguing that although both models may work, only the latter one enables people to work with others, to effect change and understand the underlying social issues and individual responsibilities. Linda Flower (1997) echoes this point. Drawing on John McKnight's (1995) analysis of social service policy, she explains that "community service has often rested on notions of philanthropy, charity, social service, and improvement that identify the community as a *recipient, client,* or *patient,* marked by economic, learning, or social deficits" (37; italics added). For that reason, one of the key components of any service-learning project must be the underlying notion of the type of relationship that will exist between the class and the "client." Rather than encourage a "client" relationship, which is hierarchical, I encourage students to work with their organizations as partners.

Although more complicated and requiring more of a commitment from the organization, students, and teacher, changing the relationship from a "client-consultant" to a three way partnership changes dynamics that have a major effect on the outcomes in terms of the way students view problem solving and their roles as problem solvers and community members. Rather than going into a relationship with the assumption that the organization is the "problem" and the university will provide the answer, students understand the importance of working together with people to meet a need (McKnight 1995).

To illustrate, I describe how I learned to make the distinction between client and partner, between technical problem solving and service. In my earliest attempts to integrate service- learning, I emphasized to students the learning and the advantages that would accrue. The projects, following a model advocated by Huckin (1997), included an initial proposal, progress reports, the project itself (for example, Web sites, newsletters, annual reports), a reflection report, and an oral presentation to the class. We began the term working with seven clients, ranging from the New River Valley Free Clinic to the YMCA at Virginia Tech. By term's end, we had met most of the needs outlined by the clients, producing products that would be used. Students applied what they learned in class about issues such as audience analysis, design, and layout. They walked away with an item for their rèsumès and, in some cases, a product they could include in a portfolio. But there wasn't much the students could say in their reflection reports about service other than statements about how they felt good about "helping" and how much that "helping" would help them later in life. Nor could I say much. I didn't get to know the clients well. Although I spoke with all of them on the phone throughout the term, I never even met two of them face-to-face. In all but one case, neither the student teams nor I formed partnerships or learned much more about the organizations, the people who worked for them, and the people they served other than what we needed to know to complete the projects. The relationships were truly consultant-client relationships, with one exception, and that exception led me to reevaluate my pedagogy to focus more on the area between service and learning. The team that opened my eyes took their project further than the others and helped me to understand the value of service. This team worked for Managing Information with Rural America (MIRA) in Christiansburg, a nearby town. MIRA,"a grantmaking initiative of the W.K. Kellogg Foundation's Food Systems/Rural Development program area, . . . seeks to draw upon the reservoirs of strength, tenacity, and civic commitment in rural communities and to help rural people use technology (electronic communications and information systems) as a tool to meet current and future challenges" (MIRA 2002); and the mission of this local chapter of MIRA was to make information accessible online. They asked for our help to create a newsletter; the team was asked to design it, write the first issue, and convert it to HTML.

Although their project was not different in kind or scope from the other projects, the advantage this team had was the energy of the larger team they joined. Most teams worked for organizations understaffed and desperate for help. In many cases, they did not have the expertise or the personnel to create the Web site or design the brochure. Thus, they asked for help and were glad to take it. They didn't have the time to supervise or, in some cases, even advise students. Thus, they were good candidates for client projects but not good ones for service-learning partnerships.

Although I didn't realize it at first, the team working with MIRA had a different situation. They became members of a larger project or team, a diverse group of local people interested in enhancing information exchange. They needed our student's expertise and help, but they wanted to work with these students, considering them as team members rather than consultants. In essence, they sought volunteers because of their expertise, and they expected that these volunteers would come to believe in the idea of the project.

Although the MIRA team had some internal problems and although working as part of a larger team had complications in terms of meeting deadlines, the students began to see that because they were involved in a dialogic, reciprocal relationship, they were learning more than just how to apply their technical skills. Because they framed their project in terms of the relationships they developed with the organization's members, they (and I) began to see a distinction between technical solutions and public action. Like the other teams, they did good work, but their approach and the assumptions they made about the organization and the people it served were different. They turned their work into service; no longer was it an act of experts providing solutions.

Instead, they joined with others to solve problems that all of them could see. As one of the students put it, "My involvement with the service-learning project changed my outlook. My work with MIRA [Managing Information with

Rural America] has had a profound impact on my commitment to volunteerism and has solidified my plans to become an active member of my community." For this student, service did not displace care; rather, service became a form of caring about the problem, the people, and the solution that he helped implement by "restructur[ing] the relationships of service around the Latin roots of the word—'feeling with' . . . [turning] service from an act of charity or authority into an act of empathy that grasps an essential" (Flower 1997, 99).

## Growth of Service-Learning in Professional Communication

When implemented in a manner similar to the one described previously, service-learning is an attractive pedagogy and a philosophy, one growing rapidly in all fields of education, at all levels. The term itself can be traced back to a group of pioneers in the late 1960s (Stanton, Giles, and Cruz 1999); and the "movement" based on the term began rather modestly in a variety of locations across the country by people with varied backgrounds. What brought them together were their beliefs that learning doesn't happen just in a classroom and education involves more than just knowledge for knowledge's sake. These individuals began grassroots organizations that have grown rapidly. Two—the Campus Outreach Opportunity League, a student-led advocacy group started in 1984, and Campus Compact, an organization of institutions of higher learning begun by the presidents of Brown, Georgetown, and Stanford Universities in 1985—have assisted the spread of service-learning, as has the creation of the Corporation for National and Community Service.

Although service-learning traces its history back to the mid-1960s, until 1997, little had been written about service-learning and courses whose subject was communication. The first few articles centered on work done in composition and advanced composition courses (Crawford 1993; Mansfield 1993; Herzberg 1994). Then, Cushman (1996) expanded the concept by talking about how working in and for the community can help to mold rhetoricians who are agents for change. Her work was followed by other articles in journals in composition studies and business and technical communication that acknowledged not only the practical value of this pedagogy in terms of how it can improve students' ability to apply what they have learned but also its value toward increasing their sense of civic responsibility (Bush-Bacelis 1998; Dubinsky 2002; Haussamen 1997; Henson and Sutliff 1998; Huckin 1997; Matthews and Zimmerman 1999; Shutz and Gere 1998). These articles outlined methods for implementing this pedagogy, its problems, and its benefits. Although problems can range from students' failing to take service seriously and copping an attitude toward skills and the workplace to having difficulty learning to speak for the organizations they're working with, the benefits, when service-learning is implemented fully, are clear. Students, working with community partners to create Web sites, write promotional or informational materials (newsletters, fact sheets, brochures, annual reports), become more committed to their communities and believe that they are better prepared to write effectively.

This recent acknowledgment of service-learning in our field is linked, in part, to an understanding that we've been practicing forms of experiential learning for several decades. Huckin (1997), for instance, states that although he hadn't heard about service-learning prior to 1997, he knows of many colleagues who had been employing project-based learning as far back as the early 1980s. It is also linked to the idea that our field has roots in classical rhetoric and the work of rhetors in classical Greece and Rome involved a commitment to the polis, to society (Dubinsky 2002). Quintilian, for instance, talked about "ideal orators" willing to put their knowledge and skills to work for the common good, who revealed themselves "in the actual practice and experience of life" (quoted in Whitburn 1984, 228).

The growth of service-learning has led to a resurgence of the importance of service. In 1999, Technical Communication Quarterly devoted an entire issue of the journal to redefining the "service" course, talking in terms of radical new pedagogy (David and Kienzler 1999), multiple literacies (Nagelhout 1999), and situated learning (Artemeva, Logie, and St-Martin 1999). The combination of service-learning and a willingness to redefine the very course often used to illustrate our menial status points to a grassroots effort in our field to slow down or even halt the attempts to make a "conceptual shift" away from service. They also illustrate reasons why even those among us calling for a new identity do not choose to throw away the old clothes altogether.

## Reexamining What We Do

The debate over the word service is old, tracing its roots in some ways to a separation between what is useful and higher knowledge, one highlighted by arguments such as Boyer's to redefine scholarship and Sullivan and Porter's to redefine the field of professional writing by breaking from a "service identity." It is a debate whose time has come.

One point of focus (Ronald 1987) is to examine our relationships with those to whom we teach these "mechanical skills" in answer to one of the questions members of our discipline often ask when discussing the nature of our work: "[Are we] helping students get jobs and promotions or [are we] helping them become critical thinkers who can change and improve their professions?" The question seems directed at some of the issues embedded in the debate surrounding service. If all we do is help students get jobs, then perhaps all we do is provide something that, while necessary, is menial. If, on the other hand, we help students become better citizens, then perhaps there is substance to our discipline.

When such questions are asked, few consider the possibility that such a question might be a false dichotomy. Regardless of how you see the question, if we're "helping," then we're being of service. By "helping," we provide not only added value but also essential knowledge and skills that students, stakeholders, and society need. We provide a procedural knowledge that helps students get jobs and that gives them the tools to improve their workplaces and their organizational cultures.

By arguing for the value of "procedural knowledge," by making a case for pedagogies such as "service learning" and for the value of "the scholarship of application," we can begin to create an environment in which those who teach these courses don't have to feel like "factory workers." Yet, these arguments will be incomplete unless we explicitly address the tacit nature of the way others and we view "service."

David Russell (1991, 71) says, "Tacit traditions have remained tacit because academia had no shared vocabulary, no institutional forums for discussing discipline-specific writing instruction." Although he isn't talking about the concept of "service" per se, he is talking about the issue of literacy, which is a goal of our "service courses." The concept that teaching writing is a service to enable the other departments to focus on the "important" tasks of teaching their content areas is such a tacit tradition. It will remain tacit as long as the underlying debate about what service means is left unaddressed.

## Conclusion

My immediate reason for addressing this topic is that I've been asked to develop a writing program to serve the needs of the many departments that believe they produce knowledge that benefits society. They see their primary mission as contained within my university's motto of "Ut Prosim" or "That I May Serve." They believe that the production of knowledge is separate from the rhetorical acts involved in such production. They see the service they do as essential and the service of those who teach writing as menial. In essence, they see a significant distinction between their kind of service and ours. What is worse, as evidenced by my brief poll, many of my departmental colleagues agree, perpetuating or extending what one scholar has called a "disciplinary Maginot Line" (Lanham 1983, 16).

To build programs in technical communication, achieve parity in institutions devoted to research, and circumvent the Maginot Line, the tacit tradition linked to the pejorative term of "service" needs to be brought out into the open for examination and discussion. We need to "see" that the forces that produced the universities and colleges many of us teach in are the same forces that created the need for our courses. We should wear the mantle of service proudly as we demonstrate the value of service to the university. We need not hide our relationship with service to claim disciplinarity. Instead, we should examine what James White (1985) calls "invisible discourse" (the implicit expectations that are part of a culture). To build and maintain programs ecologically balanced, one of our goals should be to make visible the expectations about service that our stakeholders and we hold.

I've begun to do just that by establishing a dialogue with members of other disciplines responsible for curriculum development. These discussions are playing a role in the redesign of our "service" courses, in which we're negotiating how we can integrate service-learning. By taking the lead and using service-learning pedagogy in my service courses and then publicizing the results through conversations, the ServiceLearning Center, workshops, and university newsletters, I'm opening up a dialogue about the reasons for elevating service, which include "1) the civic, moral, and cognitive development of students, 2) the improvement of the quality of life of the community as a result of university work, and 3) the campus's contribution to democracy" (Bringle, Games, and Malloy 1999, 199).

Integrating service-learning into our curriculum and working to become reflective practitioners, while also encouraging students to reflect on the work they do and the situations contributing to that work, will add to our status. When we engage in service-learning, we engage in problem solving, and as Harry Boyte (1993) says, "Problem-solving . . . is not a narrowly utilitarian term" (63). We are offering a rhetorical education that has larger purposes. By asking students to go out into the community, we enable them to develop skills and insights by focusing on real problems of real people. They learn, by working in semester-long reciprocal relationships with organizations in the community, that our society isn't perfect and that there are many ways to effect change. Specifically, they learn that the skills we teach them, when applied with care, can cause things to happen, particularly when they see that most nonprofits depend on grants and funds that come through donations (often solicited via letters or newsletters) to keep them alive. They learn to become rhetoricians for change (Cushman 1996). Consequently, they learn the value of writing well, and they apply what we teach far more enthusiastically.

In every class I've taught in which I've integrated service-learning, even earlier ones when I failed to achieve a balance between service and learning, students have overwhelmingly found the projects valuable and asked if there would be other courses with that teaching and learning strategy.8 For these students, the theoretical became practical because it was related to life. That said, the task of implementing this pedagogy isn't easy; finding the balance between service and learning is as difficult as finding the balance between theory and practice or workplace and academe. For teachers to bridge the gaps successfully, they must be aware of the need for balance between service and learning and of the potential problems associated with this need. In essence, they need to read teacher's stories such as those by Matthews and Zimmerman (1999) and Huckin (1997).

To maintain integrity and continuity of purpose, we also need to encourage our colleagues in disciplines such as communication, computer science, and graphic arts that become part of technical or professional communication programs to contribute to this dialogue about the social contexts for literacy and our obligations to students, stakeholders, and society. We should answer what service is, decide whom we serve and why, and determine what those answers mean to us and to those we serve. Once answered, we can define, develop, and defend the concept of service to argue effectively for our place in the academy. Doing so will enable us "to provide for an education for citizenship" (Newman 1985, 31), teach the process of deliberation and judgment essential to such an education (Sullivan 1990, 383), and empower students to effect change in their communities. If we accomplish those goals, we have served truly and expansively, and we'll have a unified vision of our discipline that is practical in the fullest sense and valued because of the ethical and political dimensions associated with it. Our colleagues in literature and other disciplines will see that the work we do extends beyond comma splices and forms; they'll see that our service not only teaches the skills they value but also enables students to function more fully in their workplaces.

## BREAKING VIEWING HABITS

As universities and colleges expand their reaches beyond their own walls and form partnerships with one another to bring greater variety and flexibility of courses to students within and between states, distance (or distributed) education gains prevalence. Distance education, by definition, relies on technological solutions to bring course content to students. The highly successful partnership between the University of Central Florida and Brevard Community College offers students courses taught in a variety of media, such as the World Wide Web, videotape, radio broadcasts, and interactive television. The Twin Cities campus of the University of Minnesota employs various technologies to deliver courses to and receive them from its partners—Southwest State University and the University Center Rochester—as well as its own distributed campuses in Duluth, Crookston, and Morris. In fact, a quick Internet search with the keywords "distance education" reveals the broadening scope of technology use in nontraditional learning spaces: Michigan, South Dakota, Kentucky, Idaho, and many other states and communities boast their ability to deliver classes to students at a distance.

Moreover, distributed teams in the corporate arena increasingly adopt emerging technologies to capitalize on the skills and knowledge of employees at remote locations while decreasing the need for those employees to travel—a concern of especial importance in the wake of recent terrorist attacks in New York and Washington, D.C.

As technical communicators, we appreciate the value of addressing the practical aspects of using technology in our teaching, but we also recognize the necessity of addressing the underlying social and political dynamics as well. If we do not address such concerns, we risk that students and faculty will approach "technology more as individual consumers than as collective producers" (Pew Higher Education Roundtable 1994, 3A). Focusing exclusively on the practical aspects of using a technology reinforces the primacy of the medium, rather than the educational and social needs of teachers and students. In fact, it encourages teachers and students to see the technology as inevitable, inescapable, and inflexible. As Johnson-Eilola (1997) notes, when we separate social concerns from technology, "users are discouraged from recognizing and understanding (let alone participating in) the ways technologies construct our lives" (98).

In this chapter, we propose a self-conscious, participatory approach to using technology that will allow teachers of technical communication to examine the power of a medium in collaboration with their students. In our discussion here, we focus on the technology of interactive television (ITV), a medium common in the technical communication classroom, distance education, and university-community college partnership programs, as well as corporate teleconferencing. Together, we can negotiate ITV as a cultural and historical artifact, whose realizations can be shaped according to the needs of the participants rather than the demands of the technology. Through a critical exploration, students and teachers can assume an agency denied to them through passive reception to the technology and can re-create the medium as they experience it.

Our approach includes the following three goals:
1. To understand ITV technology through collaborative discussion
2. To identify and examine underlying assumptions that define and limit our approaches to ITV
3. To explore and reinvent norms and conventions of ITV use in order to shape our own realizations of the technology

We recognize that using ITV is itself a form of technical communication, and we should therefore approach the medium not as a transaction but as an experience grounded in rhetorical sensitivity. Our approach will help students and teachers develop heightened media appreciation and, more importantly, it will encourage an informed, agency-assumed practice that can be applied beyond ITV to manage other tools still emerging in the workplace. Our intent is that even though we focus on ITV, our discussion can help participants use other technologies more effectively as well.

## The Tensions of Substantive and Instrumental Views of ITV Technology

As emerging technologies are increasingly employed in both academic and professional spheres, students need access to and education with them (Karis 1997; Shirk 1997; Tebeaux 1989; Zuboff 1988). To be successful, students, and we as instructors, need communicative and rhetorical skills, in addition to instrumental proficiency. ITV technology, as familiar and intuitive as it may first appear, is no exception to this rule.

We acknowledge the tension teachers often feel when the promise of a given technology turns into an encumbrance that counters our pedagogical convictions. As one of our instructors notes, "The technology is a barrier you're trying to mitigate, rather than a tool that will help you teach; the conditions of the ITV environment are simply not conducive to teaching." When the operational conditions of the technology and the values of our teaching clash, it precipitates a variety of responses from teachers: resignation to what we see as the constraints of the technology (Johnson-Eilola 1997); outright rejection of the technology (Gilchrist 1997); or adaptation of the technology to the teaching practices we value (Bruce and Rubin 1993). We must recognize, as Anson (1999) does, that the "key to sustaining our pedagogical advances in the teaching of writing, even as we are pulled by the magnetic forces of innovation, will be to take control of these technologies, using them in effective ways" (273). Our approach is intended to give teachers and students such control.

Unfortunately, the practical use of ITV often leads to discussions about technology as a constraint that limits our pedagogical approaches: microphones and cameras impede interaction, technology interferes with the creation and maintenance of collaborative groups, while sound delay disrupts interpersonal communication. What we find disconcerting about these discussions is that they are characteristic of what Johnson-Eilola (1997), drawing from the work of Andrew Feenberg, describes as substantive views of technology: In the substantive view, we have little choice about how to deploy specific technologies in specific instances: Once we have adopted technologies, they determine their own uses.... Like a highly communicable disease, technology remakes all it touches (and it touches all); the only alternative is to retreat. (102)

In other words, we see technology as part of a social and educational network in which we have little or no power, where the characteristics of the technology constrain our interactions and interfere with our teaching and learning. Yet, the instrumental view of technology provides even less of an alternative: in the instrumental view, "technology [is] a neutral tool for doing a person's bidding" (Johnson-Eilola 1997, 102). This view discounts the ways we shape—or can be shaped by—the technology itself and implies that all we need for success is better training, more refined skills, higher levels of competence.

A common outcome of both substantive and instrumental views is a disturbing lack of agency on the part of both students and instructors. Students and teachers feel trapped by the technology, unable to engage in natural learning and interaction. This feeling of powerlessness, however, is not inevitable. If we begin to recognize the ways in which we respond to the medium and shape ourselves to its features and capabilities, rather than vice versa, we can begin to shape technology to our needs and create the medium as we use it.

The approach we advocate is one that encourages instructors and students to identify and reflect upon influences shaping our uses of technology. It forces us out of passive, substantive ways of thinking about and dealing with the technology into active, agency-driven roles that will help us shape the way we and students use technology in the classroom. As Wahlstrom (1997) notes, "Without a sense of agency, [students and, we add, instructors] become technological determinists, failing to identify opportunities when they could initiate change" (131). Bruce and Rubin (1993) concur, adding that social, cultural, and economic realities "manifest themselves in details of classroom organization, availability of resources, mandated curricula, teacher preparation, ... and so on. These factors shape the possibilities for change in the classroom" and should, we argue, be an important part of classroom discussion and activity (Bruce and Rubin 1993, 5). In the next section, we discuss our approach more fully by demonstrating how our three goals are met and include activities and assignments that can be adapted to multiple ITV configurations as well as to other media.

## Self-Conscious, Participatory Approach in Action

We want to be clear that we deny neither the necessity nor the value of instrumental competency. In fact, we begin our approach by advocating that teachers and students learn how the technology operates, including its configuration and the physical limitations of its use. We see our approach as one that, ultimately, is practical, in the fullest, most rhetorical sense of the word. Miller (1989) suggests that we understand "practical rhetoric as a matter of conduct rather than of production, as a matter of arguing in a prudent way toward the good of the community." Such a view of practical, or practice-oriented, rhetoric as conduct will allow technical communication teachers to "promote both competence and critical awareness of the implications of competence" (23). Competence thus becomes one layer of a complex context. Understanding the complexities of that context through self-conscious deliberation and active participation—in the medium as well as in the classroom activities—encourages students not only to obtain and maintain skills but also to understand what having those skills means for them as members of our profession.

## *Understand ITV Technology through Collaborative Discussion*

Before we can exploit any medium, we need to understand how it works. We find that at the heart of students' concerns about interacting in the new class environment is fear of the unknown. Never has a student new to ITV entered the room and moved boldly to the front row without pausing and seeking reassurance. Faced with rows of monitors, microphones, and a glass-walled technicians' booth, most students back, wideeyed, out of the room and recheck the room number before returning to slink cautiously into a back row seat. The first step in our approach to teaching ITV, then, is to remove this fear by exploring the technology we see. We have found that many difficulties in using ITV can be avoided if all participants begin with a clear understanding of what ITV is and how it functions, as well as its capabilities and possible drawbacks. For example, in ITV classrooms, people who can't be heard often ask that the microphones be "turned up," as if they work as amplifiers. In truth, sound levels do not involve volume control, and adjustments are best made by moving the position of the microphone relative to the speaker. To create an effective orientation—both to the technology and its potential for use—we suggest teachers incorporate the following activities: group discovery to focus on the characteristics of the medium; demonstration of how the technology functions; and the modeling of our experiences of self-discovery to demonstrate an effective model for exploring technology.

Students need to understand right away that the space they are in is not a traditional classroom and that the medium is not commercial television. To this end, we advocate using an activity that focuses on the characteristics of the medium, developed by one of our instructors who teaches oral communication via ITV. At the beginning of the first class meeting, this instructor asks students to write their answers to one or more compelling questions (for example, "If you could work in any situation possible, what would it be and why?") and share them with the class. After students complete this exercise, she informs them that they have just completed their first ITV presentation and then asks that together they generate a list of "the unique characteristics of the ITV medium." Without fail, they are able to identify a full set of attributes that often characterize ITV: delays in delivery, voices canceling each other out, perceptions that people are not real, and so forth. We find that the students' experience of discovering ITV characteristics on their own proves more effective than just being told about those characteristics. Students are engaged, they speak to each other across sites, and because their perceptions are acknowledged and validated, they become generally more confident and less intimidated.

We suggest that instructors further take the mystery out of the classroom technology by demonstrating the controls and showing "the man behind the curtain" in more than a metaphorical sense. Students and instructors can decrease their anxiety by understanding how technology creates the characteristics they perceive, and an effective demonstration and explanation of controls can do much to remove the fear of the unknown or unexpected. A guided exploration of the control booth allows students to become more fully aware of what they usually just sense is happening around them and helps students to understand what to expect during class transmission. For example, a demonstration can explain how and why cameras move when students speak, the change in monitor display resulting from voice-activation, and the switch from overhead to straight-on cameras. Often, the technician is the person who can best explain and demonstrate how the technology works, but unfortunately, ITV participants have a tendency to ignore the technician as a contributing member of the community within the classroom. Encouraging a dialogue with technicians can help students feel more confident in front of the cameras and more comfortable in making requests regarding how they see themselves and others during ITV transmission. We encourage teachers and students to talk with technicians throughout the class and recognize that, whether through the technician or their own control, they can make changes as to how the technology is used.

We also believe that one of the best ways to support student learning is to model our experiences of self-discovery and exploration. Often, teachers who work flawlessly with ITV and produce polished presentations intimidate students with their expertise. Therefore, we remind teachers to share their stories of learning with students. To best learn about ITV, instructors should experience it both as students and as teachers and, while participating in these roles, record their observations about perceptions and interactions so they can share their discoveries with students. We suggest attending ITV workshops, touring the ITV classroom and experimenting with the controls, attending meetings of other courses, and, in general, gleaning as much information as possible by engaging in the role of student as well as teacher. We tell students about our initial perceptions of the technology and then describe how these evolved as we came to witness how and why our perceptions were rejected or confirmed. This modeling helps students to consider the dominant narratives they bring to technology.

By positioning ourselves as active and self-conscious explorers of the medium, we hope to encourage the same exploration and reflection in students. Our intent is that the purpose of orientation is not only to describe how the technology works but also to show that the medium is there for us to challenge and exploit, not to shy away from or fear. Talking with technicians and modeling our interest in learning about the technology help students grasp Miller's concept of seeing practical rhetoric as conduct, rather than as passive acceptance and application of rules.

## *Identify and Examine Underlying Assumptions Defining ITV*

As we stated earlier, participants need to understand that ITV is not a traditional classroom or commercial TV. Similarities between these "old" media and the "new" medium of ITV serve only to confuse us—and to invite comparisons between the two that inhibit our understanding and perpetuate unproductive, substantive responses to ITV. Students must not only recognize that they respond to ITV in conventionalized ways but must also understand as well why they respond in those ways.

Our second goal for our approach is to persuade teachers to take time to explore students' assumptions about ITV technology as well as their own. All participants need to understand the experience of the whole class community, and to this end, teachers need to promote activities that enrich students' understanding of what it means to be a productive, successful professional. We have found that with a self-conscious attention to student-centered pedagogy, assumptions about constraints can be turned easily into opportunities for professional enhancement in terms of both conduct and skill building.

One of students' most common assumptions about ITV is that it is little different from commercial television, or as one student puts it: "When I watch TV, I zone out." Indeed, the "interactive" aspect of ITV is the one least intuited by students. The screens in front of the class are not televisions in the common understanding of the term, but instead are monitors, even though they are the size and shape of screens commonly found in dorms and living rooms.

Perceived as commercial television, students are unwilling to interact with the people they see; after all, "talking back to the television" is not acceptable social behavior. Further, feelings of "watching television" reinforce the kind of passive behavior that is the antithesis of the active exploration we advocate. Interaction will not occur "naturally" until such assumptions are exposed and reshaped.

Another response to the medium, often a result of orientation materials that stress the avoidance of noise, is that students feel "like we're in church." They feel they must sit quietly and not fidget or make extraneous noise, or else the camera will zoom in on them and they will be placed in a very negative "spotlight." Such perceptions inhibit community building, the free exchange of ideas, and dialogues with others. Again, we've found that when students have the opportunity to discuss these fears and have the opportunity to see the reality as far less dramatic than their assumptions, they are generally more relaxed, engage the course content, and contribute more freely.

One of the best ways to understand the experience of the whole class community is to share each other's physical context. In the traditional classroom, we not only see our surroundings but also feel relatively certain that what we see and experience is pretty close to what students see and experience. This assumption is one we can't afford to make in the ITV classroom: many different classroom experiences exist, even within the confines of a single class. Each room has different monitor and microphone configurations, and the experience at our locale might be vastly different from that of our distant students, leading to unnecessary misunderstandings and unproductive misperceptions. For instance, we've all heard stories from teachers about how contrary students from distant sites can be: students move away from cameras so we can't see them or what they're doing. Our distant students, however, tell a much different story of what's happening: "We get tired of seeing ourselves on the monitor going out, so we move back from the camera to get a break." At the distance sites with which we have contact, there are two monitors at the front of the room: one that shows whoever is speaking at other sites and another that shows all the local students in their seats—a relentless (and distracting) mirror of their own activities.

Our distant students tell us of other instructor assumptions as well. Once we have gone through the process of sound and video checks with the local technician, we often take off at a run to make sure we have enough time to complete lessons and activities before the class ends and the monitors go blank. We often believe that, once checked, sound and transmission will remain fixed, that distant sites will continue to hear us throughout the class without our ever checking to ensure that they can. After all, in traditional classrooms, continued attention to sound, once established, is unnecessary. As our distant students tell us, however, this stability is not the case with ITV: "Instructors and the students at other sites don't realize we can't hear what they're saying, and we don't want to be the ones to interrupt. They need to check to see if they're being heard."

Taking the time simply to talk with students about the conditions created by the technology can be enlightening and can lead to problem-solving discussions that help students create their own solutions to the issues they identify and to which they respond. It can also open up avenues for collaboration with the technicians and for distant students' establishing themselves as site experts. We suggest that, early in the course, students at each site give a virtual "tour" of their locale, introducing the local technician and narrating the layout and the experience of working within that environment. This activity increases students' sensitivity to the multiple physical and rhetorical situations in which their class community must function and respond. It also prepares them for the variety of technological contexts they are likely to encounter beyond the classroom in corporate settings.

## *Explore and Reinvent Norms of ITV Use to Shape Our Realizations of the Technology*

Our third goal for self-conscious, participatory approaches to ITV recalls Bruce and Rubin's (1993) distinctions between a technology's idealized uses and its realization in actual use. Most technologies are developed with certain uses in mind, targeting desirable characteristics or behaviors for their users, what Bruce and Rubin call use as idealized by its designers. What often happens during actual use, however, is a realization process, or a process by which users shape the technology to their own ends. If we are to take control over the medium and have it serve us, we must learn to recognize the ways in which we shape ourselves to fit the technologies we use.

Few instructors, however, question idealizations of ITV technology. J. M. Neff (1998) notes, "For faculty in most disciplines, televised instruction poses little overt difficulty because it supports traditional methods of delivering education—lecture, discussion, examination" (136). The ideal use of ITV, then, appears to be presentation-style delivery with the teacher positioned as expert and the students positioned as passive recipients of prepackaged knowledge. This ideal is further entrenched by norms and conventions associated with commercial television, especially newscasts: stories and notes are compiled, transformed into scripts, and read by experts, who sit behind desks with graphics displayed over their shoulders.

The problem with presentation-style delivery, as both Neff and Anson point out, is that current writing pedagogy does not usually follow this teaching model. Instead, we have found that "students learn well by reading and writing with each other, responding to each other's drafts, negotiating revisions, discussing ideas, sharing perspectives, and finding some level of trust as collaborators in their mutual development" (Anson 1999, 269). In other words, we engage in highly collaborative writing workshops. To some extent, the features of ITV technology can interfere in this dynamic: time for discussion is discrete, bodies are distributed across geography, exchanging drafts must take place through other media, and distant students feel silenced because local students see it as a "hassle" to interact with them.

All these obstacles—both perceived and real—to the pedagogy we prefer indicate that we must reinvent the norms associated with ITV technology and create a realized use of the technology that supports collaboration, exchange, and interaction. Open discussions can help students become more context sensitive, but allowing them to reinvent their classroom behaviors to take advantage of the strengths of the medium will do even more: it will allow them to become better communicators, more effective collaborators in their learning experiences, and more powerful agents for change. They will begin, in short, a process of realization that will shape the technology to the social situation they create in the classroom. The following techniques offer ways of beginning a healthy process of realization for ITV technology in use.

First, we suggest that participants reconfigure their room to reconfigure conduct. Most ITV classrooms are arranged lecture-hall style: students sit in rows in front of a "stage" area equipped with a podium and an overhead projector. The idealized use of these rooms has the instructor in the traditional place of authority, at the front of the room, moving only as far as her microphone cord or camera angle will allow. Students—local and distant— sit and take notes. These are not the only possibilities for conducting an ITV class, however, even if they are the ones idealized by the designers. We suggest that teachers recognize the symbolic, authoritative space the front of the room holds and then consciously work to share that space with students by inviting, even requiring, them to participate in that space.

For example, in one of our classes, we ask that students spend some time at the front of the room at least once during the course, even if that means simply assisting the instructor. Having students work in groups from the front is especially comforting because students often find strength in numbers. To facilitate group work, we advocate forming groups across sites and assigning roles to group members—such as summarizing content, leading discussion, conducting a workshop—so they can further negotiate the authority space according to content and gain experience in collaboration with distant team members. We've found the use of agendas, which indicate time as well as content responsibilities, to be particularly helpful because students know what is expected of them, can be prepared to contribute, and can consider the adjustments they'd like made in the technology to accommodate their needs. Whatever the activity that brings students to the front, teachers need to be careful to demystify the technology: explain how controls work, demonstrate what monitors show and why, assist with sound checks, and provide time for experimenting and learning in addition to presenting.

Along with sharing the authority space, teachers should share student seats as well. Discussion times can be led by students or conducted with no one at the front of the room, to reinforce the value of students' participation and contribution. These shifts in geography can produce shifts in roles and reinforce student agency. Also, defining students' roles and responsibilities can open up possibilities for using both the room and class time more productively. If students see themselves as contributing to the flow and content of the class, they tend to take more control over the technology and the space so that their contributions are recognized and valued by others in the class.

Helping students define roles and goals can create a workplace meeting atmosphere not uncommon to many professional situations, where teams of people work together to accomplish something for the common good. From a more practical (instrumental) point of view, students are given opportunities to explore and use the technology, to present materials and lead discussions, and to experiment with camera angles and overhead devices. From a pedagogical standpoint, we are engaging with students in student-centered course design and implementation. If we support these kinds of student-led activities, the technology can be realized in ways that recognize the social, rhetorical situation while exploiting the strengths of the technology itself.

Second, we suggest that instructors be attentive to the language all of us use to describe interactions and re-create it to foster productive communication. Partly because many instructors spend most, if not all, of their time at one site, remote students often feel isolated, which surfaces clearly in their language. They describe their contributions, when in the form of questions, as interruptions of the normal flow and often begin their interruptions by apologizing. The effect of interrupting is further heightened by the cameras' sudden activation, precipitating speakers' abrupt appearance on the monitors. Local students reinforce the negative perception by turning their heads to look at the change on the monitor, emphasizing the feelings of distraction. "Interruption," as an unarticulated feeling or as a voiced complaint, fosters neither feelings of individual worth nor classroom community. Validating distant students' desire (and right) to contribute to class becomes partly a matter of changing the language students use to refer to their own activities and to those of their classmates.

Other communication scenarios beg attention when working in an ITV classroom as well. "Normal" conversation, with its overlapping turn taking and spontaneous commentary, simply doesn't work with ITV technology. Sound delays fragment or truncate people's comments, monitors and cameras make it difficult to identify who is speaking, and speakers can and do talk over one another. Therefore, we must decide on new protocols—such as students' identifying their names and site location when they speak—to ensure that students' voices do not get lost in digital deflections and electronic voids. Sometimes instructors must act as traffic controllers, but they need to be careful not to act as conduits for communication. We found it helpful to insist that students hand off the conversation to each other and refer to the author of previous contributions by name, thus requiring them to learn each other's names and reinforcing understanding that people on monitors are people, not merely virtual representations. Seating charts, for both students and technicians, help facilitate turn taking and quick location of who is speaking. We must insist as often as possible that students talk to one another directly, rather than through us, to build the interaction often lamented as missing in ITV communication.

Third, we've found that simply building in time for students to talk with one another—get some "face time," as one student put it—can break students out of their passive reception mode and increase their feelings of belonging to a unified class working toward common goals. We like to leave about five minutes at the beginning of class for people to connect a little before we get down to business, and we try to give collaborative groups (especially cross-site groups) time near the end of class to work, plan, or just plain chat. Students might also request that the "transmit auto-mute" mode, which blocks sounds, be used during videos, discussions, or breaks. Just as students find it tedious to look at themselves constantly during class, they sometimes find it tiresome to consider every word before they say it, even during informal conversations with their local classmates. Turning off the sound for brief periods of time gives students needed breaks from feeling on-camera during class.

We often hear that technology dehumanizes students and instructors. If this is so, it is because we conduct ourselves in ways less human; in other words, we gear our responses to the technology and not to the humans it connects. To emphasize the human connection, we try to initiate off-topic chatter and laughter on occasion, point out to students across sites their common interests, and allow students to move around—sometimes out of the gaze of the camera—so that they aren't sitting still for long stretches of time, feeling under surveillance. Finally, we suggest collaborating with students in exploiting the medium to get more out of it and developing media-rich contingency plans for times when the medium fails. One of the assumptions we can safely make about ITV—or, for that matter, about any communications technology—is that it will occasionally fail. Developing contingency plans is a valuable lesson for students, who will have to deal with some of these same technologies in their careers beyond the university. As Elizabeth Tebeaux (1989) points out, analytical skills and imagination are two qualities students need to develop to survive in technology-rich workplaces. Moreover, contingency plans situate agency with the users, rather than with the technology, turning substantive views of technology back on themselves.

One of our instructors registered her frustration with the fact that some of our distant sites have experienced equipment malfunctions that have prevented them from accessing class. As a preventive measure for technology-related access problems, this instructor and her students decided to make videotaping every class a consistent policy across sites. Even if remote students are unable to interact directly with classmates, they can still access the material and observe the interactions that took place in their absence. Using suggestions from her students, this same instructor has also learned to make adjustments in how she uses her course packets. Instead of filling them with readings, she includes lecture notes and other study aids to help students fill in any gaps they might experience in their ability to access class. Videotaping classes for later viewing and providing materials that will support students at a distance models proactive responses to technical difficulties. It also uses the medium's familiar commodity—information delivery—to its fullest.

Another suggestion for a backup plan is to assign note takers for every class period, one or two students responsible for taking class notes and posting them to an electronic bulletin board or class listserv. Even if the technology does not fail, students find these notes valuable study aids, in addition to the fact that they provide valuable experience in a practice common in our profession: to take, compile, format, and share notes from meetings. With a little guidance, students not only learn how to develop contingency plans for dealing with technological glitches, but they also learn about the implications of their decisions and the viability of their solutions—some of the more subtle layers of practical-rhetoric-as-conduct.

## Implications and Future Directions

Our approach answers Meyer and Bernhardt's (1998) call for a workplace literacy students need in order to understand and act upon social, organizational, and technological systems—to think critically and solve complex problems.

ITV gives the option of true practice, not just the role-playing that Meyer and Bernhardt advocate, to have students engage in, rather than act out, "scenarios where communication is likely to be difficult or strained" and to explore in collaboration with instructors the issues of power in discourse: "Who does the speaking? When? And under what rules?" (93). ITV offers the opportunity to expand our as well as students' understanding of communication media and distance delivery. This skill is an important one as communication technologies continue to overlap and become integrated: consider such new technologies as Web TV, Internet videoconferencing, electronic collaborative white boards, and other emerging technologies whose impact we can barely imagine.

One of the most important and challenging implications of our approach is that we must participate in it, which means that we must examine our assumptions, reactions, and attitudes along with students'. As Stuart Selber and his colleagues (1997) advise in their discussion about collaboration in hypertext writing, "[I]t may be important to collapse the distinctions between writers and readers, to subtly dissolve notions of who owns particular parts of a collaborative text" (263). We encourage a similar collapse and dissolution between students and teachers as we together explore ITV—a dissolution more radical, even, than that espoused by current student-centered pedagogy. Our readers should understand that exploring ITV while in use offers both instructors and students new opportunities to understand communication and media and to develop skills and ways of thinking that are clearly marketable as we face ever expanding ways to communicate at a distance. We must be willing and able to develop our sensitivity to the fact that not only these technologies, but also our very discipline and practice, are grounded in a complex world where communication itself is not just transactional or instrumental—it is transformational. It will be a difficult challenge to apply self-conscious reflection and participatory agency to ourselves in such a dizzying proliferation of technologies and communicative strategies, but we must.

We recognize, too, that our approach seems to take time away from what we see as the "content" of our classes—the lessons we'd like students to learn as they write and revise. To this concern we answer that if media are not themselves "content," then what are they? We do not expect students to learn how to run the sound boards and cameras, but we do expect them to learn to ask for what they want and to know enough about the technology to communicate their needs to the technicians responsible for running it. We expect students to learn to analyze the communicative situation and, from the constraints and opportunities presented by this situation, to realize a code of conduct through which they can not only get the job done but also articulate the values of our professional community. In short, we expect them to develop and exercise a literacy of agency by participating actively in shaping the technologies through which they communicate, collaborate, and work.

## BILINGUAL PROFESSIONAL WRITING

Professional writing instruction has changed considerably during the twentieth century as practitioners have worked to develop usable theories of technical and business communication. As a new century opens, United States demographics show Hispanics emerging as the fastestgrowing minority, already overtaking African Americans as the largest U.S. minority group. Census data indicates that "the Hispanic school-age population is growing faster than any other group in the country" (Gehrke 2002, 4A). Concentrations of Hispanics remain high in coastal states and are growing at astonishing rates in the Midwest and South. This demographic shift suggests the need for educators to adapt, create, and grow further as the century turns.

The University of Texas at El Paso (UTEP) has developed a Bilingual Professional Writing Certificate program as a method for increasing opportunities for English and Spanish bilingual graduates in the fields of business and industry. This program can serve as a model for other institutions of higher education fortunate enough to boast large numbers of Hispanic students. The model also has possibilities for adaptation to other bilingual or multilingual situations.

Located on the U.S.-Mexico border, UTEP is a comprehensive public urban institution, a midsized commuter campus located in the world's largest binational metropolitan center. The student population ranges from 60 to 70 percent Hispanic, mainly Mexican American and natives of Mexico who cross the border daily to attend classes. Approximately 3 percent African Americans and 4 percent Asian American, Native American, or international students from non-Hispanic countries comprise the rest of the non-Anglo population. This university is well situated to try new programs that encourage the success of Spanish-background students as well as other students interested in becoming fluent in the two languages.

### The Problem

Fluency in two languages should give students advantage in school and later as job seekers, but this has generally not been the case. One language tends to be dominant over the other in all students except the most totally bilingual, a rarity because dual proficiency requires the same degree of education in each language. Many Hispanics raised in the United States understand Spanish because they hear their parents, and particularly their grandparents, speak it regularly; however, they may not speak it well themselves and often do not know how to read or write it at all. Recent immigrants and Mexican nationals use Spanish as their dominant language and may have severe difficulties reading texts and producing technical or business documents in English.

The major manifestation of dual language backgrounds is that students speak and write with an accent. Rather than being an indication of a special talent and therefore an advantage, their accents hinder their classroom success and serve as an obstacle in their job search. Our program aims to change this situation and to make bilingualism an asset.

Stereotype threat presents one challenge for Hispanic learners. C. M. Steele (1997) explains stereotype threat as a situation wherein members of a minority group, even those who have been successful in school and at work, fear they will be labeled as inferior. Steele believes that "susceptibility to this threat derives not from internal doubts about their ability . . . but from their identification with the domain and the resulting concern they have about being stereotyped in it" (614). This stereotype means that even Hispanics graduating from secondary schools with high grade point averages may worry that their talents will not be recognized in college. They fear the stigma that "people like them" belong in lowpaying jobs that require only high school diplomas. Students suffering from stereotype threat need reassurance and a sure sense that their talents have worth. L. I. Rendon (1994) argues that universities must validate students. Their aim should be "to remove obstacles to learning, to instill in students a sense of trust in their ability to learn, to liberate students to express themselves openly even in the face of uncertainty, and to know that the way they construct knowledge is as valid as the way others construct knowledge" (47). Our program attempts to validate students in these ways.

Traditional teaching methods represent another challenge that confronts Hispanics in higher education. Despite many pedagogical innovations over the last decades, most college and university classes still follow the lecture-exam pattern. Some classes include discussions, and many enlightened teachers require some group work. However, as pointed out in Goodlad and Keating (1994), "the needs of students whose cultural and ethnic backgrounds tend to be outside the traditional mainstream are typically not met by what might be characterized as one-sizefits- all education" (273). Technical writing classes, falling under the jurisdiction of different departments, have been somewhat slow to incorporate new instructional pedagogy. Certainly, the language of instruction and production tends to be English and only English. The model presented here suggests a new pedagogical approach through a linking of two languages.

## The Program

The Bilingual Professional Writing Certificate program at UTEP grew out of the frustrations of attempting to teach technical writing and business communications classes to junior-level students who suffer from second-language interference. Two professors, one in English and one in languages and linguistics, surveyed students about their interest in English/Spanish professional writing courses that would satisfy a university requirement and let them practice both languages. The response was overwhelmingly favorable, and the professors began planning a pilot program.

Fortuitously, the Fund for the Improvement of Post-Secondary Education (FIPSE), sponsored by the U.S. Department of Education, issued a call for grant proposals. The guidelines seemed a close match for the pilot. UTEP's successful grant proposal provided almost $223,000 to implement a three-year trial program. The program structure is quite simple, requiring participants to complete two English courses and two translation courses and then to pass an exit exam. The entry course into the program is either a bilingual section of Technical Writing (English 3359) or a bilingual section of Business Communication (English 3355) in the Department of English or Introduction to Translation (Translation 3359) in the Department of Languages and Linguistics. One or another of the English courses is required for many majors or minors, including business, criminal justice, professional writing and rhetoric, computer information systems, marketing, and management. The translation class is the first course required for minors in translation. Thus, instructors have an opportunity to assess students' interest and expertise in bilingual situations when they are college juniors and to invite them to work toward a certificate. By taking an additional three classes in their final two and a half years, they can gain the benefits of certification.

Class requirements included the following courses:

1. Either English 3355 or 3359 (bilingual sections)
2. Translation 3359
3. English 4300 (This senior-level technical writing practicum reinforces students' abilities to write proposals and reports in both languages and places them in an unpaid internship with a local client.)
4. Either Translation 4381 (Business and Legal Translation) or Translation 4382 (Translation for Information Media) or Translation 4383 (Literary Translation)

Students must also successfully complete an exit exam that requires them to produce original documents (such as memos and letters) in both languages and to translate documents from English to Spanish and from Spanish to English.

## *Recruitment*

Students are recruited into the program through introductory courses. We also distribute informational brochures campuswide, particularly utilizing advisors in the various related departments. During registration for each semester, we post large flyers around campus and hand small flyers to registrants. We also post bulletin broadcasts on student-accessed email. The school newspaper carries articles about our program several times a year.

Although advertising brings in students, the best recruiting tool seems to be word of mouth. Students who finish a course or two and find the experience useful recommend the program to others. Our bilingual technical and business communication classes always fill early in the registration process.

## *Student Profile*

Student profiles have been gathered at the beginning and end of each bilingual section of English 3355 and 3359 throughout the three years of the program's existence. Academic majors varied for enrolled students, with the largest numbers in computer informational systems, marketing, management, and English. When questioned about their reasons for selecting the bilingual section, students reported that they were interested in both languages and that they felt good bilingual skills would be an advantage in achieving their professional goals.

Specific numbers vary from semester to semester, but in one representative survey, at the beginning of the semester 60.9 percent of enrolled students rated their fluency in conversational Spanish as excellent, and 26.1 percent rated these skills as adequate. In spoken English, 43.5 percent considered themselves excellent, and 34.8 percent rated themselves as adequate. Almost all had studied both English and Spanish in school for at least a year, but in terms of writing Spanish, only 26 percent felt capable of writing a short business letter or a technical report. Only 26 to 30 percent felt capable of producing these documents in English.

By semester's end, over 90 percent felt above adequate in speaking both languages. All students felt capable of writing a short business letter, and more than 80 percent felt comfortable writing a report in either language.

When asked what they had gained from taking the bilingual course, students in all semesters reported a positive experience:

"I actually learned how to write formal business letters."

"I gained a sense of team work and a better sense of technology."

"Technical writing skills. I learned how to focus on the audience."

"I have gained experience in writing in both languages. Also more confidence to write in a formal way."

"I've learned all the great ways to apply technology to school projects both in English and Spanish."

"A thorough understanding of the professional writer in the business environment."

The program now offers two bilingual sections per semester, with an enrollment of twenty-five each. All sections regularly enroll fully and early in the registration period.

## *Advantages*

As most enrolled students seem to recognize, this program turns the perceived handicap of learning English as a second language into the advantage of being able to function effectively in two languages. Rather than thinking of themselves, or being thought of by potential employers, as inferior because they speak or write English as a second language, certificate holders may be selected over monolingual candidates because of their special training. This undergraduate program also holds promise for students who want to enter UTEP's new Ph.D. program in rhetoric and composition, which offers a unique bilingual option, allowing students with certificates to do graduate work in translation and cross-cultural rhetoric.

The program has the further advantage of highlighting business and technical exchanges with Latin America, one of the fastest growing and most neglected economic markets. Students who can communicate across cultures and language borders will find satisfying work while improving international relations.

## Theory

Strong theoretical support underlies our model for bilingual professional writing in the areas of intercultural communications, collaboration, audience response, and writing process theory.

### *Intercultural Communications*

Technological advances in the twentieth century drew nations and cultures increasingly closer. Business and industries aiming for success in the twenty-first century must begin with the understanding that they operate within a global community unlike any before—a community demanding the fluent use of many languages. Perhaps more importantly, they need awareness of different cultures and how they do business and of the ability to hire employees who can comfortably cross physical and cultural borders. A look at statistical compilations shows that in 1997 about 335,000 Americans worked for foreign-owned companies either in the United States or overseas. More than 30,000 American companies exported goods to other countries. Even before NAFTA, the U.S. earned $33.3 billion a year from exports to Mexico alone.

Within the United States, growing numbers of Spanish-speaking buyers require advertising and marketing campaigns that differ from those designed for English speakers. They also need Spanish-language product user manuals, information sheets, assembly directions, and other documents. In the interest of safety and efficiency, multilanguage documents and signs have to be provided in workplaces that employ workers whose dominant language is Spanish. Obviously, employers need professional communicators prepared to take on the task of producing these materials.

Speaking, reading, and writing a second language go a long way toward helping employees serve the changing needs of U.S. companies in a global community. As Iris Varner (2000) points out, "If business partners do not speak a common language, the entire intercultural business communication approach will be influenced by the dynamics of interpreters" (48), which can slow down or otherwise hamper transactions. Furthermore, language skills must be supplemented with "insights into social behavior, attitudes toward morality, self-perception, and the role of hierarchy" (41). The effective cross-cultural communicator avoids stereotyping, while recognizing that members of a given culture share attitudes and practices that influence their response to outsiders. Corporate cultures differ even within the United States; in an international community, styles present much greater variety. A lack of information can cause embarrassment and loss of business, even in something as seemingly basic as setting and keeping a meeting time. Thus, educators interested in training professional writers must teach them the complexities of cultural difference.

## *Collaboration*

Teamwork and collaboration have long been staples of U.S. business and technology. Today's workers must expand the ability to work with others within their own culture to an expertise in working with people from different cultures. Students learn to cooperate on the job by experiencing collaborative learning in the classroom. Furthermore, students learn more quickly, remember better what they have learned, and form stronger bonds of friendship and mutual respect with classmates and teachers when they take part in collaborative learning communities. Theorists (Johnson and Johnson 1988; Schmuck and Schmuck 1997; Slavin 1990) show that working on group projects in semester-long teams helps minority students (women, lower-class students, nonnative English speakers, and others) gain confidence in their abilities. This confidence helps in job interviews and creates independent workers.

## *Audience Response*

When writers produce messages, they engage in a process of encoding. As they do this encoding, they assume that the recipient will be able to decode the message without significant difficulty and with a low degree of error. It is easy to see how important this can be if the message includes, for example, specifications for materials used in the construction of a bridge or calibrations of equipment for use in hospitals. Audience response theory concerns itself with the proper encoding of messages and with the importance of directing attention toward the proposed receiver. Differences between senders and receivers can cause confusion within a given company, city, state, or country because no two people have the same life experience. Confusion or misunderstanding looms even larger when the sender lives in a different country from the recipient and larger yet when one speaks a different native language from another person. Clearly, anyone engaged in bicultural communication or translation must be aware that "when a message reaches the culture where it is to be decoded, it undergoes a transformation in which the influence of the decoding culture becomes a part of the message meaning" (Samovar and Porter 1988, 21). Bilingual professional writers have to think forward to the decoding process and anticipate problems caused by ambiguity or lack of accuracy. They may need to use what has been called "back translation" (having one writer translate the document in the second language and another writer translate it back into the original) to check for potential problems (Samovar and Porter 1988). They also need to decide when this rather time-consuming operation is necessary and when it is not. Such decisions require skill that can come only with practice.

## *Process Writing*

The theory of writing as a process drives most college English composition classes and offers useful assistance to bilingual professional writers. Theorists (James Britton 1975; Lester Faigley et al. 1985; Donald Murray 1972; Janet Emig 1971; James Moffett 1968) and many others urge teachers to emphasize the way people write rather than focusing only on the final product. This matters a great deal in the field of technical communication where workers are accustomed to sending rapid email messages, memos, and letters as they conduct business. These communications in English, and even more in multilingual situations, may be poorly worded and ambiguous. Writing teachers can guard against these problems by encouraging students to think about what makes good writing. They can stress the value of putting a message aside briefly and then reexamining, revising, and correcting their writing before sending it. They can also urge writers and translators to submit work to an editor— a supervisor or coworker—to make sure it communicates effectively.

## Theory in the Classroom and Beyond

Technical communication students do not study theory in isolation. They must have opportunities to put theory into practice. Our junior and senior-level technical writing courses require students to do what they have read about. In their junior year, students work in classroom companies to complete teacher-directed projects or community projects for which their teams can produce written documents. In their senior year, students act as interns in U.S. or Mexican companies on either side of the border. Each of their projects includes creating original documents (manuals, brochures, newsletters, information sheets, and such) in two languages and/or translation of existing documents. Students at UTEP have worked for hospitals, clinics, nonprofit associations, and for profit businesses and industries both in El Paso and in Ciudad Juarez. These activities create real or realistic situations where students work together producing a bilingual product. As they collaborate, they are challenged to achieve more than they have previously and are aided in this collaboration by other group members with more experience or more skill in a particular area. This challenge is especially effective in classes like ours where some students are more proficient in English and others more proficient in Spanish. The effect is a social and professional situation that replicates the working world and encourages cognition and creativity. By working and learning as a team, all the students develop greater skill in both languages as they also develop their professional writing skills.

## Questions of Ethics

### *Essentialism*

People from one culture who work with people from another culture must always guard against the dangers of essentialism, that is, the viewing of others as a group rather than as a collection of individuals. Professional writing educators have a responsibility to teach about cultural differences while warning students that not all members of a culture are the same. U.S. citizens certainly share certain qualities and understandings, but a young white woman raised in Mississippi differs in basic ways from an elderly black man from the same state. Nor is she much like a middle-aged Hispanic raised in New York City. These people speak the same language and pledge allegiance to the same flag, but they do not fit a simple pattern. Any attempt to categorize them as "typical Americans" will lead to stereotyping and essentialism.

How much more complex is it, then, to try to put labels on Latino Americans who do not share a federal government, a monetary system, or, in the case of Brazil, even a common language. Doing business in Latin America, or anywhere in the world, requires careful study and time in a target area because "the world does not divide into neat cultural packages that can be labeled, sorted, and inspected with ease" (Brake, Walker, and Walker 1995, 80). J. Leigh (1998) reminds us that learning another language brings the learner into another world, but the learner "must be able to look into, not at, the culture of the other" (90). Professional writers must not only know about the customs of other countries but also make allowances for individual differences among citizens from those countries.

## *Translation*

The specialized work of translation presents a wide range of ethical considerations. Translators can, intentionally or otherwise, create "a screen between cultures and have the potential to apply only their meanings to the words spoken in either language" (Leigh 1998, 41). Thus, they can skew the reading of any given text. This skewing opens doors to power abuse, where the translator debases one culture or elevates another through subtle uses of language. People living and studying in the United States tend to recognize the country's many freedoms, its economic stability, and its international prominence. An incautious translation can show a preference for these qualities and the accompanying middle-class standards prevalent in the United States to the detriment of people from other countries who will read the translation.

According to L. Venuti (1998), translation is subjective and unscientific. Translation teachers must warn students to be as objective as possible and to avoid imposing their personal standards on the text and its future readers. Moreover, both teachers and students have an ethical responsibility to study and remain sensitive to social and cultural difference. The translation element of our program alerts students to the philosophical implications of navigating between languages and warns them to work carefully. Students also learn to submit their translations to ethical editors and to revise as necessary before seeing the translation into print.

Although some errors in translation can be amusing, others lose business, cost money, or endanger lives. A classic example of lost business is the well-known Chevrolet campaign to sell its Nova in Latin America. Someone should surely have realized that no va in Spanish means it doesn't go. Needless to say, the campaign did not sell many cars.

More dangerous are errors that stem from faulty understanding of vocabulary for measurements, materials, and other important specifications. Poorly translated manuals and assembly guides are annoying for consumers trying to assemble a desk or a bookcase; they can be fatal when technicians use them to assemble life-care systems or airplanes.

Bilingual professional writing programs offer excellent opportunities to teach ethics. Essentialism and translation should be discussed, but these also provide a strong introduction to more general issues of ethical practice in business and industry.

## Problems and Transitions

Faculty members of the Bilingual Professional Writing Certificate program and staff at UTEP continue to examine and modify practices. The program takes from two to three years to complete, and we find that too few students who come aboard in their junior year manage to finish all four required courses. Thus far, only one candidate has received a certificate. Others are close, but many students tend to go on to graduate school or find jobs—due partly, we believe, to the skills they gain in our courses—before finishing all certificate requirements. In an effort to get students interested in the program earlier and to plan all four classes into their last two years of undergraduate work, we will attempt to make sophomores more aware of the certificate and its benefits. We have also met with the deans from the colleges of business and engineering and have sent brochures to all faculty who advise students. We hope these faculty members will not only allow time in their class schedules for completion but also urge more students to enter the program.

Another problem that other institutions adopting our model will certainly encounter is the need for skilled bilingual faculty. Although we have been fortunate in hiring an English-Spanish bilingual professional writing teacher, we have also taught the class with a team approach, including an English professor in combination with one from languages and linguistics. We continue to train existing faculty to teach in our program, as demand for our courses increases. Flexibility should play a role in staffing certificate classes.

Currently, no textbook exists that meets the needs of a bilingual technical writing class. We have been using bits and pieces of available texts plus quantities of teacher-developed material. Elaine Fredericksen and Carol Lea Clark are writing a more suitable textbook that should be published within the next few years. This resource will include translation exercises, cultural notes, and a strong emphasis on relationships with Spanish-speakers within the United States and with Spanish-speaking countries around the world.

## Model Dissemination

We consider our program a moveable feast. Simplicity characterizes the model and makes it readily transportable to other institutions. The model also leaves room for adaptation to other target languages and to other regions. Our program focuses on two languages: English and Spanish. With qualified faculty, schools could include a number of languages in the same class, making it a multilingual rather than bilingual experience. Because our campus sits on the border between the U.S. and Mexico, students have ready access to businesses and industries working in two languages. In areas without such access, instruction can be supplemented with guest speakers, videoconferences, and email communication.

Although adopting any new program takes planning, we believe this model can be put into place with a minimum of preparation and little expense. Our experience suggests that the effort will be worthwhile.

## Conclusions

As business and industry take on a more international flavor, the need for well-trained bilingual (or multilingual) professional communicators continues to grow. These personnel can be either English or other-language dominant but must have good skills in reading, speaking, and, especially, in writing both (or all) languages. J. Gilsdorf and D. Leonard (2001) point to the advantages of hiring nonnative English employees, "including exposure to new markets and suppliers, additional talent and skill, and lower costs" (441). Bilingual professional writers reduce dependence on costly translators, improve relations with non-Englishspeaking associates and customers, and eliminate embarrassing or dangerous communication errors. Educators have placed too little emphasis on these advantages and have often overlooked the potential of bilingual students as future technical and business writers. A certificate program like the one at UTEP can give these students the impetus they need to find jobs and succeed in a global business community.

This program offers particular promise in a world where technology has changed "national and international economics, demographics, and the structure of society" (Tebeaux 1989, 138). Our program prepares students to meet these changes in positive ways. Their specialized training equips them to work in the border community where they now live and also to move into other multicultural communities as the evolving workplace requires. Rather than continuing to be identified as an underrepresented and underemployed minority, these bilingual communicators will take their place as a vital element of the contemporary workforce.

## Discipline-Specific Instruction in Technical Communication

This chapter explores possibilities for pedagogical innovation offered by interdisciplinary ventures in professional development. Introductory technical communication courses offer their instructors and host departments opportunities to link conceptually and pedagogically with representatives from disciplines across campus. Too often, however, such opportunities are not acted upon. In this chapter, we discuss our participation in a two-year project that linked technical communication and computer science courses for students entering computer-related professions. We discuss the impetus for this venture, describe the linkage of courses that resulted, and explore the advantages, disadvantages, and challenges posed by the venture. We close the chapter by offering advice to others who may be interested in launching similar projects or redefining whole programs with an interdisciplinary focus.

Our final recommendations focus on two key elements of the problems posed by interdisciplinary collaboration: identifying institutional constraints and potential sources of support and engaging in thoughtful reflection on the limitations and expertise of the faculty who hope to bring such projects to fruition. We assume that most interdisciplinary ventures will, like ours, be limited to revising specific courses. However, the project of reimagining courses leads necessarily to consideration of full curricula and opens up at least the possibility for transforming entire programs.

## The Impetus toward Interdisciplinary Pedagogy

Courses that introduce students to the fundamentals of technical or professional communication are staples of college-level curricula. Whether such courses are required components of a general education curriculum or offered as electives, they have two characteristics in common: many students do not look forward to taking them, and many faculty do not look forward to teaching them. We foster a different attitude toward the course. We see the introductory course in technical communication as an ideal site for connecting disciplines and emphasizing professional development.

Introductory courses in technical communication vary in content and strategy, but at their core, they focus in some way on the communication of information related to scientific, technical, or other special knowledge areas. Communicating information has been a perennial struggle for scientific and technical professionals. Likewise, science and technology are not the typical centers of expertise for disciplines strong in communication. Simple logic suggests that some mutual growth may result from any collaboration between these groups. Nonetheless, simple logic in this case defies institutional tradition. We believed that an interdisciplinary linkage of some sort could help students better understand both computer science and technical communication. And in the process of developing an interdisciplinary classroom venture, we hoped to learn more about our disciplinary differences and commonalities as well, especially with regard to pedagogy. As we show later in this chapter, interdisciplinarity emerged in this project in many ways, including the initial course design, the selection of a course project, the execution of our course design and, to some extent, the makeup of our project teams in the course itself. And although we recognize that the core concept of offering a discipline-specific course of this kind is not new, even at Michigan Tech's campus where we were both teaching at the time, we would argue that deep-rooted divisions among colleges, departments, and disciplines, coupled with short institutional memory for pedagogical innovation, makes projects such as ours innovative.

We agreed from the beginning that a course linkage between computer science and technical communication presented an opportunity to push students toward thinking about themselves less as students and more as developing professionals. Emphasizing professional development became our conceptual link between the subject matter of our courses. We argued that students may be able to succeed by compartmentalizing their knowledge into discrete structures (such as classes, tests), but working professionals could not. (Of course, we attempted to challenge the myth of separation in the academy as well, but that attempt is a discussion worthy of its own narrative.) The emphasis on professional development emerged in the way we presented the course to students, drew discussions back to issues of responsibility, responded to their work, and involved students in a project that asked them to serve a real client. Throughout, we addressed students as developing professionals and, in doing so, asked them to raise their expectations of themselves and their classmates to a professional level.

The time and energy we invested in this project was in part an attempt to address the negative attitudes students bring to their work in introductory technical communication classes. To some extent, we were successful in altering those attitudes. Students responded favorably in course evaluations, suggesting that we continue the practice of linking computer science to technical communication. Although many students commented that the linkage finally made the introductory course in technical communication relevant and worthwhile (and did not recognize as readily the importance of technical communication to their work in computer science), some students did understand and appreciate the full impact of our pedagogical venture. To understand the students' preconceived notions about technical communication, we need to frame the introductory courses institutionally.

## *Introduction to Technical Communication at Michigan Tech*

The Department of Humanities at Michigan Tech typically offers six to eight sections of Introduction to Technical Communication (Humanities 333) each quarter. Although a few sections are taught by tenure-track faculty, most sections are taught by graduate teaching assistants who have demonstrated classroom expertise in first-year writing and who have some interest in teaching technical communication. Sections tend to fill quickly to their twenty-five- seat capacity due to general campus demand; most majors on MTU's campus require the Introduction to Technical Communication course, and all majors can take the course as an elective. MTU students typically enroll in the university's general education technical communication course during the final year of their undergraduate curricula, when they are concurrently enrolled in upper-division courses in their majors. Students are not usually encouraged to overlap these experiences in any way. As a result, the introductory technical communication course is often viewed as the final writing course that students need "to get out of the way" before they can graduate.

The course is housed in Michigan Tech's Department of Humanities, which includes faculty from a variety of disciplines, including rhetoric, technical communication, literature, composition, philosophy, and modern languages. The department's disposition toward Humanities 333 has varied somewhat in recent history. At times, the course has been considered little more than a service course in the most limiting sense. At other times the course has generated interest from faculty and graduate students alike as a site for interdisciplinary investigation of communication practice. For a time, MTU's undergraduate Scientific and Technical Communication program was directed by a faculty member whose expertise lay outside traditional technical communication studies. In many ways, this administrator's direction introduced invigorating and transformational ideas into the overall conception of the undergraduate program. However, this administrator also questioned the significance of investing faculty time into supporting campuswide, serviceoriented courses in technical communication. As a result, the Introduction to Technical Communication course was not formally administered by any subgroup within the department. Although this hands-off policy changed under the guidance of the following administrator, several years later the department still feels the lingering effects of that decision and has been forced to retool the course because it has been reclaimed into the department's teaching culture. Despite documented early successes in writing-across-the-disciplines initiatives at Michigan Tech (see Young and Fulwiler 1986, ; Elizabeth Flynn et al. 1990), Humanities 333 has always been powerfully influenced (not always positively) by pedagogical tradition and institutionally imposed limitations. For example, due to the high concentration of engineering majors enrolled in these courses, students tend to address engineering concerns more than those of any other discipline on campus. Nevertheless, engineering and science faculty at Michigan Tech have expressed concern that Humanities 333 is too broadly defined, asking for courses that serve the particular needs of specific disciplines. Our interdisciplinary venture grew out of an initiative from computer science faculty who shared such concerns.

In the next part of our discussion, we outline the moves that took us toward establishing curricular links between computer science and technical communication at MTU.

## *A Conceptual Framework for Course Linkages*

Our interdisciplinary venture was based on the assumption that linking introductory courses in technical communication directly to the professional development programs of other curricula seems a logical move toward more effective pedagogy and more fruitful relationships among disciplines and departments. We also felt that this linkage had potential for addressing more-general workplace concerns about communication abilities among college graduates: by linking communication to disciplinary content, we hoped to spark greater interest in the subject matter and to make it more central to professional development in computer science.

Certain evidence suggests that such curricular relationships have been beneficial for both students and faculty. For example, at Georgia Tech, mechanical engineering students are introduced to technical communication by writing faculty, who teach communication within the context of engineering courses (Donnell, Petraglia-Bahri, and Gable 1999). At the undergraduate level, technical communication is taught in four courses; the curriculum design emphasizes the simultaneous development of communication ability and professional engineering expertise (114). At the graduate level, students are returned to a novice level as professional communicators, at least with respect to their transition to the role of researchers; communication is linked explicitly to professional development in a series of courses and seminars (115–116). At Worcester Polytechnic Institute, John Trimbur (1997) teaches a course called "Writing about Disease and Public Health" to students from primarily biological and technical communication backgrounds. In that course,

Trimbur asks students to evaluate the transformation of medical information in its travels from the academy to public spheres. For Trimbur and his students, understanding the delivery of information is critical to professional activity and responsibility in biological professions. The course emphasizes the awareness of professional responsibility in the presentation of information to a variety of audiences. Although these arrangements do not involve specific course linkages, as ours does, the overall motivation and impact for each course is much the same, emphasizing communication in the context of professional development.

There are good examples of course linkages as well. Brian Turner and Judith Kearns, for instance, describe the linkage between a first-year composition course and a first-year history course at the University of Winnipeg (Turner and Kearns 1996). This linkage was designed to help students adjust to the rhetorical demands of college-level writing and to help them understand the content of their history course (5). Dennis Lynch (1997), a Michigan Tech colleague, is involved with another firstyear course linkage, this one between composition and biology. Among the goals of the linked courses, Lynch identifies the study of how biologists write and communicate and what it means to become a biologist (163). In each of these course linkages, as with the examples of the conceptual and pedagogical links discussed previously, there is a sense and a hope that by introducing interdisciplinarity into science, history, engineering, and communication instruction, there will result a greater understanding of each element. In effect, the hope is that the whole really will be greater than the sum of its parts.

Among the efforts we highlight here, the consistent element to developing interdisciplinary linkages is the emphasis on professional development. That emphasis is central to our work as well. From the first, we felt that when framed as courses in professional development rather than as a series of exercises about writing forms or the mechanistic development of text, technical communication courses can become explorations of what it means to become a responsible, practicing professional. Thus, we presented communication as the social medium within which products such as software packages develop. This richer focus on communication as a social activity is likely to be more interesting and useful to people across the disciplines. It is also likely to be more rewarding for students. In the context of computer science, course linkages open opportunities to discuss the relationships in professional life among communication, product development, and customer service. We can open up opportunities to engage faculty and students in discussions about responsibility in professional life, including the ways communication knowledge provides a medium for other professional responsibility. These courses also provide opportunities for teachers to talk about the differing roles professionals may play with regard to communication, including the different ways engineering, science, business, service, or communication professionals might deal with the same body of information in different contexts.

The theme of professional development drove us to design a seamless curriculum whenever possible; that is, we wanted our two courses to feel like a single course. Therefore, instead of treating the courses as two separate but linked courses, we developed the curriculum as a comprehensive, six-credit instructional unit. In the early going, we both met with both classes. Although we maintained final instructional authority in our respective courses, we approached their design as if we were developing a single course. As a result, computer science and communication interests and issues were as fully articulated as we could make them across the two courses. We were driven in our general design by two concerns: (1) that we foreground the importance of communication in both courses, rather than encourage students to separate computing and communication; and (2) that we provide students with a "real" project that would challenge them in ways that an invented project would not. We drew on the guidelines for successful writing-across-the-curriculum initiatives offered in Toby Fulwiler's (1991) "The Quiet and Insistent Revolution." We engaged collaborative learning groups in open-ended assignments that posed real-world challenges. We addressed student writing as managers rather than as teachers, offering guidance rather than grade-oriented commentary. We shared our values as communicators, researchers, and educators by discussing our pedagogical and research goals directly with students (183–185). We also looked to service-learning scholarship for assistance in drafting our specific project goals. For example, in "Technical Communication and Service Learning," Randy Brooks (1995) suggests that "the most valuable service learning includes reciprocity of outcomes: (1) the doing helps the community solve problems or address needs, and (2) the thinking helps the student develop disciplinary skills, community responsibility (ethos), awareness of cultural diversity through the integration of theory and practice" (12).

Our planning culminated in the pilot course linkage, offered in the fall quarter of 1997. In the next section, we describe that venture in greater detail.

## Software Development in Linked Computer Science and Humanities Courses

During the spring of 1997, Philip Sweany, who was a member of MTU's computer science department at the time, initiated discussion about a curriculum revision regarding technical communication instruction. In the wake of those discussions, we began developing a course linkage that brought together the introductory course in technical communication with an upper-division software management course. Students enrolled in the linked courses worked to develop educational software for a local middle-school math class. In one ten-week quarter, we asked students to design, develop, and document a prototype software package suitable for early- development field testing. Students worked in teams of four to six people to complete several project-related items:

- software package
- user manual
- design document (software design proposal)
- functional description (description of software capabilities)
- documentation plan
- software testing documents
- software maintenance plan
- several progress reports

Only a few of the project-related tasks were completed for exclusive credit in one course or the other. Most course products received developmental feedback and grades from both instructors. When we responded to projects, especially written documents, we tried to treat the encounters as shop scenarios; that is, we responded to students' work less as teachers and more as managers. And in keeping with the shop atmosphere, students showcased their work in a "software fair" held in an open computing facility at the end of the quarter.

We prepared students as well as possible within a tight time frame to undertake their projects. As part of the learning and planning process, we asked students to evaluate existing educational software packages and their accompanying documentation. During the early part of the quarter, we connected students with subject matter experts from three areas: educational software design, small-group dynamics, and middleschool mathematics pedagogy. A faculty member from MTU's education department led a series of discussions on educational software design, including special focus sessions on developing interactivity and appealing to young audiences. A graduate student from MTU's humanities department led a series of discussions on small-group dynamics, including sessions on roles and role-playing and conflict management. Throughout the quarter, students were in contact with the math teacher who served as the project client via the World Wide Web and email. We gathered questions from students about her teaching methods, the teaching curriculum she used in her classes, and her students' experience with computers. She responded by posting information to a special section of her Web site devoted to the project.

Throughout the quarter, project-related discussions spanned issues in software and interface design, teaching and learning strategies, usability testing, and document design. We encouraged students to engage the theories they encountered in class discussions and in professional literature and, whenever possible, to extend those theories to their work. Although the software design project was the centerpiece of this linked curriculum, students participated in a variety of discussions and assignments that helped them develop the expertise they needed to complete their work.

## *Outcomes of the Software Design Projects*

Because we did not initially have a long-term commitment to the project from our department-level administrators, we did not think it wise to plan to make the class projects an ongoing effort. That is, we insisted that project groups attempt to develop, test, and deliver complete educational software packages in eleven weeks. Given this tight time frame for software development, students were forced to focus on simple design plans and to establish relatively modest goals for the complexity of interactivity they designed into their software and manuals.

Predictably, students' attempts to design software for a middle-school audience were either too simplistic or too complex. Michigan Tech students (especially those enrolled in scientific and technological disciplines) tend to be adept at solving math problems. It was difficult for them to understand the relative simplicity of middle-school math curricula. Nevertheless, most groups managed to develop projects that the client said she would be willing to field test. Most of the software packages that resulted from that first run of the linked courses focused on presenting students with information from the curriculum and then quizzing them on the knowledge they were supposed to gain. In preliminary, informal field testing, students in the client's classes were often overwhelmed with the complexity of the problems presented in students' software. However, they responded favorably to the idea of integrating computers into their curriculum for any purpose.

One project group continued its work in an independent study that extended beyond the initial quarter. That group developed a game, Lemonade Stand, that presented users with the problem of maintaining a successful beverage stand in the face of daily weather changes and fickle market demand for their product. To add an element of drama, the project group allowed users to avoid natural and social disasters (such as tornados and bullies) by solving additional math problems. This project group focused more than others on interface design and developing interactivity.

The user manuals that resulted from the software development projects were in some ways better developed than the packages themselves and with good reason. In a sense, the documentation drove the development of the software. Project groups submitted detailed written plans for their software and manuals well in advance of the completed projects. Those plans formed the basis for all of their future development. Because of the tight time frame, groups tended to stick to their original designs whenever possible so they would not have to go back and rework their documentation to fit new project developments. Thus, project groups kept to their general plans, focusing their problem-solving innovations on methods for accomplishing their original design goals. In the end, there were still last minute software changes not properly documented, but these instances were few. Overall, the user manuals were targeted more appropriately to the focus audience than the software packages themselves. Although students tended to assume that their audiences would find the software intuitive in its design, they also responded well in general to our suggestions for developing the documentation further.

Perhaps more significant than student successes in terms of their learning experience, however, was their recognition that they had all misjudged their audience in some way. The software fair was a showcase for what students learned and what they could have done, as much as it was an opportunity for students to discuss the software they actually developed. Few students were satisfied with what they had accomplished during the quarter, although most believed that their experience was not adequately represented in their final products. Unfortunately, MTU's quarter system left us with little opportunity to follow up on and encourage detailed reflection from software groups once the course ended. For many students, we could only hope that we had established a solid groundwork for such reflection and that they would engage in that process independent of their classroom experience.

We stated earlier that we believed students would benefit more from both their communication and software design courses if they were able to make connections between courses previously disconnected and to work with a real audience and purpose. And as hoped, students understood the relationship between their technical and communication responsibilities more fully in both classes than either of us had experienced prior to linking them. For example, in previous software development courses, Sweany observed discussions among groups primarily about technical issues in software development. In our linked courses, project groups discussed meeting user needs as much as they discussed solving technical problems. They argued about the logistics and merits of usability testing for both the software and its accompanying documentation. Teams in general were more concerned from the beginning about the way all the elements of the problem affected software design decisions (including user needs, information design, content, teaching strategies, learning styles).

In the end-of-the-term evaluations, students expressed a general support for the course linkage. In addition to receiving good marks in the numerically based evaluations, the course received positive qualitative comments:

*The format provided an interesting and relevant way to learn the material. It gave everything a sense of connection and direction.*

*I would definitely recommend this course. I would warn them that it does require a lot of work, but that they will learn a lot.*

*During the first week of classes, I considered dropping. It seemed that the work would be hell. At times I came close but I'm glad I stuck it out. I found that the project was fun and a good learning experience.*

These early successes not only gave us many things to think about but also left us hopeful that we were on the right track, working toward a useful, productive goal that satisfied students, administrators, and our colleagues in teaching. Despite rich possibilities for professional and curricular success, we still faced political and financial challenges in our endeavor to reinvent the introductory technical communication service course at MTU. We found that institutional momentum does not easily shift to support customized interdisciplinary education. In the next section, we reflect on some of the advantages, disadvantages, and challenges to establishing linked, interdisciplinary courses.

## Advantages, Disadvantages, and Challenges of Interdisciplinary Pedagogy

Although we believe this interdisciplinary course linkage was generally successful, it is nonetheless a venture rich with complications. In this section, we address some of the advantages, disadvantages, and challenges we have come to connect with our efforts. Although we believe that this interdisciplinary effort ought to be adopted more widely, we understand why such curricular innovations, without careful planning and energetic self-promotion in the early stages, are likely to remain isolated experiments in pedagogical design. Because we are aware of the benefits as well as the challenges for implementing this curriculum, we address the issue in our final recommendations.

## *Advantages of Interdisciplinary Pedagogy*

Our initial attempt to link courses in computer science and technical communication was met by students with increased commitment to connecting communication and computer science in their thinking about professional development. We have gathered feedback through a variety of means, including standard course evaluations from each course, anonymous questionnaires, informal interviews with students, and word of mouth. And some students have gone on to use their course projects as professional portfolio material in the job market. The linked-course project has begun to acquire a favorable reputation among first- and second-year students, many of whom now look forward to participating in the project. From the outset, we focused on four aspects of the course linkage we felt would most likely serve student interests and needs: the advantage of a comprehensive curriculum; professionally contextualized communication instruction; real-client motivation; and interdisciplinary exchange between faculty.

## *Comprehensive Curriculum Design*

We have argued here that the linkage of courses in other disciplines to the introductory technical communication course could in the best of circumstances result in a comprehensive learning experience for students. Further, linked courses offer an opportunity to focus in greater depth on the relationships among subject matter expertise, communication activities, and responsibility against a backdrop of professional development. We still see this advantage as the overarching benefit for such curricular innovation.

## *Professionally Contextualized Communication Instruction*

A consequence of linked courses is the opportunity to contextualize communication instruction with the acquisition of subject matter expertise in scientific and technological disciplines. This contextualization is more than a side effect of such pedagogical efforts; it is a real advantage to be pursued in course design and execution. We agree with students that contextualized communication instruction is far more relevant to their professional development than a course offered to a general audience of students who represent a random sampling of campus disciplines and departments. When instructors have the luxury of making technical communication courses immediately relevant to students, there is far greater potential for meeting everyone's expectations in the course.

## Real-Client and Real-Project Motivation

Although it is not a direct requirement that a comprehensive, contextualized venture such as ours be anchored by a real project with a real client, we recognized immediately that the cumulative contact time gave us the opportunity to introduce this element to the courses with some hope of success. The advantage of serving a real client is an extension of the other circumstances of our venture; nonetheless, we would recommend that anyone interested in forging such linkages pursue the possibility of connecting to a real project. Again, this helps students contextualize their work more easily in a framework of professional development and offers them added motivation to succeed. A client will see their work in the end.

We recognized the extra effort required from our client to participate in a project of our devising. To benefit from the project, she had to invest time in helping students understand her needs and the needs of her students, as well as her curriculum structure and teaching methods, and she had to make time to test prospective software packages once they were ready for their audiences. We worked hard to ensure that her efforts were rewarded regardless of the success of our project. In return for our client's participation, we offered technical support for the delivery and use of the software developed by students, the promise of revisions to potentially lucrative software packages, and the possibility of new computers from future project funding.

## Interdisciplinary Exchange between Faculty

Regardless of the classroom success or failure of a project such as this one, we feel strongly that one of the benefits of the venture, both for ourselves and students, is simple collegial exchange. To make clear our scholarly, pedagogical, and professional assumptions and goals, we had to understand them ourselves and be able to articulate them effectively. A significant element of our exchange revolved around tracing the intellectual legacy of our practices in response to the most elegant and confounding question of all: why? By going into our courses with a greater understanding of the values each of us held, we were able to anticipate how to best complement one another and when to use our professional differences constructively and creatively to spark discussion with and among students. Such pedagogical acts require trust that comes only from contextualized interdisciplinary discourse.

Although we have discussed these advantages already in this chapter, we have not addressed in any detail the drawbacks and challenges to interdisciplinary course linkages. We do that in the next two sections.

## Disadvantages of Interdisciplinary Pedagogy

We would be remiss if we did not discuss the downside of interdisciplinary ventures such as the one in which we engaged. Although we discuss only two such disadvantages here, we round out the discussion by addressing challenges in the section that follows. Here we discuss problems of time investment in curriculum development and the negative consequences of extended student-teacher contact time.

## Interdisciplinarity Demands Significant Time Investment

A course linkage such as this one demands a far greater investment of time than a standard university course preparation. Our discussions began several months prior to the first class meeting. During that time, we invested time in discussions about big-picture conceptual issues, logistical details, textbooks, guest speakers, assignment development, and other issues, including funding sources. Some of our efforts were supported by outside funding. Grants provided an alternate means of accounting for our time investment. Even so, this venture represents significant allocation of time above and beyond our typical course development.

## Extended Student-Teacher Contact Can Have Negative Consequences

We already said that the extended contact time with students was one of the advantages of a comprehensive course linkage. However, that extended contact time can also become a disadvantage for both students and faculty. Students who struggle for any reason struggle in two courses, not one. If their struggles are confined to their peace of mind in the courses, then the disadvantage is personal to them. However, such is rarely the case, especially in a team-driven, project-oriented course. The course linkage represents a significant investment for students as well, and any problems are thus magnified. Time can be an opportunity or a prison.

## Challenges of Interdisciplinary Pedagogy

In addition to the specific disadvantages of interdisciplinary course linkages, there are several obstacles to be overcome both to establish and maintain the venture. We classify them as challenges rather than disadvantages because they refer more to institutional difficulties than to pedagogical drawbacks. Each is also a call to respond innovatively to a dynamic professional context. We discuss five such challenges here: institutional obstacles; institutionalized disciplinarity; inconsistent rewards; funding; and sustaining commitment. After raising these challenges for consideration, we discuss several strategies for meeting such challenges and launching successful interdisciplinary teaching ventures.

## *Institutional Logistics Create Obstacles*

Institutions do not always respond favorably to special limitations placed on course enrollments. Standard course prerequisites are easily accounted for by scheduling personnel and software, but our course linkage created problems for the campus registrar. The introductory course in technical communication is in high demand at MTU, and students from other disciplines were frustrated that some of the sections offered were closed to people outside computer science. The registrar's office did not share our enthusiasm for the linkage experiment and so resisted our efforts to have special limits placed on our sections.

## *Institutionalized Disciplinarity*

Universities seem to be set up to encourage disciplinary isolationism, not interdisciplinarity, especially when working with undergraduate students. Students are required to take courses that range across several departments and disciplines as part of their studies, but rarely are individual courses cotaught by faculty from different departments or disciplines. We explored course linkages rather than a single cotaught course in part because we could not find a way to satisfy the university's need to assign credit for the course offerings to an individual faculty member.

Further, university faculty do not tend to encourage interdisciplinary thinking in their classes. Thus, students are not generally encouraged to build connections among courses from the complete range of disciplines they encounter during their studies. Institutionalized disciplinarity results in struggles to link courses and to get students to make connections between even similar subjects from different courses. Students are not trained to make interdisciplinary connections in their course work and thus struggle to do so when asked.

## *Inconsistent Rewards*

Pedagogy is not scholastically significant in all disciplines. Rewards for pedagogical innovation are therefore uneven. Incentives for such activities are also uneven. Engineering and science disciplines do not value pedagogical research as highly as industrially connected forms of research. Consequently, interdisciplinarity may not be rewarded for those involved, if their tenure areas are narrowly defined. English faculty may not earn any returns for publications focused on pedagogy or on interdisciplinary studies. In some cases, this obstacle may be a significant barrier presenting real concerns, especially for tenure-track faculty.

## *Funding*

Universities are not well set up to accommodate special allocations of resources. That is, when a special course is offered, such as Technical Writing for Computer Science Professionals, questions arise about who will accept financial responsibility for the course. Should responsibility remain with the department that hosts the faculty member or with the department whose special interests are being served? In our case, compromise was necessary. In university settings, funding allocations are highly political, and the issue of who pays is one best addressed early and with as much awareness of institutional politics as possible. We explored sources inside the university—through conversations with department chairs, deans of colleges, and upper-level administration—as well as outside sources for funding. Although we were able to secure sufficient support in the short run to launch the project, our results were mixed overall.

## *Sustaining Commitment*

Sustaining interdisciplinary commitment to a project such as this one is difficult. Faculty in English or humanities departments may not feel qualified to teach general courses in technical communication. It is an added burden (and source of insecurity) to ask faculty to teach such courses to a single discipline. On the other side, not all members of technical or scientific departments are likely to support the interdisciplinary effort we embarked on. Neither are all faculty from either side of these relationships likely to see the benefit of contextualized communication instruction. Thus, personnel issues are a problem with any discipline-specific pedagogy because it is difficult to sustain commitment. Once a team commits to a venture, as we did, there may be no one else in either department interested in or willing to continue the project. Thus, a good idea, a successful venture may fail ultimately due to inconsistent commitments to the idea.

Despite the drawbacks and challenges we present here, we remain firmly committed to the idea of interdisciplinary course linkages. Thus, we provide some suggestions in the next section for increasing the likelihood of success in such ventures.

## Developing Successful Interdisciplinary Course Linkages

Different strategies for sustaining interdisciplinary education will likely work better at different institutions, but there are a few things that we have found at Michigan Tech that seem to give us plenty of room for rethinking our relationships to other disciplines, while also rethinking the goals and strategies driving our introductory technical communication courses. To be of use to all stakeholders involved (students, faculty, administrators), there must be professional benefits from participating in the project. In rethinking the role of the technical communication service course for computer science majors, we engaged in several months of exploratory discussions, following a plan that might best be described by M. Jimmie Killingsworth (1997) as "pragmatic," focused in local, immediate, and serviceable needs (244–245). Although the specifics of our model may not work for all curricula, the process should be of interest to people looking for strategies to strengthen their present scientific, technological, or communication pedagogy, at either individual or programmatic levels.

In "Linking Communication and Software Design Courses for Professional Development in Computer Science," we (1999) attributed our success to seven strategies we adopted and that we think might be helpful to others who embark on similar ventures:

- Plan curriculum development time
- Plan faculty development time
- Find a real client and project
- Visit each other's classrooms
- Plan an ongoing project cycle
- Promote departmental consistency
- Engage in vigorous self-promotion

## *Plan Curriculum Development Time*

Prior to entering the classroom, we invested significant time to discussing our individual goals, project goals, and pedagogical values. We discussed external funding sources and possible project clients and how we might approach them. We outlined course syllabi, ideas for inviting guest speakers, discussion topics, and readings. We discussed the linkages between assignments, strategies for responding to student work, and creation of opportunities for encouraging client input. For our professional development, this time produced some of our most valuable and rewarding efforts. Our vision of the project emerged from hours of negotiations about the general approaches pedagogical and managerial to our courses. In the process of discussing what we could and would do together, we were forced to lay out our pedagogical theories and practices and work on crafting a compatible whole. Our discussions about the courses and the overall project helped us define and refine our teaching and researching roles and goals, including our personal, professional, and pedagogical goals, as well as our individual and collective measures of success.

## Plan Faculty Development Time

We invested significant time early in the project developing shared expertise in a variety of project-related issues, including educational software design, service-learning design, Java programming, and collaboration. Each area played its part in preparing us to enter into the project as a teaching team. Critical in these discussions was the ongoing process of assignment expertise. We did not want students to feel as if any one person involved in the project had exclusive expertise; we wanted to present as much as possible that our ideas, goals, and expertise with different project elements were complementary and overlapping. For example, we did not want to project a sense that the technical writing activities were secondary to the success of the overall project. But neither did we want to project that only technical communicators understand sound communication principles. We fostered a spirit of collaboration as much as possible in our development and wanted to portray that same spirit to and for students.

## Find a Real Client and Project

This strategy seems obvious, but projects can really vary. Although we focused on educational software, anything that gives students the opportunities to apply their talent and knowledge while helping the community can create a more enthusiastic work environment. Even simple projects can promote this commitment.

Clients themselves may come from a variety of settings—anyone who needs a project done or a problem addressed is a potential client. In our case, we set out to connect with another educator, and the local middle schools and high schools provided us with a long list of potential clients. In other courses where we have engaged in similar relationships with clients, we have sought out nonprofit organizations, community service organizations, and other faculty and staff from educational institutions. The difficulty is finding a client who recognizes that the success of projects often relies at least in part on the continued participation of the client. Absentee clients are too often surprised by the end result of student work. Clients who contribute to the success of projects without attempting to control them are more often satisfied with the results of their participation in service-learning environments.

## Visit Each Other's Classrooms

For the first part of the term, we were regular participants in each other's courses. This participation helped promote a spirit of collaboration and connectedness we felt was important to display to students. They take the courses more seriously knowing that we do too. As the courses progressed, we held regular faculty meetings to keep each other apprised of developments in our classes as well as to share observations of student performance. We were careful to communicate our collaborations frequently so students would get the sense that the collaboration continued even after the start of the semester.

## Plan an Ongoing Project Cycle

In this experiment, we carried only one project beyond the scope of the first quarter. We recruited one project group with a promising software concept and package to continue their work in an independent study. Ideally, we would have given every group the opportunity to work independently, but in this case this was not practical. Another possible source of project continuity would be to assign projects from one set of courses to groups in later sections of the same courses, asking them to contribute to the ongoing development of concept, software design, and documentation.

## Promote Departmental Consistency

We promoted this project in our home departments to encourage other faculty who teach these courses to either adopt our approach or promote similar pedagogical values. Our hope was that we could recruit others to participate and thus ensure that even without our direct participation the concept of our pedagogy could continue. It was our hope to create a model for others to follow, to offer an opportunity to reconsider the strengths and weaknesses of the whole computer science and technical communication curricula. Conversation is healthy, we feel, and well-considered change can be healthy as well. However, this effort is an ongoing struggle.

## Engage in Vigorous Self-Promotion

Part of our attempt to recruit others to the cause—other teachers, researchers, students, administrators, or funding sources—came in the form of self-promotion. We talked about the project with everyone, in meetings, in hallways, and via email. We submitted conference papers and publications. We submitted proposals for additional funding. Vigorous self-promotion is key to the success of any project and is particularly important to projects that ask people to rethink, revise, or reenvision their work if they are going to participate. Potential movement of any kind starts small and is sustained only by communication.

We recognize that interdisciplinary course linkages such as ours are not likely to become the model curriculum for computer science, for technical communication, or for professional development curricula. Unfortunate as this might be, we still feel the need to struggle to create and sustain an institutional atmosphere where such ventures are at least welcome experiments. That struggle opens up a trio of challenges for continuing investigation of questions beyond those that grow out of the discussion we have presented to this point. First, as a professional teaching community, we need to reinvent our pedagogy to fit the potential of new workplace relationships among professions. Nonacademic workplaces have often seemed more interdisciplinary than academic ones. Many projects in industry require the contribution of many disciplines and professions. Education ought to be a more interdisciplinary venture. But significant challenges remain before interdisciplinary education becomes an institutional reality. We need to identify those barriers and devise strategies for addressing them. Second, we need to create interdisciplinary places for discussion where values can come together, sometimes to collaborate, sometimes to complement, sometimes to conflict. Some conferences provide opportunities for interdisciplinary discussions, but too often our opportunities to engage with colleagues from other departments and disciplines are passed up. Certainly, our disciplinary barriers are in part a product of our disciplinary isolationism in curriculum design. Third, program administrators need to consider the short- and long-term ramifications of encouraging this interdisciplinary venture. In the short term, such projects open up pathways for focused reflection on pedagogical goals and practices. In the long term, such reflection can result in significant rewards. However, someone has to decide what resources, and in what amounts, are appropriate to commit to this project and whom among the many colleagues available it would be best to approach with this project. Again, how can we address this seemingly enormous set of challenges? This question bears further investigation, but we suggest some beginning places here in this chapter.

Interdisciplinary pedagogy of the kind we describe here is not new, but it is innovative. The present structure of colleges and universities does not make interdisciplinary work easy to develop or to succeed with. We met this challenge in the short run with hard work and hope for serving students well. Our early successes and failures provide fuel for future exploration in our work. And we end this discussion knowing that if teachers of technical communication and other disciplines can manage the potentially difficult logistics of a venture such as ours, there are real benefits for both students and faculty.

# TECHNICAL WRITING, SERVICE LEARNING, AND A REARTICULATION OF RESEARCH, TEACHING, AND SERVICE

Tensions among research, teaching, and service are real, and they are unproductive when they limit the type of work valued by the university (see Sosnoski 1994). There have been some notable attempts to rethink the work of the university and establish new ways to value a range of faculty initiatives that don't fit into the hierarchy of research, teaching, and service (for example, Boyer 1997). One of the more interesting attempts is the 1996 report by the MLA Commission on Professional Service, which takes as one of its starting places the imbalance among research, teaching, and service. The commission notes that service in particular is almost completely ignored or seen as an activity lacking "substantive idea content and significance" (171). There is nothing new either in the university's hierarchy of values or in the denigration of service. Yet this taxonomy of faculty work should be disconcerting to those of us who believe that a university must have long-term commitments to serve the community in which it is situated. But perhaps more problematic is the view of service as an intellectual wasteland.

My most general concern in this chapter is this view of service as lacking substance and significance. (I will focus, however, on community service learning rather than departmental or university service.) To be sure, the MLA Commission on Professional Service offers an intriguing rearticulation of research, teaching, and service into "intellectual work" and "academic and professional citizenship," with research, teaching, and service recast as sites of activity that can be found in both categories. I am interested in a tighter refiguring of these sites of activity for two reasons. The first is more general and is based on an argument that "service" is actually an epistemologically productive site of activity. It is this issue that serves as a framework for the chapter. My second reason for working toward a tighter configuration of research, teaching, and service comes specifically from the strengths, purposes, and applications of technical and professional writing. This discipline, perhaps more so than others, is immediately relevant to communities around a given university, is a powerful place from which to serve those communities, and is a discipline that will grow in sophistication from work outside the university. What I have described in these last few sentences is not "mere" service but also combines teaching, program design, and research into a matrix of interests and activities. My argument is this: An approach to technical and professional writing that works toward a rearticulation of research, teaching, and service is a powerful way to do academic work and can positively alter the meaning and value of technical and professional writing itself as a site of activity.

## Technical and Professional Writing, Service Learning, and Program Design

If my experiences at conferences such as the Conference on College Composition and Communication, the Association for Teachers of Technical Writing, and the Council for Programs in Technical and Scientific Communication are any indication, service learning is increasingly common.

But why? In a sense, service-learning projects are an extension of technical writing pedagogies that have been in place for some time. The use of cases in writing courses, for example, is commonplace despite the feeling of some that the fictive scenarios provide inadequate audience constructs (for example, Artemeva, Logie, and StMartin 1999). For many, including those whom I worked with at Georgia State University, cases provide a rich context for learning about writing, organizations, and other complex relations associated with writing (such as politics and ethics), and so we have written cases for a number of writing courses. Technical writing teachers have long used writing projects in which students work on solving problems for real clients, or what Huckin (1997) calls "community writing projects" (see the first few pages of Huckin's article for a sense of the number of programs that employed such pedagogical practices in the late 1990s). Yet, at the time Huckin wrote his article on technical writing and community service, he knew of no technical writing programs that employed service learning. That situation has certainly changed, and there are two reasons for this, I think: service learning has caught fire across the university within the last ten years, and technical and professional writing programs have been well positioned to embrace and enhance the pedagogy. Because of the focus on complex problems and real clients, then, service learning is in many ways a natural extension of pedagogies common in technical and professional writing classes.

My concern in this chapter isn't primarily with service learning, but rather with programmatic connections to service learning. Still, servicelearning teaching is at the core of the changed practices I'm arguing for here, and so I begin with my approach to service learning. Like Huckin (1997), who articulated his goals for service learning in technical writing as (1) helping students develop writing skills, (2) helping students develop civic awareness, and (3) helping the larger community by helping area nonprofits, my goals for service learning are to take part in long-term community change by meeting the needs of community partners and to provide rich and compelling contexts for student learning. These goals are actually quite complicated in how they play out. In fact, they bleed into all aspects of our writing program and my work at Georgia State.

Setting up service-learning projects takes some time. The ultimate goal is to make service-learning programmatic (more on this later), but currently I am the only faculty member who consistently teaches courses with service-learning components. The process actually runs throughout the year. I have contacts at my university's office of community service learning who occasionally funnel projects my way. I am sometimes asked by our AmeriCorp program to speak at training and information sessions with members of community-based nonprofits. These opportunities often result in new projects and relationships. And I have created a network of contacts in Atlanta, with whom I have been working for nearly four years now. These efforts are essential because through them I am trying to build long-term relationships with organizations in the community that make a difference in people's lives; likewise, I am trying to make our professional and technical writing program an organization that also makes a difference in people's lives.

Depending on my teaching and that of interested colleagues, I work with my contacts to come up with seven to fourteen projects each semester, which meet the following criteria:

- The projects meet a real need as articulated by our community partner
- The projects are sophisticated and writing related3
- The projects fit into the course time frame (about ten weeks)

The heart of the criteria is that these projects must be of service to the people with whom we are working. When these criteria are met, I begin to address other constraints. Once potential projects are identified, I visit my contacts at their locations to learn about the organization, make sure the site and neighborhood are safe and accessible to students, and further discuss the contours of the project. If my contact person expresses the desire to proceed, I write a letter of understanding, which is based on my university's standard intern contract. This letter is then rewritten by the contact person, if need be, and eventually is given to students as well (who can also add to the letter). Finally, the contact person is invited to class for the first day of the project to see the university, to see the space where students work and learn, and to meet with the group of students who will be working with them.

The students who participate in these projects are diverse in terms of age, race, class, and gender—"typical" students at Georgia State. Although the course serves students from across the university, the majority of students are juniors and seniors from the business school. Technical writing, on the other hand, isn't a true service course. About half the students in technical writing enroll to fulfill requirements for majors other than English; the other half plan to be technical writers upon graduation. The diversity of student experience is useful for service-learning projects because not only do these students have a range of interests and expertise but many also work as professionals and so bring rich histories and skills to our classes.

My approach to service learning is somewhat different from the model typically presented in composition and some technical and professional writing forums. The difference is not really in the pragmatics of setting up or teaching a service-learning project; rather, it is in the institutional framework I am trying to create. Therefore, I am more interested in relationships between the writing program and community-based organizations than I am in student–community agency relationships. In composition studies in particular, the common service-learning model is to have students find projects to work on or to choose from a wide array of projects—usually more projects than can be addressed in a given semester. Student choice, student agency, student voice are valued and for good reason (see Bacon 1997). One goal of service learning is to educate for citizenship and to transform students' understandings of and relationships with the world around them. But my concern with such an approach is that it too often sounds like a low-level colonization of the communities around a university. I question, in other words, both the pragmatics and ethics of such an approach. I wonder if students can find appropriate projects with community organizations within the time frame allotted. But more importantly, my experience with nonprofits suggests that students continually coming to them looking for projects takes valuable time and tends to raise expectations that might not be met. These expectations can create situations that hurt rather than help university-community relationships. In other words, I have serious doubts about that ability of service learning to accomplish either its service or its learning goals without a solid institutional home. Communities can indeed be hurt if they are in fact burdened by responding to numerous students looking for projects, particularly if there is no solid commitment that the project will be completed. The primary goal, after all, is to help community-based organizations help their communities; it is to participate in community change. Yet, when the primary motivation and concern is student agency, student learning, and student growth, I think service learning runs a serious risk of doing harm.

To avoid harm (at the very least), service learning in technical and professional writing needs to be part of the writing program. And so let me outline here the theory of institutional design necessary for creating that home. First, meaningful service is connected to long-term and community-driven attempts at change. Students, by the very nature of their position, cannot make the long-term commitments necessary to participate in meaningful community change. Faculty and programs can and so should make themselves available to help communities; we shouldn't be sending students into communities, like missionaries, to find problems. Second, ongoing processes of community and institution building are integral to community change (see Kretzmann and McKnight 1993 for much more on community building and change). Writing teachers and students can participate in community building and change, but only to the extent that we move away from an individual service ethic, which I tend to equate with academic charity (individual classes and students serving others, for example), and toward a community-situated ethic that seeks sustainable change, which I tend to link to (communitydefined) issues of justice. Writing programs are far more useful to communities than to individual students and faculty because they provide a context for meaningful student and faculty work. They can do so, however, only if they are designed with a community interface.

I am primarily interested is the relationship between communitybased organizations and the writing program because such an institutional relationship is more powerful and potentially more transformative. Service learning must primarily benefit the community partners with whom we work—they must be given preference—and the best way to ensure that this preference happens is to develop meaningful, longterm relationships with them. These relationships must be institutional to be effective. They cannot depend on the charisma of individual students or the commitments of individual faculty members, although they almost always start that way.

At Georgia State, we are attempting to institutionalize service learning within the writing program. At the undergraduate level, we situate service-learning experiences in both technical and business writing classes. Although service learning has never been limited to these classes, they are concentrated within these curricular slots to ensure that students have the option of service-learning experiences during their time with us, an option we encourage. In a larger sense, then, relationships between the writing program and the community are part of the identity of the writing program. Such relationships affect not only what happens in the classroom but also the kinds of experiences we offer students, the types of classes we offer (and will offer), and ultimately, the work we do as a faculty and a program. Service and community involvement, then, flow into other categories of work, and each site of activity—service, teaching, and research—is potentially transformed. In the next section, I will use two service-learning projects to demonstrate this possibility.

## Refiguring Research, Teaching, and Service

The two cases I discuss in this section began with relationships connected to my service-learning efforts. Each case shows how "service" activities can have intellectual substance; how "teaching" can both serve and foster research; and how "research" can serve and instruct.

The first case concerns my involvement with rethinking public policy efforts associated with the local Ryan White Planning Council (see Grabill 2000 for a more complete discussion). The Planning Council is a federally created body that makes decisions with respect to HIV/AIDS care in Atlanta. Most urban areas have such councils. The Planning Council must be composed of individuals who fit a number of categories (everything from health care providers to government officials), and at least 25 percent of the local Planning Council must be made up of individuals affected by the disease. In addition, the composition of that 25 percent must match the current demographics of the disease (which has become increasingly low-income, non-white females). The theory here is that those most affected by the disease ought to have a significant say in making policy about their care. However, meaningful client involvement isn't easy. In fact, the feeling of many involved with the Atlanta Planning Council is that meaningful client involvement hasn't been achieved: the council hears from too few clients, who represent a rather narrow range of those affected by the disease.

I became involved with the project to address problems of client involvement through a student's service-learning project in one of my technical writing classes. The project in question was completed with Kuhrram (Ko) Hassan, an adolescent-HIV/AIDS educator, who worked for one of the service providers funded by Ryan White legislation. Ko was concerned with generating and documenting client involvement at his agency, which became the focus of the student project. For part of a semester, the student worked with Ko to understand his position, the policies and procedures of the organization, and ways in which he and others at the organization interacted with clients. The student's goal was to create with Ko and others a process by which involvement with clients could be easily facilitated, recorded, and then written about and shared with others.6 She (the student) produced a short procedures "manual" (a process-flow chart, really), some job descriptions relevant to this process, and a formal report documenting her research and arguing for her work (a "product" and a report are typical of the deliverables for projects like this).

The student project was complicated, and in many respects, the student never finished it (although she did well within the context of the course). During the course of the student project, however, Ko and I began to discuss the larger problem of client involvement that was affecting the Planning Council's policy functions. Our conversations eventually evolved into a research project with two interconnected goals: (1) to improve client involvement in policy making by creating with clients procedures that overcame current barriers and (2) to create documentation of client involvement for use in policy discussions and reports of compliance to the government. So I was invited to help address a problem, and this invitation was framed as research, which was important for the Planning Council because it gave credibility to voices too easily dismissed as isolated, to evidence from clients too easily ignored as anecdotal, and to client concerns too often dismissed as complaints. For obvious reasons, framing my involvement as research was important to me as well. The time I devoted to this project was significant, and to frame it as "service" or even "teaching" within an institution that still maintains a hierarchy of research, teaching, and service was unwise. More to the point, however, the work I did with the Planning Council was research. But it was also a service to that organization and to the people with whom I worked, and initially it was an explicit part of my teaching.

The Planning Council project is important for other reasons as well. Because the project was one of my first service-learning experiences, what I learned changed how I teach technical and professional writing classes. I began to look for technical and professional writing practices in community-based contexts. I began to more fully understand the role of writing and research in public policy processes. And I began to rethink the common ways in which technical and professional writing identified itself as a discipline. For example, I have started to think about what might happen to technical and professional writing if we fully embraced civically focused, nonacademic writing and writing in noncorporate and governmental organizations as a critical concern. Certainly, the kinds of questions we would seek to answer in response to these different contexts would change. We would also teach different sorts of writing to a new group of students and collaborate with units within the university we don't currently work with—public health, city planning, and public policy programs, for example. Our writing program designs would similarly change. Service outside the university has been fertile intellectual ground for me because it has forced me to rethink the identity and social value of technical and professional writing both at Georgia State and within the discipline at large.

The second case concerns work that is ongoing. As part of the regular conversations I have with community-based organizations, I became involved with the United Way, who wanted to list our writing program as a "technical support resource" for their grant programs. Through these programs, the United Way funds grassroots organizations that form to solve specific problems in neighborhoods throughout Atlanta. We have worked with a couple of organizations funded by United Way grant programs. In 1998, I was appointed to an ad hoc United Way committee investigating the use of

Geographic Information Systems (GIS) technologies to provide data-based maps of neighborhoods and communities to be used by the United Way and other organizations for decision-making regarding needs and services. Students were to provide research and writing expertise to this project. Although that project was soon shelved, I developed a working relationship with Patrick Burke of The Atlanta Project's Office of Data and Policy Analysis, the group supplying the GIS and planning expertise. We agreed that some kind of Web-based interactive database would indeed be a useful tool to neighborhood and other community-based organizations. Such a tool could help them participate more effectively in planning decision- making processes that demanded information and analysis that was tough to acquire (see Sawicki and Craig 1996 for one version of the theory driving this effort).

Work on this project still continues. Our goal is to design with stakeholders from community and neighborhood organizations a Web-based queryable database that returns data in the form of maps. The tough part, of course, is designing it in such a way that it is usable by people with varying experience and literacy levels. In addition, our initial feedback suggests that this tool will be even more useful if it serves more communicative functions—if, for example, it contains spaces for exchanging ideas and spaces for matching people with people and people with resources. For me, this database is a major research project. But it has also become a regular part of my teaching and, through my teaching, a service to some communities.

Early in the project, when Patrick Burke and I were just exploring possibilities, a group of students helped me with research related to access to computers in the city of Atlanta. Our focus was on libraries and other centers that allowed free public access to computers and computer networks. For a Web-based database to work for people associated with grassroots and community organizations, there must be infrastructural access and a host of literacy-related accesses. The student project was focused on mapping infrastructural access in certain neighborhoods and gauging the literacy support (such as documentation) that would be necessary to use Web-based tools. What the students discovered was depressing at best, and it was an eye- opening experience for them, both in terms of the uneven distribution of information technology and in terms of how such inequality deeply affects the project we were working on. Students began to understand that although it would have been easy to design these Web-based tools in a vacuum, such a resource would have failed.

Later, once we had developed a prototype of the Web site, another group of students took on the task of designing the usability research necessary to write the online help, and one of these students, during a later independent study course, took on the task of writing an initial version of the help system. Like the first group of students, this group was forced to confront the complexity of a "real" project; their experiences were both frustrating and exciting. The richness of these contexts for instructional purposes cannot be overstated. The teaching benefits are substantial because they place students in complicated writing contexts and ask them to deploy many of their intellectual skills as writers toward developing a solution. Students also get an opportunity to work closely with faculty on research. This work is not only a relatively rare opportunity but also an intellectually meaningful one. Students don't often get to see what we do, and this observation strikes me as an important part of their education. At the same time, students are given an opportunity to understand aspects of their community and participate in community service. I highlight this project because, like the public policy project, it is an example of how service engagements are productive; and furthermore, it is an example of how students can participate in faculty research, thereby enhancing instruction.

I hope these projects have provided a deeper understanding of the transformative possibilities of service learning, but, more importantly, I hope they illustrate how a tight integration of research, teaching, and service begins to blur distinctions among these three areas, infuses each site of activity with shared energy and actions, and makes the work of students and faculty in technical and professional writing more meaningful and, in my mind, potentially one of the most radical sites of activity in the university.

## *Implications and New Directions*

My suggestions for rethinking research, teaching, and service begin pragmatically with service learning. The process of service-learning design that I urge others to consider looks something like this model:

- Develop relationships with others inside and outside the university who are supportive of service learning, who want to participate in service learning, and who are willing to assist in the development of service learning in technical and professional writing.
- Work to integrate service-learning experiences into the writing program.
- Begin slowly and small with a few service-learning partners and one writing class; make sure beforehand that the projects serve the needs of the partner, are curricularly appropriate, and can be completed within a term's timeline.
- Frame the service-learning projects appropriately in the classroom by showing how such work is meaningful for writing instruction and how service-learning experiences are one way to achieve the larger goals of

the university. (Students, in my experience, need to be persuaded to take risks. Persuade them and then reward them for doing so.)
- Follow up with students and service-learning partners to honestly gauge the student's intellectual and service experiences (reflection) and the nature of the benefit to the partnering agency or organization.
- Maintain relationships.

This process is one way to institutionalize service learning and increase the possibility that such experiences transform the work of the university. Over time, what counts as "curricularly appropriate" will likely change as views of writing change based on experiences with community organizations. In addition, research opportunities will abound. I see more interesting projects each year than I can possibly do. These opportunities can also filter into graduate programs and theses and dissertations. My point, again, is that embracing and then institutionalizing community involvement is one way to transform the work of university faculty in substantial ways. Research, teaching, and service, as I hope I've shown, tend to blend into one another to more fully become sites of activity where one can teach, serve, and research at the same time.

There are certainly limitations to the approach I have presented. It is time consuming, and project selection and management can be difficult. In addition, when projects don't work well, it causes significant problems for students and community partners. And because the service elements focus on organizations (when we work with organizations that serve the homeless, for example, students may not work directly with the homeless), students don't always see their work as service and don't always reflect on their work in ways that are meaningful. In terms of the larger argument I have been making, it is also telling that I still feel the need to validate the time spent and the work accomplished in terms of my ability to generate research from community-based projects. Finally, my insistence that the more transformative aspects of refiguring research, teaching, and service depend on institutionalizing service learning places a burden on writing programs that some may see as too significant. It remains to be seen whether we can handle the burdens here at Georgia State. I see these problems as program design specifications, and I think the following specifications, which move beyond the more concrete service learning suggestions at the beginning of this section, are more generally useful design heuristics:
- Service learning is unsustainable within and outside the university as an individual initiative; it does not respond well to community-driven needs and will exhaust individual faculty. Service learning must therefore be part of the writing program's design and therefore integrated into the curriculum (but not just slotted into classes; it can and should transform

how classes are taught), given administrative support, and rewarded as part of faculty work, perhaps much like the single course release given to most internship supervisors.

- Service learning must be seen as substantive and intellectually rich work and so must be visible and presented in these terms. Its meaningful presence in the writing program and curriculum is one type of visibility, as is its ability to generate research. Service must also be visible in other ways as well, such as a university Web presence in which those involved with service learning can describe its value to the community (through the use of project evaluations, letters of thanks, and project artifacts, for example). Like all good programs, technical and professional writing programs can and should argue for their social value. Service-oriented writing programs help.

Community based work in technical and professional writing allows technical and professional writing students and faculty to work across a number of contexts, with diverse audiences, and on projects of civic significance. I see technical and professional writing as a site of truly radical activity because of our ability to redefine the work of university faculty and students, because of our ability to move among the university, the corporation, and the community, and because of our ability to understand the powerful ways in which writing constructs institutional systems and changes them. We do work of "substantive idea content and significance," and we do it across sites of activity long artificially separated. Continuing this work should be at the center of who we are as teachers, researchers, and citizens.

## NOTES TOWARD A "REFLECTIVE INSTRUMENTALISM"

The faculty of Clemson University's MAPC program—rhetoricians and professional communications specialists of various kinds—gather this Monday, as we do weekly, to continue our work: designing, implementing, and enhancing the "MAPC," our M.A. program in professional communication. Rich in theory and practice, it's a program benefiting from the attention provided by frequent faculty discussions. Our current task is one that continuing graduate programs take up periodically: reviewing and revising a reading list for a comprehensive exam, in our case the MAPC oral exam keyed to the MAPC reading list.

Today, we begin our discussions by focusing on a central programmatic issue for all technical communication programs, raised in an email sent by a new colleague, Sean Williams:

*I had two students in my office this week trying to figure out just what on earth social construction has to do with writing a memo and why they need to know Cicero to write a good proposal. "Just give me the format, Dr. Williams, and*

*I'll write it,"* they say in not so many words. I think this is a huge curriculum issue, too, at the grad level because the perceived bifurcation (is that word too strong?) of the program begs the question of "fundamental" knowledge for proceeding in the program. Why aren't students required to take 490/690, "Technical Writing," but are required to take classical rhetoric? I don't mean to imply that they should be separated because I don't think they should be.

*However, I'm not sure that we as a faculty are clear on exactly how the areas are connected, and the result is confused students and perhaps a confused faculty. We need, IMHO, to articulate, in writing, goals that unite the two threads in a mission statement or something like it because this type of focused attention on "What do we do?" necessarily precedes "How do we do it?" Revising the reading list is a "How do we do it?" consideration. And, not to be too selfaware, but would defining "what do we do?" be reflective instrumentalism?*

In his recent Collision Course: Conflict, Negotiation, and Learning in a College Classroom, Russel Durst (1999) tracks the competing agendas of students and faculty in first-year composition studies classrooms. Like our MAPC students, Durst's composition students want practical help; like Durst's colleagues, we faculty want theory and critique as well. It's another version of the theory/practice divide, with faculty on one side, students on another, what Durst—and before him, Patrick Moore (1996, 1999), Carolyn Miller (1979, 1996) and Robert Johnson (1998a, 1999), among others (see Bridgeford 2002)—couches as a conflict between two impulses: on the one hand, students' "instrumentalism" and on the other, faculty theorizing.

Durst's (1999) curricular reply to this tension is what he calls "reflective instrumentalism," which, he says, "preserves the intellectual rigor and social analysis of current pedagogies without rejecting the pragmatism of most . . . students. Instead, the approach accepts students' pragmatic goals, offers to help them achieve their goals, but adds a reflective dimension that, while itself useful in the work world, also helps students place their individual aspirations in the larger context necessary for critical analysis" (178). Which leads us to ask the following questions:

Would Durst's concept of reflective instrumentalism provide a useful way of framing our program in professional communication?

If so, what changes to the program might it recommend? Would other concepts already part of the culture of the program—such as "professionalism" or "reflective practice"—provide framings more congruent with the program?

What changes might they recommend, particularly if they were made a more explicit or integral part of the program?

Are there other ways we might think about the program, especially about the relationship we seek to establish between rhetoric and technology?

How might we use these framings to develop a language to explain our expectations to students—and to ourselves?

In the pages that follow, we'll take up these questions as we narrate the process of revising the reading list for the MAPC. We'll approach this task as participant-observers of our program and our processes of curricular design. Additionally, in narrating the processes that we used in our curricular decisions, we'll explore the possibilities for representing these processes textually and our rationales for why we choose to represent them as we do. Our reading list is, of course, only one of many representations we could make of our process: other representations include MAPC recruiting materials, our MAPC handbook, and MAPC graduates themselves. In conducting this study, then, we hoped to build an understanding of

1. the processes we used to review our program
2. the ways we represent that process textually in different rhetorical situations
3. a consideration of what those representations do to the process and our understanding of it

In other words, we want to consider a final reflective question: what does the means of representation suggest about the program itself, and how will it affect the very program under scrutiny?

Equally important, we hope that, in creating this reflective account of our revision process, we make a successful argument that other programs might also try such a collaborative revision themselves. Such curricular revision isn't often consciously observed or reported on, nor is it often theorized, yet (ironically) given its influence on students, it's critical. The key factor, as we found, is to work together. In other words, we chose not to assign this task to a subgroup of a larger committee or to a special task force, but to take it up as a committee of the whole. We knew in proceeding this way that the process would take more time, would be more cumbersome, would require considerable negotiating skills. We understood that, vested as we all are in what we think is important, we were taking a risk, that negotiations could break down, even fail. At the same time, we found, and we think others will as well, that both process (articulating together our goals for the program and ways these are realized in a set of readings) and product (the revised list) are worth the risk and effort.

We have many ways to narrate the story of our process, all of which comment differently on the values of the program itself. We could simply record it, for instance, by noting that we began work on the reading list in the fall and concluded in the spring. We met weekly, some of us routinely, others as time and other responsibilities permitted—as we taught classes, wrote papers, attended conferences, recruited new faculty, developed a new undergraduate Writing and Publication Studies major. Representing the process this way indicates that major curricular issues are a matter of course for the committee of the whole, responsibilities that we took up seriously. That itself is both claim and statement about the program.

We could also tell our story through numbers. We began with twelve categories, including among them topics that were identical with our five core courses: Visual Rhetoric; Workplace Communication; Classical Rhetoric; Introduction to Professional Writing; and Research Methods in Professional Communication. Included as well were other categories that seemed to play a role in the program, although the role wasn't always clear: Literacy, Technology, International Communication. We began with forty-four items and were committed to maintaining that number, to resisting the impulse to grow the list. To accommodate the impulse, yet stay close to our target number of items, we created an archival list of all the items that could be included and worked from those. We also spoke as though all the categories were equal, although as individuals we had preferences, and it wasn't difficult to discern what those were. Given the number of items and the number of categories, each category—from Classical Rhetoric to International Communication—seemed eligible for about four entries. Representing the process this way would indicate that we value a certain conservative structure, that we like to explore the possibility of expanding our reach, but that at the end of the day we like to come home to the familiar, where everything has its place.

We could also tell our story through understandings, specifically our understandings about the process we should use for revision. Some of us thought that we should use the old list as a point of departure and should proceed by revising this list, understanding that to add a new text, we had to drop an old one. Some of us thought we should work from a blank slate to build a new list. Some of us thought we should focus on certain underrepresented areas—technology and diversity among them. Some of us felt passionately about our favorite figures and texts and thought that others should see the list through our theoretical lenses. And when passions were strong, we used our communication symbol—a "Fight Club" button, a promotional pin from Brad Pitt's movie by the same name popular at the time—to signal that an individual had become overly invested in their personal preferences. The "Fight" button—which even now is seen by some as sign of negotiation, by others as sign of friction—became a part of the process, a material token of the work to which we are all committed.

We are choosing, however, to tell our story primarily through our individual voices, in part because this individualism is ultimately what we value in the MAPC program and hope to teach students: a respect for a multiplicity of voices, perspectives, personalities, and passions. In part, we hope, through this way of telling the story, to work in palimpsest (de Certeau 1984; Barton and Barton 1993), to include in our collective story here traces and vestiges of how it came to be. In other words, the new reading list itself is one map to the program. But how that map was created can itself be mapped, and that too is our aim. Our listserv makes such a representation possible. Listen in as we enter in medias res to Mark Charney, the chair of MAPC, summarizing the review of one meeting:

Dear Kathleen (and MAPC Committee): Here are the best notes I can muster up from the meeting you missed. Please forgive me if I've misrepresented anyone! We discussed primarily visual communication, and plan next week to discuss professional communication theory, ideology, and teaching/pedagogy, so please, MAPCers, come to the meeting with good notes about what you want to do with each of the next three fields.

Sean began the meeting not only with great ideas about vis comm, but also samples and examples of each of the following.

1. Jacqueline Glasgow's "Teaching Visual Literacy for the 21st century" for its emphasis on decoding images, making passive observers active, and its explanation of semiotics.

2. Williams and Harkus's "Editing Visual Media" for its emphasis on the verbal vs. the visual, especially its practical bent (and the good example of a ball vs. a basketball, etc.)

3. A PRIMER OF VISUAL LITERACY, Chapters Two and Three: one offers guidelines for visual literacy, a good overview, and the other, basic elements of visual communication.

4. Edward R. Tufte's new chapter 2 in VISUAL EXPLANATIONS, and chapters 4 and 5 in the old book to keep terms like Chat Junk, etc.

5. DESIGNING VISUAL LANGUAGE by Kostelnick and Roberts, especially chapters 1 and 2 which tie rhetoric to visual.

Now here is where I break down in terms of who suggested what. Both Tharon and Chris had a say here, and all three agreed, as did the rest of the committee there, about the worth of the [texts] below. It wasn't a fight club situation at all, and we got through this in record time, so much so that it surprised us into being unprepared to move on, so we adjourned early! (well, ok, only a few minutes early)

6. Kress and Van Leduwen's READING IMAGES, Chapters 2 and 3 about narrative theory and visual communication, especially the linguistics of visual design. Also, possibly chapter 4 which deals with modality.

7. Karen Schriver's DYNAMICS IN DOCUMENT DESIGN, pages 168–181 (this was Tharon's I remember), which deals somewhat with usability studies and technical brochures.

8. Carl mentioned a new book by Kenneth Hager with one chapter on Visual Communication. He plans to give us the exact reference next week.

9. Sean encouraged us to keep the Elizabeth Keyes already on the list, while everyone finally agreed to keep everyone already there, especially Barton and Barton, who everyone agreed was a clear introduction for uninitiated students, and Maitra/Goswami, the Kostelnick on the list, etc.

10. Also, EDITING: THE DESIGN OF RHETORIC, the final chapter about typesetting and production, was mentioned as something that may help basic students. By Sam DRAGGA and GWENDOLYN GONG.

*Some discussion ensued about how this was often the first class most students took and how it has to begin very basically. The Hilligoss book was mentioned by Barbara Heifferon, who uses it successfully in the classroom, but using it would break our rule not to use our own texts in the classroom.*

*Finally, we agreed to make two lists—one the reading list for orals, and the other, a list of all of these related texts, each significant to students in the field and to students researching theses and projects. Such a list could be updated every year for the orientation MAPC book, making that list a current one from which we could update the orals list anytime we wanted.*

*I apologize if this is rough, or if I've given credit to anyone for something he or she may not want! See you next, and every Monday . . .*

*Mark Charney*

Sometimes discussions that seemed to be about one issue—the one previously mentioned about visual rhetoric, for instance—turned out to be about others; and always in the background was the question: Who is the MAPC student?

*It would be almost impossible to define the ideal student.*

*Beth Daniell*

*I agree. What I'm driving at in using this term is actually something like "what should every MAPC student leave the program with?" I'm not thinking here in terms of discursively forming ideal students, but rather of a minimum set of qualifications and knowledge that all students should possess, much like the list that you offered: theory, practice and technical expertise. The tricky part is figuring out what "theory," what "practice," and what "expertise" we're talking about. Is theory rhetorical theory or is it professional communication theory? They're related certainly, but not by any means the same. Is practice, writing seminar papers or creating multimedia? Again, they're related, but not the same. Is expertise a theoretical expertise or knowing how to use computers well? The separations are a matter of emphasis and it seems to me that this emphasis needs to be fleshed out a little more by having conversations like that we had today. It was EXTREMELY helpful in helping me to understand the way the people in this program view what the program does. Now that I have a little more context on "what it is that we do" I can make more informed choices about what to include/exclude from the reading list.*

*Sean Williams*

Who is the MAPC student? This question haunted the process, as we understood our role in defining and constructing that figure. Still the student, as Beth Daniell suggests, eludes us.

*Continuing to beat this poor horse, I don't think we can always be more specific. I want students to have some sense of technology. What does that mean? I don't think it means everyone has to design Web sites. I think a lot of it is what the student wants it to mean. They are agents in this process, not empty containers. While I understand your need for definition, I have been teaching way too long to think that my categories or yours are adequate to cover all the students. We set up the framework in which individuals and teachers work. The outcome is not up to us. I'm constantly amazed at what my students come up with—and like you, they often complain that I am not being clear enough.*

*Beth Daniell*

At some point, our negotiations on who is the MAPC student turned from abstract to particularized as we began to horse-trade—"I'll trade you a Landow for a Plato"—to represent what we thought every MAPC student should know. To accomplish this, we all forwarded nominations for each category, not to select winners, but to show patterns. We called them tallies. (Language matters.) It wasn't a flawless process, and it provided a set of questions that continue to beguile us.

How to negotiate?

As implied previously, having a written record helps; here Kathleen Yancey provides context for understanding the tallies.

## Draft of Nominations for Reading List for MAPC

Context: Not everyone sent in tallies. Not everyone voted for three per category, so I just counted the number up to three. Not everyone sent only three per category, so I just counted the first three. If you numbered them, I took the top three.

A couple of suggestions appeared that had not been mentioned or discussed previously. I did not include them on the list.

Issues: Presence?

Absence?

The categories: do we need all of them? Two folks mentioned that they would dispense with teaching, one that we could dispense with literacies.

Should all categories be equally weighted? What's the role of the current list?

How do these items compare to what's on the current list?

Some items are repeated—Faigley and Barton and Barton—come to mind.

Can we cross-reference some items?

Is diversity sufficiently represented?

Is technology sufficiently represented?

When we look at the list, what student have we constructed?

In the background, as we sorted through the tallies, discussions related to our questions continued. A major discussion involved the relationship of rhetoric to professional communication, as Martin Jacobi explains:

*I guess I'm wondering still what constitutes "rhetoric" for you. I'm hoping it's not something like "bombastic discourse having no relation to the real world, to what professional writers—whoever they may be—do for a living." I'm trying to imagine the nature of "professional documents outside the frame of rhetoric" but I'm coming up empty. When Ornatowski talks about the engineer who has to write a report that will sell to potential customers an engine that will not start in cold weather, he talks about the rhetorical choices—and ethical choices (since any action, as opposed to motion, is necessarily ethical invested)—that the engineer is making. It's clearly a rhetorical document that Ornatowski's engineer is talking about.*

*I would agree that reading Aristotle is not the most effective way of teaching or learning ethics, but what's your point? If you're saying that pro com uses case studies and not theory to do things, then aren't you contradicting your earlier claim that pro com is theoretically sophisticated? Aristotle pointed out that he wrote his Art o' Rhetoric because teachers of rhetoric were only using something like case studies for their students.*

Sometimes in the middle of all this discussion would arrive a listserv post from somebody outside our dialogue that reminded us that we were hardly alone in sorting out these issues:

*Last spring in Time or Newsweek there was a big article on Careers [,] and Technical Writing was featured heavily as a good bet for college students. We used it to help us bolster our argument for an interdisciplinary graduate certificate in professional writing.*

Irene Ward, from WPA-L (listserv)

The horse trading continued. It was smart; it was social; it was (of course) rhetorical. We made connections between other professional contexts and this one; we used such comparisons to think about what would best help students.

*I'm thinking ahead to our next meeting and urging everyone come with a text or two to "be flexible" on. I think we are good enough horse traders to do this? Our task is not as daunting as it may seem. I counted 54 texts, and if we get down to 45 (shoot for less and see how that goes), that's only 9 to give up. I came up with that number because we are doing fewer chapters in Latour and Woolgar (e.g.) and others.*

*I'm also reading for absences. As peer reviewer for TCQ . . . I've reviewed a number of tech comm pieces. . . . My reviews have included some alarm about lack of awareness of something other than our good ol Yanqui point of view (I realize how strange this sounds in S[outh] C[arolina]). When I get the reviews back with other reviewers' comments as well, they are picking up on the same thing. All this to say that I'm concerned that we may not yet represent a voice of someone other than ourselves for the good of our students who will go out and work in a world that, surprise, does not look exactly like us. Thus we need at least Freire on board or someone that makes this point. There may be a better rep. I'm open. Unless I missed something on the list, I don't see us doing this.*

*I wouldn't mind trading a Doheny-Farina and Harraway for a chapter from Harding that addresses a couple of absences. The one that covers standpoint theory (also one of Tharon's lenses in his book) might serve. It's at home, I'll send the chapter # later. Harraway is so dense, though God(dess) knows I love her, she makes Vitanza read like a Sunday school picnic (most likely an abominable mixed metaphor).*

*Barbara Heifferon*

Trading itself, of course, isn't an easy process. We understood our choices as signs, as representations. We read multiple gestalts into such a list, as Chris

Boese self-referentially suggests:

*Chris won't give up Harraway. And Chris wants Freire. Classic struggle with canons. You know what it is. For new points of view to come in, something sacred has to go. I'm not trying to be intransigent here, but I have a different point of view on the list. The old list is dangerously deficient in the area of technology. Quite a bit needs to go in there to bring it up to speed with what is going on in the world. I am as much of a horsetrader as anyone, but I don't think technology should be the thing that has to "give" as much as other areas do. Of course reasonable people may disagree. But if serious room for technological issues and technology criticism isn't made on the list, I believe there will be major credibility problems with it. Other areas have long held place on the list. Like Rhetorical Theory. They are the 900 pound gorillas. Technology scholarship is newer and having great impact in the field, changing the landscape of the field even as we speak. If our list doesn't make room for it, it won't be because tech is a yearling gorilla, it will be because those of us who advocate for it haven't done a good enough job in making the case. The field is changing, with or without us. We just have to decide if we want our list to actually reflect that change.*

In the end, as Barbara Heifferon's concluding post attests, the process worked—

*I wanted to tell you the good news in case no one else had.... At MAPC today, after a meeting that lasted under an hour, we went from a reading list of 62 down to 46!! Trades were made and collegiality remained intact after a few vigorous conversations.... I think it's a great list. I took notes as did Mark, and someone will get the final list ready for fall!! We did cheat a bit (folding a few readings of same authors together, just a couple)*

—if by "worked" we mean that we had a new list that most of us would agree was better and that we had negotiated well. The list: it's appended. It's not perfect. But most of us would agree, on most days, that it's better. And it's different: some eleven items are new. Some of our favorites—from Harraway to Bakhtin—didn't make it. But they are on the archival list, and they are available for another (negotiating) day. And although second-year graduate students have been given the transitional option of using the old or new list, the new students are using this list, and we are finding it a better fit for most of the core courses. As Sean Williams, Barbara Heifferon, and Kathleen Yancey (2000) put it at CPTSC 2000, "Students who have seen the new list make positive comments about it because the list manages to bring what seem to be opposite poles—reflection and instrumentalism—into a single reading list that represents the current state of our discipline."

We began this chapter, as we began the revision of the list, with an interest in bringing theory and practice together. The new list doesn't completely resolve this divide because we ourselves are still resolving it; probably we should have understood that it's too large and too complex a divide for this single curricular practice to resolve. But we have seen that we can negotiate: we can compose a list that constructs a student we'd like to see develop within our program and whose development is fostered by our new reading list. The program, in other words, is dynamic: it is able to accommodate both change and the tensions accompanying such change.

As Bernadette Longo puts it,

> Now that we've gone through one iteration of this process for revising the MAPC reading list, it seems that we've played out the issue that motivated this revision in the first place: "the perceived bifurcation . . . of the program" between theory and practice. We entered this process on high theoretical ground, positing topics that should be included in a reading list that reflected the important conversations in our field. (Actually, I'm not sure we agree on what our field is, but that's another chapter.) We all put forward readings in these categories based on theories and philosophical points of view informing our own research and teaching. But as weeks went by and the discussions ground on, it seemed that we slipped unnoticed into the arena of practicalities as the size of the list and the pressures of compromise constrained us. By the end of the year, many of our discussions were shaped by the need to keep the list at about 44 items and also to include representative works from all 12 of our original topic areas. . . .
>
> The intent of revising the list was theoretical, but the revision process turns out to be mostly practical. Once again, questions of "how do we do it" seemed to overwhelm questions of "what do we do." As Sean has mentioned in postrevision discussions, I'm not sure we have a handle yet on the question of what we do (as a program) when we shape our MAPC students' graduate studies. I think we have come up with a more current reading list through this process, and that's good. I'm not convinced, though, that we have better articulated the intent and objectives of our graduate program. Maybe that discussion needs to take place separately from the reading list revision process.

Which, of course, it has, through our later discussions—on exams, on projects and theses, on discussions about the kinds of experiences we hope to offer students. Ultimately, that we didn't resolve the theory/practice split, or that Durst's (1999) construct didn't inform the entire process, or that we all feel there are still some gaps in the list doesn't matter as much as it may appear: this is not an exercise in Katz's (1992) expediency. What ultimately matters is that in the processes of (1) renegotiating our reading list and (2) negotiating the way we have chosen to represent it here, we discovered that we can practice what we preach to students: that successful communication, even involving the creation of reading lists, requires recognition and negotiation among many competing voices. In Durstian terms, we have had it both ways: in instrumental terms, we both accomplished the task and continued to reflect on the list, on the program, on the processes informing it, and on ways to weave together theory and practice into a coherent curricular whole.

In thinking about how and why such a process might be useful for others, we'd observe

- that participating in such a curricular revision can be a significant socializing activity, certainly for new faculty members, but also for more senior faculty as they interact with their new colleagues and with the possibilities for curricular revision;
- that it provides all faculty with a chance to examine how the field—and even the definition of the field—has changed since the last list was constructed;
- that engaging all program faculty in developing and maintaining a graduate program seems to require the kind of commitment realized in curricular negotiations and that these negotiations may entail friction and require delicacy and humor;
- that after having participated in this process, faculty understand the rationale explaining why individual readings are on the list as well as how the readings relate to each other, and they therefore are more inclined to see the list as a total package (rather than a set of disparate readings) and can explain this to students;
- that a reading list is just that, only a list; in a healthy curriculum, any list is necessarily and always penultimate given its contextualization within many other readings and experiences and the fact that it too will be revised;
- that the value of the list is likewise never fully understood until it is used by students and faculty together; and
- that what we have outlined here—by specific observations and linguistic montage—is a process, one more difficult and less efficient than if we had tasked it to a smaller group, but one more rhetorically productive. We created an opportunity to bring people together to communicate about things that matter: to write the program representing us and constructing students.

In short, we modeled for students the ways we'd like them to behave. The best we could do for students is to maintain a vestige of this idea in the reading list—and we did. We think this, too, may be one of the benefits of a collaborative curricular design.

## STORY TIME: TEACHING TECHNICAL COMMUNICATION AS A NARRATIVE WAY OF KNOWING

Telling stories is the basis of how I teach—not just technical communication but any subject—composition, editing, literature, and publications management. I don't tell these stories simply to entertain students or to keep them interested—although certainly stories can perform that function. I tell stories because stories are a part of the practices of everyday life; they make it possible to articulate these practices. We know each other, our communities, and the world through the stories we tell each other about what we know, how we know what we know, and why we know what we know. Specifically in my technical communication classes, I ask students to read a particular story as a context for assignments and discussions. This approach helps students to contextualize the constructs and implementation of knowledge demonstrated in technical documentation—audience analysis, invention, information design, and documentation. In this chapter, I describe this approach, providing some example assignments and student writing in order to demonstrate how stories help me realize my pedagogical goals.

This approach is heavily influenced by Michel de Certeau's (1984) concept of stories as the articulation of everyday practice and Jerome Bruner's (1981 and 1990) discussions about hermeneutic composibility— how stories are made. These two perspectives provide the foundation for the construction of technical documents from a narrative perspective.

First, telling stories, or what Michel de Certeau calls the "narrativizing of practices," is a "textual way of operating" or "way of thinking" that involves a meshing of what one knows (theory), how one knows what one knows (practice), and how one applies that knowledge to situations (metis). The telling of stories is characteristically concerned with the "style of tactics" (79), or a way of operating that traverses schemas into opportunities for action. Because tactics are opportunistic, they belong, de Certeau says, to the classical concept of metis: a "form of intelligence that is always 'immersed in practice,' which combines 'flair, sagacity, foresight, intellectual flexibility, deception, resourcefulness, vigilant watchfulness, a sense of opportunities, diverse sorts of cleverness, and a great deal of acquired experience'" (81). To be effective, stories must demonstrate this level of cleverness in their realization.

Stories are realized in the act of telling. Because a story "makes a hit (a coup) far more than it describes one," "its discourse is characterized more by a way of exercising itself than by the thing it indicates" (79). In this way, narrativizing is an "art of saying," or a "know-how-to-say," "characterized more by a way of exercising itself than by the thing it indicates" (de Certeau

1984, 78, 79): it is an "art of speaking . . . which exercises precisely that art of operating" and "art of thinking" (77). Stories provide, de Certeau says, the "decorative container of a narrativity for everyday practices," which "provide a panoply of schemas for action" (70). In other words, stories both describe and hypothesize everyday practices.

Second, stories connect us to each other as human beings. Telling stories is a process of knowledge construction that all humans share and in which all humans have some measure of competency because "we store, categorize, and process knowledge mainly in the form of narrative" (Bruner 1991, 4). In other words, we process and categorize knowledge in narrative form. Given this premise, consider the hammer. It is impossible to understand "hammer" without imagining it within a context of some kind. For me, the hammer is a symbol of my dad's identity—a master craftsman. I understand a hammer in this context: as part of the many tools that defined my dad's craft; as part of my dad's tool belt; as an extension of his hand as he built one of the many hutches or homes for which he was most known; as part of the many lessons about construction ("Hickory is the best wood for constructing hammers"); and as part of how we buried him—with his hands wrapped around the same hammer he used to begin his career. Although each of these parts could lead to a number of stories that explain better what a hammer is, the story most effectively describing its particular characteristics occurred during my dad's wake. After paying his respects, one of my dad's colleagues greeted us and said, "It's a shame to bury him with that hammer.

It was just getting broken in" (the hammer was then forty years old). This statement makes sense only when one considers its context: it made sense to us because to me a hammer is not simply a tool; it is a narrative construction of who my dad was.

In "The Narrative Construction of Reality," Bruner (1990, 1991) says that stories are "a form not only of representing but of constituting reality" (1991, 5) that work by constructing a dual landscape involving both consciousness (a way of thinking) and action (a way of operating), constructions that "occur concurrently" (1990, 51). Similarly, in Acts of Meaning, Bruner (1990) indicates that the human "capacity to render experience in terms of narrative is not just child's place, but an instrument for making meaning that dominates much of our life in culture" (97). He describes how the mental powers of narrative make it possible to frame experience in ways that enable us to both remember and make sense of human happenings"; in fact, he argues that "what does not get structured narratively suffers loss in memory." Narrative frames, Bruner says, provide a "means of constructing the world, of characterizing its flow, [and] of segmenting events within that world," without which we'd be "lost in a murk of chaotic experiences" (56). Human beings, he says, do not "deal with the world event by event or with text sentence by sentence," they frame events and sentences in larger structures" (64). However, simply reciting what happened does not constitute a narrative construction of reality because the "act of constructing a narrative . . . is considerably more than 'selecting' events either from real life, from memory, or from fantasy and then placing them in an appropriate order. The events themselves need to be constituted in light of the overall narrative" (1981, 8). This "part-whole textual interdependence" is a defining property of hermeneutics, because the "telling of a story and its comprehension as a story depend on the human capacity to process knowledge in this interpretive way" (8). This property is what makes narrative constructions of reality "different from logical procedures"—"they must be interpreted" (1991, 60).

Stories have more to do with context than with text, with the conditions of telling than with what is told. In other words, the events must be interpreted in order to tell the story. Hermeneutics is the study of interpretation, that is, how interpretation happens. Narratives have to do with people acting in situations. Making sense of a story (either in the telling of or listening to a story) requires making connections between characters' intentional states (beliefs, desires, theories, values, and such) and "the happenings that befall them." To make this connection is to state "reasons," not "causes," for behavior, a process Bruner calls hermeneutic composability. The term hermeneutic, Bruner says, implies an attempt to "express" or "extract" a meaning, which further implies that "there is a difference between what is expressed in the text and what the text might mean." This hermeneutic process is required "when there is neither a rational method . . . nor an empirical method" for "determining the verifiability of the constituent elements that make up the text" (Bruner 1981, 7). Because interpretation is dependent upon an individual's ability "to achieve mastery of social reality," the "best hope of hermeneutic analysis," Bruner says, "is to provide an intuitively convincing account of the meaning of the text as a whole in light of the constituent parts that make it up," a process "nowhere better illustrated than in narrative" (8).

Narratives are not self-evident. They "do not provide causal explanations" for a character's actions; what they do supply is a "basis for interpretation," that is, a basis for "assigning meaning" to a text (Bruner 1981, 7). Events are meaningless without interpretation because the veracity of a narrative depends on the ability of the storyteller to situate a story within a context and to interpret the meaning of those events based on a particular context and to convince a listener to accept that version of reality. Because of this interlocutionary interaction, Bruner says, interpretation is "studded with" two problems that have to do more "with context than text, with the conditions on telling rather than with what is told": intention (purpose) and background knowledge (ability to judge veracity). Intention refers to the reasons a story is told, how and when it is told, and how it is interpreted "by interlocutors caught in different intentional stances themselves." Narratives (or their interpretations) are not created unintentionally: text, context, and situation converge to influence meaning for both the storyteller and the listener. Equally important is the background knowledge on which both the storyteller and the listener rely to judge the verisimilitude of a narrative account: typically, we presuppose that what an interlocutor says in replying to us is topic relevant and that we most often assign an interpretation to it accordingly in order to make it so" (10). Both these contextual issues hold "important grounds for negotiating how a story shall be taken . . . or how it should be told" (11), and both depend on the abilities of the storyteller and the listener to "fill in" information as necessary for comprehension (10). The capacity to complete information is the "human push to organize experience narratively" (Bruner 1990, 79).

A story is successful if it can convince listeners to accept its version of reality as "narrative truth"—if it can "sensitize us to experience our own lives in ways to match" (Bruner 1981, 13)—a truth "judged by its verisimilitude rather than its verifiability" (13). In this way, narratives are "centrally concerned with cultural legitimacy" (15); that is, they grow out of and reenforce cultural norms and encapsulate background scripts, implicitly inscribing the norms and behaviors of a culture. Because narrative is "centrally concerned with cultural legitimacy," stories not situated within a culture's norms seem "'pointless' rather than storylike" (11). But these scripts provide only the background necessary for comprehending the facts of the story; they do not constitute the "story" or its tellability. The "tellability" of a story depends on "what happened and why [a story] is worth telling" (12). To be worth telling, Bruner argues, a "tale must be about how an implicit canonical script has been breached, violated, or deviated from in a manner to do" harm to an implicit canonical script (11). In much the same way that de Certeau (1984) says an audience understands the metis component of storytelling, that is, the point of manipulation within the story that marks its unusualness, Bruner (1981) says that the moment a "hearer is made suspicious of the 'facts' of a story or the ulterior motives of a narrator"—an element of breach—she becomes "hermeneutically alert" (10). This state of mind comes from narrative necessity, which sets up the story in such a way that it "predisposes its hearers to one and only one interpretation" (9). These are the stories worth telling and worth listening to because they compel us into what Bruner calls "unrehearsed interpretative activity," or using what is known to understand what is unknown.

But, what does all this have to do with technical communication? How does a narrative way of knowing work in technical communication classrooms? For one thing, technical documents appear to be neutral, decontextualized texts that should require no interpretative activity (some scholars argue that this "objectivity" is the objective of technical documents—to limit interpretation; see Moore 1996, for example). Many textbooks focus on this aspect of technical communication, which I think doesn't address the content (how writers understand what they are saying) at a level in which students feel connected with the text. Stories, I think, do just that—connect with students at a level that all humans share. I don't simply tell stories about myself in classes. I assign a specific piece of literature as a context for assignments, which provides a way for students to make connections between what they already know—in a form they already know it (narrative)—and what they are learning about technical documentation.

Throughout the rest of the chapter, I describe how to structure a pedagogy designed as a narrative way of knowing, the procedures I use for helping students read and understand literature from a technical communication perspective, some individual and collaborative assignments I've used, and the evaluation methods used to assess student performance. I conclude this chapter with a discussion about some lessons I've learned from using this pedagogy.

## Establishing A Narrative Way of Knowing

### Course Focus

As a pedagogical approach, a narrative way of knowing begins with a theme (or focus), around which all assignments and discussions revolve (such as agriculture communication or environmental communication). This theme provides the focus for discussing and creating technical documents and depends on a teacher's own interests and goals for the class. The introduction of this theme should start with a representative technical document for a particular kind of communicative activity. The document could be a policy statement (government, corporate, nonprofit, or community), an application (such as for loans, admission, or adoption), a letter (such as Bush's recent letter to China), a proposal (such as for a national park or a legislative bill), a report (such as Accreditation Board for Engineering and Technology [ABET] 2000), and so on; there are endless possibilities. I generally start with a technical document because from a surface inspection, it appears to be neutral, objective, and decontextualized. Since adopting this approach, I have used such documents as the Agriculture Adjustment Act of 1933 (AAA), a piece of legislation that guaranteed farmers restitution if they planted only a percentage of their acreage, or the Environmental Protection Act of 1970 (EPA), which established the Environmental Protection Agency.

## *Literature*

After selecting a technical document, I choose a piece of literature—or what I'm calling a narrative way of knowing—that provides a common context for thinking about the technical document. Providing a context for that document involves judiciously choosing a piece of literature that contextualizes the communicative activity implicitly embedded within the seemingly neutral technical document. The literature chosen should provide various perspectives (how characters think and interpret), situations (of collaboration), and actions (decisions made about communicative problems). This choice of literature could be one or more short stories, a novel, a film, a poem, or song lyrics—but whatever its genre, it must provide a comprehensive, complete story about a particular situation.

With the Agriculture Adjustment Act, for example, I used various short stories depicting farm life, values, and beliefs and a short excerpt from Lois Philips Hudson's (1984) The Bones of Plenty, which provides a lively scene in which North Dakota farmers attend a town hall meeting to discuss the merits of the Act with a government representative. With the Environmental Protection Act, I used Scott Russell Sanders's Terrarium (1985), a futurist novel depicting an overpolluted earth that forces people to move into Enclosures (globe-like structures that offer protection from the elements of climate) in order to sustain human life. Together, the technical document and the literature provide the context in which assignments and discussions revolve.

I use literature because its self-enclosed construction provides what Barbara Mirel (1998) calls "entry and exit points" that help students situate themselves within a context as a basis for interpretation, as a basis for "figur[ing] it out" (or as a student once described it—"it makes us use our minds"). The literature frames discussions about technical documentation in ways that situate students into what Bruner (1981) calls "unrehearsed interpretative activities" (9). Teaching technical communication as a series of parts without constituting them within the whole shortchanges students and encourages them to leave your classroom knowing only a particular skill—such as how to format a memo (placement of heading, formatting of body text, and so forth), which teaches them what to think, not how to think about communicative problems.1

Using literature as a context encourages students to consider thoughtfully the perspectives of characters in terms of the communicative action in the story as well as their and others' perspectives in the class.

In class, these perspectives are shared through in-class activities requiring students to discuss their interpretations in order to complete the assignment and through display of student writing on an overhead. For example, during an in-class writing activity, I asked students to work in groups of three or four to write parenthetical, formal, and expanded definitions for such terms as farm, agriculture, tractor, combine, homestead, and barn from the perspective of a character in Wil Weaver's (1989) "A Gravestone Made of Wheat" (such as the farmer, the farmer's wife, the sheriff, the farmer's son or daughter, the county clerk, the FHA agent, or the judge). My intention with this activity was to encourage students to pay attention to the implicit canonical scripts—embedded within the story and within students' personal narrative constructs—suggested by terms like "farm" and "farmer." By asking students to write technical definitions from a particular character's point of view, I had hoped they would expand their awareness of different contexts that affect the construction of knowledge and audience. In his end-of-thequarter reflection memo, one student demonstrated this expanded awareness.

*I think that reading and discussing the required literature had an effect on the technical writing I did in this course. . . . I think that the biggest thing the reading did for me was to enlighten me on writing for different audiences. . . . As a specific example of this, I remember on one of our workshop days when we had to write technical definitions of certain farm-related terms for a character in "A Gravestone Made of Wheat." My group chose to write the definitions with the judge as the audience. I did not realize how much different it would be to write the definitions for the different characters. From doing the reading, I learned that the judge was well educated, knew little about farming, and seemed to have some biases towards farmers. These facts dramatically changed the way we defined the terms. We decided that we could use fairly technical terms to make the definitions because he must have been fairly well educated to be a judge, but we need to go into great detail in defining the terms because he did not have any experience in farming. The hardest part about defining the terms for the judge was trying to deal with the biases he had about farmers and farming. We ended up portraying farming in a somewhat negative way to make him better understand what we were saying because of his biases.*

*Anthony (pseudonym)*

To realize that language use changes with the audience and the situation, Anthony had to interpret the circumstances of the story to come to an understanding of the judge's attitude toward farmers; he had to, essentially, figure out what is implicitly provided about the judge. Anthony's expressive "I did not realize how much different it would be" statement indicates his engagement in "unrehearsed interpretative activity" in ways that challenged his conceptions about the objectiveness of technical documents. He clearly sees the judge, the term, and technical communication differently. Although pedagogical design of a narrative way of knowing should begin with the selection of a technical document, decisions about the document and the literature more often occur concurrently. For example, The Bones of Plenty excerpt focuses specifically on the concept of agriculture adjustment, which led me to the AAA of 1933, and Terrarium mentions a fictitious "Enclosure Act," which led me to the EPA of 1970— both of which led me to the technical documents. Other possibilities include adoption policies of Native American children with Barbara Kingsolver's The Bean Trees, immigration policies with Helena Vermontes's Under the Feet of Jesus, a Search for Extraterrestrial Intelligence (SETI) report with Maria Doria Russell's The Sparrow, the Communications Act with The Net, or a NASA report with parts or all of the HBO miniseries From the Earth to the Moon.

For the purposes of this chapter, I focus my discussion on my use of the Environmental Protection Act of 1970 and Scott Russell Sanders's Terrarium.

## *Procedures*

For literature to work as a context successfully, students need to understand its purpose in conjunction with technical communication. To help students situate the literature, in this case Terrarium, within the language of technical communication, I associate the communicative practices with those in the workplace by creating procedures for reading the literature (see appendix A). I use the term procedures for three reasons: (a) because it provides a lens through which students can view the context from the perspective of technical communication practices, (b) because it emulates the language and sensibilities of engineers and technical communicators, and (c) because the students at Michigan Technological University, where I was teaching at the time, tend to be extremely systematic and respond well to assignments that provide an identifiable foundation. The creation of these procedures grew out of my concern that because the assignment included a piece of literature, students might be tempted to adopt a literary studies perspective and read it in terms of its value as a literary artifact. I developed these procedures to help students focus their attention on the context the literature provides and how narrative ways of knowing transmit implicit knowledge.

Explanation of these procedures occurs on the day the schedule requires students to finish reading Terrarium. Column 1 (appendix A) names the procedure according to the cognitive function involved, column 2 provides heuristic questions that help students figure out the procedure described, and column 3 equates the activity with workplace activities. Although this discussion does focus primarily on Terrarium, when first explaining the procedures, I usually add to the discussion with examples from my work experience (such as when the small midwestern college I worked for in the early 1990s considered dissolving my public relations position, arguing that one marketing representation was enough for all six colleges in the region; in defense of my position, I was asked to write a brief statement about the value of this public relations position). After explaining the procedures, I ask student to work in groups of three or four, writing a one-to-two sentence statement for each procedure, using Terrarium as a context. I then ask each group to write one of their answers on the board and discuss it with the entire class.

The first procedure, Comprehending the Story, asks students to consider the meaning of the story as a whole. The biggest hurdle to overcome here is students' tendency to focus on the plot, such as "Terrarium is a story about how a group of people escape from the Enclosure" or "Terrarium is about good versus evil." The second procedure, Determining the Rhetorical Situation, asks students to consider the circumstances and the context of the story and how they affect the meaning of the story as a whole. Students also tend to describe the plot here, but this activity should focus on why the situation is important. Identifying the Exigency of the Situation, the third procedure, is the most confusing for students, mainly because of the term exigency. This procedure helps students identify the action or burden called for by the situation.2 The fourth procedure, Identifying the Stakeholders, asks students to identify the people involved in the situation and the significance of their participation. This procedure emphasizes the importance of audience analysis in the creation of technical documents. The last procedure, Reflecting and Connecting the Story to Technical Communication, is intended to help students equate their interpretative activities with the activities associated with creating technical documents such as audience analysis, gathering and organizing information, and determining ethical dilemmas. This last step has proven to be the most difficult for students, I suspect, because this discussion occurs early in the term and because they try to see Terrarium as a technical document.

## *Assignments*

To be successful, assignments based on the literature must address some kind of exigency—some reason or purpose—for providing the information that suits the context of the story. In other words, students should respond to a particular communicative problem not just answer a question with a particular form. Assignments require writing scenarios in which students more or less interact with characters. This interaction gives them a sense of audience in ways that simply naming "your boss" or "a client" cannot. It also allows them to imagine themselves acting in the situation. Assignments should not identify for the students the appropriate communication required (report, memo, or letter of application, for example), although there are some exceptions; rather, assignments should require students to interpret the situation and determine the appropriate action—to make rhetorical decisions. Appendix B lists some representative assignments I have given in conjunction with The Bones of Plenty and Terrarium.

What's important to keep in mind when creating assignments are the connections the students make between this imaginary "playacting" and the kind of communicative interactions in which students will be expected to participate in the world of work. These assignments must involve appropriate and recognizable workplace situations, actions, and contexts with which students connect the rhetorical action—or exigency— between what they know or have been told about the workplace, whether that knowledge is from personal experience, from professors in major classes, or from professionals in the fields, and the kind of thinking and writing involved in the assignments.

I generally focus the first part of the term on individual and in-class collaborative assignments, which are intended to help students practice writing in the genres of technical communication and understanding those "genres as social action" (Miller 1984) and as constructions of knowledge (Berkenkotter and Huckin 1995). During the last half of the term, students work in collaborative groups of four or five on a major project in which they emulate the contextual approach I demonstrated during the first half. The purpose of the major project is, obviously, to evaluate students' abilities to generate content for a specific audience, to organize and shape that content, and to present this information in a readable fashion—to assess their communicative competency.

## *Individual Assignments*

Assignments like those listed in appendix B are individual assignments that take place during the first half of the term. They all rely on the story as a context and require that students interpret a character's intentions, motivations, and actions. Assignments involve two kinds of communicative activities—individual and collaborative—both of which provide students with opportunities to practice articulating what they know, how they know what they know, and why they know what they know.

Pragmatically, these assignments involve creating documents such as letters of application and memos, fact sheets, short reports, technical descriptions, and processes and procedures. On a more conceptual level, to create these documents, students must interpret the circumstances embedded in the story in order to generate the content for the documents, contextualizing and organizing that content within the constraints of the assignment and the audience. These interpretative activities include topics such as identifying and characterizing problems, situations, and actions; analyzing and assessing problem-solving strategies and reflecting on those problems; and describing and evaluating collaborative processes, procedures, and instructions. Assignments based on Terrarium, then, are constructed in such a way that students are required to make genre decisions, to generate content, and to format and organize information—to conduct themselves as a member of that community—based on their assessment of the situation, the audience, and the exigency of the assignments. Although the technical forms assigned are fairly standardized (for example, memos, letters, reports, and proposals), the content for those forms must come from students' interpretations of the circumstances of the story. In this way, students not only practice the interpretative task of assigning meaning to an event, but they also unmask the nature of practice within a community.

To complete any of these assignments, logistically, students must make genre decisions, invent content appropriate to the situation, and present this information in an appropriate form, style, and tone. These decisions require students to identify the rhetorical situation (such as a second interview or an expert review), the exigency (what's required to get a particular position or request for evaluation, for example), and select the appropriate form, content, and style, based on this situation (for instance, applying for a job requires a formal letter of application or pitching an idea requires a proposal). More conceptually, students must interpret the circumstances of the story, invent content from their interpretations, and organize that information in ways that make sense to the audience defined—all in terms of the purpose and exigency of the assignment. To do this kind of conceptual thinking, students must see themselves practicing imaginatively within the context of the story.

To be effective, individual assignments based on the literature need to be contextualized within some kind of exigency—some reason or purpose—for providing this kind of information. In other words, the assignments should provide a scenario in which students are responding to a communicative problem, not just answering a question. One assignment, for example, asked students to apply for a position with a character from Terrarium:

*You have applied for an engineering position with The Enclosure Group by answering a blind ad in the Enclosure Gazette. So far, you've had one introductory meeting with several Enclosure representatives and feel confident that they liked you. You received a letter today from Dr. Zuni Franklin, the Supervising Engineer, at 3980 Enclosure #1, Portland City, CA 00001, indicating that you are one of five applicants competing for the job. She has asked you to respond to the scenario below in writing to determine if you will be called for a second interview. Using Terrarium as a context, write a letter to Dr. Franklin* indicating your continued interest in the position and identifying, analyzing, and evaluating three problem-solving strategies from the list below. Also indicate which strategy you think works best and why.

*Death of Sol*

*Phoenix's fear of Terra*

*Avoiding the health patrollers*

*Repairing the enclosure*

*Zuni's retirement*

*Teeg and her father*

*Teeg and her mother*

In a related example, but not nearly as successful, I asked students to use Terrarium as a context and to create a fact sheet intended to convince people like Judith Passio (a known adversary of the Enclosure—the globe-like structure into which humanity was moved when the earth became so polluted that it could no longer sustain life) to accept the inevitability of enclosures. In the novel, Passio is a holdout, refusing to move into the enclosure throughout the story and, aside from twenty or so pages toward the end of the novel, Passio's character is known only from diary-like vignettes between chapters. Passio is, as a lawyer might surmise, a hostile witness (or audience), firmly believing in her rejection of technology as the sum total of humanity's problems—the enclosure representing the furthermost extent of this problem. To write this fact sheet, students needed to interpret her character as hostile in order to use language that could actually convince her to move into the enclosure. Although most students wrote "effective" facts sheets from a technical communication perspective in terms of clarity, organization, and design of information, most of them did not consider the reality of Passio's character in their use of language. Many of them used a "let'sbe-friends" voice, highlighting the benefits of enclosure life, many of which Passio had openly criticized.

Although most of the assignments typically succeed (that is, students write clear, effective documents based on the context of the story), when they do fail, it is not always the students who demonstrate bad judgment. With the application letter assignment described earlier, students generally accurately addressed a letter of application to Dr. Gregory Passio and competently identified, described, and analyzed three problem-solving strategies. However, they also referred to events that this character couldn't possibly know because he was long since dead when they occurred. Because the students had seemingly understood the idea of literature in the technical communication classroom and had successfully integrated content from the story in previous assignments, I was confounded that in their character analysis, they had missed such an obvious point. I didn't expect to have to discuss character analysis in this way. So, I asked students why they referred to things the character couldn't possibly know. One student raised his hand and said, "Well, all the scenarios you listed for the assignment happened after his death. We just assumed you brought him back to life for the assignment." Evidently, I had.

## *Collaborative Assignments*

The major project requires students to work collaboratively in groups of three or four, asking them to create a microcosm of their field of study through the lens of a technical document indigenous to the field. Some groups, however, involve more than one major. The technical document created should represent some larger concept indicative of that field ( the ethics of artificial intelligence, for instance). Students must figure out a focus for their projects, whether the group consists of similar or dissimilar disciplines, in ways that bring the three fields together, such as a piece of technology (a transistor) or a concept (project management). And because a group's complement does not always consist of students with the same majors, they must create a document that represents two or more fields. They then must choose a story that provides a context for the technical document they are creating, in much the same way that I use Terrarium as a context for the Environmental Protection Act.3 Within these constraints, each group completes a number of ancillary assignments intended to broaden their knowledge and understanding of the concept through research and development. These ancillary assignments include a proposal, a journal report, an audience-analysis report, a visual report, and individual and group activity logs.

The audience for the assignment consists of technical communication teachers who want to know more about the different disciplines on campus in order to better teach technical communication. This major project includes a variety of ancillary assignments that inform their thinking about the content of the document: a proposal, a journal report, an audience-analysis report, two progress reports, a cover memo, and a final presentation. These assignments accompany and support the technical document students create. Appendix C shows some representative projects students have completed during the past four years.

As part of this assignment, students are expected to include, either within the project itself or as part of the appendices, presentation materials and a summary and analysis of the story and how it works as a context for their document. Although I was concerned in the beginning that I'd have to provide too much input in the selections of stories, my input has been minimal. I was especially worried that students would have difficulty successfully articulating the connection between the document and the story. Although some groups tended to engage in plot summary more than interpretation of the story in the context of their project's focus, most groups competently analyzed the story from the perspective of their project's focus. One group that called itself the AI Group, for example, effectively connected the chosen story (Bladerunner) to their topic—artificial intelligence—by drawing on their background knowledge in computer science.

Artificial Intelligence, being a relatively new area of study (middle of 20th century), has largely extended it's interest into a variety of different disciplines. It can be loosely defined as: the quest to understand thought patterns and recognition processes present in the mind of living organisms, and to somehow reconstruct these thought processes in such a way that a machine (computer) can mimic parts or all of the process attained in living thought. Such a philosophical definition leaves much unanswered, as is the case in Artificial Intelligence.

Considering what intelligence is, AI researches have found much resistance in modeling brain thought and learning. Often, even simple tasks which most all people can achieve without much "intelligence", prove to be large obstacles in AI. For example, most people have the ability to clean the dinner table and do dishes after a meal. Such a task is a large problem for an Artificial Intelligent machine to complete without assistance.

Such implications lead us to believe a living brain uses more than intelligence for many everyday applications. Extending intelligence to include such things as feelings or environmental awareness in contextual situations (a common unconscious process in the human mind), drives AI research to include such things as body and natural language. These topics have become much more complex than originally projected, and thus have driven the interest of Artificial Intelligence into many areas of study.

They also include links to Web pages that provide more background information and list resources for future reference. In connection to this background knowledge, they clearly indicated how the focus of their project connected to their story by emphasizing the ethical considerations involved in development of this kind of technology:

In a number of ways computer science and engineering are like the law profession, all three rely on precedents to make decisions. A computer scientist always wants to go into new situation prepared by a prior precedent. Unfortunately in the rapidly developing field of computer science, precedents are not available, or they are of limited use. The solution to the short fall is the world of fiction. Fiction allows the computer science community to explore the ethical implications of their work, even if the necessary advances will not be available for years to come. By creating an ethical precedent, the computer scientist will be prepared for the road ahead, and he/she will be unhindered by the limited existing "real world" precedents. The ability to be forward looking makes fiction an extremely important aspect to a well rounded Computer Scientist.

This group identified fiction—specifically science fiction—as one way to fill the gap created by unavailable precedents in the fairly new field of computer science. Because science fiction often depicts computerized societies, it creates, according to this group, an "ethical precedent." By focusing on the ethics of artificial intelligence, they attend to the contexts relevant to such a technology and address the humanistic components that interest technical communication teachers. Interestingly, they did not ignore their second audience—other students in the class who would be in attendance for their presentations. In both cases, these students addressed attitudes, motivations, skill, education, and interest of their audience in order to "relate the presented material to the audience on a personal level."

Similarly, a student from an early class focused his report on the idea of progress by tracing the history of the engine from combustible to fuel-injected. For context, this student selected the jalopy in John Steinbeck's The Grapes of Wrath and its Western theme so he could show the "struggle between human and machine." He also placed his discussion within the larger context of the conflicts between humans: "While the struggle between human and machine was a relatively simple battle, the struggle of humans against nature and the battle between humans proved to be much more difficult to win." He defended his choice in literature appropriately by saying that the novel "portrays how humans struggle with machines" (the Joads are forced to repair their engine along the way to California), as well as how humans have struggled against nature (the Joads lost their land in the Dust Bowl). He argues that the Joad's won this struggle because "they were ultimately able to repair the engine and continue along the road," which represented their future. He associates this struggle with what he sees as the aim of mechanical engineering, that is, "to solve problems that deal with humans against machines," and demonstrates that connection by illustrating and describing the dynamics of a fuel-injected system. By contextualizing the theme of progress within The Grapes of Wrath and the Western narrative of progress, he demonstrates for teachers one of the underlying struggles important to mechanical engineers. Another group focused on the role of regulations in the field of civil engineering. To do this, they characterized the building of the Hoover Dam, "when regulations concerning the environment [were] nonexistent," as an impossibility today in light of "public awareness." As a context, they pointed to Upton Sinclair's The Jungle, which led to the "passage of the Pure Food and Drug Act of 1906, less than a year after the novel's publication." They equated the way The Jungle "illustrated how changes in society's perspective can lead to changes in regulations" with the necessity for engineers "to understand how to identify and analyze. . . public opinion, environmental laws and regulations." The connection between their historical example of Hoover Dam and The Jungle shows how today's civil engineers must pay more attention to factors such as public opinion, preservation, and environmental protection "prior to construction"—all which help technical communication teachers better understand the nature of work in civil engineering.

The major project works much like the individual assignments in that both operate from a narrative way of knowing. Individual assignments help students learn to identify, describe, and evaluate practices from a critical perspective. They require interpretative acts in the construction of knowledge, encourage connections through contexts, and enable articulations of knowledge in a recognizable form. With the major project, students have an opportunity to engage in, as de Certeau (1984) says, a "narrativizing of practices" that encourages them to consciously consider what work means in their field, how it operates in that field, and their role in completing that work. The triangulating aspect of the major project—the bringing together of the field (or fields), the issues (journal), and the story, or as de Certeau might say, their art (its theory and practice)—demonstrates their ability to engage in narrative ways of knowing. The successful projects demonstrated what Bruner (1981) called a story's "verisimilitude," that is, the story's tellability, what makes it worth telling" (13). Their ability to "assign meaning" to their work through narrative constructions included well-designed, content-rich documents that illustrated their competency—their alertness—in conveying technical information to an audience, while engaged in unrehearsed hermeneutic activities.

## Conclusion

Instructors adopting a narrative way of knowing as a pedagogical approach need to know that using literature in the technical communication classroom is not necessarily new (see, for example, Kilgore 1981; Karis 1989). These scholars argue, and I agree, that literature can provide both examples of and a context for technical communication; however, they do not encourage the production of technical documents out of the context literature provides. Teaching technical communication as a narrative way of knowing does just that: it not only provides opportunities for helping students develop an understanding of technical information as constructed from a context but also encourages reflective and critical perspectives about that information.

When choosing literature, instructors need to consider carefully whether the literature chosen is conducive to the construction of technical documents. The story should contain examples of collaborative activities, demonstrating limited and full participation and various levels of conflict and cooperation. The action depicted in the story should involve several aspects of people working together, of negotiation of meaning, and of application of that negotiation to a problem. The mutual participation depicted in the story should involve characters trying to figure out the circumstances of their lives, their work, and their world in conjunction with other characters within a context of practice. Stories that are more character-driven might not be able to demonstrate as effectively the kind of mutual participation necessary to engage students in the practices of that community.

If adopting this approach, instructors need not be rhetorical, literary, or narrative theory experts, although they should be able to explain how a particular story provides a context for a particular technical document. When instructing students about the use of literature, instructors should adopt a rhetorical criticism approach, rather than a literary analysis approach, because its emphasis on audience, purpose, and situation better fits the socially constructed theories common today in technical communication discussions. Instructors might find it useful to read current theories about how communities of practice use narrative ways of knowing to sustain relationships within a community (see, for example, Wenger 1998).

More than anything else, I feel compelled to warn instructors adopting this approach that preparing for class and assessing and evaluating course documents can be time consuming, at least in the beginning. Creating scenarios for assignments requires a great deal of creativity: you must situate students within the context of the story in ways that require them to act (through the creation of a technical document). You must also be prepared for the various interpretations students present. I've used this approach for almost five years and inevitably a few students will write on their evaluations that they had difficulty figuring out what I want. These statements come from, I think, their understanding of my written comments on their documents as arguments with their interpretation (rather than as a response to the clarity of their statements).

One technique I recently adopted has helped me better help students evaluate and assess their work in my class. Before completing assignments, I have students engage in an assessment workshop—a method for evaluating technical documents holistically. This method encourages them to exercise their judgment—before completing an assignment—by evaluating a technical document according to an assessment rubric that I include in the course materials. In this assessment workshop, the instructor's role is one of guide; she does not score or critique the document herself. Although I have only just begun using this method, I am already discovering that students generally identify the same problems with a document that I would, that students are much more critical than I would be, and that students write better and require fewer revisions because they have an idea about how their documents will be evaluated. Overall, I have found that the longer prep times for course discussions, as well as for the assessment workshop, pay off in time spent responding to and grading students' documents.

Certainly, I can't prove that telling and using stories make students better writers or communicators. I simply believe that stories are a more interesting way to learn. When I run into students after the completion of a class, they inevitability remember Terrarium before they remember my name. They always remember the stories.

# HYPERMEDIATING THE RESUME

## Introduction

Popken (1999) suggests that the resume as a genre was codified in the 1920s and 1930s in various business communication textbooks, becoming part of technical writing textbooks in the late 1970s (95).1 Today, resume writing is an assignment deeply woven into the technical writing curriculum. Most contemporary technical writing textbooks include a unit on letter and resume writing in some form, as do most classes.

The appeal of resumes (and letters of application) as a beginning assignment in a technical writing class is not hard to see. Many students approach such a course with a good deal of apprehension. Often they have done little substantive writing since first-year composition and have at best a limited sense of the role written communication will play in their professional lives. These students realize that resumes are important documents and are usually motivated to work on the assignment. The appeal to teachers is also not hard to see. A resume is an enormously flexible form. It is a brief, compact document that can be used to foreground virtually any theoretical or practical aspect of technical writing.

## Innovative Practices and the Resume

Although the resume continues to be an attractive assignment, much has changed since the late seventies. Indeed, the technological and social contexts of resume writing have changed dramatically in just the last few years. The resume assignment in a technical writing course is in need of innovation to align it with current practice.

One of the goals of a traditional resume assignment has been to produce a resume that could be skimmed on a first reading by someone looking to separate candidates who clearly are not qualified from those who deserve a more careful look (McDowell 1987).2 Traditionally, a job candidate could not count on more than ten to twenty seconds of a human resource person's time during this initial screening. Faced with a stack of two hundred resumes and a limited amount of time to identify a pool of promising candidates, what choice was there? Screening to eliminate candidates first was and still is a form of survival.

In the late 1980s, one of the attractions of desktop publishing technology was its ability to transform a typewritten resume into an easy-toscan typeset document. Today, a visually attractive typeset paper resume is still an important component of a job search, but at the same time, students are increasingly asked to email resumes or to submit resumes using Web forms that strip out all formatting. In addition, in many large companies, computers now do the task of initially screening candidates. A large insurance company headquartered near my university routinely scans every print resume it receives using the software package Resumex. They place the scanned resumes into a database so that initial pools of promising candidates can be generated via keyword searches.

In preparing a print resume for Resumex scanning, less is no longer more. Because an overworked human resources (HR) person is no longer doing the initial screening, job candidates can cram their resumes with text containing the keywords that they hope are likely to generate hits and help them make the initial cut. However, these job seekers still need an attractive, traditional paper resume to share with the (for now) human manager who actually interviews them.

Finally, the World Wide Web makes it possible to produce a resume that can be both scanned quickly and linked to increasingly more complex detail about a job candidate. Such a resume/electronic portfolio can function at many different levels and meet a variety of purposes.

## Hypermediating the Resume

These changes suggest that a single print resume is no longer enough. In this postmodern world of fragmented identity, students need a hypermediated resume that exists in several different versions designed for different media and different purposes. The resume, of course, has always been a hypertextual genre. Its stylized, scannable, nonlinear nature invites multiplicity in the sense that Bolter and Grusin (1999) have defined it. The symbiotic relationship of a resume to a letter of application also reflects Bolter and Grusin's notion of "immediacy"— the idea that through media we strive to create the illusion that the reader/viewer is part of the experience rather than separate from that experience. In a job search, the need for immediacy is filled by the letter of application in which the job applicant interprets the resume and attempts to make him or herself come alive for the reader, while the resume complements this immediacy with a nonlinear, selective, hypermediated explication of that background. The letter of application and the resume are deeply intertwined, just as immediacy and hypermediacy are intertwined, each depending on the other.

In the hypermediated resume assignment, not only do the print letter and resume play off one another, but different electronic versions of the resume further complicate the assignment. Specifically, this assignment repurposes the traditional paper resume into three (and sometimes four and five) different documents:

A more or less traditional print resume that uses visual form, space, and typographic emphasis to create a resume that a human can scan in ten to twenty seconds to identify a candidate's strengths

*A text-only resume (with line lengths limited to sixty-five characters) that has no formatting and is suitable for submission via an email message or a Web-based form*

*An HTML version of the resume published on the Web*

In addition to these three required versions of the resume, students may optionally submit a scannable version of their resume, create an Acrobat PDF version of their print resume, and do a more complex, HTML-based portfolio resume as a project later in the course.

## The Print Resume

The initial document in this project is a print resume pretty much like the print resumes students have always produced. No innovation here. Large companies may be moving to Web-based forms and resume databases, but most small companies still sort through resumes by hand. A clearly written, attractive, effectively organized resume is as important now as it has always been. Scanning software may be able to process densely-packed resumes full of keywords, but managers will always prefer a lean, focused, attractive resume that tells a story. If there has been any change in the design of print resumes, that change has been toward more visually conservative forms. Because design elements such as graphics, rules, tints, and unusual fonts limit the effectiveness of OCR software, many students elect to avoid them. A resume with a simple, straightforward visual design can, however, still be a complex rhetorical document; giving up fancy tints and rules does not mean giving up design.

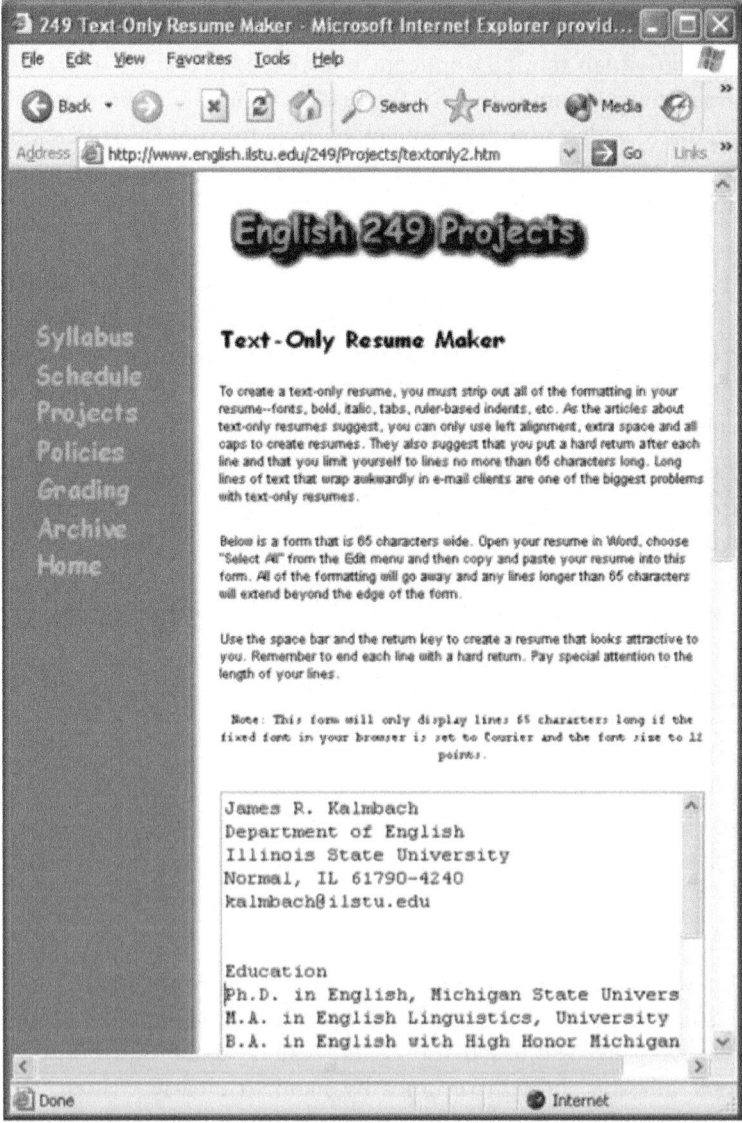

**Figure 1.** Web form used to create a text-only résumé. Lines that extend beyond the edge of the form will not wrap correctly when emailed.

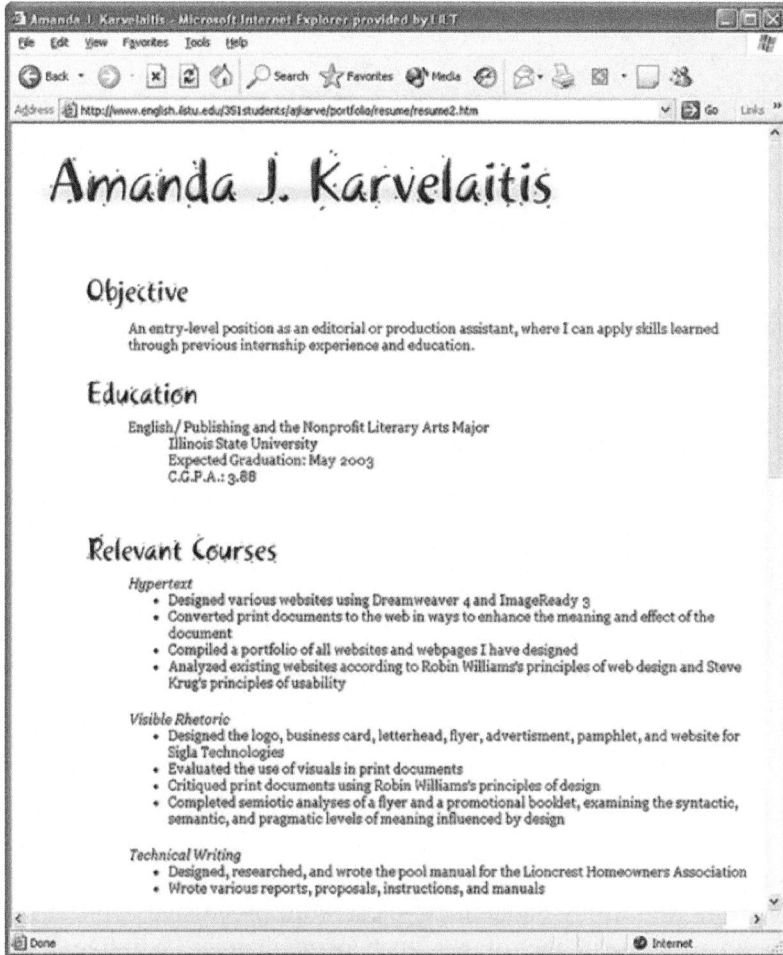

**Figure 2.** Screen-shot of an HTML-based résumé.

## *The Text-Only Resume*

As more and more job recruiting takes place over the Internet, students are increasingly asked to submit resumes via Web-based forms that support only ASCII text, or they may be asked to submit a resume via email. Currently, the only reliable way to submit a resume by email is to paste a text-only version of the resume into the body of a message. Sending resumes via attachments to email messages can be a nightmare of incompatible word processing formats; the person processing the resume may not have the right fonts in his or her system to render the resume correctly; and the resume file may inadvertently carry macro viruses.

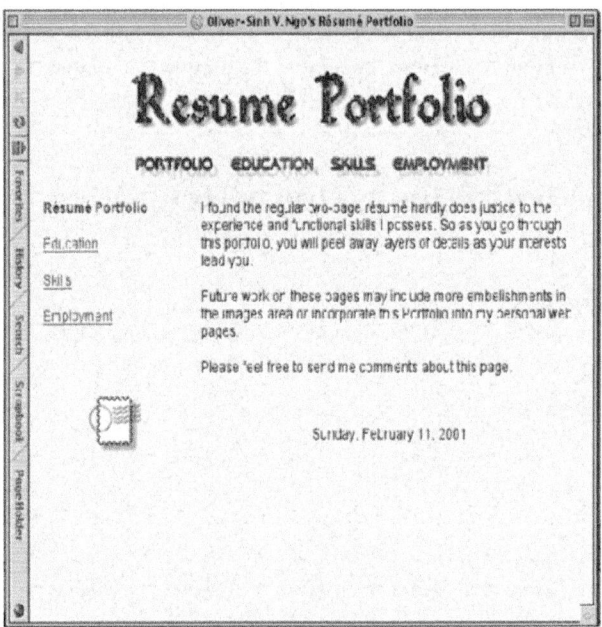

**Figure 3.** HTML-based portfolio résumé/portfolio.

Indeed many companies routinely delete without opening any resumes sent to them as attachments (Nemnich and Jandt 1999).

Teaching students to create a text-only resume is harder than one might think. Even when students save their resume as text-only files in Word or use a program like Notepad, they still have access to fonts and characters not supported in Web forms. In addition, most word processing applications use word wrap, resulting in lines of text much longer than the sixty-five- character lines displayed by email programs. As a result, a text-only resume might look fine when viewed on the screen or printed from Notepad but turn into an unreadable jumble when pasted into an email message.

Creating a text-only resume in a mail program can also be dicey. Although Web mail clients tend to be safer choices, mail clients such as Eudora, Outlook, and Outlook Express support HTML formatting within mail messages. As a result, students can add formatting to their email without being aware that they have done so, and the resulting resume will be filled with HTML code that at best makes the resume hard to process and at worst makes it incomprehensible if a reader's email program does not support HTML encoding and instead shows the message with its underlying code.

My solution has been to use a Web-based form for converting Word documents into text- only resumes. The form in figure 1 is set to a width that displays sixty-five characters of a normal-sized nonproportional font. To use the form, students open their resume in Word, copy the text, and paste that text into the text area. All non-ASCII formatting disappears, and any line that extends beyond the edge of the form must be shortened because it is too long to display properly in an email program. Students use returns to shorten those lines, and they add space between sections and upper-case headlines to create more emphasis. They then email me the text-only resume, and we go through several rounds of revision.

## *HTML Resumes*

Because I also teach my department's Web-authoring class, I have always been on the lookout for ways to incorporate more Web-based publishing into my other classes. I began including an HTML resume in technical writing courses as a way of doing more with the Web and to give students the confidence to attempt a Web-based project later in the class, but I discovered that an HTML resume can also be part of a job search. Many students report receiving inquiries as a result of having their resume online. Moreover, the Web is a medium in which students can experiment with design elements such as color, line art, and even photos, not typically available in print resumes (see figure 2).

Publishing on the Web can also expand students' notions of what is possible in a resume. An HTML resume can both tell a story in ten to twenty seconds and provide links to more detailed information in different topics. For example, in the HTML resume pictures in figure 3, the links along the left side of this resume lead to levels of increasing detail about the student's education, skills, and work experience. This sort of resume is both scannable by a human and packed with information should the reader wish to know more.

Whereas the text-only resume is an exercise in minimalism (students explore just how much formatting they can strip away from their resume) the HTML resume is an exercise in expansion. Students experiment with the different ways they can use digital media to add design elements to their HTML resumes while still telling a compelling story.

## Integrating the Hypermediated Resume into the Technical Writing Classroom

Teaching so many different forms of the resume has also meant innovating the ways the assignment is sequenced. Instead of teaching a single unit in a three-week block of time, I teach the unit in two parts: at the beginning of the semester and again after midterms. The initial week is spent introducing the assignment, workshopping first drafts of letters and resumes, and talking about formatting issues. After this week, we turn our attention to writing first a report and then a manual. While working through these projects, students turn in a new draft of their letter and resume each week until those resumes are clearly written, attractively formatted, and error free.

After this period away from the project, we return to the hypermediated resume. We spend one day converting print resumes to text-only resumes and the next five class periods converting text-only resumes into HTML resumes.

Using a discontinuous structure has been particularly helpful in this assignment. It gives students the time to work through various writing and design issues as they create an effective print resume. Once that resume is done, they can turn to repurposing it in other media.

Although the assignment as described here is closely tied to my particular institutional context and my style of teaching with technology, the hypermediated resume can be used in a variety of pedagogical contexts. Successfully incorporating such an assignment will depend on three issues: the nature of your students, the technological resources available, and the pedagogical goals that you bring to your courses.

## The Nature of Your Students

The single most important factor in deciding whether to teach the hypermediated resume in a technical writing course is the nature of your students. A resume project works best with students who are just beginning or are in the early part of their major coursework. These students are often in their third or fourth year of college. They are beginning to take their major courses and may have completed or are about to begin an internship or co-op experience.

A letter and resume project tends to be much less useful in classes where most of the students are beginning their college careers. Writing an effective resume means conceptualizing one's major in terms of a professional community that lies outside the classroom and telling a story that communicates strengths as a potential member of that community. A student taking mostly general education courses (and who may not know what his or her major will be) is usually not ready to think about a professional identity within a professional community.

I have also had less success using a resume project with graduate students, adult learners, or students in their last semester who are actively involved in a job search. Although such students may need help with their resume, they often have so much invested in that resume (they may have used that resume successfully in several job searches) that they resist the rhetorical rethinking and remediation required of a hypermediated resume.

## *Available Technology*

In most cases, access to technology is not a problem in a hypermediated resume project. Most students have or can get access to a quality word processing application and an ink jet printer. Similarly, most students come into class knowing how to use email so the process of creating textonly resumes tends to go smoothly once students make the conceptual leap of removing formatting to create rhetorical emphasis. Only for HTML resumes does technology continue to be an issue.

Mauriello, Pagnucci, and Winner (1999) have written about the difficulties of incorporating Web-based writing assignments into their classes. These difficulties start with the software used to create HTML resumes. Six years ago, when my students first started doing Web-based projects, I taught them how to use code-based HTML programs such as Home Site or BBEdit; it was an enormously time-consuming and intellectually exhausting process. In recent years, however, the quality of Web-authoring software has improved dramatically. Programs such as Macromedia Dreamweaver, Microsoft FrontPage and Adobe Go Live have all but eliminated the need for students to work with the HTML code underlying their Web-based resume. After trying out a variety of these programs, I have standardized the Web-authoring program that comes with Netscape: Netscape Composer. It is simple and straightforward for creating a simple, one-page document like a resume, and any student who has Netscape has Netscape Composer on his or her computer. Once students have created HTML resumes, they can visit clip-art sites on the Web (such as www.clipart.com) for backgrounds, rules, and other graphical elements, and they can use online tools (such as www.3dtextmaker.com) to create graphical headers.

Of course, creating an HTML resume is one thing. Getting that resume on the Web is another. In the past, using an FTP program to transfer files over the Internet has been a stumbling block. Learning the grammar of transferring files over the Internet was more technology than many students were prepared to learn. In response to this problem, my university instituted a set of Internet services, including a common WINS-based logon process so that students, faculty, and staff can use the same user id and password to log on to computers and access their mail. In addition, each student has been given a ten-megabyte Web folder on an Apache Web server, and the University computer labs are configured so that these shares are mounted as networked volumes when students log on. Anything a student saves to his or her Web share is published on the Web. These changes have eliminated the need to FTP files. Instead of mastering a new program, students publish to the Web using the same grammar of "Save/Save As" that they use to save all of their files.

Even if your institution does not offer a similar "Save As" Web-publishing process, many Web sites offer free Web publishing via simple file upload forms or DAV file sharing. From Web authoring to graphics to Web publishing, appropriate technologies to create HTML resumes are available to anyone with access to the Internet.

## Supporting Pedagogical Goals

The final issue to think about when considering a hypermediated resume project is how such an assignment can support your pedagogical goals. You need to reflect on why you are using the resume if you want to integrate the assignment effectively into your course. Here are some of the many different pedagogical goals a hypermediated resume can support.

## The Resume and the Writing Process

The resume can be used to foreground the importance of revision. For me, the core experience in learning to write well is revising a text you care about over and over again until it is as good as you can make it. The resume is a form brief enough and a topic important enough to merit repeated revision.

## The Resume as Negotiated Social Space

In writing a resume, students get advice from their technical writing teacher, from members of their department/profession, from on-campus career services, from their roommates, and from the companies they are applying to.9 Students may have already prepared a resume in one or more other classes. The many different voices heard in the process of creating a resume—the resistance, the conversation, and the negotiation— can be used to talk about the social nature of writing as students negotiate a form for their resume in a manner that will satisfy many different interests.

## The Resume as Rhetorical and Narrative Form

One of the appealing features of resumes to teachers (and frustrating features for students) is that there is no one correct format. The resume is a most highly rhetoricized genre. There are broad principles of resume writing for students (for example, entry-level people almost always lead with their education), but within those broad principles, the range of possible rhetorical forms is enormous.

A resume is not a neutral display of a student's life history; it is a selective look that should be tailored to each student's strengths as a job candidate. Consequently, the nature of the categories a student includes in a resume, the names a student gives those categories, and the sequence in which those categories appear all depend on the student's unique background. One student may have a particularly strong sequence of course work and course-related projects, another student may have impressive extracurricular activities, another may have co-op or internship experience, while another may have a particularly impressive work history. Each student must decide what story their resume will tell and what sequences of topics and content can tell that story effectively. If you teach the report or the manual as narrative forms, the resume can be used to introduce the idea of narrative in technical writing to the class.

## *The Resume as Visual Form*

The resume is also a very visual form. Content and purpose are shaped by choices in layout and typographic emphasis. Visual issues do not, however, have to be only about aesthetics (making it look pretty) or about usability (making the resume scannable for someone taking ten to twenty seconds to decide whether to toss your resume in the trash). You can also talk about how the visual choices students make in a resume mark them as members of a particular professional community. Thus, the resume can be a starting point for talking about (and getting students to experience) the interplay between the visual, the aesthetic, the cognitive, the political, and the social forces that pull against one another in the shaping of a document.

## *The Resume and Correctness*

The resume can be used to reinforce the importance of proofreading and spelling checking when producing final drafts and to foster an appreciation for the role of correctness in documents written for real readers. I tell the story of a student who was turned down for an internship at a major corporation and the reason that they gave us was that she had misspelled the name of the company in her letter. The rapid transition from early to late drafts in resume writing, the briefness of the form, and the obvious importance of its appearance make the resume a natural place to talk about the difference between reflectively reading early drafts for organizational and conceptual issues and meticulously and obsessively reading late drafts to eliminate error.

## *The Resume and Overlapping Projects*

I have found that most of my students are used to sequential projects in their classes. They work on one project, get a grade, and then work on another project; or they study material, take a test, and study more material. Most professionals, however, must juggle many different projects at once (paying more or less attention to each project as it matures) rather than finishing one project and starting another in a sequential manner. The discontinuous nature of the hypermediated resume assignment (starting a project, going on to other things, and then returning to that project) can be used to introduce the conception of nonsequential writing projects.

These various goals and purposes really just scratch the surface. Technical writing teachers need to be clear about what they value and why they want to include a hypermediated resume in their class if they are to use the assignment effectively.

## *Remediating the Resume*

Inevitably, a hypermediated resume assignment like the one described here leads to remediation: "the representation of one media in another" (Bolter and Grusin 1999, 45). Each of the different versions of their resume students create represents and appropriates the forms of the others. Each critiques and informs the other. The ultimate value of a hypermediated resume assignment may well be the reflection and the critique such an assignment encourages.

Reflection should not, however, be limited to students; the hypermediated resume invites teachers to reflect on our practices as well.

Quoting from Marshall McLuhan, Bolter and Grusin (1999) argue that "the 'content' of any medium is always another medium" (45). So, too, the content of any pedagogical activity is always another pedagogy. Innovation in teaching is a form of remediation, a form of representing and appropriating old practices in new. What we learn in teaching the hypermediated resume ultimately emerges out of this remediation, out of the conversations between approaches.

I have argued elsewhere that the history of teaching with technology is a history of remarkably similar patterns (Kalmbach 1997). What teachers did with typewriters in the 1930s and the arguments made for the use of that technology are virtually identical to what teachers did with computers in the classroom in the eighties and the arguments that we made for this technology. From these patterns, I developed the slogan: "Technology changes, pedagogy stays the same." This slogan suggests that the fundamental role of technology in the classroom may well be to create new spaces in which students and teachers can revisit old arguments, old conversations about teaching.

From the perspective of the hypermediated resume, however, we might better argue that teachers use technology not to duplicate but to repurpose and remediate past practice, to revisit and make those practices our own. The versions of the resume I present here will probably change, perhaps dramatically, in the next few years. Technology will provide us with new ways of understanding this genre and its social consequences. No matter; we will create new forms and new practices. As teachers we will repurpose and remediate. That is what we do.

# USING ROLE-PLAYS TO TEACH TECHNICAL COMMUNICATION

## Introduction

The techniques and assignments described in this chapter grow from the authors' own academic interests in constructivist pedagogy, the learning plays of Bertolt Brecht (1968), and Augusto Boal's (1968) Forum Theater. We use role-plays to generate both oral and written assignments, which fulfill two constructivist precepts. First, students learn communications best from authentic problems. Second, learning communication skills is a fully engaging activity: communication is both physical and mental. Specifically, we generate written and oral assignments from role-plays written by students and drawn from their experiences with technical communication problems.

At our school, we teach technical communication to electronics technology students. Our graduates interact with rapidly changing computer and communications technology and must demonstrate high-caliber customer service skills. Traditionally, employers value our graduates because their "hands-on" technical education enables them to "hit the ground running." Upon graduation, however, many students enter company training programs. Increasingly, these programs emphasize customer service and teamwork skills. This emphasis is because, instead of servicing mostly large-scale projects and government contracts, the electronics industry increasingly serves smaller consumers, developing, supplying, and maintaining sophisticated electronic equipment for small businesses and even individual households. Several years ago, an industry representative told one of the authors that companies are almost ready to recruit field technicians from liberal arts programs; companies were willing to provide technical training to applicants who had developed the ability to communicate with customers. In response to these changes in industry, we have developed classroom techniques and assignments to prepare the electronics technician to "come out from behind the machine" and interact with the customer.

Briefly, in our technical communication classes, students role-play personal incidents of failed communication. This role-playing creates the opportunity for a critical distancing of their lived experience. Like Brecht's

(1968) estrangement-effects—V-Effekten (680)—our role-playing technique gives the audience (and in our case, the student/actor/author) an opportunity to break out of habitual ways of seeing and to observe and engage with the rhetorical choices made by the characters. The intention is for students to develop a sense of control over aspects of their lives that have reified under layers of habit and assumption. Using the techniques of Augusto Boal's (1968) Forum Theater, which developed as a critique of Brechtian theory and practice (139–142), students present and critique their role-plays. The presentation techniques of Forum Theatre empower students to critique their habitual styles of communication. The role-play exercises then become rehearsals for success.

From these role-playing exercises, opportunities for writing naturally emerge. The most usual motivation for writing is somehow to repair or prevent the problems presented in the role-plays. Because they have role-played these problems, students can better visualize the goals of their writing. Those visualizations can then be described, analyzed, and revised, in words as well as in action. Specifying the location for the roleplay—on the job or within an organization—assures that issues of organizational and technical communication become the focus of the roleplays. As teachers, we can respond realistically to this writing, posing questions about how the real audience (the audience as presented in the role-play) would react to content, style, and presentation. We become editors positioned between the writers and the audience, which is our preferred teaching position. Thus, our classes become student centered; we become facilitators of learning rather than lecturers, and students become actively and critically engaged in authentic problems of organizational and technical communication.

The following sections describe our use of role-plays, our sources, and some of the broader implications that we think this model has for college pedagogy. In the first section, "The Structure Of The Actor's Work: Creating A Classroom For Role-Plays," we discuss how we prepare students for the work role-plays will demand of them and suggest ways the teacher and class structure can model the dramatic principles and rhetorical discretion inherent in role-plays. In the next section, "The Arsenal: Tools for the Student Creating the Role-Play," we describe a typical sequence for staging and responding to the students' first role-plays of the semester. We refer to the performance concepts of Boal (1968) and Brecht (1968) to clarify the principles and goals of this method of delivering a course in technical communication. In the next section, we describe how role-plays can lead to authentic writing assignments or enrich students' responses to more traditional, textbook-based assignments, including discipline-specific research papers. In a later section, we close with some reflections on how our experience with role-plays has guided our professional lives outside the classroom, including our responses to writing across the curriculum, case-studies initiatives, the pressures of traditional grading, and textbook selection.

## The Structure of the Actor's Work: Creating a Classroom for Role-Plays

If we set the scene carefully in the beginning weeks, many classes become self-directed, and we simply guide the work students have already committed to. We begin by introducing fundamental concepts similar to those of most technical communication classes. As we do this, we deliberately model the audience awareness and adaptation we expect from students. The objective of our first class meetings is to get students to articulate their judgments and build their confidence. If we succeed, students articulate authentic situations that guide their work for most of the semester (the subject of the next section), and they commit themselves to finding workable solutions to these situations.

### *Introducing Rhetorical Analysis*

Our technical communication course begins with an introduction to rhetorical analysis. We want to make students aware of the considerable repertoire of rhetorical skills they already have. We lecture briefly about language acquisition and use simple, hands-on demonstrations of the power their language skills give them to organize and communicate information. A simple but powerful example: We give them a list of eight words to memorize in order. As they attempt that, we write the same words on the board so that they form a sentence and ask them to memorize the words again. The sentence is memorized as a unit, almost instantly. They experience, hands-on, one of the most elemental and powerful innate abilities of the human brain. In lecture, we also present some tools for rhetorical analysis, ranging from the basic, traditional author-subject-audience triangle to more complex methods such as Killingsworth and Palmer's (1999) context of production/context of use (3–20).

The level of sophistication of this introduction depends on our sense of the audience we have before us. If the class is anxious to "do something," the introduction is more like a pep talk. More reflective classes do more discussion. We are ready and willing to adapt our presentation, to observe students, and, at any time, to ask the question: "Do you want to do a role-play now?" This willingness to adapt instantiates the basic lesson of our course: An effective communicator responds to the real needs of an audience. From our first meeting, we explicitly model that skill for our classes by eliciting their responses to our plans for the course and our assumptions about communication. This method does not constitute a fundamental change in most teaching styles.

Most teaching is as responsive as it is directive, and our approach does not fundamentally alter the mechanics of teaching; instead, it tries to lay bare these fundamentals for students to see and use.

The goal of our introduction is, finally, to prepare students to turn technical data into technical information and to develop from knowers into teachers. Thus, our introductory lecture- demonstrations also have to build students' confidence in their ability to do the work of teaching. Sometimes, technical communication can intimidate even students with a substantial record of success in their technical courses. Technical communication is different from their technical courses both in subject and structure, and we don't try to smooth over the differences. Instead of encountering brand new technical content and a clean slate to write on, students in our courses are made to question some deeply held beliefs and break some old habits. One of these habits is eschewing ambiguity in the search for the one right answer, the one method, for solving all their communication problems. From the first day of class, our work is a matter not of finding the one right answer, but of choosing the best answer from many possible answers. We model for students the need to adapt, and we introduce a range of tools, including our textbooks and other reference material, for informing our judgments and making effective rhetorical choices.

We don't want our introductory classes or our textbook to preempt the students' own decision-making process. We want them to develop confidence by discovering and exercising the rhetorical skills they were born with. We are then able to demand that students test and revise the solutions they suggest to real problems. We try to convince them that human beings are sophisticated rhetoricians long before they are trained technicians.

## *Integrating Role-Plays*

The way we integrate role-plays into our classroom varies from semester to semester and section to section, precisely because the rhetorical situation we face as teachers changes with each set of students. Some semesters, role-plays may serve as a warm-up for a more traditional "genre studies" class. Other semesters, a set of role-plays may bring up issues so complex that we will spend the better part of the semester on them, covering material from textbooks by way of the role-plays and conducting necessary research. In every case, however, by midsemester most classes, whether based on textbook readings or role-plays, have covered the same range of material required by our department's course description. Revision, proofreading, ethics, letter format, memo format, technical descriptions, and so forth emerge from a class centered on roleplays as consistently as they emerge from a syllabus designed around a textbook; but, in a class centered on role-plays, the control over these topics becomes a shared enterprise between teacher and students. Students who emerge from classrooms where role-plays have controlled the syllabus are as well prepared for our departmental writing assessment as those who emerge from classes that more closely follow the structure of the textbook. This preparation is because they have internalized problem-solving strategies that enable them to creatively and confidently address a broad range of technical communication tasks.

A short description will illustrate how our method can structure a semester. One semester, our classes took on the project of revising the labs in their technical courses. This project took the entire semester. It emerged during the first weeks of role-plays. In role-plays based on inschool communication problems, it became clear that students felt they were receiving poor "customer service" in the lab. When they began to explore the systematic causes of this situation, they discovered that the way the labs were written predisposed teachers and lab assistants to offer poor customer service. For instance, cautions and diagrams were not included. When they began to rewrite the labs, they had to consider themselves and their fellow students seriously as an audience. But they also had to consider the larger academic systems within which labs are written and revised. They discovered students in the lab were not their only audience; so were the teachers who would teach (and approve) the changes, the dean who would approve the cost of recopying the labs, and so forth. Each class session began with the question, "Did we get the labs changed?" Answering this question took the entire class session and set the homework for the week. The class agenda and schedule were set by the students' real need to resolve a real problem. They used their communication textbook and their class time as resources to help them effect change, not as ends in themselves. Two products emerged from their work: new labs and a new awareness of their technical classrooms as rhetorically complex environments where students and professors have myriad roles. This authentic writing situation also supported the formal academic requirements for technical communication: students who participated in this project wrote memos, technical descriptions, procedures, and directions; they created charts, diagrams, and visuals; they learned to format documents on the computer; they made oral presentations; and they practiced audience analysis, revision, editing, and proofreading.

The students in this classroom, and in other classes where a role-play lasts a few minutes or a week, have faced the questions of engagement and responsibility crucial to generating and evaluating writing both in the classroom and the workplace. It is easy for students to dismiss rhetorical problems in which they are not fully engaged. Every teacher has worked with students who write merely to complete an assignment and please the teacher. These students can't understand why you are not satisfied when they have done everything you asked—everything, that is, except commit themselves. When presented with a communication problem in a classroom setting, such students confidently ignore it and turn it into something easier to handle, but irrelevant. A problem-solving letter will degenerate into a tirade and end in an inappropriate action, or it will degenerate into a polite, powerless, but structurally perfect "letter of complaint" and end in inaction. However, once students experience the sophistication of their rhetorical powers, they are more prepared to reconsider their first knee-jerk responses to the communication problems we present. For this reason, the problems we present for students' consideration must be fully engaging, both mentally and physically. Such engagement emerges from student-generated role-plays based on situations often ongoing in their lives and on significant events in their working lives. Thus, even if the entire semester does not revolve around role-plays, we find them a useful way to introduce the content, structure, and expectations of our course.

## The Arsenal: Tools for the Student Creating the Role-Play

Once we have set the scene for the actors' work by introducing the fundamentals of the communication situation and establishing student engagement, we turn our attention to generating the actual role-plays that are the meat of the course. We begin with a basic process, which we modify depending on the students and the progress of the semester. Students begin by generating ideas, which we review and categorize to create structure in the course. Students rehearse briefly, and the class is given a topic to consider as they observe the role-play. After each roleplay, students discuss the focus topic, and then the players replay the scene, suggesting alternative actions.

### *Generating "Scripts"*

Crucially, students generate the ideas and scripts for the role-plays from their experiences, using a process based on Augusto Boal's (1997) Forum Theater. When students generate, select, and present the situations, they become "spect-actors" rather than spectators (17). This technique empowers them to establish the problems to be addressed and leads them to take responsibility for their communication strategies. This technique also assures an authentic experience of rhetorical problem solving.

It is a relatively simple technique. For the first set of role-plays, we often ask students to describe a time they have seen or experienced a failed attempt to communicate in the workplace. For each role-play, we give the class at most a half hour to produce a script. We leave the definition of "script" wide open. The idea of student-generated, and therefore authentic, scenarios comes directly from Boal's Forum Theater (1968) technique (132). Some students create scripts that simply sketch the outlines of events; others write out complete dialogues. Once they begin to perform their role-plays, the students soon learn that the end result of either script is the same because they must perform without the script.

Especially for the first role-plays, we generate some discussion to prepare students to write their role-plays. A couple of students almost always immediately understand the assignment; thus, as soon as we are done describing the assignment, we ask the class for an idea for a role-play, and we discuss its characteristics. Soon the whole class understands, and everyone can begin to produce a script. Usually, in a class of twenty-five we have found that only one or two have trouble getting a situation after a little thought. Students in our classes are probably older than most, and almost all students have jobs, so results may vary, but we suspect not by much. After all, the sense of what constitutes a rhetorical problem has its roots in an innate human ability to use language. Asking college students to identify a communication problem at work merely taps into the rich and varied experience they already have with language. After everyone has written a script, we collect the scripts and take them home to read and categorize. We look for three categories of circumstances because in the next class we break students into groups of three to work on their role-plays.

## *Discovering the Curriculum*

Discovering these categories requires us to relate the rhetorical lessons we teach to the experiences of the people we are teaching. Like our course introductions, the categories we find vary from class to class, but we have never failed to find a relevant set of categories. For example, one class's scripts were divided into "failed communication between supervisor and employee," "failed communication between employees," and "failed communication between customer and supplier." Another class's scripts divided into "intentional deceptions," "ignorance about the subject of the communication," and "unintentional misunderstandings." (Sometimes we skip the classification step altogether and just go with the flow. At these times, we enjoy the rich and varied scripts and the challenge of on-the-spot analysis and act like a director or a drama critic, identifying the central agon, critiquing the plot.)

When we choose to find categories, as we usually do, these categories need to honor the students' authentic experiences and their ways of naming and understanding these experiences. At this point, we exert control over the curriculum. We could choose role-plays we think will lead to technical definitions or technical descriptions, proposals or recommendations. However, imposing categories like these from our textbook or departmental requirements risks diminishing the role-plays' potential for helping students uncover meaning and practice authentic problem-solving. Asking for a role-play that produced a "technical description" situation will not work because situations do not occur to students as instances for the textbook's exegesis; otherwise, they wouldn't need our course. We have learned to trust that discussions of topics like the "extended technical definition" will emerge naturally out of the work on the role-plays. This delay of academic classification helps students discover the issues and strategies of technical writing on their own and thus to adopt them as their own. The relevance of the contents of a textbook has to be discovered, with the teacher serving as facilitator, not lecturer. Indeed, concentrating on basic rhetorical problem solving makes the teaching of genres and types easier and faster because the genre is taught at the moment students are intellectually prepared for it. Once you recognize that an extended definition will solve your problem, the technique becomes as obvious as a hammer: you pick it up and use it.

At the next class meeting, after the scripts have been classified, students begin to perform their role-plays. First, we point out that the roleplays take place in "real time," so that students need to focus those scripts down to their key moments in ways that take no more than about four minutes. We return each student's script with just a number—1, 2, or 3—on it, and students form groups of three. Each group includes the author of a "1" script, a "2" script, and a "3" script, so that each group will—to the extent possible—work with one script from each category we have defined. (We do not tell the students what these categories are.)

The group then reviews each of its scripts, chooses one, and creates a role-play for it, focusing on the crucial actions. For us, this process of focusing is an application of Brecht's (1968) concept of the gestus, a social comportment captured in gestures, and Boal's (1968) use of participant-generated action (689). This focusing on the essential action of a scene is a wonderfully complex act of rhetorical analysis. Students accomplish it with ease. The whole process of reviewing, selecting, and "rehearsing" the actions estranges them in ways that make them more available for student interventions. This process can reinforce the students' sense of control and competence. It also prepares students to write more detailed narratives and descriptions. At the end of their "rehearsal" time, each group will have discussed three role-plays, one from each student, and practiced one for presentation. This whole "rehearsal" is remarkably easy and quick.

The first time a class does the exercise, the selection and rehearsal can take about half an hour. After one experience, the role-plays can usually be selected and prepared in less time. Giving more time can even be counterproductive. Students' impromptu responses are most effective at communicating the main issues as soon as the "actors" have a sense of the reality of a scene. Practice here may sometimes dull the edge because students tend to want to soften the conflict. It is often the restless, nonreflective student who produces the most compelling roleplay, while the more diligent student sometimes takes fewer risks and produces a two- dimensional representation with a prepared solution. As we said, humans are naturally masterful rhetoricians and, given enough time, students will take any "case" and try to define the rhetorical problem out of existence, especially when it involves written communication. Students who resist role-plays want to wave a wand at the problem; they say, "I wouldn't write; I'd just talk to the guy" or "That's just the way it is; there's nothing I could do about it" and believe it will go away. This ability to "resolve" challenges by redefining the issues is not unrelated to Boal's (1968) concept of "magic." Magic, in Forum Theater, describes proposed solutions that are unrealistic. In Forum Theater, the facilitator, called the Joker, may interrupt a scene by calling out the word "magic" when some proposed resolution seems unreal, such as resolving an oppression by appealing to the oppressor's sense of brotherhood (139–42). The need to overcome this remarkable human ability to sidestep rhetorical challenges is one of the things that brought us to roleplays, and especially to impromptu role-plays, which do not allow students the time or distance they need to bury the key rhetorical issues in diversions and vagaries. In addition, we extend the power of the Joker mutatis mutandis to the whole class: that way, even when a student does trivialize his or her role-play, we get a teaching moment. First, the student's attitude is usually the result of an insensitivity (or oversensitivity) to the issues involved. Second, other students can often see the threat and the opportunity that the author is ignoring.

Before we let the students present the first role-play to the class, we usually introduce a focus for the discussion that will follow. For our first set of role-plays, we usually ask students to observe the responsibility each persona in the role-play has for the failure of the communication. Introducing a theme like responsibility just before students see a roleplay helps focus the discussion of alternative actions that follows the presentation. If we don't introduce a focusing issue to encourage students to stop and analyze, their innate ability to redefine rhetorical problems sometimes will preempt a discussion of the actual action of the role-play. We like the issue of responsibility because it is central both to the students' work lives and to their comportment in the writing classroom. Raising the issue of responsibility early helps them to find the connection between themselves and writing. For instance, in one roleplay, the student had refused to shovel on a work site because he thought it was unsafe. A fellow worker did as he was told and ended up in the hospital. The focus question allowed the discussion of this incident to center on responsibility, not blame: What were the responsibilities of each worker and of their supervisor? A central problem in getting students to recognize the need for rhetorical analysis is teaching them to fix the problem, not the blame. After students are comfortable with the role- play process, we can set a focus for the class discussions at various points in the process: before students begin to script, after we return scripts, or before students rehearse.

## *Performing the Curriculum*

After scripting, rehearsal, and focusing, the actual performance of the first role-plays occurs. Students perform without referring to the written scripts. When we first started using this form of role-playing, we allowed the students to take a copy of the written script with them for a first runthrough, but then we had them replay the scene without the script. Students quickly saw that effective role-playing was easier than they thought and could even be fun. On their own, they abandoned the written scripts after rehearsal.

Sometimes, we videotape the role-plays to help resolve disputes about which action caused which reaction. Also, information about body language and physical expression is absorbed in the form of a "dramatic" image, and we have seen what a powerful effect the internalizing of this projected self-image can have on the development of interpersonal skills. We prefer to use a video projector rather than a TV for playbacks. Perhaps because they are small or because the format is so familiar, television screen images do not seem to capture the attention or have the impact of the near life-size image of a student projected onto a screen. We are always amazed at the ability of these images to hold the class's attention for extended periods. We have videotaped several roleplays from one class session (our classes run usually two hours) and held discussions that did not require the use of the film, and yet the students were ready and eager to sit through a replay of all the role-plays at the end of the class. We have also used videotaped role-plays as the basis of exams, asking students to view the tape and then write an analysis of the situation presented. Videotaping is a useful option, but it is not essential; and we wouldn't insist on reviewing a tape before we began the discussion section of our role-play exercises, especially because these discussion may lead back into role-playing as described later.

A discussion of a role-play usually follows immediately after its presentation and can take different forms. The discussions can be short and limited to one aspect of analysis. Often, in the first set of role-plays for a semester, we run through the role-play discussions with just one task: to name the responsibility each persona had in the failure of the communication. We want to reinforce the idea that even the most obvious villain—the boss with a chip on her shoulder or the alcoholic co-worker— to some extent may be enabled by the responses of other actors. On the other hand, the discussion of one role-play could be material for more than one class session. It might open up topics like teamwork, management, or information flow that may require research or reference to the textbook. This dynamic is the same as the one that traditional case-study techniques engage.

Eventually, discussion may lead to alternative ways to envision and enact the role-play. In the style of Boal's (1968) Forum Theater, the students become "spect-actors": not passive observers, but active participants, and therefore active learners. In our discussions, students are able to intervene in a role-play after its first run-through to test out different strategies. For example, in one role-play a student is fired for handling a customer when it wasn't part of his job description. In this situation, the policy conflicted with best practice/ policy implementation—an authentic and complex situation. Originally, the student author/actor had not tried to keep his job. Presenting the event as a role-play enabled him to revise his personal history. It was too late to change the outcome, but seeing what he might have done increased his sense of control. He actually considered contacting his former employer, but decided that instead he would accept it as a lesson learned. Thus, during the discussion phase, we employ Forum Theater techniques to allow class members to stop the role-play at critical junctures to introduce other possibilities and reject alternatives as magical. Following Forum Theater practice, we sometimes play each intervention through until we see a real solution or until we come to another intervention that revises the scene or advances the action to move us closer to a resolution of the core problems (Boal 1968, 139–42).

The essential part of the role-play is its function as a rehearsal, estrangement, and deliberation, all which Brecht (1968) and Boal (1968) name as essential to the dramatic process. For example, in one student-generated role-play, this question was posed: How do you respond when a group member isn't pulling his or her weight? Students role-played it two ways. First, they lectured and punished, and the delinquent student-actor naturally (unrehearsed) pulled away and acted worse. Next, they included him, asked for his input, and he responded positively. Rehearsing their response allowed them to respond more deliberately and more effectively. As Brecht observed about his learning plays, this role-playing is a rehearsal for real life.

## Listening to What We Hear/Seeing What We Look at: Finding Writing Within the Role-Plays

Using the process described previously, students generate a wide range of role-plays, practice their interpersonal and self-presentation skills, and discuss thoughtfully many rhetorical issues that arise in technical communication. But students also need to write. Like role-plays themselves, the writing assignments that emerge from them are complex. They invite student investment and revision, place the teacher in the role of facilitator, and teach the principles of technical writing as surely as textbook assignments. These writing assignments, in fact, prepare students for more traditional academic assignments, such as research papers, which we sometimes assign in the second half of the semester. In fact, by midsemester, students are prepared to see their academic writing as role-play, a strategy that gives them the rhetorical tools, sophistication, and confidence to succeed as academic writers.

## *Writing a Solution*

At some point, a group's role-play will generate a writing task, either as a follow-up to the event role-played or as an alternative to the failed strategy of the role-play. This task usually emerges naturally in discussion but can be prompted by questions such as "What needs to happen now?" or "How could this have been avoided?" These questions serve as a springboard for all our writing assignments, which may include letters or memos from one persona to another or to a figure implied by the action. In this way, the writing situation is authentic, visible, and motivated. Students begin to see writing as a natural by-product of life, not as an academic exercise. At the same time the writing assignment remains a common topic for all students in a section, which is practical for our grading purposes and for documenting our adherence to institutional course requirements.

As students draft their writing assignments, we can return to role-playing to test the efficacy of their writing. A follow-up role-play can test the effect of the writing on the intended audience. This role-playing peer review can make clear when a student has tried to solve a complex problem with a sledgehammer. In a particularly effective scenario, one of the students, playing himself, insulted his supervisor's mastery of English. The student then sent the supervisor a memo about the encounter. In a follow-up role-play, the supervisor called the employee into his office after receiving his memo about the encounter. The supervisor first impugned the employee's own mastery of written English and then fired him for insubordination. The class cheered. They love a good payback.

## *Writing Research*

Even if we move to more traditional presentation modes, like academic research projects for a technical course, later in the semester, we find the students' work with role-plays enriches their academic work. Once students understand the communication process within an authentic workplace environment, they are prepared to see the academic genres and classroom learning as authentic. For example, in the first assignments, we use a Total Quality Management customer/supplier model to discuss rhetorical issues (Schmidt 1992, 37). In this model all work relations, both internal and external, are identified as occurring between customers and suppliers. Just as a customer comes into a store to get what he needs to do his job, coworkers within a company act as both customers and suppliers to one another; a key to one's professional life in this model is identifying one's myriad customers, their needs, and the effect one wants to have on them. Later in the semester, we may employ this same model to work with students on a research project assigned from one of their technical courses. We ask students, who are used to seeing themselves as customers of the teacher, to see themselves as suppliers of the research project. We begin with the questions that we often use to focus role-plays: Who are the customers in this situation? What effect do you want to have on them? Using the experience of role-playing, the simplistic answer, "My teacher is the customer" gives way to a more complex discussion: How are the students in your research team also your customers? How are the students in your class customers of your research? How can you make a potential employer the customer of your research? Recently, two of our former students told us that they went to a job fair and told recruiters about their research, which led them to job interviews. It was the role-playing in our class that led them to understand that someone in the real world could be interested in what they had done in an undergraduate research project. They were able to see themselves as suppliers of information to potential employers. That is the lesson we think role-playing teaches well: to become an effective part of an organization, you have to understand the role your communication skills do and can play.

With an improved understanding of research and writing as a commodity that an employer might need, rather than a retelling of old information to prove they have done the required reading, students begin to take more responsibility for their research. In our classes, the purpose of research projects becomes to teach the class, as well as the teacher, something about a technical subject that will be relevant to their lives and work. In this way, with the class as a real audience, the research project becomes a rehearsal for life. As part of the project, students present a proposal to the class before they begin. The class has to approve the topic and suggest what it is they might want to know about the proposed topic. After conducting the approved research, the student must then deliver an oral report to the class and a written report to the professor who assigned the project. This assignment creates two very different audiences. The textbook issue of the complex audience thus arises out of an authentic assignment. Our expansion of the primary customer from professor to fellow students also helps the class resist the urge to see research as facts lifted from books or the Internet. The whole project is now defined by the need to teach a specific audience specific material and to respond to the real needs of the customers. At the end of the student's final presentation and the question and answer period, the class takes a quiz on the material, designed by the presenter. The success of the class on the test factors into the final project evaluation. This test situation is a more authentic situation than a research paper alone. It has a specific but complex audience (with equal or less knowledge than the writers) and measurable results. It also sensitizes students to their responsibility to an audience and to the extent of their control over both situations and information.

## Doubts and Certainties: The Teacher as Learner

The previous sections tried to made clear the value we find for role-plays in students' academic lives, but they have not touched on the value this approach has for our academic and professional lives. Role-plays create a classroom environment that engages us equally as it engages students, allowing us to reflect on the questions we find essential to our lives as teachers and academics. At the same time, they streamline the procedural and administrative work of teaching because they make it clear both to us and to students our function in the classroom. We find our work with role-plays has made us reconsider our position on academic issues, such as writing across the curriculum and case-studies initiatives. Role-plays have also forced us to reflect on some of the essential power dynamics of the classroom embodied in traditional grading and textbooks.

### *Rethinking Writing across the Curriculum and Case Studies*

For us, use of role-plays developed out of our experience with two movements in the teaching of college writing: writing across the curriculum (WAC) and case studies. When the authors first became colleagues, we worked on developing a WAC program for the college. We began by engaging technical faculty in joint writing projects. Though we succeeded in developing joint writing projects, our commitment to constructivist ideas about student-centered classrooms soon created problems. The assignments from the technical courses were not in tune with a student-centered approach. The research projects were not well adapted to the students' technical interests or research skills. The lab reports were mostly fill-in exercises with a paragraph or two of discussion and conclusions. As described earlier, we adjusted one research project to make it more authentic, but we were and are still dissatisfied with the results. The technical component in these projects remains fully defined by traditional course content. The students are given a list of technical topics to select from, all which are covered in the textbook. Our WAC projects were subordinating the authentic rhetorical needs of students to course content. In response, we initiated our technical projects, such as the semester-long lab revision project described previously. Our frustrations with WAC projects made clear the advantages of the more authentic approach to role-playing that we now use. Role-playing, in turn, influenced our revision of WAC projects.

Subsequent and connected to our work with WAC, which continues, was the opportunity to work on a collegewide case-studies initiative. We collected and developed a set of cases for use in technical and general education courses. In the end, the process of preparing cases for unprepared instructors in existing courses was unsuccessful because the cases we developed looked like the cases that many newer professional/technical writing textbooks provided. These cases, conceived in terms of specific book chapters and discussion points, were not authentic learning experiences for the students. They led students to specific material at specific times, instead of bringing material to students only when discussions require it, which is the traditional method of case-studies courses. In the case-study classroom, the development of the course content should be subordinated to the needs of the case work. This is not what happened in our case-study initiative, for two reasons, we think. First, the institutions, discipline, or self- definition of most technical teachers does not allow them the creativity and close attention to an unfolding class dynamic that being a case facilitator requires. Second, the method used to prepare these cases was inappropriate for our classes. Either they were too sophisticated, requiring too much subject knowledge to be effective, or they had to be stripped down to match the professional knowledge of students. The Harvard Business School case-studies model, which underlies many case-study projects, is probably not a good one for undergraduate students or for students without equivalent professional background and experience.

We were frustrated by WAC and prescriptive case studies because we felt they did not go far enough toward a student-centered pedagogy. Then, at a meeting with representatives of the Field Services Managers Association, we asked what we could do to prepare students for employment and got the response, "Teach them to use role-plays." We combined the role-playing technique with the idea of a student-centered classroom, and the result was the technique we have been describing. The work of Brecht (1968) and Boal (1968, 1997) then gave us the theoretical direction and practical tools for dramatizing our technical writing courses. Role-playing has dramatized the classroom for us. In the process, it has challenged our traditional academic assumptions about assessment, student success, and textbooks.

## *Rethinking the Power Dynamics of the Classroom*

Their initial role-plays unintentionally prepared students and ourselves to interrogate the validity of traditional grading methods in the face of authentic experience. This interrogation is a natural by-product of raising authentic issues of purpose and presentation within a traditional classroom. Students will ask, "If I got the job done, how can you grade me?" Or, "If the other student responded the way I wanted in the roleplay where I presented my letter, how are you going to grade me down?" The role-plays help students see the relativity of communication, which in turn complicates grading, with its basis in error rather than achievement. In doing so, role-plays create an opportunity for students to begin to consider their methods for assessing their personal effectiveness.

Perhaps this opportunity is one reason that bad students often succeed at role-plays in ways that force us to redefine the behaviors we categorize as "good" and "bad." The success that low- achieving students experience in role-playing makes us conscious of the artificiality of these labels. Role-plays often help the bad students by validating their active, personal approach and by helping them use it mindfully to get what they want. As teachers of adults, we probably cannot ignore their habits, but we can make them aware of these habits and help them bring them under their control.

Good students often create inappropriate role-plays, tests, and presentations; bad students often create dynamic, engaging, and authentic role-plays, tests, and presentations. For instance, good students will create tests with many multiple-choice questions about specific numbers. Bad students will ask for definitions of basic terms. Good students will "hide" their questions within the presentation; bad students tend to advertise them in neon as the presentation unfolds (writing them on the board before they begin, giving cues such as "This is an important word to remember"). One semester a group of good students complained fiercely because a group of bad students got a better grade. How unfair! How unheard of! Role-plays disturb students because the usual structure that determines how one earns an "A" isn't there, and they don't know what to do. They have to think about the rules. (In theory, role-plays have given them a tool to do this and to revise how they see rules.)

There seem to be several reasons bad students excel. Bad students help each other more in ways that attempt to leave none behind. Good students often see a locus of control in the material or the professor and define presentations and assignments as "telling knowledge." They see everything in the technical field as talking to someone who knows more than they do and to whom they must prove their command of the material. Role-plays do give these students a language with which to name more diverse audiences, but these students often balk at role-plays and research-for-their-peers because it risks undermining the academic structure in which they have found success and safety. Their presentations tend to be complex and their quizzes too subtle. Bad students, on the other hand, often see the locus of control in their peer groups. What other students think of them is more important than what the teacher thinks of them. This perspective is in some ways actually a more realistic worldview. We believe it leads them to seek success in what their peers can get from them. These students, of course, do recognize the locus of control in the material or professor, but they appear to be so intimidated by the control they perceive in these places that they opt out of the structure to be in control of an alternative, "loser" reality/structure. They are the students who say, "I'll do what I can," instead of "I'll do what I'm supposed to" (which the good students say). This attitude is a way of designing and controlling a situation that often results in effective analysis of our role-play problems.

## *Rethinking the Textbook*

Finally, using role-plays has made us examine and change how we use textbooks in our classrooms. In classes structured around role-plays, we do not use textbooks to plan lessons. Instead, we use them to support students in the work that they have set for themselves. The genre parts of the text (for example, how to write a letter) become reference guides to students after writing assignments emerge from role-plays and discussion. We incorporate the sections on audience, user testing, ethics, and so forth into our daily classroom practice. These sections provide a common vocabulary and ethos with which the class can discuss and understand the rhetorical aspects of their experiences inside and outside the classroom.

We have observed that technical writing textbooks are becoming rhetorically sophisticated in their choice of subject. They discuss more thoroughly issues of audience awareness and ethics. The challenge is to create a way of generating assignments that raise these issues with the same sophistication. Turning our classroom into a more student-centered experience by creating student-directed, problem-solving contexts has helped us to make use of the rhetorical thoroughness of the latest generation of texts. The challenge and opportunity is to capture students' authentic communication experiences. As the field of technical communication changes from a static, codified genre, students' needs have pressured the discipline to reenvision what a textbook should be and what it's capable of doing. Our classroom methods are an attempt to make available to students the possibilities of the new texts and to demonstrate the relevance of rhetorical education.

# WHO ARE THE USERS? MEDIA REPRESENTATIONS AS AUDIENCE-ANALYSIS TEACHING TOOLS

*If all else fails, read the manual.*

*Consumer of High-Tech Product*

Although usually meant to be humorous, this clichè underscores a truism: Instruction manuals are often unhelpful and difficult to understand. In fact, the quote's bitter tone suggests that customers feel alienated from technological products and that they blame such alienation on flawed instruction manuals. Of course, the technical communicators who write these instruction manuals do not set out to alienate customers; in fact, just the opposite tends to be true—most technical communicators consider themselves to be user advocates.

Nevertheless, many technical manuals are, indeed, unintelligible to their intended readers. This problem affects two kinds of stakeholders. Obviously, unintelligible documentation affects technology consumers, the primary audience for documentation. But it also affects technical communicators, whose reputations and job satisfaction hinge on producing products that users can relate to. Audience analysis is touted as the way to get in touch with the users of technical documents; however, this mainstay of technical communication pedagogy and practice has changed very little in the past thirty years or more, despite all the technological changes that have occurred during that time period. Even a cursory review of the audience-analysis chapters in a selection of recent technical communication textbooks reveals that regardless of the theoretical allegiances of the authors, all textbooks recommend practically the same procedures for analyzing audiences. In most cases, textbook authors recommend a classification model like the one outlined by Karen Schriver (1996, 153). Such seeming agreement among textbooks concerning audience analysis implies that technical communicators have settled on the best way to understand readers. As Jan Youga (1989), author of The Elements of Audience Analysis, puts it, "When the concept [of audience] is explained to us, we can all nod in agreement at this commonsense notion." However, I suggest in this chapter that the taken-forgranted classification method of audience analysis, while necessary, is not sufficient, especially given recent and continuing changes in both the technological landscape and the users who populate it. As Youga puts it, "to really understand what audience is and how it affects a piece of writing, we need to look at it more closely" (2).

To look more closely at audience analysis in technical communication, I characterize it in terms suggested by J. MacGregor Wise's (1998) concept of the differentiating machine and Bruno Latour's (1993) concepts of purification and hybridity. I propose an alternate or supplemental approach to understanding audiences that blends figural analysis, a method drawn from cinema studies, with what Schriver calls intuition- and feedback-driven audience-analysis methods (1996, 153–154). This alternate method involves regarding as representative users the figures who populate media representations such as advertisements, news reports, and cartoons.

## Why are Technical Documents Difficult to Understand?

It's easy to blame technical communicators for inadequate technical documents and for the accompanying alienation that readers experience, as captured in the familiar saying with which I introduced this chapter, "If all else fails, read the manual." A number of authors, probably unintentionally, ratify such blame by recommending that technical communicators address documentation shortcomings by reconsidering how we teach and conduct audience analysis (for instance, Dobrin 1989; Alred, Oliu, and Brusaw 1992; Schriver 1996; Holland, Charrow, and Wright 1988).

Besides blaming readers' alienation on the writers who produce technical documents, one might also logically blame the readers themselves, reasoning that they are responsible for their technological weaknesses. Expressions such as "idiot-proof" and acronyms such as "ESO condition" ("Equipment Smarter than Operator," a term I learned from a student who formerly worked at a home electronics superstore) point unsympathetic fingers at users who do not understand technological devices.

But professional user advocates and interaction designers disagree with both these blame games. The problem with technology, these experts assert, is not that users—or technical communicators—are incompetent, but that technologies are needlessly complex (Norman 1990, 1994; Cooper 1999; Johnson 1998b; Head 1999; Mirel 1993). Users will remain alienated from technology and from technical documents, this line of thinking asserts, until those users have a say in how technological tools are designed. In recent years, a few forward-thinking companies have begun to implement user-centered design (UCD) in which representative users are involved in the design process from the beginning. Other progressive companies perform usability testing, usually late in the product development cycle, in an attempt to intercept and correct major usability problems before the product is released. But neither user-centered design nor usability testing has become widespread enough to prevent end-user alienation, especially because technology use itself has simultaneously intensified. If technical communicators, interface designers, or other user advocates were in control of their companies' product development processes, the transition to a more user-centered product development process might pick up speed. Unfortunately, such control usually rests with professionals like programmers or operations managers, whose priorities are elsewhere (and who coined terms like "idiot-proof" and "ESO"). However, technical communicators can influence segments of the product development process over which they exercise control, including audience analysis, to lessen the impact of customer alienation.

## Alienation

Just as I don't believe that technical communicators deliberately alienate computer users from technology, I likewise don't believe that computer users have always been alienated in this way. Such alienation appears to be a relatively new phenomenon, fueled by two recent and related technocultural developments. First, there is the sheer proliferation of technology in myriad forms, from cell phones to ATMs to computers.2 Everyday lives in Western societies are increasingly organized and overdetermined by technology: "Like the purloined letter, technology is 'there'" in plain view, yet it "cannot be located in any one place" (Ormiston 1990, 102). Not so long ago, the typical computer user was a professional computer scientist, engineer, technical researcher, or advanced technical student. In J. Macgregor Wise's (1998) terms, a differentiating machine was in place that successfully organized—or differentiated—technological artifacts and their users, so as to create easily distinguished categories of technology expertise (67). Today, on the other hand, ordinary citizens participate alongside technological specialists in the effects of technological growth and overdetermination.

*Traditionally, the more complex a mechanical device was, the more highly trained its operators were. Big machinery was always locked away and operated by trained professionals in white lab coats. The information age changed everything, and we now expect amateurs to manage technology far more complex than our parents ever faced. (Cooper 1999, 34)*

Even as both work and leisure activities compel us to operate, manage, and—we hope—also understand an unprecedented array of complex technological systems, information about technology comes to us, unbidden, from a variety of sources. Given all of this complexity, perhaps the instructional manual is the least influential source of technology information for most people. Although it is the mainstay of technical communication work, we have already established that the general public is granted license—by each other and arguably also by the media—to ignore instructional manuals, to read them only "if all else fails."

The previously mentioned proliferation of technology has led to a corresponding proliferation of users, who are now more fully diversified than ever before in terms of the traditional audience-analysis categories of educational background, profession, age, gender, race, and economic status (Cooper 1999). With the increase in technology use and the accompanying increase in users, then, a differentiating machine that functioned adequately in the past no longer creates useful categories of technological expertise (cf. Rubin 1994, 5–6).

Despite recent changes in technology habits, technical communicators still rely upon a simplified binary differentiating machine to classify audiences. First, readers are usually classified with respect to their tool proficiency, such that the tool separates novice from expert. This audience-analysis system prevails in textbooks aimed at technical communication majors (for example, Alred, Brusaw, and Oliu 1992), as well as in textbooks designed for technical communication service courses (such as Burnett 1994; Lay et al. 1995).

The differentiating machine also places writers in contention with their audiences (Youga 1989, 39). Like the binary that attempts to distinguish novices from experts, the writer/audience binary emphasizes difference and opposition. Technical communication scholarship and pedagogy often suggest a user-advocacy role for technical communicators (see, for example, Redish 1993; Dobrin 1989; Cilenger 1992; Wells 1986). But I submit that the contentious writer/audience relationship outlined previously discourages technical communicators' user- advocacy role; thus, despite their best intentions, technical communicators may contribute to users' feelings of incompetence and alienation.

## Hybridity

For an alternative to habitual binary constructions, we might turn to Bruno Latour's (1993) work in We Have Never Been Modern. Latour posits hybrids, "mixtures of nature and culture," as a counterpoint to so called "purified" categories such as binary oppositions, which are mutually exclusive; that is, they do not overlap and cannot be conflated (30). Latour argues that the modernist paradigm disavows the simultaneous existence of purified and hybrid categories. Although he demonstrates that hybrids exist in a modernist world, Latour claims that they are not acknowledged. They are "invisible, unthinkable, unrepresentable" (34).

Novice and expert are purified binary categories.3 I submit that the privileging of purified categories limits current audience-analysis pedagogy (and may also limit practice, although additional research is required to verify this hypothesis). Like Latour, I believe in hybrids. In fact, I regard today's computer users as hybrids. Changes in the distribution and use of technology—changes that have led to the emergence of the hybrid user—suggest a need for technical communication teachers to develop an audience-analysis pedagogy that disrupts the binary differentiating machine's work, that contaminates the purified categories of novice and expert. One way to do this is to introduce students to media representations of computer users through a figural-analysis methodology, which involves close examination and speculation about the characteristics and motivations of the figures depicted in media representations.

Studying media representations in the technical communication classroom has several benefits. For one thing, media representations can suggest metaphors with which to frame instruction sets. If groups of technical communication students are assigned to survey technological metaphors used by journalists or advertisers, the resulting awareness of how technologies are described in the media can help them understand how their readers are taught to conceptualize technology. Moreover, such a focused attention on technological metaphors can suggest strategies for countering unproductive metaphors as well as opportunities for building on sustainable metaphors. If the media use a particular term or concept to describe a technological process, for example, perhaps that term should be included in a document's index as a cross- reference to the term that the product employs. How do popular magazines refer to Web navigation strategies? If "surfing," "browsing," and "searching" are all popular terms, then all should be indexed. Similarly, hardware technical writers who observe that a competitor's ads promise an interesting feature that is perhaps not fully developed may be better prepared to explain the drawbacks of such a feature to their intended readers.

Moreover, as the figural-analysis methodology outlined in this chapter suggests, studying the figures presented in media representations of technology can give technical communicators a sense of a broader cultural view of the technology user. If popular culture represents society thinking about itself (Asimow 2000, n. 90), then images of technology users in popular culture represent what society thinks those users are (or should be) like. Asimow (2002) authorizes the study of popular culture in professional contexts: "The fact that works of popular culture tend to reflect (at least in distorted form) popular attitudes, misconceptions, and myths is itself important and justifies the study of these works as a barometer of public opinion" (550).

Of course, technical communicators are not accustomed to seeing relationships between their work and media representations. But in fact, the media engage in cultural pedagogy: they teach us, in multiple and diverse ways, how we are to understand and interpret culture and its contexts, including the contexts in which technical communication takes place. When I teach figural analysis in my technical communication classes, I begin with two cartoons that appeared about eighteen months apart in two different publications (Newsweek, February 27, 1995, 21, and the Chronicle of Higher

Education,, September 20, 1996). Both cartoons depicted white, middle-aged, middle-class men struggling to use their computers. In the Newsweek cartoon, the man is working on his home computer; he complains to his wife that he can't figure out how to install a piece of software and then asks, "What's that neighbor kid's name again?" In the Chronicle cartoon, a curmudgeonly older man—presumably a professor—works at his office computer with a younger female colleague, who explains mouse operation in patronizing baby talk.

In both these instances, the male figures bear marks of success, such as the ability to make major purchases and work in well-appointed offices. But when a computer comes into the picture, the men's status as insiders is called into question. In both cases, the men are forced to learn prefiguratively— from a younger, less-experienced person, instead of in the more traditional postfigurative manner, from an older person (Mead 1970, 1).

On the surface, the cartoons can be seen simply as a commentary on the ineptitude so many otherwise competent adults feel when confronted with even the most run-of-the-mill computing tasks. For technical communicators, however, they provide anecdotal evidence of an inversion of the classic novice/expert binary. Analysis of the cartoons, including figural analysis, suggests that a purified novice/expert binary is still highly valued in Western technoculture while acknowledging that such a binary no longer functions as before. Thus, when technical communicators attempt to define expertise, they must acknowledge that so-called experts may have uneasy relationships with technology. Moreover, elders are expected to guide, protect, and educate younger people; however, especially in the Newsweek cartoon, age no longer guarantees status: in fact, it may hinder the achievement of certain kinds of status. Scrutinized through a technological lens, both cartoon computer users are found wanting, despite the status they have obviously achieved in other areas. But the prevailing educational model—Mead's postfigurative model in which adults teach and children learn—does not accommodate their learning needs.

Each cartoon character represents what I would call a hybrid user of computers. But the media, relying on purification, depict them as novices and denigrate their limited technological expertise. Similarly, technical communicators faced with writing manuals for these men, and reliant upon purified categories of audience, would also characterize them as novices on the basis of their lack of computer knowledge. However, addressing them as novices denies their achieved status and life experiences that originate outside the high-tech realm, in much the same way as does speaking in baby talk to a university professor. The cartoons offer two choices to adults struggling with technology: either they can suffer experts' patronizing attitudes, or they can step aside and permit experts to do the complex tasks for them. Neither approach suffices; the boundaries between novice and expert are fluid and shifting.

A figural analysis may also be conducted on news representations. By examining news reports, wherein words and illustrations work together, we can see that expertise with technology is again inscribed quite differently from a perceived lack of expertise. For example, the August 8, 1994, issue of Newsweek, which featured a Woodstock cover story, also included an article titled "The Birth of the Internet." The article explains that in 1969, while others were enjoying Woodstock, a "small group of computer scientists" was busily inventing the Internet, thereby "changing the future of computing" (Kantrowitz and Rogers 1994, 56–58).

Most of the people who developed the Internet in the 1960s are relatively unknown to us today; a few of the names are recognizable to computer industry insiders, but others mentioned in this article have faded into obscurity. These Internet pioneers had to learn from each other, in Mead's cofigurative mode, because there were no elders to lead them in their groundbreaking quest. The cofigurative, or apprenticeship, learning model, with its accompanying disdain for hierarchies, is commonplace throughout the computer industry (Levy 1984) and resonates to this day.

The 1960s Internet pioneers have led lives of relative obscurity. Given the fame and fortune enjoyed by today's Internet developers, one might expect some resentment to be expressed by the 1960s experts, but, as team member Robert Kahn asserts, he "doesn't like to dwell on the past." Moreover, the optimistic idealism of the men quoted in this article makes today's Internet heroes' work seem even more crassly commercial. Kahn, for example, optimistically privileges the myth of progress, as this closing quote from the Newsweek article attests: "Those were very exciting days, but there are new frontiers in every direction I can look. . . . A quarter century later, the future still looks bright" (Kantrowitz and Rogers 1994, 58).

This bright future, the foundation of which was laid by the 1960s Internet gurus, is now enjoyed by the experts who have more recently made their mark on the commercial Internet, and the latter-day experts didn't wait thirty years for their achievements to be recognized. But, as a figural analysis of the Internet pioneers illustrates, the experiences of the earlier experts differed greatly (and continue to differ) from the prominence and wealth enjoyed by today's well-known experts. For instance, the most famous of today's Internet gurus, Microsoft's Bill Gates, routinely appears on the covers of Time and Newsweek. This exposure is perhaps not surprising; he is, after all, among the world's richest men and his company arguably has set the stage for our turn-of-the-century computing environment.4 But other technology figures also attract popular media attention. Netscape developer Mark Andreessen was featured on the cover of Time magazine (February 19, 1996) and touted as one of a group of "Golden Geeks." This hero of the cyber-revolution amassed, almost overnight, a wealth of $58 million. Time's cover depicted the barefoot, twenty-four-year-old Andreessen wearing a crown and seated on a throne and responded to readers' interest, not only in Andreessen's and the other Golden Geeks' technological achievements but also in their private lives and their cultural influence: "They invent. They start companies. And the stock market has made them instantaires. Who are they? How do they live? And what do they mean for America's future?" Andreessen's overnight wealth is democratic, the article implied, because anyone with comparable intelligence, luck, and timing could achieve a similar status. The myth of progress resonates throughout the article, yet luck seems to play a role as well. These "instantaires" are not just ordinary folks who have achieved the American Dream; they are computer geniuses blessed with an incredible sense of timing. Barefoot, baby-faced Andreessen remains decidedly down-to-earth and modest despite his success.

On the one hand, then, in the mid-1990s, both the Clinton administration and the media were promoting the Internet as a culture-changing technology. Excitement surrounding the commercial prospects of the Internet intimated that no particular expertise would be required to take advantage of easy, in-home access to information, commerce, politics, and entertainment and that unprecedented economic growth would follow the acquisition of new global markets and the invention of innovative communication products and services.

On the other hand, however, in concurrent ads, magazine covers, and news and feature articles, the media presented the people who understood these new technologies as endowed with special powers not available to the average adult. This vision of "golden geeks" suggests a binary differentiating machine at work in a polarized Internet environment. Just as attention to Latour's work suggests, technology expertise retained a special prominence, with "golden geeks" and "instantaires" as the poster children of this exalted and purified category. Because hybrid computer users are invisible to a culture predisposed to see purified categories, then, hybrids' wide-ranging, diverse, and idiosyncratic attributes, skills, aptitudes, and needs are unrepresentable as such in the media.

## Representing Hybrid Technology Users

As Latour (1993) suggests, hybridity may be masked by the expectation that there are only purified categories of expertise—namely novice and expert. But if we know to watch for them, we can find media representations of hybrid computing expertise. In fact, hybrids are present in two advertisements that appeared in Web Week magazine in August 1995. Web Week is a Web developers' magazine, aimed at experienced computer users. The center spread of that issue featured an advertisement for the Apple Internet Server Solution. Four experienced professionals of varying ages, races, and genders—marketing manager Lawson Clarke, biology department chair Lisa Honea, yarn shop owner Debbie Heick, and freelance artist Joe Rosales—are pictured in and addressed by the ad.

The advertisement's headline poses a question and answers itself with another question: "Looking for a compelling reason to set up an Internet Web site? How about the fact that you don't have to be a propellerhead anymore in order to actually do it?" Immediately, then, the ad sets up the binary between expert ("propellerhead") and novice (you, the reader). The ineptitude of novices is further alluded to in the ad copy, which begins, "It's called the World Wide Web (WWW). But that doesn't mean that you have to get tangled up in it." In language that alternates between technical jargon and comforting, respectful reassurance, the advertisement explains that the Apple Internet Server "represents the easiest, most affordable way for people to make their information widely accessible on the Internet." Expecting that readers will identify with one of the figures pictured in the ad, the copywriter allays some of their concerns: "Virtually anybody can now create a WWW site" that is "full of hyperlinked text, graphics, video and sound," and that site can be "up and running in minutes at less than half the cost (not to mention the headaches) of a typical UNIX-based server." As we keep in mind that this ad predated free-access Web sites like Geocities and Angelfire and WYSIWYG HTML editors like Dreamweaver and Front Page, a final statement in the ad perhaps reveals the company's attitude toward its target audience: "The sample Home Pages can even be customized," the ad copy reassures us—as though customizable home pages, even in the early days of the Web, were unusual.

Each of the portrayed figures is a hybrid—an expert in his or her own field of art, science, marketing, or crafts, but inexperienced with computers. However, the ad ends up ignoring their hybridity and addressing them as novices based on their technology expertise alone. This is especially evident in that last sentence, but can be seen elsewhere in the ad as well. For example, the costs of mounting a Web site are mentioned, but no hard data are provided. Similarly, the ad mentions, but does not define, the volume of site traffic that can be considered "heavy." In short, the advertisement seems to expect that the reader will uncritically (perhaps naively) accept its claims—that is, that he or she will adopt a novice's mentality.

In contrast, the intended reader of a second two-page ad in the same issue of Web Week is addressed as a technological expert in charge of an existing company Web presence. Again, the ad copy makes a number of claims about the capability of the server being promoted—in this case, a Silicon Graphics UNIX-based Web FORCE server. The ad suggests that Web managers must build speedy Web servers to attract and retain customers. If potential customers must wait to enter your site, the ad copy admonishes, "they'll probably move on," which means lost customers and revenue.

The ad appeals to a different kind of hybrid: a system administrator or other technical professional who has assumed Web design and maintenance responsibilities. This techie is the person user advocates would least like to see running a company's Web presence. Lacking in user sensitivity, the techie interpellated by this ad is concerned with maximizing the technical capabilities of the company's Web site. The ad appeals to this reader by mentioning special customer analysis and tracking tools that can enhance a company's efficiency and competitive edge. "These days, it's not enough to set up a home page and wait and see what happens," the ad notes; in addition, you must build a "valuable database of who's visiting and what they are doing" so that you can "generate Web pages on the fly" to meet the specific needs of individual customers or particular categories of customers. The "unrivaled throughput and scalability" of Web FORCE systems "give your creative teams the tools they need" to make your site "attract and retain a crowd."

The image that accompanies the Silicon Graphics ad is particularly startling: it portrays site visitors as a flock of sheep trying to fit through a narrow bridge. By assuming that techies look down on less-experienced users, the ad gets away with referring to customers as sheep.5 In short, the ad can be interpreted as saying that visitors to a business's Web site, like sheep, will always follow the flock. With text written in a coconspiratorial voice, the ad invites the techie who doubles as a Web master to regard potential customers as sheeplike; furthermore, these customers, although they apparently cannot make a decision for themselves, must be cultivated and flattered by high-speed connectivity and by compelling and individually responsive content, so that they will return to the site and ultimately purchase the product or service being marketed there. In short, we are left with the unsettling impression that Silicon Graphics regards the end users of commercial Web sites as passive consumers easily swayed by technological wizardry.

## A Pedagogy for Addressing Hybrid Users

The media representations featured in this chapter were gathered over a four-year period from 1993 to 1997, as the Internet was emerging as a commercial force. Because I have worked with them for a long time, my interpretations are fairly detailed and may sound definitive, perhaps suggesting that meaningfully incorporating media representations into technical communication classes requires sustained attention and perhaps even some special semiotic expertise. However, if you pay attention to the content of your daily media dose, whether it consists of newspapers, magazines, television, radio, or billboards, you'll find more examples than you can use. Take Apple's iMac campaign, for example. To be sure, some of the ads in that campaign focus on hardware attributes (like "The New iMac," which appeared on the back cover of Time's April 6, 2002, issue). However, another thread of that campaign features emails allegedly sent to Apple by average people who recently switched from a PC to the iMac. In the June 17, 2002, issue of Time, Mark Frauenfelder, a freelance writer and illustrator, writes that he switched because "I wanted a better computing experience than I had with my PC." Mark, pictured on the left-hand page of a two-page spread, at first resisted switching platforms because he thought it would be too much trouble. "I thought, why make the leap? It's like being stuck in a bad relationship: It works on some level, so you don't want to make the effort to change." In the end, though, switching was no trouble at all, and he writes, "I'm GLAD I switched." The iMac, he claims, can do everything he needs it to do—except make coffee in the morning.

Mark is portrayed as a hybrid; although he's tied into computers for his work, we get a picture of him as an individual. We can relate to his comments about bad relationships and the body's need for coffee. He's not rich or glamorous—in fact, his picture shows a downright nerdy guy who, we might conclude, was photographed before he had brewed his morning coffee. Another figure in the iMac ad campaign is Aaron Adams, who says he works as a PC LAN administrator. In his email, he writes, "At work, I deal with PCs all day long and I can say without exaggeration that keeping those Windows machines running is a constant struggle." This ad, which appeared in Time's July 2, 2002, issue, demystifies the work of the system administrator—the definitive techie—by revealing that Aaron regards his work as "fighting with computers." He doesn't mind doing so "on my employer's time" but wants an easier, friendlier computer to play with at night.

Buried in Apple's iMac campaign is an emphasis on cross-platform compatibility and ease of use. By featuring users' difficulties with the complexity of computers, the campaign suggests that even people we regard as experts struggle with computers and maintains that the iMac computer solves user frustration because it "just works" without a fight. One might say that the iMac ad campaign has incorporated hybrid users—people not defined solely by their technology expertise—but it does not yet displace purified categories of novice and expert. IBM's countercampaign bears out this observation. Structurally similar to the iMac campaign, in that a typical user is pictured on one page with information about the circumstances of that person's use on the facing page, IBM's series of ads features the ThinkPad, a laptop that is the choice of "some of the world's most successful people," including Charles Nolan, a designer for Anne Klein. Nolan is pictured conferring with a colleague at a point "halfway through the fall/winter line." While the IBM ad calls upon us to emulate IBM ThinkPad users who have achieved success in their fields, the iMac ad incorporates the "authentic" user voice of regular working people from a variety of disciplines who have abandoned their PCs in favor of the more usable and flexible iMac. Although polarized novice/expert categories are not absent, in this genre of ads, we are introduced to hybrid users.

In proposing ads such as these as tools for audience analysis in upperdivision technical communication courses, I might ask students to answer a rather simple question: "Who does the ad want us to be?" They articulate excellent and detailed descriptions of Aaron and Mark and Charles—the figures in the ads become very real to them. Nonetheless, in more general discussions of audience, some students proclaim that there's no excuse for user frustration; technology is just part of what we do as members of Western technoculture, they assert, so users need to get over their frustrations and get with the program. Thus, media representations of frustrated technology users are countered for many of them by their experience as successful technology users—graduating seniors in a technical communication program. The digital divide doesn't affect them much; in fact, every student in the class owns a latemodel computer with Internet access, and class is held in a computer lab equipped with state-of-the-art computers and recent versions of key software. Although they hear about the digital divide—the "haves" polarized against the "have-nots"—these students don't have direct experience with that divide. Moreover, despite several years of classroom talk about audience analysis and user advocacy, some of them still exhibit a "blamethe-user" mentality. Media representations can be cited as the source— or at least as a reinforcement—for such a mentality. A case in point is Robert J. Samuelson's editorial, "Debunking the Digital Divide" (Newsweek, March 25, 2002, 37). In the middle of a technology-oriented issue of Newsweek that featured a cover story entitled, "Silicon Valley Bytes Back," Samuelson concludes his editorial as follows:

*The "digital divide" suggested a simple solution (computers) for a complex problem (poverty). With more computer access, the poor could escape their lot. But computers never were the source of anyone's poverty, and as for escaping, what people do for themselves matters more than what technology can do for them. (37)*

It's hard to argue with Samuelson's contention that we are being overly simplistic if we assume that the application of computers will solve all the problems that the "digital divide" encapsulates. But isn't Samuelson also oversimplifying when he denies any connection between computers and poverty? Samuelson's essay highlights problems with our typical audience-analysis methods in ways that students and teachers should reflect upon in the context of the technical communication classroom.

In this chapter, I've suggested some ways of thinking about media representations in light of technical communication and outlined a few ideas for including media representations in the technical communication classroom—as aids to audience analysis and as sources of prevailing technological metaphors. Other innovative approaches to integrating cultural representations into technical communication pedagogy remain to be unveiled.

## WHAT'S UP, DOC? APPROACHING MEDICINE AS A CULTURAL INSTITUTION IN THE TECHNICAL COMMUNICATION CLASSROOM BY STUDYING THE DISCOURSES OF STANDARD AND ALTERNATIVE CANCER TREATMENTS

### Introduction

Scientific and technical communication has, over the past few years, been witness to a call for research more culturally informed (see, for example, Longo 1998 and Herndl 1993b). This type of research takes into account—and indeed regards as primary—the notion that science is, more than anything else, a powerful cultural institution that has profound and real effects on individuals. Indeed, Herndl (1993a), for one, states that "cultural studies assumes that no undertaking, including science, is autonomous and that any discourse is inherently ideological." Discussing a branch of biology as a specific example of a scientific cultural institution, he adds, "cultural critics might ask how evolutionary biology participates in the whole political and social process of organizing life and legitimizing knowledge and power" (66). In addition, this research recognizes the cultural institution of science operates discursively, thus complicating largely service course–oriented notions of scientific and technical communication as being driven by documents and Web sites analyzed or produced in isolation. Because culturally informed research recognizes texts as a manifestation of cultural institutions and because we as scientific and technical communicators are by and large keenly aware of this connection, we are both well qualified and well positioned to study the discourse of science and to use those analyses to comment on how science functions in the society at large. In fact, we are even ethically obligated to do so, given that science has such a significant impact on our lives and those of students. Although some attention has been given to the need for and conduct of culturally informed research in institutions and organizations in which scientific and technical communication takes place, less work has been done on its pedagogical counterpart.1 However, although she discusses research methodology rather than pedagogy, Longo (1998) has provided some insight into how such a pedagogy might be modeled: she states that researchers in technical communication need to use cultural studies research strategies "to illuminate technical writing issues . . . such as effects of institutional relationships and expanded notions of culture . . . as well as the cultural power of knowledge" (54). For us as instructors of technical and scientific communication to fulfill our missions of highlighting the importance and the effects of scientific discourse and teaching students how to analyze and produce this discourse effectively, we must use ideas such as Herndl's and Longo's and develop innovative pedagogies to ensure that students understand that science is—like education, government, religion, the market, and the media, as our colleagues who teach in first-year writing programs have shown us—a cultural construct that impacts students (and us) significantly and repeatedly. Science reflects and reinforces cultural biases, and it operates on the basis of negotiation and persuasion within specific ideological contexts. Students need to understand the wherefore and the why of these biases and contexts so that they can work with and within them as informed participants, be that as professional scientific and technical communicators or as private citizens. Armed with such an understanding, it is my hope that students can read science-related texts with a clearer awareness of what is going on between the lines, figures, tables, and other elements and produce science-related texts that stand an improved likelihood of accomplishing their rhetorical objectives.

In this chapter, I demonstrate how the discourse of medicine, a branch of the cultural institution of science that not only profoundly shapes individual consciousness but also may soon, as a result of the Human Genome Project, actually create it as well, can be used in introductory scientific and technical communication classes, as well as medical writing courses, to help students understand that the cultural institution of medicine operates with specific (but not necessarily always consistent) economic, political, and social agendas that help to form all our subjectivities. I accomplish this by first demonstrating how I would attempt to convince students that medicine is a cultural institution that operates discursively and that has an impact on identity. I then explain how I have asked my undergraduate students, using a set of four questions I derived from work in cultural studies and in rhetoric and technical communication, to characterize the cultural institution of medicine as a result of their interaction with discourses on standard and alternative cancer treatments. My goal in this research was to determine whether the characterizations differ on the basis of the type of discourse that the students engaged and, if so, why these differences occurred.

Whether a difference appears or not, the more complex understanding of medicine that results from the awareness gained by comparing standard and alternative cancer discourses will, I believe, enable students to take more ownership of their health and that of others close to them, to stand a better chance of succeeding professionally as writers, editors, and designers because they understand more broadly the purpose and potential implications of their work and to effect meaningful change in the cultural institution of medicine as a whole by, for example, critiquing and improving existing genres and suggesting and developing new ones when the rhetorical situation demands it. Whether producing or analyzing texts, the ability to engage medicine more meaningfully at both a personal and an institutional level as a result of cultural-context awareness would, in turn, make possible the ability to engage the broader institution of science more successfully (for instance, to ask questions such as "Who paid for this research?" and "Who benefits from its conclusions?"). Indeed, in our life experience, many profound legislative, judicial, and corporate decisions are made on the basis of scientific research, ranging from gauging the effectiveness of college entrance exams such as the SAT to diagnosing a child with attention deficit disorder. Because Western culture is so utterly dependent on science, students must possess a critical consciousness of these institutions to participate fully in the workings of society.

## Show Me the Theory: Convincing Students that Medicine Operates as a Discursively Governed Cultural Institution

Medical discourse affects students directly. College students are often asked, in the form of surveys, about health concerns considered important to them: alcohol and drug use, physical health, psychological health, and sexual attitudes (Sax 1997). In addition, college health centers and wellness programs use the Web extensively to provide healthrelated information and promote prevention practices (see Fulop and Varzandeh 1996, for example). That medicine is a powerful cultural institution there can be little doubt, and I would try to persuade students to agree by introducing some cultural studies terms and figures as follows. By cultural institution, I mean that medicine can be understood, for example, as an Althusserian ideological state apparatus. Althusser (1971) defines such entities as "a certain number of realities which present themselves to the immediate observer in the form of distinct and specialized institutions" (143). Althusser does not include medicine in his list of ideological state apparatuses, but it certainly meets the criteria he establishes for them. Indeed, medicine produces a product— health—and, simultaneously, reproduces the means and conditions of its production (128), in that, even as it finds a cure or treatment for some condition or disease, another previously unknown ailment has likely been identified to challenge researchers and clinicians anew.

As do all cultural institutions, medicine affects individuals (see Berlin 1996 and George and Shoos 1992 for a discussion about how, by way of signifying practices, cultural institutions such as media and the market achieve this impact). That is, it significantly influences subjectivity, and, of course, in the classroom I would emphasize student subjectivity. Perhaps no better way can be found to demonstrate this subjectivity than by briefly examining with students the Human Genome Project, which is the largest scientific undertaking of our time. Similar to those who worked on the development of the atomic bomb in the 1940s and early 1950s or on the Apollo missions of the 1960s, scientists working on the Human Genome Project often see themselves as part of a grand, noble endeavor that will inalterably change the way people understand science and medicine. Myers (1990) has demonstrated how the gene has become a cultural icon that people look to as a source of, among other things, individual identity. Because icons can be understood as "a sign in which there is a relationship of resemblance between signifier and signified" (Myers 53), one can argue that we are reaching the point in Western society in which we are defined by our DNA (see such recent films as Gattaca—a film relatively popular with students, I've found—for examples of how this idea plays out in popular culture). DNA dictates physical characteristics, such as hair and eye color and genetic susceptibility to disease, and may, according to some, substantially contribute to personality traits as well. Thus, the ability to manipulate DNA at will has the potential to profoundly shape and even create identity, starting with selecting a gender and moving on from there.

In addition to impacting individuals directly, cultural institutions operate discursively, and the cultural institution of medicine is no exception. Within technical and scientific communication, Lutz and Fuller (1998) have focused specifically on the discursive operations of the cultural institutions of "orthodox" and alternative medicine; they explore how the discourses of alternative and complementary medicine work "through language to gain credibility against, through, and around" the more stable and entrenched institution of orthodox medicine. I would introduce students to these two distinct institutions of medicine. On a more practical level, I would also share with students research such as Koski's (1997), which states that between twenty-five and forty percent of the stories in daily newspapers are health-related. Of even greater importance for students, of course, is the Internet, which is replete with health-related sites. Even in 1997, the popular search engine site Yahoo! listed some

15,000 health-related sites; as of May 2002, that number had risen to over 21,500.

I would ask students to consider that medical information is often couched in scientific terms and is thus able to "partake of the cultural power residing in scientific knowledge" (Longo 1998, 59). Indeed, even Foucault (1977b) contends, "'Truth' is centered on the form of scientific discourse and the institutions which produce it" (73). Because it is often obtained during a time of crisis, many people want to believe that the medical information they procure is true and reliable; when this information is presented within a scientific context, it is more likely not to be questioned critically. Such trust can create problems that can be illustrated for students. The authority with which medical information is vested contributed a great deal, for example, to the ongoing controversy over mammography, which pits a National Cancer Institute–sponsored panel of oncologists against radiologists in a bitter dispute over the necessity of mammography for women in their forties. Essentially, the oncologists found that there was no proven long-term survival benefit gained by mammography screenings of women between the ages of forty and fifty. In fact, the oncologists added that an annual mammography for these women may actually have drawbacks.

The oncologists recommended that women begin mammography at age fifty. The radiologists, who, it must be pointed out, benefited significantly from providing annual mammography to women forty years of age and over, fiercely contested this conclusion and pointed to their studies, which demonstrated that women who started annual mammography screenings at age forty were much more likely to detect cancer early, when it is most treatable. Especially exasperating to followers of this controversy was the fact that both of the groups involved in the mammography controversy had mountains of "scientific" evidence to back up their claims. I would ask students whom they would believe. Indeed, many people did not have a legitimate mechanism to evaluate the competing conclusions. As a result, many women—not to mention their physicians—were unsure whom to believe: these competing discourses had the all-too-real effect of causing confusion and anxiety over an extremely important and personal medical decision.

## An Application: Standard and Alternative Cancer Discourses

I asked students in my undergraduate, 200-level technical and scientific editing course, who major in technical and scientific communication, English, speech communication, media arts and design, or chemistry, to examine discourses representative of standard and alternative or complementary cancer treatments as part of a discussion of editing Web sites for development of ethos. I consider discourse about a standard cancer treatment to be representative of the cultural institution of Western medicine, while I consider discourse about a nontraditional (at least from a Western perspective) cancer treatment to be representative of the cultural institution of alternative and complementary medicine. For an example of standard cancer treatment, I chose Web-based lung cancer treatment information provided via the National Cancer Institute's (NCI's) CancerNet. Part of the federally funded National Institutes of Health in Bethesda, Maryland, the NCI is regarded as the world leader in conducting and supporting cancer research, treating cancer, and supplying information about cancer to patients, their families, the general public, and health professionals. This lung cancer treatment information on the NCI Web site displays characteristics typical of traditional Western medical discourse: it is written in third-person passive voice, it is presented as factual, and no narrative is used. Instead, focus is on the "disease" or "cancer cells."

As an example of the discourse of alternative cancer treatment, I chose a Web site8 that advertised and advocated the use of Tian Xian liquid, developed in China by Wang Zhen Guo, for the treatment of lung cancer. I consider the discourse of this Web site to be "alternative" or "complementary" because it is an "intervention not taught widely in U.S. medical schools or generally available in U.S. hospitals" (Eisenberg quoted in Lutz and Fuller 1998). In addition, the site contains—and in fact highlights—elements not characteristic of traditional Western medical discourse, such as testimonials and an award gallery. The Tian Xian liquid itself is described as "an alternative dietary food supplement to help destroy, control and inhibit Cancer by strengthening the body's immune system"; the liquid consists of essences of roots and stems of various herbs and plants such as ginseng (see http://www.tianxian.com/english/ingredients.shtml).

I chose cancer because it is an especially well-known condition, or set of conditions, that receives a great deal of public support in the form of, for example, tax dollars. (Indeed, for fiscal year 2001, NCI has asked for $3.5 billion [http://www.nci.nih.gov/legis/fy2001.html].) Although comparatively few children or adolescents are stricken with cancer, many students know of an older relative or family friend who has battled the disease. In addition to (or perhaps because of) its being widespread, I chose cancer because a large number of alternative and complementary therapies are practiced to treat the disease. A great deal of information on alternative and complementary treatments is readily available; one largescale study found that nine percent of cancer patients use these therapies instead of or in addition to conventional treatments (Lerner and Kennedy 1992). These therapies have received widespread attention and mixed reviews; although treatments such as laetrile have generally been dismissed by the mainstream medical community, a 1997 National Institutes of Health consensus conference endorsed the use of acupuncture to treat side effects of chemotherapy (see http://cancernet.nci.nih.gov/). I chose Web sites rather than print sources for two reasons: first, students are, of course, much more likely to use the Web for research than they are to use print sources. Second, and less obvious, I think that it is oftentimes easier to gain information about the organizational context in which the information is presented (and hence answer the questions more completely) from a Web site than from a print source. For example, a student looking at the NCI site on the treatment of non–small cell lung cancer can easily move to other screens that contain information about the National Cancer Institute; however, a print copy of the same information obtained via the NCI's CancerFax service allows no such opportunity I developed a set of four questions to ask students about each Web site. These questions grow out of (a) composition-based work in cultural studies, such as that by Berlin (1996), and (b) work that ties together rhetoric and technical and scientific communication, such as that by Ornatowski (1997) and Halloran (1978). The questions (discussed elsewhere in more detail) are based on the following cultural-studies premises:

- Institutions, operating discursively, impact individual consciousness and action significantly

- Individuals, in their daily lives, attempt to make sense of multiple and competing discourses produced by these institutions.

- Individuals ascribe a level of credibility to the institutions on the basis of the perceived quality of the discourses and on the basis of previous experience with such institutions, if any.

The basic premise that links cultural studies with rhetoric—and, in this case, the rhetoric of medical discourse—is that cultural institutions operate discursively; thus, rhetoric plays an unmistakably critical role in the advancement of these institutions. Ornatowski (1997), in his chapter, "Technical Communication and Rhetoric," explains that the discourses of science and technology are often used for, among other things, the following purposes:

- To coordinate the activities of groups and individuals

- To promote the progression of institutional tasks

- To control activities

- To monitor output

- To make an individual's work advance the established objectives of an institution

I read these purposes as typical of those of any cultural institution's discourse; indeed, they can be understood to correspond to Foucault's (1977a) description in The Order of Discourse of the ways discourse is controlled. In this work, Foucault says that control of discourse is achieved by, among other things, the limitation of discourse by disciplines. Disciplinary discourse, says Foucault, must "address itself to a determinate plane of objects" and "be able to be inscribed on a certain theoretical horizon" to be considered "in the true" (1160). Discourse that does not meet these criteria is excluded from the discipline. The correspondence between Foucault's description and Ornatowski's five purposes then plays out like this: the persons in power who control the content and flow of discourse in disciplines (which are, in the case of science and technology, cultural institutions) in turn use this discourse to perform Ornatowski's purposes. All five of these purposes are innately tied to the maintenance and, perhaps, expansion of cultural institutions through discourse, and they have the potential to affect individuals.

The four questions, which I piloted with students from two other courses, are as follows:

1. Which of the sites do you find to be more credible?

2. What specific features of the sites ( rhetorical features such as textual and visual content, document design, and use of persuasive appeals) contribute to your conclusion?

3. What other experiences can you draw on from your life experiences that help you reach this conclusion?

4. What would you do to the sites as a Web editor to boost their credibility?

I sent students the questions and the URLs for the two sites in an email message and asked them to respond in kind.

## Responses from Students

Responses from students were revealing and centered primarily on issues of credibility. Credibility was, for the students, inextricably intertwined first with what they perceived as the mission of the two Web sites. Students stressed that the NCI Web site provided information, while the Tian Xian Web site tried to sell a product. (Indeed, one of the students characterized the difference as an audience issue, saying that the NCI site was targeted at "information gatherers," while the Tian Xian site was targeted at "somewhat superstitious people.") The perceived marketing mission of the Tian Xian site immediately caused many students to react negatively to the site; several students mentioned that the ".gov" extension associated with the NCI site URL gave it more credibility than the ".com" extension of the Tian Xian site URL. "The Tian Xian Liquid Web site," stated one student, "is provided by Green and Gold International Exports, which indicates that their interest is in solely making a profit." Another said that the Tian Xian site is "a commercialization for the fears of cancer victims, and may be nothing more than a pyramid sales scheme for a product." Similarly, one student claimed that Tian Xian was simply "an impulse buy for Web surfers" and that he was "suspicious" of the product.

Credibility was also tied closely to content. One student stated that she preferred the NCI site because it contained no shopping cart, as did the Tian Xian site, while another stated that she was impressed by the "skillful use of medical language" on the NCI site. The first student went on to say that he was "skeptical of anything [he sees] on a commercial site, because [he knows] that information such as statistics will get skewed in order to better influence customers." Several students stated that the NCI site is more comprehensive because it contained information on cancer in different parts of the body, and they pointed out that contact information, complete with a toll-free telephone number, is provided as well. In addition, although some students found the Tian Xian text easier to understand than the NCI text, the fact that the NCI site contained a dictionary of terms tended to boost its credibility. Visually, some students complained that the Tian Xian site contained too many pictures and that many of these pictures were of poor quality. The proportion of pictures to text was apparently too high for several students and detracted from the ethos of the site; one said that the pictures were distracting.

The content of the two sites contributed directly to their tone. One student focused specifically on this issue, saying that the NCI site "is kind of reserved, like a wise old person, not shouting in your face [as the Tian Xian site does]. . . . The NCI page looks like . . . an encyclopedia page." Several other students maintained that the NCI Web site was much more balanced in tone—presenting both positives and negatives of various treatments—than the Tian Xian Web site, which was described as "cheesy," as looking similar to a "talk show," and not listing "side effects." The NCI site did receive its share of criticism, though, being characterized in tone as "choppy, clinical, and dull" and as "morbid."

With regard to credibility, students also commented frequently on the perceived trustworthiness of the sources of information contained in the Web sites. For example, the information in the NCI Web site came from "reliable sources that go through a rigorous process of drug testing," said one student. Another insisted that the NCI site "had a lot of good information that was supported by medical proof." Although there was a section of the Tian Xian Web site called "Lab Test Results" that listed several Western-style scientific studies, complete with graphs, tables, and references, many students insisted that the products advertised on the Tian Xian Web site needed to undergo "legitimate" scientific testing and peer review in the U.S. and have results published by an American medical journal. The mechanism by which the Tian Xian products act, they said, needs to be identified, clinical trials need to be conducted, and confounding variables need to be identified. Students objected to the narratives ("Testimonials") on the Tian Xian site, which they saw as the main source of evidence used by the company for the efficacy of the Tian Xian liquid. "Instead of providing facts and figures to support the [Tian Xian] drug," one student said, "they gave emotional 'success' stories." Another stated that "Under the testimonials for lung cancer, there are 9 stories of success, a small number to base an effective treatment on." A second student called the Tian Xian liquid a "miracle elixir" with no proof, and a third complained that the ingredients were not listed (in fact they were). "Factual errors" were also noted: one student pointed out that the Tian Xian site contained the phrase "genes entering cells"—a scientific impossibility because genes are present within cells. This same student, however, noted that translation problems (the Tian Xian site is available in six languages) might have contributed to this mistake. Finally, a student dismissed positive reviews of the Tian Xian liquid reprinted on the site, saying that the newspapers involved—Manila Bulletin and the Philippine Daily Inquirer—sound "similar to the National Inquirer," while another commented that awards given to the manufacturers of Tian Xian and listed on the site were from "non-nationally recognized organizations."

In terms of authorship and credibility, the students appeared to take the authority of the NCI Web site (and studies listed therein) authors for granted. They attributed a great deal of credibility to the sponsorship of the U.S. government for the NCI Web site, saying that the government has access to knowledge and financial resources that the Tian Xian manufacturers did not. Indeed, the NCI Web site designers also ensured that users would get this thought in their minds by placing a banner reading "Credible. Current. Comprehensive." across the top of the CancerNet splash page. The Tian Xian Web site did not fare as well. Several students noted that one author (and the only author affiliated with an American institution) on some of the studies listed on the Tian Xian Web site was a professor at Capital University in Washington, D.C.; these students claimed to have never heard of this institution. (Given that a large percentage of students at the institution at which I teach are from the Washington metropolitan area, I would expect that some of them would know it.) Other authors listed were affiliated with a Taipei, Taiwan–based institution; this fact did not seem to make the Tian Xian site any more credible for the students.

Not all the news was positive for the NCI site, however. It was faulted for being too "texty" and "looking like a hospital." Another student complained that the site was "lackluster" and "monotonous." And, ironically, the same student who lamented the lack of facts and figures in the Tian Xian site previously described faulted the NCI site for being too impersonal, saying that "I don't think they showed any pictures of people or told any personal stories." Another student shared an aesthetic concern, stating that the site should "use more colors besides blue and white." Finally, one student found the NCI site difficult to get around because of its sheer size and scope.

Perhaps the most surprising aspect of students' reactions to the Web sites was the notion that if they were faced with terminal cancer, the students indicated that they wouldn't hesitate to try the Tian Xian liquid if conventional treatments failed. "If I'm desperate," concluded one student in response to question 3, "this might be something that I would want to try." It seems, perhaps, that entrenched cultural codes can be dismissed more easily if one faces an imminent risk of death.

## Discussion and Conclusions

Students' respective reactions to the NCI and Tian Xian Web sites reflect a thoroughly entrenched, culturally implemented and maintained belief in Westernized scientific and medical practices. In terms of science, the students are—as am I—especially cognizant and supportive of rigorous testing, large sample sizes, peer review and publication, and reproducibility. The vast majority of students accept and embrace the compartmentalized approach of Western medicine, finding that, for example, the NCI site is more credible because types of cancer corresponding to different parts of the body were much easier to find there.

I used students' responses to prompt class discussion in an attempt to illustrate culturally associated assumptions and contradictions that arose in the responses. For example, no student observed that the treatments discussed in the NCI Web site also cost money—much more money than the Tian Xian products—but that these treatments often may be paid for (that is, recognized by) Western insurance companies. I asked students to consider whether making money in the form of federal budget allocations was important to the National Cancer Institute, to ponder whether or not the makers of Tian Xian were interested in helping people, and to think about the similarities and differences between Tian Xian and Western pharmaceutical companies.

Also in the ensuing discussion, students repeatedly reinforced the sense of credibility they gained from the text of the NCI site. Given the extent to which Western society has become a visually based rather than a text-based culture—

at least if we are to believe what we are being told—I was struck by how much students praised the voluminous, often fairly technical, and dense NCI text and criticized the perceived large number of visuals in and the colorful design of the Tian Xian site. One student's written response to question 2, which I used to start this part of the discussion, typifies this belief. According to this student, "The site by the National Cancer Institute looks more professional. There is a lot of text, virtually no visuals. . . . The Tian Xian site looks like the center for the next Olympics. The visuals do not go with the seriousness of cancer. It has too many colors and not enough info./text." On the basis of this comment, it appears that we have a ways to go before a primarily visual, colorful design is accorded the same level of respect given to oldfashioned, boring, black and white text when both are associated with scientific and technical content. In addition, our entreaties as technical and scientific communication instructors for brevity and lack of jargon as characteristics of effective, respected discourse do not seem to be having their desired effect as yet.

Although the discussions with students were intriguing and illuminating, I cannot, of course, claim that students can dismiss thoroughly entrenched cultural codes associated with powerful cultural institutions simply as a result of comparing two medical Web sites and then discussing assumptions underlying their conclusions about these sites; nor should students be expected to subsequently dismiss their beliefs even if they are recognized as being culturally constructed. However, by approaching medicine (as well as science and technology more broadly) as a discursively operating cultural institution in a technical and scientific communication course, students can begin to gain the necessary critical tools to demystify and make sense of the myriad claims and counterclaims inherently a part of these discourses and to begin to understand how the discourses affect them individually. Because health is such a vital part of an individual's subjectivity, it is especially important that students understand the contexts in which the discourses associated with the cultural institution of medicine are produced, especially, for example, in terms of who stands to gain what with respect to political or economic power, of recognizing that results of medical research can often be interpreted in different ways, and of realizing that for every voice heard, there are many other voices that are not.

Additionally, students will write, edit, and design more effectively if they know something about the cultural baggage that discourse—no matter what cultural institution it is a part of—always and already carries. In this particular study, attention to medicine as a cultural artifact does not detract from my goal of teaching students to produce effective, rhetorically successful medical discourse. Indeed, a better understanding of the rhetorical situations of which these discursive events are a part most likely increases the chances for students composing discourse that achieves its desired results. This realization also helps students to predict the ethical implications of their writing, an area that Hartung (1998) has pointed out as seriously lacking in our pedagogy. As a result, they can understand more clearly the mechanisms by which they are influenced and, in turn, gain a more complex understanding of and critical appreciation for the medical discourse.

In this study, students were able to recognize assumptions about Western science and its manifestation as a cultural institution by contrasting an example of Western scientific discourse with its counterpart from a different cultural context. Such a contrast invites a relatively rapid and invigorating response. An intriguing and challenging followup to such an assignment would be to ask students to then focus on a piece of Western scientific discourse on its own, without the benefit of contrast to help sharpen the assumptions, to determine if the critical skills they gained via the National Cancer Institute/Tian Xian comparison can still be applied. For example, the instructor could ask students to find some relevant Western research that relates to a health issue that they, a family member, or friend is facing and to develop a series of critical questions not explicitly addressed or answered in the research.

## COLLABORATING WITH STUDENTS: TECHNOLOGY AUTOBIOGRAPHIES IN THE CLASSROOM

### A Story

As this volume suggests, all sorts of instructional innovations are possible. As a result, it is sometimes hard to tell which way to move. Where should we put our energies, limited as they are? In this chapter, I suggest that we might go about productively innovating our technical and professional communication pedagogy and curricula by paying attention to students' literacy skills as they come into our classes and programs. In particular, we might want to attend to their technological literacy skills, attitudes, and approaches to learning. A short anecdote might be instructive.

My observations of student's technological literacies and their impact on technical communication (TC) courses are reflected nicely by the experiences of one of my former colleagues at Michigan Technological University, Dr. Dale Sullivan. Sullivan was teaching a Web design class in the spring of 2000 when he commented on an unexpected turn the class had taken:

*I discovered that the coding ability of the students tended to be very advanced. The problem is that we don't know where students are, and one class in Web design will attract a very wide array of abilities. For 80 [percent] of the class,*

*I should have been teaching perl and cgi script applications and xml and asp. For 20 percent I should have been teaching very basic html and how to put a Web page on a server. . . . So I simply resorted to teaching basic principles of user-centered design, architecture, navigation, user interface design and user testing, and turned the class into a group work operation. (Email correspondence, May 5, 2000)*

This chapter suggests that the flexibility and nimble curricular redesign that Sullivan was able to manage in this class is becoming more and more the state of affairs in many technology-rich TC courses.1 His note caught my attention because the experience so closely matched my observations: there have been surprising fluctuations in technological skills, approaches, and attitudes in student population over the past several years.

## Practicing What We Preach

It's a good day when students write back to their home institution and let teachers know how their lives are going. Several years ago, one such message came across my screen, and I've used it ever since in all of my TC courses. It came from a young woman who had graduated a few years before and for whom I had great respect. I asked her about the most important three lessons she had learned in her tenure as a technical communicator. She said, "Know your audience; know more about your audience; and really get to know your audience." I've used her quote many times in the classes I teach.

We ask students to know their audience at every turn in the technical communication curriculum, occasionally providing them with methods for such analyses. In light of the changing technological experiences that Dr. Sullivan encountered in his course and the obvious need for communication specialists to know their audiences, I began to realize that I should have been following my advice. After all, as a teacher, I am continually constructing learning "interfaces" for students: interfaces that consist of online environments, content material, composing processes, in-class activities, and so forth. It occurred to me that I should also be making a stronger effort to know these students and to construct learning experiences with them, not just for them.

This chapter proposes a method—an autobiographical assignment focused mostly on past technological experiences—that might well benefit students and our class and curricular planning. As assignments, technological autobiographies (TA) are wonderfully functional. They provide an interesting glimpse into the attitudes, experiences, learning strategies and levels of expertise that students bring with them into our classes. They are writing samples; they are introductory narratives that help form our understandings of each other as people, workers, and learners. They help us and students get to know, know more, and "really" know an audience that we often use in our TC classes: the class members themselves.

But, in addition, these assignments can be part of a participatory design "method": technology autobiographies are windows into student lives in an age of rapidly changing technologies, technologies that have become central to our educational and professional endeavors on and off campus. I am certainly not the first to claim that we need to adopt and adapt user-centered, participatory design methods to the design of classes (Soloway 1994). In his article about designing online courses, Stuart Blythe (2001) makes it clear how difficult the academic setting makes this method. His solution to these difficulties comes in two forms. First, we have to imagine, as usability advocates have for years, that enduser (student) participation in the design of our classes is ongoing and formative. It should be an expected component of the ongoing redesign of our classes, not a one-time usability event. Second, he provided opportunities for each generation of students taking his class to choose the focus of projects in its class. Thus, his "assignment" becomes part of a participatory design method that will inform not only the class at hand but also the next improved, technology-rich, instructional experience that he helps construct.

## The Technologies in Our Discipline

But students' changing technological literacy practices aren't the only reason for adopting participatory design methods. As I've suggested in other publications, our culture is currently experiencing an overdetermined state of technological change. This change is particularly true in our discipline (see, for example, R. Selfe 1998). One graphic method of characterizing the overdetermined nature of this state of affairs is through the guillotine chart originally constructed by IBM in 1979, then revised by Dwight Stevenson in 1984 and Roger Grice in 1987. No doubt the blade has gotten longer and sharper since then.

Roger Grice, in his 1987 dissertation Technical Communication in the Computer Industry: An Information-Development Process to Track, Measure, and Ensure Quality, describes how in 1979 the IBM Human Factors Task Force met in Atlanta, Georgia, to "discuss and chart future actions" (50). Among other actions, they defined the role of technical communicator as "information developer" and created a guillotine chart much like the one presented in figure 1 that shows the growing responsibilities included in that role. In 1979 only the first four columns were represented. In 1984 Dwight Stevenson's prescient expansion of the chart showed the technical communicator "moving into the area of system design, especially design of the user- system interface" (Grice 54). It's hard to argue that Stevenson wasn't entirely correct in his assumptions that information developers would soon be engaged in video and film production, product development, database design, and software development, to name just a few of the additional "skills" suggested by his chart. And this, of course, was before the meteoric rise of the World Wide Web as an interactive, multimedia information delivery device.

*Information Development Job Description and Direction*

1960 → 1985

|  | Designed After | Designed With | Designed as an Integral Part | Systems Design |
|---|---|---|---|---|
| Purpose | Product Description | Functional Description | Task-Oriented Use Description | Process Design and Description |
| Development Emphasis | Content | Development and Schedule | Field and Customer Cost | Product and Process Evolution |
| Objective | Completeness | Technical Accuracy | Ease of Use and Total Cost | Efficiency, System Optimization |
| Product | Books | Libraries | Information | Information, Especially Electronic |
| Volume | Low | Medium | High | High in Volume, Complex in Nature |
| Skills | Document Writing / Editing | Computer Hard/Software Engineering Writing Editing Planning Graphics Text Management Testing for Accuracy | Retrievability Writing Editing Planning Graphics Management Text Management Testing for Accuracy and Usability Audience Definition Measurement Financial Human Factors Media Packaging Distribution Publishing Task Definition | Substantive Editing Substantive Writing Graphics Layout and Production Video and Film Training Interpersonal Communication Organizational Behavior Planning Text Management Computer Text Production Testing Financial Analysis / Management Product Distribution Product Development Online Documentation Computer Graphics Information Research Database Design and Management Legal Protection Cross-Cultural Communication Software Development Software Management Public Policy Research Design Research Synthesis |

**Figure 1.** Grice Guillotine Chart (adapted from Stevenson 1984).

## Participatory Design and the TC Curriculum

If anecdotal evidence (Sullivan and Blythe, for example) suggests that changing technological literacies will or should change the courses we teach and if the increasing technological complexity of the discipline itself will encourage us to adapt our courses, one might then ask, "What do we mean by participatory design?" I would suggest that it is more of an attitudinal change than any one particular method. That attitude will then lead us to innovative pedagogical approaches and implementations. In a special issue of Human-Computer Interaction on "Current Perspectives on Participatory Design" (PD), Randall Trigg and Susan Anderson (1996) suggest a common theme among the many approaches found in this design rubric. In PD, there is "a fundamental respect for the people who use technology and for the right of people to have a direct influence on decisions that affect their lives" (181). Changing technological literacies are so fundamental to the TC curriculum that we will probably find traditional usability methods—focus groups, questionnaires, controlled usability testing—useful but "not sufficient to the development of genuinely useful systems [in this case, educational systems]" (Blomberg, Suchman, and Trigg 1996, 239). As we design technical communication programs or classes, we are in essence aiming at a moving target, one moving on several dimensions at once. At least two of those dimensions seem obvious: students bring a rapidly changing set of technological literacies practices into our classrooms each term, even as the technologies we are asked to use change around us.

As a result, we need to rethink our relationship to students. They are, after all, the workers in an educational system, a system that is, in my experience with the program at Michigan Technological University over the past fifteen years, constantly in the process of being redesigned. TC academics face a growing list of skills designated by commercial representatives and changing theories of the communication process. One might reasonably ask, then, another question: "Isn't it enough that TC teachers and curricula designers consider the suggestions of theorists, industrial advisory boards, employers, and technology experts in the redesign of our programs and classes?" The answer for those working on technical literacy projects is, of course, "No." In a research report submitted to the Society for Technical Communication in March of 2000, called "Studying the Acquisition and Development of Technological Literacy," Cynthia Selfe and Gail Hawisher summarized the problem we face this way:

*So, here is a problem: We know very little about how and why particular individuals acquire and develop, or fail to acquire and develop, technological literacy.*

*And, here is another problem: We know very little about how large-scale historic, cultural, economic, political, or ideological movements act and interact to shape individuals' acquisition and development of technological literacy— or how individuals' literacy practices and values help constitute these macro-*

*level trends.*

*And here is a really big problem: Despite our lack of knowledge about these important matters, literacy experts, educators, and policy makers continue to set standards for technological literacy (National Educational Technology Standards for Students, 2000; Standards for the English Language Arts, 1996), create educational and workplace policies about technological literacy (Getting America's Students Ready for the Twenty-first Century, 1996); and design programs and curricula that teach technological literacy in schools and in the workplace (National Educational Technology Standards for Students, 2000). In sum, we're basing big decisions on minimal information. (1)*

As suggested in Selfe and Hawisher's comment, TC curriculum designers, myself included, have habitually relied on system-centered approaches as they face the escalating curricular requirements driven by diverse skill sets like those represented in Grice's guillotine chart (see figure 1). We attend to our favorite theorists, available industrial representatives, and technology specialists, but rarely the student populations who inhabit our programs. We "black box" their changing literacy practices at the risk of becoming increasingly irrelevant or at least disconnected not only from students and their learning habits but also from the youth culture in general.

## The Autobiographic Assignments

The story that Dr. Sullivan tells about his Web design class strikes a chord with me because my ability to predict what students will bring into the class has likewise been unsettled. I have clearly overestimated and underestimated their abilities in the past. At the same time, literacy scholars like Deborah Brandt have come to some interesting conclusions about changing literacy expectations. In "Accumulating Literacy: Writing and Learning to Write in the Twentieth Century," Brant (1995) interviewed sixty-five participants with the goal of discovering the "institutions, materials, and people" that inform the acquisition of "practices that haunt the sites of literacy learning" (651, 661). One of her findings suggests that there is an increasing "escalation in educational expectations" on literacy practices both in the home and in the workplace (650) as a result of recent, incessant technological "innovations." The technology autobiography and related assignments developed in this chapter are generally beholden to scholars like Brant. More specifically, they have been developed in detail and practice by my colleagues Karla Kitalong and Michael Moore. In a forthcoming publication, we speculate that "these heightened expectations [are] articulated by a wide variety of educational stakeholders, including the media, state legislatures, industry, and any number of special-interest groups." Our approach highlights "the contradictions and ambiguities between institutional goals and the communicative acts and literacy practices of students, articulated in their own words" (Kitalong, Selfe, and Moore forthcoming).

In the following section, I discuss how I instituted versions of the autobiographical assignment in classes with two different populations of technical communication majors: one set of assignment responses came from junior and senior undergraduates and the other from masters-level graduate students in a different professional communication program. In both cases, the course name was the same: Publications Management. As you might expect, each set of responses to the assignment taught both me and the students a slightly different lesson. For that reason, in the next section, after describing the assignments themselves, I'll explore possible implications gleaned from each collection of responses. The implications I drew from these student reflections provided the impetus for immediate classroom innovations and were valuable as I planned future courses and programmatic proposals for modifying the undergraduate and graduate programs in which I work.

The process I used in both classes (graduate and undergraduate) was similar:

1. I assigned the autobiographical activities described later.

2. I combined their reflections into a class booklet (hardcopy and .pdf versions) to be used as a text in the class.

3. I asked students, after reading the class booklet, to speculate on the range of learning styles, attitudes, technological skills, and experiences (LATEs) they saw in the combined document. (I also participated in this process.)

4. I worked with them to determine how these LATEs should influence the technology modules (instructional documentation) they would be producing for the class.

For the purposes of this chapter, I'll touch briefly on step 4 but focus primarily on the value of step 3. I, of course, learned at least as much as the students from their responses to this assignment. Students were informed that the autobiographies were also part of a classroom research project that would be used to help reconfigure this and other TC courses and used to make recommendations that I hoped would influence technical and professional, undergraduate and graduate communication programs in the future. The technology autobiographies, then, had two primary purposes:

1. To help the students learn more about an audience that they would be addressing in future assignments

2. To help me better understand students and their relationship to technology and course content

In both classes students were asked to respond to the following question sets in informal, autobiography assignments.

## *Questions Leading to the Undergraduates' Technology Autobiographies*

1. Write and/or draw an autobiography in which you recall your earliest experiences with technological devices or artifacts. What were they? What do you remember about using them?
2. What were the popular gadgets in your house while growing up?
3. Who[m] do you identify as being most technologically "literate" in your life?
4. What's on your desk at home?
5. What technological devices are you carrying now?
6. What's on your technological "wish list"?
7. How do you expect to deal with new technologies in the future?
8. What sort of documentation works best for you? (Artistic representations [are welcome] and need to be accompanied by a written statement explaining the work.)

Notice that the eighth question—"What sort of documentation works best for you?"—was not directed so much at the technological portion of this assignment as it was at the content of the course. The upcoming assignment would ask students to design, test, and produce a technology documentation for the people using a local computer lab. You will see that I expanded this section in the next iteration of the autobiography assignment (for the graduate class). I included an entirely new focus for student reflection: the publishing autobiography. I quickly realized that it would be useful to know more about students' past experiences not only with technology but with the course content as well. In both cases, I hoped to find ways of involving students more intimately in the design of assignments and products that come out of the class. A version of the assignment as I explained it to students follows:

## *Technology and Publishing Autobiographies*

These two pieces of writing are meant to be fun and interesting to your classmates and myself. We need to know a bit about you. I would like you to write a personal technological autobiography (TA) and a publishing autobiography (PA). We'll start this assignment in class and then, after you complete your autobiograph[ies], distribute them electronically (in .pdf format) as a booklet. The class will have the weekend to read them. It's a lot of reading but by the second class, we will all know something about each other and our collective technology and publishing experiences. These TAPAs will NOT be graded other than to note that you handed them in. . . . To complete the assignment, respond to the following prompts:

## *Technology Autobiography (TA)*

Write and/or draw an autobiography in which you recall your earliest experiences with technological devices or artifacts. What were they?

- What do you remember about using them?
- What were the popular gadgets in your house while growing up?
- Whom do you identify as being most technologically "literate" in your life?
- What's on your technological "wish list"?
- How do you expect to learn and keep up with new technologies in the future?
- What technological workshops are you willing to develop for me and your classmates?
- What technologies do you need to learn in the near future?
- (Artistic representations of your relationship to technology are very welcome and usually very interesting. I would appreciate a short written statement explaining the work.)

## *Publishing Autobiography (PA)*

- What experiences in your past have gotten you excited about publishing?
- What informal or formal (work-related) publishing experiences have you had?
- What specific publishing expertise do you bring to the class: organizational, audience analysis, technological, experience with types of publications, . . . ?
- What sort of publishing NOW interests you? In other words, imagine

yourself working for a company, organization, or start-up that you really believe in: describe what kind of work they would do and what sorts of publishing they would engage in.

Write both the TA and PA with your classmates' interests in mind. What examples would be most interesting to them? How much time do they have to read about your experiences? What do they need to know about you and your abilities?

## *Why start with this information?*

Almost every professional/technical communicator I talk to about her/his job mentions the need to know more, more, and still more about the audience being addressed when creating a publication. In other words, knowing your audience very intimately is more important to a successful publication than almost anything else. Your first individual project will be to construct a technology module for users of your home computer lab. And if my experience holds true, even those of you who have worked in this lab know very little about the literacy skills and learning habits of those around you.

## Implications from Autobiography Assignments in Upper-Division and Graduate TC Courses

### *The Technological Ambivalence in an Undergraduate TC Course*

In both classes, I was introducing students to the publishing industry and, in that process, relied on real client projects. Because of the need to use imaging and publishing software and hardware in both classes, it seemed important to identify what students already knew and what they could add to the class (because many students came in, as was the case in Dale Sullivan's class, with skills more advanced than the teacher's). I also wanted to better understand what attitudes and learning styles they had adopted in the past. The technology autobiography assignment for the undergraduate class was one way of collecting this type of information and incorporating it into the planning of subsequent courses and sessions within this particular course.

### *Learning about Each Other: An Aside*

Because of a subsequent assignment, it was important that these students learn a great deal about each other, and the autobiography booklet provided that opportunity. The assignment asked them to develop "technology modules" (instructional documentation) that would be useful to students working in the drop-in lab that they frequented. The students in the class would be, as a result, both the creators of helpful technology modules and representative users of those same modules. Not surprisingly, these informal autobiographies were remarkably useful in our audience analyses ("really get to know your audience") for this assignment. After receiving their short autobiographies, I constructed a single document that contained the entire class set (thirty pages long). That booklet became a reading assignment out of which the students were asked to develop a user profile for their technology modules. The technology autobiographical document gave us the exigence for discussing the nuances of audience needs, expectations, and learning styles at a level well beyond the generalities I often received in students' previous audience analyses.

But the autobiography assignment gave me and the students information about the technological literacy makeup of the class that seemed just as or more valuable at pedagogical and curricular levels.

Perhaps because these students were young, burgeoning professionals and just beginning to realize the full extent of what communication technologies would mean to them in the future, this set of autobiographies, as a whole, illustrated the ambivalence that students have for their technology-rich futures. In a future publication, Karla Kitalong, Michael Moore, and I discuss this ambivalence in more detail (forthcoming). Here, I'll summarize some observations that seem to have implications for TC classes and programs in the midst of pedagogical and programmatic change.

## *A Diversity of Experience*

One observation common to all the sets of technology autobiographies that I have reviewed over the past two years (our research team and others have been asked to apply this type of assignment to a number of technology-rich English-studies classes) is that students bring a wide range of technological experiences to bear in the TC classroom. This might be best illustrated by a student's description of what I call generational compression of technological experience:

*My little brother, who is four years younger than I am, just graduated from high school with more knowledge of computers and technology than I will ever learn. He just built himself a computer from scratch and is currently attending [XXX] State to study computer networks and systems. My sister, on the other hand, is only two years older than I am. She spent 4 years in college without ever having to turn a computer on. (Paula, pseudonym)*

Students realize that there are radical differences in experience levels. Those variations in experience, however, don't necessarily reduce the opportunities for hard-working, self-motivated students, as the next quote indicates:

*[A] calculator was my only real link to technology [in high school] until I managed to actually touch computers again in college. I was overwhelmed when I got here. I had no clue what computers could do. At the time I was an electrical engineering major. Now, I'm a computer science major [and one of the most technologically adept students in the class]. (Otto)*

But for the average student entering our technology-rich programs, we can't assume that they will all simply "catch up" magically. They worry about, and we should worry about, how our classes might better facilitate the catch-up process, and, at the same time, we should continue to challenge those students who come in with Paula's brother's level of experience.

## *A Backgound of Gaming*

A second component to the technological ambivalence in these undergraduates' TAs is a growing experience with gaming systems. In all sets of technology autobiographies, educational and purely entertainment-level gaming has a strong representation. To a follow-up question to students who claimed a strong gaming background came these responses. "Believe it or not, games can make children less frightened of technology. I thought of computers as a toy for years before it actually became a tool." (Johnson, email correspondence, Sept. 22, 1999) Not only did they suggest that gaming reduces computer anxiety, they hinted that specific learning strategies were encouraged by games. The following is an extended quote from a young woman's reflections on gaming:

*What gaming taught me is that there are always little tricks to doing things. For example, when i played supermario bros. i learned how to "warp" to different worlds and that meant that i could skip 4 levels of playing without losing points. So i would always try to do new things regardless if there was a hint that i could do it or not. . . . The hidden shortcuts really got to be fascinating. . . . But what is also key is that i learned a lot of tricks from my friends. . . . So that is getting a reward [from others'] experience with the game. (Glenda, pseudonym, email correspondence, Sept. 22, 1999)*

These two short comments suggest that students with gaming experiences might be more willing to approach new technologies fearlessly, try techniques regardless of whether those techniques seem possible or not, and seek out shortcuts and tricks on their own and with friends. The questions that come to mind first include the following: How can students, who are designing instructional modules, or how can we, who are devising technology-rich classroom activities, take advantage of this playful, exploratory attitude? Will someone with this type of background approach technology instructions or our classroom activities in interesting and unique ways? As this type of gaming experience becomes more common than exceptional (nine of nineteen students in 1999 claimed to have had substantial gaming experiences), how will our approach to online and print-based learning systems and documentation change? How should our approaches to teaching change? What will this mean for technical and professional communication departments at a programmatic level? The ambivalence here resides mostly in my concerns, not students'.

## *Learning Styles Differ Radically*

The technology autobiography assignment asks explicitly about how students learn or plan to learn new technologies; this led to the third component: students' technological ambivalence, which came out of the undergraduates' reflections and which has to do with radically differing learning strategies. Though a certain percentage of students have a tinker's mind-set—one that encourages them to understand the underlying workings of the technologies they use—most admit to short-term, just-in-time learning patterns that allow them "to stay current with those things that pertain to my field or are positioned in it" (Randall).

Students will apparently come to us, not surprisingly, with a number of learning strategies, some of which won't be a comfortable fit for many of technical and professional communication teachers: students will be crisis learners; fearful, reluctant learners; stealth learners willing to make the trade-off between their depth of understanding and the practical art of getting the job done. They are also aware of the trade-offs they may have to make if they are going to commit to learning new technologies thoroughly.

*I have a hard time throwing off other, maybe older, values for the sake of my computer literacy. I recognize that it takes a tremendous time commitment to stay fluent. I don't know what other part of my life I want to give up so that I can learn yet another piece of software. I will probably manage the learning of future skills by crisis, doing only what I have to do to remain literate enough. (Diana, pseudonym)*

These comments only hint at the ambivalence students sometimes express about their future with constantly changing computing technologies. They sometimes speak about enslavement, painful values, reluctant learning, impersonal lifestyles, and rude online behavior. All are words and phrases that make it clear why students might approach our use of communication technologies with some reluctance. Our job, as a result, would seem to go well beyond the introduction to new— sometimes useful, sometimes painful— bleeding-edge technologies. Technical and professional communication instructors may well need to begin asking themselves what strategies they themselves adopt to stay reasonably and appropriately current. More difficult might be to imagine innovative approaches that make those strategies an explicit part of our instruction. To summarize, this one set of technology autobiographies led me to reimagine several components of TC courses and programs. The first is to question how we accommodate the wide (some would say "ever widening," C. Selfe, 1999) technological experiences that students bring into our classes. The second is to imagine how the substantial online experiences with gaming systems will change the way students work and learn in our classes. The third is to build a robust set of strategies for adopting new technological systems into our curriculum and for adapting to them. These concerns are not necessarily going to emerge in all technical and professional communication courses. The autobiographies do, however, give me data and an agenda to take back to our curricular committee, which is endlessly reconfiguring and reconstructing the requirements and courses in our program. I assume that other programs, having collected their data, might well come up with unique (innovative) concerns that they might address in their curriculum as well.

One of the most interesting aspects of collecting these autobiographies over time and courses, however, is that patterns begin to appear. As I read through the technology and publishing autobiographies (TAPAs) from a graduate professional communication course, not only were patterns evident, but potential pedagogical solutions also seemed to present themselves in the anecdotes and descriptions students provided.

## Learning from the Technology and Publishing Autobiographies (Tapas) From a Graduate Professional Communication Course: Reassessing the Course Itself

### *Content Feedback: Another Aside*

You might have noticed that the second autobiography assignment added questions aimed at better understanding not only the technological literacy of the class but also the content experiences of students (in this case, publishing autobiographies that detailed their experiences with print publications). In future classes, I plan to use the content questions to help organize that portion of the class as well. Students' varied publishing experiences in this set of autobiographies have convinced me, for instance, of the value of several strategies:

1. I might ask students to recruit expert consultants to visit the class physically or virtually during the term.
2. Productive interviews with working professionals (again either face-to-face or virtually) will enrich the class and subsequent classes.

3. It should be possible to develop sustained relationships with some of these professionals to set up lively online discussions that provide professional relevance and contact with industry professionals even in the remote north woods of Michigan Technological University.

But the more generalizable and important innovations for technical and professional communication programs would seem to be located in the technology autobiographies of these students.

## *Adopting and Adapting to New Technologies*

Although there is always a great deal to glean from the technological experiences that students describe in their autobiographies, each set seems to provide some insight into particular or related portions of the courses I teach. The informal TAs assigned to this graduate publication course in the fall of 2000 made it clear that students from both courses were quite concerned about one issue in particular: the need to develop strategies for adopting and adapting to new technological systems.

*I read these journals and magazines advertising new software and technologies and wonder how on earth I am supposed to stay competitive in the job market when I haven't learned the old stuff before they introduce the new. (Brown)*

*Ms. Merrill says,*

*I did eventually get my hands on a word processor, which was replaced by an actual computer when I was starting college.*

*What do I remember about using them? Fear. Trepidation. I remember being more than a little daunted by those computerized thingys with all their buttons and options and programs. This reluctance did not last long, however. Without ever really consulting the instruction manuals except in extreme desperation, I figured out how to work them through guess-work and trialand-error.*

Statements of anxiety seem common to many students coming to technology late in their academic careers. The lucky ones are thrown into an institutional setting where they are required to learn new systems quickly to survive. Usually, they have no structured way to develop any systematic method of learning new technologies and so are thrown back on survival strategies: just-in-time learning, trial-and-error efforts, guesswork learning patterns. These are the lucky ones. Unlucky students may not even have these opportunities. Students' anxiety was compelling possibly because theirs reflected mine so accurately. They made me wonder whether together we couldn't devise some alternative models that would better serve their technological literacy needs. As I read their stories, I began to imagine some possibilities.

## Resources and Procedures for Staying Abreast

*I try to stay educated about technological trends, though. I peruse magazines, engage in conversations about what's "out there", and play enough video games to understand the implications of new technology to the entertainment industry. To this day, I still relate my experiences of technology through my obsession with entertainment, because I have learned the most about technology through this medium, and I honestly think entertainment drives technology more than any other single factor. (Bonhan)*

Obviously, Bonhan hasn't been exposed to high-end military applications or he might change his mind slightly. But his claim about gaming might also be closer to the truth than I might think. His comment suggests to me that we might incorporate explorations like the ones he mentioned during class by asking students to find reliable sources for technological news relevant to the class and share summaries of their visits (to Web sites), articles, posts, and so forth with the class. If one of Bonhan's techniques is to "play enough video games to understand the implications of new technology," then we might ask him and other gaming aficionados to bring the implications they draw from that experience to class. If TC instructors make this type of activity an explicit part of our exploration, we might all be able to imagine how the gaming industry can provide some positive, productive protocols to technical communication professionals interested in instructional systems and online interaction.

## Setting Up Collective Learning Experiences

One approach to reducing anxieties and providing students with strategies for learning new technologies is to set up appropriate technological learning experiences within our classes. The sixth question for the masters-level class was supposed to help me set up this type of learning experience. (What technological workshops are you willing to develop for me and your classmates?) Surprisingly, even those experienced with some technologies often responded this way: "At this time, I don't feel that I have enough expertise to lead a technical workshop" (Julie).

Students are justifiably concerned about teaching their peers. If public speaking is one of the most anxiety-producing events in a person's life, consider how nerve-wracking public teaching must be! Students often don't believe that they are the most technologically savvy person in the class and so feel incapable of leading a technology session. I haven't given up on this approach, however. Instead, it has become my job to convince them of the kind of workshop they can develop and lead, not whether they can lead one. To pave the way, I might

1. provide them with a model interactive learning situation appropriate for the class,
2. survey them and identify the expertise in the class around which they can form teams,
3. help them construct interactive learning modules that will help bring the entire class (including the teacher!) up to some baseline understanding of a particular software, hardware, or netware environment; we could then . . .
4. implement those learning activities systematically during the course.

Not only will we all learn a great deal about relevant technologies, but these activities are also full of opportunities for typical technical communication compositions (textual, visual, aural, animated, and so forth), oral presentations, interactive instructional presentations, and the development of online help systems and Web-based constructions.

## *Technological Mentoring Programs*

*The second event that changed the way I look at technology occurred when I became friends with the guy I am now dating. He was raised in a technologically advanced environment, so computers are quite the norm for him. (Loftin)*

Though we are unlikely to intentionally set up close personal relationships between students, there is every reason to believe that it might be productive to add a mentoring experience to capstone classes for graduating seniors. A technological mentoring assignment may provide a way to harness the expertise of seniors and pass it along, at some level, to our younger students. On the other hand, if the technological compression described earlier holds true, these graduating seniors might also find themselves learning a great deal about new technologies from the younger students. And they will certainly learn a bit about relating to younger colleagues, a skill of some significance in the workplace.

For years, I've encouraged teachers in professional development workshops to recruit their best, most enthusiastic former students as technical resource collaborators. These students can help implement a version of the technological mentoring program within a single class. Though it takes some preplanning and organizational finesse, it is possible to recruit former students to work with your current class as volunteers or for small stipends or for independent study credit. I've seen even the most technologically savvy teachers use mentoring programs within their classes successfully.

## *Stand-Beside Consultants*

An idea closely related to the technological mentor is the stand-beside consultant. When asked what software or hardware they might explore with the class, surprisingly, most students expressed unease at the prospect of leading a technology demonstration for their peers. But they were quite willing to offer help to novices as they worked. Programmatically, we might want to consider in-class or out-of-class activities that pair those new to specific systems or software with experienced students as they work on class projects. Using these students as "standbeside" consultants will give consultants valuable teaching experience that they will no doubt need in the workplace. Both novice and consulting participants can be asked to produce reflective writing that details the kind of collaboration and consulting that worked well. Collected, these reflections could be combined into a "text" to be read and discussed by the whole class.

This begs the question, however, of how to push the more experienced students in the class. Perhaps we should be making time in the course for technologically advanced students to push their skills along by collaborating with out-of-class consultants if the teacher can't provide the expertise. We might contact former students, local professionals, or students from other majors as we attempt to recruit these consultants. Part of the assignment for advanced students could be to create a learning experience for the rest of the class that will introduce us all to the new systems they will be learning.

## Concluding Statements

### *The Method*

A great deal of the "method" involved in applying participatory design processes to our classes and programs has yet to be developed. I look forward to dialogues with other TC professionals as we try to imagine how learner-centered design might best be applied to the technology-rich instructional environments.

### *The Work Load*

Resource assignments, collective learning experiences, mentoring, and stand-beside consultant programs are all the more work for the teacher or more planning for the program director. As such they have to be weighed against the already substantial responsibilities of teachers, administrators, and students. As this volume makes abundantly clear, all innovative pedagogies seem to carry the same onus: they are typically more work than the status quo. But if we have to make choices about how we manage our courses and curricula, technology autobiographies at least give us vivid and contextualized "data" to use as we challenge our traditional pedagogical practices in a changing technological landscape.

## *The Context*

As I mentioned early, the speculation about how we might draw on the observations from technology autobiographies to redesign classes and curricula is still quite preliminary and must be placed in unique programmatic contexts. What seems appropriate in a TC program at a technological university located in a rural, isolated region of the north woods (Michigan Technological University) and what seems essential to students living near the research triangle of North Carolina (Clemson University) are quite different. I look forward, however, to exploring the patterns of common student experiences with colleagues from around the country (and worldwide) as a prelude to innovating and making relevant technical communication programs of the twenty-first century.

## REFERENCES

1. Aristotle. Excerpt from On Rhetoric: A Theory of Civic Discourse. Trans. George A. Kennedy. New York: Oxford U P, 1991. (Book 1, chapters 1–3 [25–51]; Book 2, chapters 18–26 [172–214]).
2. Barton, Ben F., and Marthalee S. Barton, "Ideology and the Map: Toward a Postmodern Visual Design Practice," Professional Communication: The Social Perspective. Eds. Nancy Roundy Blyler and Charlotte Thralls. Newbury Park: Sage, 1993. 49–78.
3. Bitzer. "The Rhetorical Situation." Philosophy-and-Rhetoric 1.1 (1968): 1–14. Bizzell, Patricia. "Foundationalism and Anti-Foundationalism in Composition Studies." PRE/TEXT 7.1–2 (1986): 37–56.
4. Blyler, Nancy Roundy, and Charlotte Thralls. "The Social Perspective and Professional Communication: Diversity and Directions in Research." Professional Communication: The Social Perspective. Eds. Nancy Roundy Blyler and Charlotte Thralls. Newbury Park: Sage, 1993. 3–34.
5. Bolter, Jay David. Either Chapters 1, 2, and 13 from Writing Spaces, or Chapter 1 from Remediation. Brandt, Deborah. "Accumulating Literacy: Writing and Learning to Write in the Twentieth Century." College English 57 (1995): 649–68.
6. Brown, Stuart. "Rhetoric, Ethical Codes, and the Revival of Ethos in Publications Management." Publications Management: Essays for Professional Communicators. Eds. O. Jane Allen and Lynn H. Deming.

Amityville: Baywood Publishing, 1994. 189–200.

7. Burbules, Nicholas. "Rhetorics of the Web: Hyperreading and Critical Literacy." In Page to Screen. Ed. Illana Snyder. Burke. Kenneth. "Terministic Screens." Language as Symbolic Action. Berkeley, CA: U of California P, 1966. 44–62.

8. An Excerpt from Grammar of Motives. Debs, Mary Beth. "Corporate Authority: Sponsoring Rhetorical Practice." Writing in the Workplace: New Research Perspectives. Ed. Rachel Spilka. Carbondale: Southern Illinois UP, 1993. 158–70.

9. Doheny-Farina, Stephen. "Confronting the Methodological and Ethical Problems of Research on Writing in Nonacademic Settings." Writing in the Workplace: New Research Perspectives. Ed. Rachel Spilka. Carbondale: Southern Illinois UP, 1993. 253–267.

10. Duin, Ann Hill. "Test Drive-Techniques for Evaluating the Usability of Documents." Techniques for Technical Communicators. Eds. C. Barnum and S. Carliner. NY: Macmillan, 1993. 306–35.

11. Faigley, Lester. "Nonacademic Writing: The Social Perspective." Writing in NonAcademic Settings. Eds. Odell, Lee, and Dixie Goswami. New York: Guilford P, 1985. 231–48.

12. And Chapter 1 of Fragments of Rationality. Flower, Linda, et al. "Revising Functional Documents: The Scenario Principle." New Essays in Technical and Scientific Communication. Eds. Anderson, Paul, R. John Brockman, and Carolyn Miller. Farmingdale, NY: Baywood, 1983. 41–58.

13. Foucault, Michel. "Order of Discourse." In Bizzell and Herzberg, The Rhetorical Tradition. Freire, Paulo. "The Adult Literacy Process as Cultural Action for Freedom and education and Conscientizacao." Harvard Educational Review 68.4 (Winter 1998): 480–520.

14. Gorgias. "Encomium of Helen." The Rhetorical Tradition: Readings from Classical Times to the Present. Ed. Patricia Bizzell and Bruce Herzberg. Boston: Bedford Books of St. Martin's P, 1990. 40–42.

15. Herndl, Carl. "Teaching Discourse and Reproducing Culture: A Critique of Research and Pedagogy in Professional and Non-Academic Writing." College Composition and Communication 44 (1993): 349–63.

16. Johns, Lee Clark. "The File Cabinet Has a Sex Life: Insights of a Professional Writing Consultant." Worlds of Writing: Teaching and Learning in the Discourse Communities of Work. Ed. Matalene, Carolyn. New York: Random House, 1989. 153–87.

17. Kaplan, Nancy. "Ideology, Technology, and the Future of Writing Instruction." Evolving Perspectives on Computers and Composition: Questions for the 1990s. Ed. Gail Hawisher and Cynthia Selfe. Urbana, IL: NCTE, 1991. 11–42.
18. Katz, Steven. "The Ethics of Expediency: Classical Rhetoric, Technology, and the Holocaust." College English 54 (1992): 255–75.
19. Killingsworth, M. Jimmie, and Jacqueline Palmer. "The Environmental Impact Statement and the Rhetoric of Democracy."Ecospeak: Rhetoric and Environmental Policies in America. Carbondale: Southern Illinois UP, 1992. 162–91.
20. Kostelnick and Roberts. Chapters 1–2 of Designing Visual Language: Strategies for Professional Communicators. Allyn and Bacon, 1998. 3–78.
21. Kostelnick, Charles. "Cultural Adaptation and Information Design: Two Contrasting Views," IEEE Transactions on Professional Communication 38.4 (December, 1995): 182–96.
22. Kuhn. Preface and Intro to The Structure of Scientific Revolutions. Kynell, Teresa. Chapter 6, "1941–1950: The Emergence of . . ." Writing in a Milieu of Utility. Ablex, 1996. 75–88.
23. Latour, Bruno, and Steve Woolgar. Chapters 1, 4 and 5 of Laboratory Life: The Construction of Scientific Facts. Princeton, NJ: Princeton P, 1986. 15–233.
24. Laurel, Brenda. Chapter 1 from The Computer as Theatre. Addison-Wesley, 1993. MacNealy, Mary. Strategies for Empirical Research in Writing. NY: Allyn and Bacon, 1999.
25. Maitra, Kaushiki, and Dixie Goswami. "Responses of American Readers to Visual Aspects of a Mid-Sized Japanese Company's Annual Report: A Case Study." IEEE Transactions on Professional Communication 38.4 (December, 1995): 197–203.
26. Miller, Carolyn. "What's Practical about Technical Writing?" Technical Writing: Theory and Practice. Eds. Fearing, Bertie, and W. Keats Sparrow. New York: MLA, 1989. 15–26.
27. Perkins, Jane. "Communicating in a Global, Multicultural Corporation." Plato. "Phaedrus." Trans. W. C. Helmbold and W. G. Rabinowitz. New York: Macmillan Publishing Company, 1956.
28. Myers, Greg. "Texts as Knowledge Claims: The Social Construction of Two Biology Articles." Social Studies in Science 15 (1985): 593–630.
29. Nielsen, Jacob. Chapter 2 "Page Design" In Designing Web Usability.

Indianapolis: New Riders Publishing, 1999.
30. Redish, Janice, Robbin Battison, and Edward Gold. "Making Information Accessible to Readers." Writing in Non-Academic Settings. Eds., Lee Odell and Dixie Goswami. New York: Guilford P, 1985. 129–53.
31. Schmandt-Besserat. "The Earliest Precursor of Writing." Scientific American 238 (1978): 50–59.
32. Schriver, Karen. Excerpt from Dynamics in Document Design Creating Texts for Readers. New York: John Wiley and Sons, 1997. Pages 168–181.
33. Selfe, Cynthia L., and Richard Selfe. "The Politics of the Interface: Power and Its Exercise in Electronic Contact Zones." College Composition and Communication 45.4 (1994): 480–504.
34. Sullivan, Patricia. "Taking Control of the Page: Electronic Writing and Word Publishing." Evolving Perspectives on Computers and Composition: Questions for the 1990s. Ed. Gail Hawisher and Cynthia Selfe. Urbana, IL: NCTE, 1991. 43–64.
35. Tebeaux, Elizabeth. "Technical Writing in Seventeenth-Century England." Journal of Technical Writing and Communication 29.3, 1999. 209–54.
36. Tufte, Edward. Chapters 4 and 5 of The Visual Display of Quantitative Information. Cheshire, CN: Graphics P, 1983. 91–105, 107–21.
37. And Chapter 2 of Visual Explanations. Cheshire, CN: Graphics P, 1997. 27–54.
38. Vitanza, Victor. "Historiography." Winsor, Dorothy. "Engineering Writing/Writing Engineering." College Composition and Communication 41.1 (Feb 1990): 58–70.
39. Yates, JoAnne. Chapters 1–2 of Control through Communication: The Rise of System in American Management. Baltimore: John Hopkins UP, 1989. 1–64.
40. Adams, E. J. 1993. A Project-Intensive Software Design Course. SIGCSE Bulletin 25:112–16.
41. Allen, J. 1989. Breaking with Tradition: New Directions in Audience Analysis. In Technical Writing: Theory and Practice, ed. B. Fearing and W. K. Sparrow. New York: MLA.
42. ———. 1992. Bridge over Troubled Waters? Connecting Research and Pedagogy in Composition and Business/Technical Communication. Technical Communication Quarterly 1:5–26.
43. Allen, N., and G. A. Wickliff. 1997. Learning Up Close and at a

Distance. In Computers and Technical Communication: Pedagogical and Programmatic Perspectives, ed. S. Selber. Greenwich CT: Ablex. Almstrum, V. L., N. Dale, A. Berglund, M. Granger, J. C. Little, D. M. Miller, M. Petre, P. Schragger, and F. Springsteel. 1996. Evaluation: Turning Technology from Toy to Tool. In Integrating Technology into Computer Software Environments Conference Proceedings. Barcelona: ACM P.

44. Alred, G. J., W. T. Oliu, and C. T. Brusaw. 1992. The Professional Writer: A Guide for Advanced Technical Writing. New York: St. Martin's Press.

45. Althusser, L. 1971. Lenin and Philosophy and Other Essays. New York: Monthly Review Press. Anderson, P. 1985. What Survey Research Tells Us About Writing at Work. In Writing in Nonacademic Settings, ed. L. Odell and D. Goswami. New York: Guilford.

46. ———. 1995. Evaluating Academic Technical Communication Programs: New Stakeholders, Diverse Goals. Technical Communication 42:628–33.

47. Andrews Knodt, E. 1988. Taming Hydra: The Problem of Balancing Teaching and Scholarship at a Two-Year College. Teaching English in the Two Year College 15:170–74.

48. Anson, C. M. 1999. Distant Voices: Teaching and Writing in a Culture of Technology. College English 61:261–80.

49. Arbaugh, J. B. 2001. How Instructor Immediacy Behaviors Affect Student Satisfaction and Learning in Web-Based Courses. Business Communication Quarterly 64:42–54.

50. Aristotle. Politics. 1941. The Basic Works of Aristotle. Trans. Ed. Richard McKeon. Benjamin Jowett. New York: Random House

51. Artemeva, N., S. Logie, and J. St-Martin. 1999. From Page to State: How Theories of Genre and Situated Learning Help Introduce Engineering Students to Discipline-Specific Communication. Technical Communication Quarterly 8:301–18.

52. Asimow, M. 2000. Bad Lawyers in the Movies. Nova Law Review 24.2 (winter). Available online at http://tarlton.law.utexas.edu/lpop/etext-/nova/asimow24.htm#92 [cited September 28, 2002].

53. Avery. U.S. News and World Report. 1998. Best Jobs for the Future. 84–85.

54. Avery, D., M. Charski, D. Floyd, M. Loftus, M. B. Marcus, A. Mulrine, S. Schultz, and K. Terrell. 1998, October 26. "20 Hot Job Tracks" US News and World Report.

55. Bacon, N. 1997. Community Service Writing: Problems, Challenges, Questions. In Writing the Community: Concepts and Models for Service Learning in Composition, ed. L. AdlerKassner and R. Crooks. Urbana IL: NCTE.
56. Baker, M., and C. David. 1994. The Rhetoric of Power: Political Issues in Management Writing. Technical Communication Quarterly 3:165–79.
57. Barton, B. F., and M. S. Barton. 1993. Ideology and the Map: Toward a Postmodern Visual Design Practice. Professional Communication: The Social Perspective, ed. N. R. Blyler and C. Thralls. Newbury Park CA: Sage.
58. Bellah, R., R. Madsen, W.M. Sullivan, A. Swidler, and S. M. Tipton. 1985. Habits of the Heart. Berkeley: University of California Press.
59. Bellotti, V., S. Buckingham Shum, A. MacLean, and N. Hammond. 1995. Multidisciplinary Modeling in HCI Design. In Proceedings of CHI'95 ACM Conference on Human Factors in Computing. Boulder: ACM P.
60. Berkenkotter, C., and T. N. Huckin. 1995. Genre Knowledge in Disciplinary Communication: Cognition/Culture/Power. Hillsdale NJ: Lawrence Erlbaum.
61. Berlin, J. A. 1993. Poststructuralism, Semiotics, and Social-Epistemic Rhetoric: Converging Agendas. In Defining the New Rhetoric, ed. T. Enos and S. C. Brown. Newbury Park NJ: Sage Publications.
62. ———. 1996. Rhetorics, Poetics, and Cultures. Urbana IL: NCTE.
63. Bevan, N. 1998. Usability Issues in Website Design. In Proceedings of Usability Professionals' Association (UPA). Bloomington IL: UPA.
64. Birkerts, S. 1994. The Gutenberg Elegies: The Fate of Reading in an Electronic Age. New York: Fawcett Columbine.
65. Blakeslee, A. 2001. Bridging the Workplace and the Academy: Teaching Professional Genres Through Classroom-Workplace Collaboration. Technical Communication Quarterly 10:169–92.
66. Blomberg, J., S. Suchman, and R. Trigg. 1996. A Work-Oriented Design Project. HumanComputer Interaction 11:237–65.
67. Bloomberg News. 2001. Sharp to Challenge Palm, Pocket PC with Linux PDA. http://news.cnet.com/news/0-1006-200-5023907.html.
68. Blyler, N. 1993. Theory and Curriculum: Reexamining the Curricular Separation of Business and Technical Communication. Journal of Business and Technical Communication 7:218–45.
69. Blyler, N., and C. Thralls. 1993. Professional Communication: The Social Perspective. Newbury Park CA: Sage. Blythe, S. 2001. Designing

Online Courses: User-Centered Practices. Computers and Composition 16:329–46.
70. Boal, A. 1968. Theatre of the Oppressed. Trans. C. A. McBride and M. L. McBride. New York: Theatre Communications Group.
71. ———. 1997. Games for Actors and Non-Actors. Trans. A. Jackson. London: Routledge.
72. Boiarsky, C., and M. Dobberstein. 1998. Teaching Documentation Writing: What Else Students—and Instructors—Should Know. Technical Communication 45:38–46.
73. Bolter, J. D., and R. Grusin. 1999. Remediation. Cambridge: MIT Press. Bosley, D. 1995. Collaborative Partnerships: Academia and Industry Working Together. Technical Communication 4:611–19.
74. Boyer, E. 1981. Higher Learning in the Nation's Service. Washington, D.C.: Carnegie Foundation for the Advancement of Teaching.
75. ———. 1990. Scholarship Reconsidered. Princeton: Carnegie Foundation for the Advancement of Teaching.
76. ———. 1997. Scholarship Reconsidered: Priorities of the Professoriate. Pittsburgh: Carnegie Foundation.
77. Boyte, H. 1993. What is Citizenship Education? Rethinking Tradition: Integrating Service with Academic Study on College Campuses. Denver: Education Commission of the States.
78. Brake, T., D. M. Walker, and T. Walker. 1995. Doing Business Internationally: The Guide to Cross-Cultural Success. New York: Irwin.
79. Brandt, D. 1995. Accumulating Literacy: Writing and Learning to Write in the Twentieth Century. College English 57:649–68.
80. Brecht, B. 1968. Kleines Organon f,r das Theater. Gesammelte Werke Schriften zum Theater vol.16:2. Frankfurt A. M.: Suhrkamp
81. Bridgeford, T. 2002. Narrative Ways of Knowing: Re-imagining Technical Communication Instruction. Ph.D. diss., Michigan Technological University.
82. Bringle, R. G., R. Games, and E. A. Malloy. 1999. Colleges and Universities as Citizens: Reflections. Boston: Allyn and Bacon.
83. Bringle, R. G., and J. A. Hatcher. 1996. Implementing Service Learning in Higher Education. Journal of Higher Education 67:221–39.
84. Britton, J., et al. 1975. The Development of Writing Abilities (11–18). London: Macmillan.
85. Brooks, R. M. 1995. Technical Communication and Service Learning:

Integrating Profession and Community. In 1995 Proceedings of the Council of Programs in Technical and Scientific Communication, ed. M. M. Cooper. Houghton MI: Council for Programs in Technical and Scientific Communication.

86. Bruce, B., and A. Rubin. 1993. Electronic Quills: A Situated Evaluation of Using Computers for Writing Classrooms. Hillsdale NJ: Lawrence Erlbaum. Bruffee, K. 1986. Social Construction, Language, and the Authority of Knowledge: A Bibliographic Essay. College English 48:773–90.

87. Bruner, J. 1991. The Narrative Construction of Reality. Critical Inquiry 18:1–21.

88. ———. 1990. Acts of Meaning. Cambridge: Harvard University Press.

89. Burnett, R. E. 1993. Conflict in Collaborative Decision-Making. In Professional Communication: The Social Perspective, ed. N. Blyler and C. Thralls. Newbury Park CA: Sage.

90. ———. 1994. Technical Communication. Belmont CA: Wadsworth.

91. ———. 1997. Technical Communication. 4th ed. Belmont CA: Wadsworth.

92. Bush-Bacelis, J. L. 1998. Innovative Pedagogy: Academic Service-Learning for Business Communication. Business Communication Quarterly 61:20–34.

93. Campbell, K. 1999. Collecting Information: Qualitative Research Methods for Solving Workplace Problems. Technical Communication 46:532–45.

94. Cates-Melver, L. 1999. Internships and Co-op Programs: A Valuable Combination for Collegians. Black Collegian 20:85–87.

95. Cha, S., and M. Rothman. 1994. Service Matters. Providence: Brown University

96. Charney, D. H., and R. Rayman. 1989. The Role of Writing Quality in Effective Student resumes. Journal of Business and Technical Communication 3:36–53.

97. Chickering, A. W., and S. C. Ehrmann. 1998. Implementing the Seven Principles: Technology as Lever. American Association for Higher Education. Available online at http://www.aahe.org/tech-nology/ehrmann.html.

98. Chickering, A. W., and Z. F. Gamson. 1987. Seven Principles for Good Practice in Undergraduate Education. AAHE Bulletin 39:3–7.

99. Cilenger, E. N. 1992. Controlling Technology Through Communication:

Redefining the Role of the Technical Communicator. Technical Communication 39:166–74.

100. Clark, G. 1990. Dialogue, Dialectic, and Conversation: A Social Perspective on the Function of Writing. Carbondale IL: Southern Illinois University Press.

101. Clemens, L. 1999. Preparing Technical Communication Ph.D. Students to Teach at a Distance: Guidelines and Principles. Master's thesis, University of Minnesota.

102. Cohen, A., and F. Brawer. 1989. The American Community College. 2nd ed. San Francisco: Jossey-Bass.

103. Cohen, J., and D. Kinsey. 1994. Doing Good and Scholarship: A Service-Learning Study. Journalism and Mass Communication Educator (winter: 4–14).

104. Coney, M. B. 1997. Technical Communication Theory: An Overview. In Foundations for Teaching Technical Communication: Theory, Practice, and Program Design, ed. K. Staples and C. Ornatowski. Greenwich CT: Ablex.

105. Cooper, A. 1999. The Inmates are Running the Asylum: Why High Tech Products Drive Us Crazy and How To Restore the Sanity. Indianapolis: SAMS.

106. Cooper, M. M. 1996. The Postmodern Space of Operator's Manuals. Technical Communication Quarterly 5, no. 4 (fall): 385–410.

107. Coppola, J. F., and B. A. Thomas. 2000. A Model for E-Classroom Design Beyond "Chalk And Talk." T.H.E. Journal 27:30–36.

108. Couture, B. 1998. Toward a Phenomenological Rhetoric: Writing, Profession, and Altruism. Carbondale. Ill.:Southern Illinois University Press.

109. Crawford, K. 1993. Community Service Writing in an Advanced Composition Class. In Praxis I: A Faculty Casebook on Community Service Learning, ed. J. Howard. Ann Arbor: OCSL Press.

110. Cushman, E. 1996. The Rhetorician as Agent of Social Change. College Composition and Communication 47:7–28.

111. David, C., and D. Kienzler. 1999. Towards an Emancipatory Pedagogy in Service Courses and User Departments. Technical Communication Quarterly 8:269–84.

112. Deal, T., and A. Kennedy. 1982. Corporate Culture: The Rites and Rituals of Corporate Life. Menlo Park CA: Addison-Wesley.

113. De Certeau, M. 1984. The Practice of Everyday Life. Trans. S. Rendall.

Berkeley: University of California Press. Denning, P. 1992. Educating a New Engineer. Communications of the ACM 35:83–97.

114. Dicks, R.S. 1999. Technical Communication in Academia and Industry: The Cultural Gaps That Prevent Understanding. Paper presented at the second annual meeting of the Association of Teachers of Technical Writing, Atlanta, Ga.

115. Dicks, R. S., and B. Mehlenbacher. 1999. Usability Testing "Ask NC State." Summary Report for North Carolina State Extension, Research, and Outreach Project, October 15–June 30. Raleigh, N.C.: North Carolina State, October 15-June 30.

116. Dobrin, D. N. 1989. Writing and Technique. Urbana IL: NCTE.

117. Donnell, J. A., J. Petraglia-Bahri, and A. C. Gable. 1999. Writing Vs. Content, Skills Vs. Rhetoric: More and Less False Dichotomies. Journal of Language and Learning across the Disciplines 3:113–17.

118. Dragga, S. 2001, summer. Ethics in Technical Communication, special issue. Vol. 10, #3

119. Dubinsky, J. 1998. Learning the Möbius Loop of Theory and Practice: Reflections on the Techné of Teaching Writing. Ph.D. diss., University Of Ohio. Oxford, Ohio.

120. ———. 2002. Service-Learning as a Path to Virtue: The Ideal Orator in Professional Communication. Michigan Journal of Community Service Learning 8.2(2002):61–74.

121. Duin, A. H., L. Baer., and D. Starke-Meyerring. 2001. Partnering in the Learning Marketspace. San Francisco: Jossey-Bass. Durst, R. 1999. Collision Course. Urbana IL: NCTE.

122. Eastman, D. V. 1998. Adult Learners and Internet-Based Distance Education. In Adult Learning and the Internet, ed. B. Cahoon. San Francisco: Jossey-Bass.

123. Ecker, P. S., and K. Staples. 1997. Collaborative Conflict and the Future: AcademicIndustrial Alliances and Adaptations. In Nonacademic Writing: Social Theory and Technology, ed. A. H. Duin and C. Hansen. Mahwah NJ: Lawrence Erlbaum.

124. Ede, L. 1984. Audience: An Introduction to Research. College Composition and Communication 35:140–54.

125. Ede, L., and A. Lunsford. 1984. Audience Addressed/Audience Invoked: The Role of Audience in Composition Theory and Pedagogy. College Composition and Communication 35:155–71.

126. Ellsworth, N. J., C. N. Hedley, and A. N. Barbatta, eds. 1994. Literacy: A

Redefinition. Hillsdale NJ: Lawrence Erlbaum.

127. Emig, J. 1971. The Writing Process of Twelfth Graders. Urbana IL: NCTE. English, D., and D. Koeppen. 1993. The Relationship of Accounting Internships and Subsequent Academic Performance. Issues in Accounting Education 8:292–300.

128. Faber, B. 1999. Intuitive Ethics: Understanding and Critiquing the Role of Intuition in Ethical Decisions. Technical Communication Quarterly 8:189–203.

129. Faigley, L., R. Cherry, D. Joliffe, and A. M. Skinner. 1985. Assessing Writers' Knowledge and Processes of Composing. Norwood NJ: Ablex.

130. Fearing, B. E. and W. K. Sparrow. 1989. Technical Writing: Theory and Practice. New York: MLA.

131. Flower, L. 1997. Partners in Inquiry: A Logic for Community Outreach. In Writing the Community: Concepts and Models for Service-Learning in Composition, ed. L. Adler-Kasner, R. Crooks, and A. Watters. Washington DC: AAHE/NCTE.

132. Flynn, E. 1997. Emergent Feminist Technical Communication. Technical Communication Quarterly 6:313–20.

133. Flynn, E. A., R. W. Jones, D. Shoos, and B. Barna. 1990. Michigan Technological University. In Programs that Work: Models and Methods for Writing across the Curriculum, ed. T. Fulwiler and A. Young. Portsmouth NH: Boynton/Cook Heinemann.

134. Forman, J. 1993. Business Communication and Composition: The Writing Connection and Beyond. Journal of Business Communication 30:333–52.

135. Foucault, M. 1977a. The Order of Discourse. Trans. I. McLeod. In The Rhetorical Tradition, ed. P. Bizzell and B. Herzberg. Boston: Bedford Books.

136. ———. 1977b. Truth and Power. In The Foucault Reader, ed. P. Rabinow. New York: Pantheon Books. Fulop, M. P., and N. N. Varzandeh. 1996. The Role of Computer-Based Resources in Health Promotion and Disease Prevention: Implications for College Health. Journal of American College Health 45:11–17.

137. Fulwiler, T. 1991. The Quiet and Insistent Revolution: Writing across the Curriculum. In The Politics of Writing Instruction: Postsecondary, ed. R. Bullock and J. Trimbur. Portsmouth NH: Boynton/Cook Publishers.

138. Garay, M. S., and S. A. Bernhardt. 1998. Expanding Literacies: English Teaching and the New Workplace. New York: SUNY. Gazzaniga, M.

1998. How to Change the University. Science 282:237.

139. Gee, J. P., G. Hull, and C. Lankshear. 1996. The New Work Order: Behind the Language of the New Capitalism. Boulder CO: Westview Press. Gehrke, R. 2002. Hispanic School-Age Population Fastest-Growing, Report Says. El Paso Times, June 20, 4A.

140. George, D., and D. Shoos. 1992. Issues of Subjectivity and Resistance: Cultural Studies in the Composition Classroom. In Cultural Studies in the English Classroom, ed. J. A. Berlin and M. J. Vivion. Portsmouth NH: Boynton/Cook Heinemann.

141. Gilchrist, C. 1997. Faculty Attitudes and Perceptions Toward Using Interactive Television: A Case Study. Ph.D. diss., University of Minnesota, Twin Cities.

142. Giles, D.E., Honnet, E. Porter, and S. Migliore. 1991. Research Agenda for Combining Service and Learning in the 1990s. Raleigh NC: National Society for Internships and Experiential Education.

143. Gilsdorf, J., and D. Leonard. 2001. Big Stuff, Little Stuff: A Decennial Measurement of Executives' and Academics' Reactions to Questionable Usage Elements. The Journal of Business Communication 38:439–75.

144. Goodlad, J. I., and P. Keating, eds. 1994. Access to Knowledge: The Continuing Agenda for Our Nations' Schools. New York: College Entrance Examination Board.

145. Grabill, J. T. 2000. Shaping Local HIV/AIDS Services Policy Through Activist Research: The Problem of Client Involvement. Technical Communication Quarterly 9:29–50.

146. Grice, R. 1987. Technical Communication in the Computer Industry: An Information- Development Process to Track, Measure, and Ensure Quality. Ph.D. diss., Rensselaer Polytechnic Institute.

147. Halloran, S. M. 1978. Technical Communication and the Rhetoric of Science. Journal of Technical Writing and Communication 8:77–88.

148. Hanna, D. E. and Associates. 2000. Higher Education in an Era of Digital Competition: Choices and Challenges. Madison, Wisc.: Atwood Publishing.

149. Hansen, C. 1995. Writing the Project Team: Authority and Intertextuality in a Corporate Setting. Journal of Business Communication 32:103–23.

150. Harris, E. 1980. Response to Elizabeth Tebeaux. College English 41:827–29.

151. ———. 1982. In Defense of the Liberal-Arts Approach to Technical Writing. College English 44, no. 6:628–36.

152. Hartung, K. K. 1998. What Are Students Being Taught about the Ethics of Technical Communication?: An Analysis of the Ethical Discussions Presented in Four Textbooks. Journal of Technical Writing and Communication 28:363–83.

153. Haussamen, B. 1997. Service-Learning and First-year Composition. Teaching in the Two Year College: 24, no. 3:192–98.

154. Hawisher, G., and C. L. Selfe, eds. 1999. Passions, Pedagogies, and Twenty-First Century Technologies. Urbana: NCTE.

155. Hayhoe, G. F. 1998. The Academe-Industry Partnership: What's in It for All of Us? Technical Communication 45, no. 1:19–20.

156. Head, A. J. 1999. Design Wise: A Guide for Evaluating the Interface Design of Information Resources. Medford NJ: Cyberage Books.

157. Henson, L., and K. Sutliff. 1998. A Service Learning Approach to Business and Technical Writing Instruction. Journal of Technical Writing and Communication 28:189–205.

158. Herndl, C. 1991. Writing Ethnography: Representation, Rhetoric, and Institutional Practices. College English 53:320–32.

159. ———. 1993a. Cultural Studies and Critical Science. In Understanding Scientific Prose, ed. J. Selzer. Madison WI: University of Wisconsin Press.

160. ———. 1993b. Teaching Discourse and Reproducing Culture: A Critique of Research and Pedagogy in Professional and Non-Academic Writing. College Composition and Communication 44:349–63.

161. ———. 1996a. Tactics and the Quotidian: Resistance and Professional Discourse. Journal of Advanced Composition 16:455–70.

162. ———. 1996b. The Transformation of Critical Ethnography into Pedagogy, or the Vicissitudes of Traveling Theory. In Nonacademic Writing: Social Theory and Technology, ed. A. Duin and C. Hansen. Mahweh NJ: Lawrence Erlbaum.

163. Herzberg, B. 1994. Community Service and Critical Teaching. College Composition and Communication 45:307–19.

164. Hogan, Harriet. 1983. Distinguishing Characteristics of the Technical Writing Course. In Technical and Business Communication in Two-Year Programs, ed. K. W. Sparrow and N. A. Pickett. Urbana IL: NCTE.

165. Holland, V. M., V. R. Charrow, and W. W. Wright. 1988. How Can Technical Writers Write Effectively for Several Audiences at Once? In Solving Problems in Technical Writing, ed. L. Beene and P. White. New York: Oxford University Press.

166. Honebein, P., T. M. Duffy, and B. Fishman. 1993. Constructivism and the Design of Learning Environments: Context and Authentic Activities for Learning. In Designing Environments for Constructivist Learning, ed. T. M. Duffy, J. Lowyck, and D. Jonassen.

167. Heidelberg: Springer-Verlag. Huckin, T. 1997. Technical Writing and Community Service. Journal of Business and Technical Communication 11:49–60.

168. Hudson, L. P. 1984. The Bones of Plenty. St. Paul MN: Minnesota Historical Society Press.

169. Huizinga, J. 1990. The Nature of Play. In Philosophic Inquiry in Sport, pp. 3-6. International Society for Technology in Education. 2000. National Education Technology Standards for Students: Connecting Curriculum and Technology. Eugene, Ore.

170. Johnson, D. W., and R. Johnson. 1998. Cooperation and Competition: Theory and Research. Englewood Cliffs NJ: Prentice Hall.

171. Johnson, R. R. 1998a. Complicating Technology: Interdisciplinary Method, the Burden of Comprehension, and the Ethical Space of the Technical Communicator. Technical Communication Quarterly 7:75–98.

172. ———. 1998b. User-Centered Technology: A Rhetorical Theory for Computers and Other Mundane Artifacts. Albany: SUNY Press.

173. ———. 1999. Johnson Responds. Technical Communication Quarterly 8:223–26.

174. Johnson-Eilola, J. 1996. Relocating the Value of Work: Technical Communication in a PostIndustrial Age. Technical Communication Quarterly 5:245–71.

175. ———. 1997. Wild Technologies: Computer Use and Social Possibility. In Computers and Technical Communication: Pedagogical and Programmatic Perspectives, ed. S. A. Selber. Greenwich CT: Ablex. Jorn, L., A. H. Duin, and B. J. Wahlstrom. 1996. Designing and Managing Virtual Learning Communities. IEEE Transactions on Professional Communication 39:183–91.

176. Kaasbøll, J. J. 1998. Teaching Critical Thinking and Problem Defining Skills. Education and Information Technologies 3:101–17.

177. Kahne, J., and J. Westheimer. 1996. In Service of What? The Politics of Service Learning. Phi Delta Kappan 77:593–600.

178. Kalmbach, J. 1997. From Liquid Paper to the Typewriter: Some Historical Perspectives on Technology in the Classroom. Computers and Composition 13:57–68.

179. Kantrowitz, B., and A. Rogers. 1994. The Birth of the Internet. Newsweek, August 8, 56–58.
180. Karis, B. 1997. Building Relationships to Garner Technological Resources and Support in Technical Communication Programs. In Computers and Technical Communication: Pedagogical and Programmatic Perspectives, ed. S. A. Selber. Greenwich CT: Ablex.
181. Karis, W. M. 1989. Using Literature to Focus Attention: Rhetorical Models and Case Studies. The Technical Writing Teacher 16:187–94.
182. Karras, T. 1999. The Mammogram Screening Controversy: When Should You Start? http://www.cnn.com/HEALTH/women/9909/27/bcam.mammography/.
183. Kastman Breuch, L. 2001. The Overruled Dust Mite: Preparing Students to Interact with Clients. Technical Communication Quarterly 10:193–210.
184. Katz, S. 1992. The Ethics of Expediency: Classical Rhetoric, Technology, and the Holocaust. College English 54:255–75.
185. Keene, M. L. 1997. Education in Scientific and Technical Communication: Academic Programs that Work. Arlington, Va.: Society for Technical Communication.
186. Kendall, J. C. 1990. Combining Service and Learning: An Introduction. In Combining Service and Learning: A Resource Book for Community and Public Service, ed. J. C. Kendall and Associates. Raleigh NC: NSEE.
187. Kienzler, D. 2001. Ethics, Critical Thinking, and Professional Communication Pedagogy. Technical Communication Quarterly 10:319–40.
188. Kilgore, D. 1981. Moby-Dick: A Whale of a Handbook for Technical Writing Teachers. Journal of Technical Writing and Communication 11:209–16.
189. Killingsworth, M. J. 1997. Developing Programs in Technical Communication: A Pragmatic View. In Foundations for Technical Communication: Theory, Practice, and Program Design, ed. K. Staples and C. Ornatowski. Greenwich CT: Ablex.
190. Killingsworth, M. J., and J. S. Palmer. 1999. Information in Action. 2nd ed. Boston: Allyn and Bacon. Kim, L. And M. J. Albers. 2002, August. "Web Design Issues When Searching for Information Using Handheld Interfaces". Technical Communication. Vol. 49, no. 3.
191. Kitalong, K. S., D. Selfe, and M. Moore. Forthcoming. Technology Autobiographies and Student Participation in English Studies Literacy

Classes. Teaching/Writing in the Late Age of Print, ed. J. R. Galin, C. P. Haviland, and J. P. Johnson.

192. Kresskill NJ: Hampton Press. Knouse, S., J. Tanner, and E. Harris. 1999. The Relation of College Internships, College Performance, and Subsequent Job Opportunity. Journal of Employment Counseling 36:35–44.

193. Knox, E. L. 1997. The Pedagogy of Web Site Design. ALN Magazine vol.1, no. 2. http://www.aln.org/alnWeb/magazine/issue2/know.htm.

194. Kolb, D. A. 1984. Experiential Learning: Experience as the Source of Learning and Development. Englewood Cliffs NJ: Prentice Hall.

195. Koschmann, T., A. C. Kelson, P. J. Feltovich, and H. S. Barrows. 1996. Computer-Supported Problem-Based Learning: A Principled Approach to the Use of Computers in Collaborative Learning. In CSCL: Theory and Practice of an Emerging Paradigm, ed. T.

196. Koschmann. Mahwah NJ: Lawrence Erlbaum. Koski, C. A. 1997. Down the Rabbit-Hole: Exploring Health Messages on the World Wide Web. Journal of Technical Writing and Communication 27:49–55.

197. Krause, T. 1997. Preparing an Online resume. Business Communication Quarterly 60:159–61.

198. Kretzmann, J. P., and J. L. McKnight. 1993. Building Communities from the Inside Out: A Path Toward Finding and Mobilizing a Community's Assets. Chicago: ACTA Publications.

199. Kryder, L. 1999. Mentors, Models, and Clients: Using the Professional Engineering Community to Identify and Teach Engineering Genres. IEEE Transactions on Professional Communication 42:3–12.

200. Kunin, M. 1997. Service Learning and Improved Academic Achievement. Service Learning, ed. J. Schine. Chicago: NSSE.

201. Kynell, T. 1996. Writing in a Milieu of Utility. Norwood NJ: Ablex. Landauer, T. K. 1995. The Trouble with Computers: Usefulness, Usability, and Productivity. Cambridge: MIT Press. Lanham, R. 1983. One, Two, Three. Composition and Literature, ed. W. Horner. Chicago: University of Chicago Press.

202. Latour, B. 1993. We Have Never Been Modern. Trans. C. Porter. Cambridge: Harvard University Press. Laurillard, D. 2002. Rethinking Teaching for the Knowledge Society. Educause 37:16–25.

203. Lay, M. M., B. J. Wahlstrom, S. Doheny-Farina, A. H. Duin, S. B. Little, C. D. Rude, C. L. Selfe, and J. Seltzer. 1995. Technical Communication. Chicago: Irwin. Lee, Y. S. 1998. University-Industry Collaboration on

Technology Transfer: Views from the Ivory Tower. Policy Studies Journal 26:68.

204. Leigh, J. W. 1998. Communicating for Cultural Competence. Boston: Allyn and Bacon. Lerner, I. J., and B. J. Kennedy. 1992. The Prevalence of Questionable Methods of Cancer Treatment in the United States. CA-A Cancer Journal 42:181–91.

205. Levy, S. 1984. Hackers. New York: Dell. Longo, B. 1998. An Approach for Applying Cultural Study Theory to Technical Writing Research. Technical Communication Quarterly 7:53–73.

206. Lutz, J., and M. Fuller. 1998. The Cure From Within: The Rhetoric of Alternative Medicines. Paper presented at the Conference on College Composition and Communication, April.

207. Lynch, D. A. 1997. Email in an Interdisciplinary Context. In Electronic Communication across the Curriculum, ed. D. Reiss, D. Selfe, and A. Young. Urbana IL: NCTE.

208. Mansfield, M. A. 1993. Real World Writing and the English Curriculum. College Composition and Communication 44:69–83.

209. Marchionini, G., and C. Hert. 1997. Usability Testing Large Institutional Websites. Usability Testing World Wide Web Sites: Position Papers From a Two-Day Workshop at CHI 97. March 23–24 in Atlanta, Ga.. Available online at http://www.acm.org/sigchi/webhci/ chi97/testing/marchion.htm.

210. Markel, M. 1997. Ethics and Technical Communication: A Case for Foundational Approaches. IEEE Transactions on Professional Communication 40:84–99.

211. ———. 1999. Journal of Business and Technical Communication 13:208–22.

212. Markus, G. B., J. P. F. Howard, and D. C. King. 1993. Integrating Community Service and Classroom Instruction Enhances Learning: Results from an Experiment. Educational Evaluation and Policy Analysis 15:410–19.

213. Martin, W. B. 1977. Teaching, Research, and Service—But the Greatest of These is Service. Redefining Service, Research, and Teaching, ed. W. B.

214. Martin. San Francisco: Jossey-Bass. Matthews, C., and B. B. Zimmerman. 1999. Integrating Service Learning and Technical Communication: Benefits and Challenges. Technical Communication Quarterly 8:383-404.

215. Mauriello, N., G. S. Pagnucci, and T. Winner. 1999. Reading between the Code: The Teaching of HTML and the Displacement of Writing Instruction. Computers and Composition 16:409–19.
216. Mawby, R. G. 1996. The Challenge for Outreach for Land-Grant Universities as They Move into the Twenty-First Century. Journal of Public Service and Outreach 1:46–56.
217. McCafferty, D. 2002. Dude, What's in Your Car? USA Weekend 26:6–7. McCormack, C., and D. Jones. 1998. Building a Web-Based Education System. New York: Wiley. McCune, J.C. 2000. Training Drain. Management Review, March 30. Available online at http://web7.infotrac.galegroup.com.
218. McDowell, E. E. 1987. Perceptions of the Ideal Cover Letter and Ideal Resume. Journal of Technical Writing and Communication 17:179–91.
219. McEachern, R. 2001. Problems in Service Learning and Technical/Professional Writing: Incorporating the Perspective of Nonprofit Management. Technical Communication Quarterly 10:210–24.
220. McKnight, J. 1995. The Careless Society: Community and Its Counterfeits. New York: Basic Books. Mead, M. 1970. Culture and Commitment: A Study of the Generation Gap. Garden City NY: Natural History Press/Doubleday.
221. Mehlenbacher, B. 1997. Technologies and Tensions: Designing Online Environments for Teaching Technical Communication. In Computers and Technical Communication: Pedagogical and Programmatic Perspectives, ed. S. A. Selber. Greenwich CT: Ablex. Meister, J. C. 2000. Savvy Learners Drive Revolution in Education: The Case for Corporate Universities. Financial Times (London), April 24, 2000. Available online at http://web.lexis-nexis.com/universe.
222. ———. 2001. The Brave New World of Corporate Education. Chronicle of Higher Education, February 9, B10–11.
223. Mellander, G., and N. Mellander. 1998. Corporate America: Inroads Realizing the Dream; Corporate Internships Benefit Thousands. Hispanic Outlook in Higher Education 8:19.
224. Meyer, P. R., and S. A. Bernhardt. 1998. Workplace Realities and the Technical Communication Curriculum: A Call for Change. In Foundations for Teaching Technical Communication: Theory, Practice, and Program Design, ed. K. Staples and C. Ornatowski. Greenwich CT: Ablex.
225. Michaels, A. 2000. Companies Get Hit by the Learning Bug: The Growth in the Number of Corporate Universities Reflects a Sea of Change in the Training of Executives and Employees. The Financial Times (London),

April 24, 2000. Available online at http://web.lexis-nexis.com/universe.
226. Miller, C. R. 1979. A Humanistic Rationale for Technical Writing. College English 40:610–17.
227. ———. 1984. Genre as Social Action. Quarterly Journal of Speech 70:151–67.
228. ———. 1989. What's Practical about Technical Writing. In Technical Writing: Theory and Practice, ed. B. E. Fearing and W. K. Sparrow. New York: MLA.
229. ———. 1996. Comments on "Instrumental Discourse Is As Humanistic As Rhetoric." Journal of Business and Technical Communication 10:482–86.
230. Miller, G. 1996, Oct. 7. Gap exists between net awareness and use. Los Angeles Times, online at http://www.latimes.com MIRA (Managing Information with Rural America). 2002. Project Scrapbook, May 31. Available online at http://mira.wkkf.org/about.htm.
231. Mirel, B. 1993. Beyond the Monkey House: Audience Analyses in Computerized Workplaces. In Writing in the Workplace: New Research Perspectives, ed. R. Spilka. Carbondale and Edwardsville, IL: Southern Illinois University Press.
232. ———. 1998. "Applied Constructivism" for User Documentation: Alternatives to Conventional Task Orientation. Journal of Business and Technical Communication 12:7–49.
233. Mirel, B., and R. Spilka. 2002. Reshaping Technical Communication: New Directions and Challenges for the Twenty-First Century. Mahwah NJ: Lawrence Erlbaum.
234. MLA Commission on Professional Service. 1996. Making Faculty Work Visible: Reinterpreting Professional Service, Teaching, and Research in the Fields of Language and Literature. Profession, 161–216.
235. Moffett, J. 1968. Teaching the Universe of Discourse. Boston: Houghton. Moore, P. 1996. Instrumental Discourse Is As Humanistic As Rhetoric. Journal of Business and Technical Communication 10:100–118.
236. ———. 1999. Myths about Instrumental Discourse: A Response to Robert R. Johnson. Technical Communication Quarterly 8:210–26.
237. Moran, M. H., and M. G. Moran. 1985. Business Letters, Memoranda, and Resumes. In Research in Technical Communication, ed. M. Moran and D. Journet. Westport, CT: Greenwood.
238. Moulthrop, S. 1999. Everybody's Elegies. In Passions, Pedagogies and Twenty-First Century Technologies, ed. G. Hawisher and C. Selfe,

Urbana IL: NCTE.

239. Mowbray, N. 2000. The Rhetoric of Acupuncture. Master's thesis, James Madison University, Harrisonburg, Virginia.

240. Murray, D. 1972. Teach Writing as a Process Not Product. The Leaflet: 11–14. Myers, G. 1990. The Double Helix as Icon. Science as Culture 9:49–72.

241. NCTE and the International Reading Association. 1996. Standards for the English Language Arts. Urbana IL: NCTE

242. Nagelhout, E. 1999. Pre-Professional Practices in the Technical Writing Classroom: Promoting Multiple Literacies through Research. Technical Communication Quarterly 8:285–300.

243. National Cancer Institute. 2000. Available online at http://cancernet.nci.nih.gov.

244. Neff, J. M. 1998. From a Distance: Teaching Writing on Interactive Television. Research in the Teaching of English 3:136–57.

245. Nelkin, D. 1995. The Press on the Technological Frontier. In Selling Science: How the Press Covers Science and Technology. New York: W. H. Freeman.

246. Nemnich, M. B., and F. E. Jandt. 1999. Cyberspace Resume Kit. Indianapolis: JIST.

247. Newman, F. 1985. Higher Education and the American Resurgence. Princeton NJ: Carnegie Foundation for the Advancement of Teaching. Nielsen, J. 1994. Heuristic Evaluation. In Usability Inspection Methods, ed. J. Nielsen and R. L. Mack. New York: John Wiley and Sons.

248. ———. 1997. Usability Engineering. In The Computer Science and Engineering Handbook, ed. A. B. Tucker, Jr. Boca Raton FL: CRC Press. Noble, D. F. 1997. Digital Diploma Mills: The Automation of Higher Education. New York: Monthly Review Press. Norman, D. 1990. The Design of Everyday Things. New York: Doubleday.

249. ———. 1994. Things That Make Us Smart: Defending Human Attributes in the Age of the Machine. Cambridge MA: Perseus Publishing.

250. Øgrim, L. 1991. Project Work in System Development Education. In Information System, Work, and Organization Design, ed. P. van den Besselaar, A. Clement, and P. Jårvinen. Amsterdam: North-Holland.

251. Ormiston, G. L., ed. 1990. From Artifact to Habitat: Studies in the Critical Engagement of Technology. Bethlehem PA: Lehigh University Press.

252. Ornatowski, C. M. 1997. Technical Communication and Rhetoric. In Foundations for Teaching Technical Communication, ed. K. Staples and

C. Ornatowski. Greenwich CT: Ablex.

253. Parker-Gwin, R., and J. B. Mabry. 1998. Service Learning as Pedagogy and Civic Education: Comparing Outcomes for Three Models. Teaching Sociology 26:276–91.

254. Perelman, S. J. 1976. Insert Flap "A" and Throw Away. In Humor in America: An Anthology, ed. E. Veron. San Diego: Harcourt Brace Jovanovich. Pew Higher Education Roundtable. 1994. To Dance with Change. Policy Perspectives 5:1A–12A.

255. Phelps, L. W. 1991. Practical Wisdom and the Geography of Knowledge in Composition. College English 53:863–85.

256. Phillips, G. W., and L. Metzler. 1991. The Corporate-Academic Relationship: Risks and Returns. Fund Raising Management 22:26–30. Pirsig, R. M. 1974.

257. Zen and the Art of Motorcycle Maintenance. New York: Bantam.

258. Plauche, C. 2000. The J.M. Smucker Company Named to Fortune's List of "100 Best Companies to Work For" For Third Year in a Row. Available online at www.smucker.com/news_fortune.html.

259. Popken, R. 1999. The Pedagogical Dissemination of a Genre: The resume in American Business Discourse Textbooks, 1914–1939.

260. Journal of Advanced Composition 19:91–116.

261. Porter, J. E., and P. Sullivan. 1996. Working across Methodological Interfaces: The Study of Computers and Writing in the Workplace. In Electronic Literacies in the Workplace: Technologies of Writing, ed. P. Sullivan and J. Dautermann. Urbana IL and Houghton MI: NCTE/Computers and Composition. Porter, L. 1997. Creating the Virtual Classroom: Distance Learning with the Internet. New York: Wiley.

262. Powers, D. R., M. F. Powers, F. Betz, and C. B. Aslanian. 1998. Higher Education in Partnership with Industry: Opportunities and Strategies for Training, Research, and Economic Development. San Francisco: Jossey-Bass. Press, E., and J. Washburn. 2000. The Kept University. The Atlantic Monthly 285:39–54.

263. Quibble, Z. K. 1995. Electronic resumes: Their Time Is Coming. Business Communication Quarterly 58:5–9.

264. Redish, J. C. 1988. Reading to Learn to Do. The Technical Writing Teacher 15, no. 3(fall): 223–33. Reprinted in IEEE Transactions on Professional Communication 32, no. 4(December): 289–93.

265. ———. 1993. Understanding Readers. In Techniques for Technical Communicators, ed. C. M. Barnum and S. Carliner. Needham Heights

MA: Allyn and Bacon.

266. ———. 1997. Understanding People: The Relevance of Cognitive Psychology to Technical Communication. In Foundations for Teaching Technical Communication: Theory, Practice, and Program Design, ed. K. Staples and C. Ornatowski. Greenwich CT: Ablex. Rehling, L. 1998. Exchanging Expertise: Learning from the Workplace and Educating It Too. Journal of Writing and Technical Communication 28:385–93.

267. Rendon, L. I. 1994. Validating Culturally Diverse Students: Toward a New Model of Learning and Student Development. Innovative Higher Education 19:33–51.

268. Reynolds, J. F., C. B. Matalene, J. N. Magnotto, D. C. Samson, and L.V. Sadler. 1995. Professional Writing in Context: Lessons from Teaching and Consulting in Worlds of Work. Hillsdale NJ: Lawrence Erlbaum.

269. Rogoff, B. 1990. Apprenticeship in Thinking: Cognitive Development in Social Context. NY, NY: Oxford University Press. Ronald, K. 1987. The Politics of Teaching Professional Writing. Journal of Advanced Composition 7:23–30.

270. Rooney, A. 1997. Warning: Do Not Put This Column in Water. Daily Mining Gazette, July 26, 4A. Rubin, J. 1994. Handbook of Usability Testing: How to Plan, Design, and Conduct Effective Tests. New York: John Wiley and Sons.

271. Russell, D. R. 1991. Writing in the Academic Disciplines, 1870–1990.

272. Carbondale and Edwardsville IL: Southern Illinois University Press. Samovar, L. S., and R. E. Porter. 1988. Intercultural Communication: A Reader. Belmont CA: Wadsworth. Samuelson, R. J. 2002. Debunking the Digital Divide. Newsweek, March 25, 37.

273. Sanders, S. R. 1985. Terrarium. Bloomington and Indianapolis: Indiana University Press.

274. Savery, J. R. 1998. Fostering Ownership for Learning With Computer-Supported Collaborative Writing in an Undergraduate Business Communication Course. In Electronic Collaborators: Learner-Centered Technologies for Literacy, Apprenticeship, and Discourse, ed. C. J. Bonk and K. S. King. Mahwah NJ: Lawrence Erlbaum.

275. Sawicki, D. S., and W. Craig. 1996. The Democratization of Data: Community Groups and Information Technology in the Next Decade. Journal of the American Planning Association 62:512–23.

276. Sax, L. J. 1997. Health Trends Among College Freshmen. Journal of American College Health 45:252–62.

277. Schank, R. C. 2000. A Vision for Education in the Twenty-First Century. T.H.E. Journal 27:42–45.

278. Schmidt, W. H., and J. P. Finnigan. 1992. The Race without a Finish Line: America's Quest for Total Quality. San Francisco: Jossey-Bass.

279. Schmuck, R.A., and P. A. Schmuck. 1997. Group Processes in the Classroom. 7th ed. Boston: McGraw-Hill.

280. Schön, D. A. 1983. The Reflective Practitioner: How Professionals Think in Action. New York: Basic Books.

281. ———. 1987. Educating the Reflective Practitioner: Toward a New Design for Teaching and Learning in the Professions. San Francisco: Jossey-Bass.

282. Schriver, K. A. 1996. Dynamics in Document Design: Creating Texts for Readers. New York: John Wiley and Sons.

283. Schutz, A., and A. R. Gere. 1998. Service Learning and English Studies. College English 60:129–49.

284. Selber, S. A., ed. 1997. Computers and Technical Communication: Pedagogical and Programmatic Perspectives. Greenwich CT: Ablex.

285. Selber, S. A., J. Johnson-Eilola, and B. Mehlenbacher. 1997. Online Support Systems: Tutorials, Documentation, and Help. In The Computer Science and Engineering Handbook, ed. A. B. Tucker, Jr. Boca Raton, Fla.: CRC Press.

286. Selfe, C. L. 1999. Technology and Literacy: A Story About the Perils of Not Paying Attention. College Composition and Communication 50:411–36.

287. Selfe, C. L., and G. Hawisher. 2000. Studying the Acquisition and Development of Technological Literacy: Research Report. The Society for Technical Communication.

288. Selfe, R. 1998. Critical, Technical Literacy Practices in and around Technology-Rich Communication Facilities. Ph.D. diss., Michigan Technological University.

289. Selzer, J. 1983. The Composing Processes of an Engineer. College Composition and Communication 34:178–87.

290. Sherer, H. M. 1984. Effective Entry Level Organizational Communication as Assessed Through a Survey of Personnel Recruiters. Ph.D. diss., Indiana University.

291. Shirk, H. N. 1997. New Roles for Technical Communicators in the Computer Age. In Computers and Technical Communication: Pedagogical and Programmatic Perspectives, ed. S. A.

292. Selber. Greenwich CT: Ablex. Shneiderman, B. 1998. Designing the User Interface: Strategies for Effective Human-Computer Interaction. 3rd ed. Reading MA: Addison-Wesley Longman.
293. Sigmon, R. 1994. Linking Service with Learning in Liberal Arts Education. Washington DC: Council of Independent Colleges. Slavin, R. 1990. Cooperative Learning: Theory, Research, and Practice. Englewood Hills NJ: Prentice Hall.
294. Soloway, E., M. Guzdial and K. Hay. 1994. Learner-Centered Design: The Challenge for the Twenty-First Century. Interactions: 4 no. 2:36–48.
295. Sosnoski, J. J. 1994. Token Professionals and Master Critics: A Critique of Orthodoxy in Literary Studies. Albany: State University of New York Press. Spiro, R. J., P. J. Feltovich, R. L. Coulson, and D. K Anderson. 1989. Multiple Analogies for Complex Concepts: Antidotes for Analogy-Induced Misconception in Advanced Knowledge Acquisition. In Similarity and Analogical Reasoning, ed. S. Vosniadou and A. Ortony. Cambridge: Cambridge University Press.
296. Spiro, R. J., W. P. Vispoel, J. G. Schmitz, A. Samarapungavan, and A.E. Boerger. 1987. Knowledge Acquisition for Application: Cognitive Flexibility and Transfer in Complex Content Domains. In Executive Control Processes in Reading, ed. B. K. Britton and S. M. Glynn. Hillsdale NJ: Lawrence Erlbaum. Stanton, T. K., D. E. Giles, Jr., and N. I. Cruz. 1999. Service-Learning: A Movement's Pioneers Reflect on its Origins, Practice, and Future. San Francisco: Jossey-Bass.
297. Staples, K., and C. Ornatowski. 1997. Foundations for Teaching Technical Communication: Theory, Practice, and Program Design. Greenwich CT: Ablex. Steele, C. M. 1997. A Threat in the Air: How Stereotypes Shape Intellectual Identity and Performance. American Psychologist 52:613–29.
298. Sullivan, D. 1990. Political-Ethical Implications of Defining Technical Communication as a Practice. Journal of Advanced Composition 10:375–86.
299. ———. 2000. Email correspondence, May 5. Sullivan, P., and J. Porter. 1993. Remapping Curricular Geography: Professional Writing in/and English. Journal of Business and Technical Communication 7:389–422.
300. ———. 1997. Opening Spaces: Writing Technologies and Critical Research Practices. Greenwich CT: Ablex. Swift, C., and R. Kent. 1999. Business School Internships: Legal Concerns. Journal of Education for Business 75:23–7.
301. Tebeaux, E. 1980. Let's Not Ruin Technical Writing, Too: A Comment

on the Essays of Carolyn Miller and Elizabeth Harris. College English 41:822–25.

302. ———. 1985. Redesigning Professional Writing Courses to Meet the Communication Needs of Writers in Business and Industry. College Composition and Communication 36:419–28.

303. ———. 1989. The High-Tech Workplace: Implications for Technical Communication Instruction. In Technical Writing: Theory and Practice, ed. B. E. Fearing and W. K. Sparrow. New York: MLA.

304. ———. 1996. Nonacademic Writing into the Twenty-First Century: Achieving and Sustaining Relevance in Research and Curricula. In Nonacademic Writing: Social Theory and Technology, ed. A. H. Duin and C. Hansen. Mahwah NJ: Lawrence Erlbaum.

305. Tiffin, J., and L. Rjasingham. 1995. In Search of the Virtual Class: Education in an Information Society. London: Routledge.

306. Tocqueville, A. de. 1974. Democracy in America. New York: Penguin. Tovey, J. 1991. Using Visual Theory in the Creation of Resumes: A Bibliography. Bulletin of the Association for Business Communication 54:97–99.

307. ———. 2001. Building Connections between Industry and University: Implementing an Internship Program at a Regional University. Technical Communication Quarterly 10:225–39.

308. Trace, J. 1985. Teaching Resume Writing the Functional Way. The Bulletin of the ABC 48:74–76.

309. Trigg, R., and S. Anderson. Introduction to This Special Issue on Current Perspectives on Participatory Design. Human-Computer Interaction 11:181–85.

310. Trimbur, J. 1997. Whatever Happened to the Fourth C?: Composition, Communication, and Socially Useful Knowledge. Paper presented at the Conference on College Composition and Communication, Phoenix. Available online at http: www.hu.mtu.edu/~cccc/97/trimbur/. Turner, B., and Kearns, J. 1996. Writing and Reading History: Teaching Narrative in a Linked Writing Course. Journal of Teaching Writing 15:3–24.

311. United States. 2000. National Environmental Policy Act. Title 42, chapter 55. Order no. 42. U.S. Code. Sec. 4321. Available online at http://archnet.uconn.edu/archnet/topical/crm/usdocs/nepa1.htm [cited September 19, 2000]. United States. 2000. Agriculture Adjustment Act. Title 7. U.S. Code. Sec. 601. Available online at http://www4.law.cornell.edu/uscode/7/601.html [cited September 19, 2000].

312. U.S. Department of Education. 1996. Getting America's Students Ready for the Twenty-First Century: Meeting the Technology Literacy Challenge, A Report to the Nation on Technology and Education. Washington DC.
313. United States. 1998. Science and Engineering Indicators. GOP (NSB 98-1) National Science Board. Division of Science Resources Statistics. Http://www.nsf.gov/sbe- /srs/seind/start/htm
314. Varner, I. 2000. The Theoretical Foundation for Intercultural Business Communication: A Conceptual Model. The Journal of Business Communication 37 (January): 39–57.
315. Venuti, L. 1998. The Scandals of Translation. New York: Routledge.
316. Wahlstrom, B. J. 1997. Teaching and Learning Communities: Locating Literacy, Agency, and Authority in a Digital Domain. In Computers and Technical Communication: Pedagogical and Programmatic Perspectives, ed. S. A. Selber. Greenwich CT: Ablex.
317. Walsh, M. E. 1977. Teaching the Letter of Application. College Composition and Communication 28:74–76.
318. Watson, K. 1992. An Integration of Values: Teaching the Internship Course in a Liberal Arts Environment. Communication Education 41:429–40.
319. Weaver, W. 1989. A Gravestone Made of Wheat. In A Gravestone Made of Wheat. St. Paul MN: Graywolf Press. Weinstein, L. A. 1993. Moving a Battleship with Your Bare Hands: Governing a University System. Madison WI: Magna Publications.
320. Wells, S. 1986. Jürgen Habermas, Communicative Competence, and the Teaching of Technical Discourse. In Theory in the Classroom, ed. C. Nelson. Urbana IL: University of Illinois Press.
321. Wenger, E. 1998. Communities of Practice: Learning, Meaning, and Identity. Cambridge: Cambridge University Press.
322. Werner, M., and D. Kaufer. 1997. Guiding Technical Communication Programs through Rapid Change: The Cycle between Technological and Curricular Change. In Computers and Technical Communication: Pedagogical and Programmatic Perspectives, ed. S. A. Selber. Greenwich CT: Ablex.
323. Whitburn, M. 1984. The Ideal Orator and Literary Critic as Technical Communicators: An Emerging Revolution in English Departments. Essays on Classical Rhetoric and Modern Discourse, ed. R. J. Connors, L. S. Ede, and A. A. Lunsford. Carbondale and Edwardsville IL: Southern Illinois University Press.

324. White, J. 1985. Heracles' Bow: Essays on the Rhetoric and Poetics of the Law. Madison WI: University of Wisconsin Press.

325. Wickliff, G. A. 1997. Assessing the Value of Client-Based Group Projects in an Introductory Technical Communication Course. Journal of Business and Technical Communication 11:170–92.

326. Williams, S., B. Heifferon, and K. B. Yancey. 2000. Reflective Instrumentalism as a Possible Guide for Revising a Master's Degree Reading List. CPTSC: Available online at http://www.cptsc.org/conferences/conference2000/Williams.html.

327. Williamson, W. J., and P. H. Sweany. 1999. Linking Communication and Software Design Courses for Professional Development in Computer Science. Journal of Language and Learning across the Disciplines 3:103–6.

328. Wilson, R. 2001. A Higher Bar for Earning Tenure. Chronicle of Higher Education, January 5, A12–14.

329. Wise, J. M. 1998. Exploring Technology and Social Space. Thousand Oaks CA: Sage.

330. Wojahn, P. 2001. Blurring Boundaries between Technical Communication and Engineering: Challenges of a Multidisciplinary, Client-Based Pedagogy. Technical Communication Quarterly 10 no. 2:129–48.

331. Youga, J. 1989. The Elements of Audience Analysis. New York: Macmillan. Young, A., and T. Fulwiler, eds. 1986. Writing across the Disciplines: Research into Practice. Upper Montclair NJ: Boynton/Cook.

332. Young, J. R. 2000. David Noble's Battle to Defend the "Sacred Space" of the Classroom. Chronicle of Higher Education, March 31, A47–49.

333. Young, R., A. Becker, and K. Pike. 1970. Rhetoric: Discovery and Change. New York: Harcourt Brace Jovanovich.

334. Zimmerman, D. E., and M. Long. 1993. Exploring the Technical Communicator's Roles: Implications for Program Design. Technical Communication Quarterly 2: 301–17.

335. Zuboff, S. 1988. In the Age of the Smart Machine: The Future of Work and Power. New York: Basic Books.

# Chapter 3

# CONTEMPORARY RESEARCH METHODOLOGIES IN TECHNICAL COMMUNICATION

Brian McNely[1], Clay Spinuzzi[2] and Christa Teston[3]

[1]University of Kentucky
[2]University of Texas, Austin
[3]Ohio State University

Many tools, technologies, spaces, and practices of technical communication today bear little resemblance to those of the late 1990s, when *Technical Communication Quarterly* published its last special issue on research methods and methodologies. On the surface, this seems significant, for in the life of writing as a technology 15 years is not so long. As Schmandt-Besserat (1986) illustrated, 5,000 years transpired between the first appearance of symbolic clay tokens and their impressed and incised signs in written systems of accounting and commerce (pp. 32–34). Similarly, humans have used various combinations of ink and paper for around 5,000 years (Fischer, 2011). Pen and paper persist for contemporary technical communicators, but new writing technologies have developed dramatically over the last two decades. The workflows of today›s technical communicators are mediated by conditions that either did not exist or were not prevalent in the late 1990s: by new tools (always connected smartphones and touch screen devices, widely available eye-tracking systems for usability research, inexpensive and expansive digital storage); by new technologies (instant/text/multimedia messaging, social media, real-time collaborative document editing, nimble content management systems, Darwin information typing architecture); by new spaces (hybrid work locations, coworking venues, virtual offices); and by new practices (contextual design, user centered design, interaction design, single sourcing).

Recent special issues of this journal have explored many of these developments (Ding & Savage, 2013; Kimme Hea, 2014; Pullman & Gu, 2008; Spinuzzi, 2007; Swarts & Kim, 2007). Although advances in technical communication research methodologies and methods have been substantial, the last special issue devoted to methodologies was published in 1998. In her introduction to that issue, Goubil-Gambrell argued that "defining research methods is a part of disciplinary development" (p. 7). We agree that methodological approaches act as markers for disciplinary identity and changes to practices and theories of technical communication since the late 1990s serve as powerful exigencies for this special issue on contemporary research methodologies. Goubil-Gambrell claimed that articles in the 1998 special issue illustrated "where we are now" (p. 7); the work of authors in this special issue provide indicators of where we are in 2015, and how we are responding to substantive change in our field.

More important, the articles in this special issue not only respond to these changes but innovate and map future methodological approaches to technical communication. Since their work looks forward, we briefly look back—to some of the key methodological developments that have shaped our field›s current research identity. We begin with sociocultural theories of writing and communication that were coincident with the 1998 special issue on research methodologies. This body of work inspired and built from qualitative studies of communicators in context. Next, we explore associative theories and methodologies that developed in parallel, but that carried alternative assumptions, methods, values, and aims about communicative actors, tools, and contexts. This body of scholarship and methodological practice changed ways in which researchers of communication explored and theorized human agency and mediation. We then consider recent work in the new material turn, a related but diverse set of approaches that is changing the ways that technical communication researchers study and understand contexts, distributed work, and collective labor. Last, we touch briefly on evolving adaptations of traditional qualitative methodologies; mixed methods approaches; and reconciliations of increasingly large technical communication data sets with situated, contextual research methods. We do all this as a way to situate the methodological contributions made by the articles in this special issue.

## SOCIOCULTURAL THEORIES

Scholars such as Bazerman (1988, 1994, 1997, 2013) Prior (1998, 2006, 2009), and Russell (1993, 1995, 1997a, 1997b, 2009, 2010) have been strong proponents of sociocultural theory in a variety of communicative contexts, and their work has influenced approaches in technical communication. "Sociocultural theory," according to Prior, "argues that activity is *situated* in concrete interactions that are simultaneously *improvised* locally and *mediated* by prefabricated, historically provided tools and practices" (2006, p. 55; emphasis in original). Sociocultural theory has clear implications for methodologies and methods, influencing what objects and practices—beyond texts—are germane to researchers. Bazerman, Prior, and Russell draw on traditions of scholarship in social psychology, symbolic interactionism, and learning theory. For Prior (2006), attention to local contexts of situated activity is thus foundational to sociocultural theories. Writing is a protean form of situated activity, mediating and communicating abstract knowledge, practical know-how, and ways of being in the world. In sociocultural approaches, the material surroundings of communicators matter because everyday activities are carried out and mediated by heterogeneous artifacts and tools (Prior, 2006).

In technical communication and related fields such as human–computer interaction (HCI) and computer-supported cooperative work (CSCW), similar methodological and theoretical approaches to contexts, artifacts, and human activity have been deployed. For example, situated action models (Brown, Collins, & Duguid, 1989; Lave, 1988; Suchman, 1987) were grounded in contextual theories of learning and everyday practice. Nardi (1996) argued that a focus on practical activity and its epistemic effects in this approach "deemphasizes study of more durable, stable phenomena that persist across situations" (p. 72). In theories and studies of distributed cognition (see, for example, Norman & Hutchins, 1988, and Hutchins, 1991,1995), however, the focus extends to tools, artifacts, and concepts that move across design problems (Nardi, p. 78). In distributed cognition, attention to the coordinative roles of tools, artifacts, and cognitive constructs stretch beyond particular situations and are reused and adapted to new or ongoing challenges (Nardi, p. 86). Scholars in rhetorical genre studies, also influenced by sociocultural theories, have explored such typification and durability in the form of genres (Artemeva & Freedman, 2007; Bawarshi & Reiff, 2010; Miller, 1984). The more recent synthesis of rhetorical genre studies and activity theory (known as writing, activity, and genre research or WAGR; see Russell, 2009; Spinuzzi, 2010) brings the durability and nomothetic potential of genres together with situated and ideographic explorations of specific contexts.

Indeed, Nardi (1996) argued that activity theory is a sociocultural approach that allows researchers in HCI and CSCW to study complex, situated contexts while producing findings that are generalizable (p. 70). Activity theory, which was introduced to professional communication via Bazerman (1988), Russell (1995, 1997a), and Berkenkotter and Huckin (1993), has been widely used in technical communication to study how genres are durable, suasive, and mediatory within specific activity systems (Fraiberg, 2013; Kain & Wardle, 2005; McCarthy, Grabill, Hart-Davidson, & McLeod, 2011), across linked activity systems (Gygi & Zachry, 2010; McNair & Paretti, 2010), and in broader networks (Ding, 2008; Propen & Schuster, 2010; Sherlock, 2009;

Spinuzzi, 2008, 2012). (For more detailed overviews of studies involving genre and activity theory, see Russell, 1997b; 2009.) Activity theory posits a clear asymmetry between communicators and their tools and technologies. In technical communication, activity-theoretical approaches have emphasized the motives and intentionality of individuals or collectives, positioning human subjects and material objects as distinct, yet interoperative. As Nardi argues, a key emphasis of activity theory is consciousness and motive, "which only belong to humans" (p. 86). Spinuzzi (2008) detailed another foundational perspective of activity theory that has particular methodological salience: Grounded in the work of social psychologists such as Vygotsky and Leontiev, activity theory is fundamentally genealogical and its accounts of human actions and intentions are therefore developmental.

Within those developmental parameters, sociocultural theories such as activity theory have anchored various methodological approaches in technical communication. For example, Mirel (1998, 2004) drew on sociocultural theory to outline her approach to interaction design, and Spinuzzi (2003, 2013) developed genre tracing as a methodology for information design. More recently, Sun (2012) drew on activity theory, genre theory, and articulation theory to develop Culturally Localized User Experience. In a 2006 interview with Zachry published in *TCQ*, Nardi described that in her article "Objects of Desire" she was trying to stay "really close to the data" (p. 493) and, to do so, paired activity theory with grounded theory (GT). Grounded theory approaches (Corbin & Strauss, 2008; Farkas & Haas, 2012; Glaser & Strauss, 1967/2007; Strauss & Corbin, 1990) afford analytic granularity and generalizable, formal theory building (for additional examples of GT approaches in technical communication, see Cooke, 2003; Mirel, Barton, & Ackerman, 2008; Schuster, Russell, Bartels & Kelly-Trombley, 2013; Scott, 2008; Spafford & Schryer, 2010; Teston, 2009, 2012; Whithaus, 2012). Some of these approaches tend to draw on variations of interventionist methods and methodologies popularized in sociology, anthropology, cultural psychology, and computer-supported cooperative work.

Yet, developmental approaches have their limitations. In particular, they assume a purposeful human actor who retains agency during processes of technical communication. However, this outlook is not the only productive one; other approaches have explored how agency, similar to cognition, can be understood across humans and nonhumans that have become associated in a system.

## ASSOCIATIVE THEORIES

Associative theories analyze humans and nonhumans as parts of intersubjective systems across which agency and motives are stretched. Such theories do not necessarily deny individual agency or cognition, but they deemphasize the roles of individual human beings to avoid overdetermining human agency and underdetermining roles played by other parts of the system under consideration. By the 1990s, technical communication scholars had begun drawing in earnest from associative approaches such as articulation theory (Johnson-Eilola, 1997; Slack, Miller, & Doak, 1993), rhizomatics (Selfe & Selfe, 1994), distributed cognition (Freedman & Smart, 1997; Winsor, 2001), and actor–network theory (Winsor, 1994). Of these, actor–network theory (ANT) has had perhaps the most uptake in technical communication and rhetoric, being used in a range of studies with various methodological commitments (Fleckenstein, Spinuzzi, Rickly, & Clarke Papper, 2008; Fraiberg, 2013; McNely, 2009; Potts, 2009; Jeff Rice, 2009, 2012; Spinuzzi, 2005, 2008; Swarts, 2009, 2011).

Like other associative theories, ANT takes the position of *symmetry*—a methodological stance that ascribes agency to a network of human and nonhuman actors rather than to specific human actors. Methodologically, therefore, researchers focus on associations among nodes in an actor–network. And since associations themselves are the focus, things that they associate are considered network effects. Symmetry does not involve anthropomorphizing nonhumans or seeing humans as agentless media; instead, it involves focusing on how associations among them generate new possibilities.

This stance has implications for technical communication research methodologies that have been developed in different ways. For example, Jeff Rice (2009, 2012) applied ANT descriptively, tracing associations across networked and offline media to explore how identities emerge from these networks. Swarts (2009, 2011) focused on aspects of translation and network-building in writing environments, and demonstrated how everyday issues such as technological literacy and reuse are developed rhetorically. Liza Potts (2009, 2014; see also Potts, Seitzinger, Jones, & Harrison, 2011) took a modeling approach by mapping different actants and how they relate in networks across social media. Last, scholars such as Fleckenstein and colleagues (2008) and Spinuzzi and colleagues (2006) used an ecological approach that provided a holistic examination of texts-in-use and compared different moments of that use. These strands are not exclusive, and they draw on different methodologies to apply ANT insights in different ways.

## THE NEW MATERIAL TURN

Associative approaches such as actor–network theory expand not only technical communication contexts but potential actors involved in such work. Latour (1992) suggested that nonhuman actors, in particular, are among the "missing masses" of collective life that participate in and shape experience (p. 152). Recent research across several disciplines (namely science and technology studies, political science, rhetoric, and philosophy) has extended associative and relational approaches to more directly engage the missing masses of nonhumans, taking seriously their potential role in affecting human work, and effecting ostensibly human activities and outcomes. In contrast to sociocultural theories, these approaches share a radically symmetrical perspective on relationships between humans and nonhumans—between people and *things*, whether those things are animal, vegetable, or mineral. Agency, from this perspective, is a function and emergent property of collectives: It is distributed and interdependent. Latour's (2013) term for this phenomenon is interagentivity—the capacity of humans and nonhumans to affect and effect one another beyond a subject–object bifurcation (p. 5). The development of these theories, we argue, will affect technical communication theory and methodology in years to come.

Emerging from a broad body of work in philosophy and political science (Barad, 2007; Bennett, 2010; Coole & Frost, 2010) and scholarship often collected under the umbrella known as *object-oriented ontology* (not to be confused with *object-oriented programming*; see Bogost, 2012; Bryant, 2011; Harman, 2002, 2005, 2011; and Morton, 2007, 2013) these approaches constitute a new material turn. This scholarship is labeled "new" materialism because it considers materiality as something much more than the simple substrate upon which human designs and activity play out. In new materialisms, then, "things are not simply projections by, containers for, or artifacts of human activity: not fetishes but actors" (McNely & Rivers, 2014). Although some have called this brand of materialism new, others (in particular, those who align themselves with feminist materialism) would suggest there is nothing new at all about it. Yet, although research in technical communication and rhetoric has often focused on discursive relations and effects they generate among human actors, the radical symmetry of new materialism explores interagentive potentials by asking how things relate and produce effects as assemblages. Bennett (2010), for example, considers electrons, electromagnetic fields, and power lines as formidable actors in what we experience as "power" or "electricity" (p. 24). These actors are often unwilling to be shaped by human designs and intentions (Latour, 1988, p. 197); an interagentive view of electricity (and related technical communication concerns such as energy policy and usage restrictions), therefore, sees agency emerging from the human–nonhuman assemblage rather than from human actors alone.

In scholarship of the new material turn, which increasingly influences work in technical communication and rhetoric (see, for example, Cooper, 2011;

Gries, 2013; Hawk, 2011; Mara & Hawk, 2009; McNely & Rivers, 2014; Jenny Rice, 2012), things matter in robust ways, and nonhumans have suasive potentials that have been obfuscated by subject–object bifurcations (Latour, 2013). Rickert (2013), for example, invites us to reconsider information as not only a material context in which work is done, but also as "an ensemble of material elements bearing up, making possible, and continually incorporated in the conducting of human activity" (p. 93). In Rickert's "ambient rhetoric," human activities such as technical communication are "a stitchwork of material, practical, and discursive relations" (p. 93). From an ambient perspective, technical communication research and practice is often extractive: Our methods and methodologies seek salience about a particular concern—usability, collaboration, motives—allowing us (or, in a more cynical view, forcing us) to bracket the complexity of practical activity. In new materialist approaches, usability, collaboration, and motives of technical communicators are inseparable from the material environs in which knowledge work is practiced.

These theories, in short, have important methodological implications in the research of technical communication. Scholarship in the material turn has troubled how researchers should bound off and study objects and practices, given the potentially formidable roles such objects and material environs play in everyday work and in practical attunements of technical communicators to those environs (Rickert, 2013). New materialisms ask us to reconsider kinds of methodological commitments and values we should deploy when attempting to capture the complexity of objects and their role in everyday ontologies. For example, Dourish and Bell (2011) make a case for infrastructure as an object of study, and, when exploring mess and myths associated with ubiquitous computing, they adopt an ethnographic approach. They eschew, however, the editorial imperative to, upon completing the ethnography, make recommendations for improvements upon technological design. For them, ethnography is "scenic fieldwork" (p. 67) and serves to "reveal certain underlying logics of social practice" (p. 69)—not render recommendations for the elimination of a problem.

## LOOKING FORWARD: PREVIEWING THE SPECIAL ISSUE ON RESEARCH METHODOLOGIES

In some ways, associative theories and work in the material turn bring us back to where we began: theory building about social practices of technical communication—including all their messiness, failures, and fraught, mutually constitutive associations. Methodologies influenced by new materialisms and associative theories, however, broaden the scope of social and rhetorical aspects of technical communication and encourage us to consider tools, technologies, and environs as potentially interagentive elements of practice. Although the three broad theoretical trends we have briefly outlined have shaped methodologies in technical communication, so too have innovations in qualitative approaches. For example, work in action research (Blythe, Grabill, & Riley, 2008; Grabill, 2003), work in participatory design (Evia & Patriarca, 2012; Simmons, 2007; Spinuzzi, 2005), and work in visual methods (Evia & Patriarca, 2012; McNely, 2013; McNely, Gestwicki, Gelms, & Burke, 2013; Varpio, Spafford, Schryer, & Lingard, 2007) have adapted and extended traditional qualitative approaches for nuances of contemporary technical communication. In addition, given the increasing importance of so-called "big data" in a variety of knowledge work fields, mixed methods and statistical approaches to technical communication are likely to become more prominent. We believe a formidable methodological challenge in coming years will be to explore increasingly large data sets with innovative methods while remaining grounded in the values and aims that have guided technical communication methodologies over the previous three decades. In the hot-air balloon view of our discipline, methodological and theoretical pluralism reveals the rich and diverse tapestry of opportunities for research and practice.

The 1998 special issue of *TCQ* on research methodologies established new directions in how technical communication researchers, teachers, and practitioners would understand and explore the field's objects of study, research ethics, and metrics (see Table 1). In this 2015 special issue, each contribution reflects how technical communication›s methods and methodologies have developed further—and along various paths—to better address many new objects of study, new aspects of research ethics, new metrics that have emerged alongside developments in theory, new research opportunities and modes, and new technologies.

**Table 1:** Comparing *TCQ*'s 1998 and 2015 Special Issues on Research Methods and Methodologies Based on Key Methodo-Communicative Issues

| Methodo-Communicative Issues | 1998 | 2015 |
|---|---|---|
| OBJECTS OF STUDY. How do we account for contexts, people, things, objects? | Longo is attentive to contextual nature of technical communication. | Read and Swarts are attentive to networks and knowledge work. |
| ETHICS. How do (and should) we cross borders? | Blyler deploys critical (e.g., feminist; participatory action) methods vs. descriptive/explanatory methods. Johnson sees interdisciplinarity as an ethic. | Walton, Zraly, and Mugengana see visual methods as a way to deploy ethically sound cross-cultural, community-based research. |
| MEASUREMENT. What's our metric? What counts as data? | Charney asks, what does empiricism, romanticism afford us? | Graham, Kim, DeVasto, and Keith ask, what does statistical genre analysis of larger data sets afford us? |

This special issue extends some of these theoretical and methodological trends in innovative ways, describing and deploying perspectives that allow us to better apply their insights to technical communication research questions (see Table 2).

**Table 2:** The Current Issue's Contributions to Methodo-Communicative Issues

| Methodo-Communicative Issues | 2015 | What's New (or "Where Are We Now?") |
|---|---|---|
| *OBJECTS OF STUDY.* How do we account for contexts, people, things, objects? | Read and Swarts model how to study networks and knowledge work. | Networks are an object of study; network analysis is one method for capturing their complexity.<br>*Theoretical ancestry: science and technology studies; actor–network theory; social network analysis* |
| *ETHICS.* How do (and should) we cross borders? | Walton, Zraly, and Mugengana model visual methods as a way to engage ethically in cross-cultural, community-based research. | Values and validity should be considered in cross-cultural research; visual research methods as a way to do that.<br>*Theoretical ancestry: anthropology* |
| *MEASUREMENT.* What's our metric? What counts as data? | Graham, Kim, DeVasto, and Keith model how to conduct statistical genre analysis of larger data sets. | Larger data sets can be analyzed rhetorically using statistics' methodological affordances.<br>*Theoretical ancestry: rhetorical studies, linguistics, science and technology studies, statistics* |

In "Visualizing and Tracing: Research Methodologies for the Study of Networked, Sociotechnical Activity, Otherwise Known as Knowledge Work," Read and Swarts address the question of how to conduct a principled network analysis. Taking the network as their object of study, they bring together and place into conversation two very different methodological perspectives, using actor–network theory and social network analysis to develop a synchronic view of how work is distributed spatially, temporally, and disciplinarily at an interdisciplinary, project-based research environment called the CIRCUIT Studio. Moreover, Read and Swarts provide visual tools for understanding this distributed work, and their methodological innovation offers incisive implications for how we understand knowledge work in such organizations.

Walton, Zraly, and Mugengana explore methodological processes in "Values and Validity: Navigating Messiness in a Community-Based Research Project in Rwanda." In particular, they consider the issue of how to develop and enact research ethics in community-based, translingual fieldwork. Qualitative fieldwork is inherently messy, and community-based, translingual research may involve additional considerations for technical communication research, such as adjusting mutually with community stakeholders throughout the research process. Walton, Zraly, and Mugengana describe how to negotiate research objectives while democratically sharing power with community stakeholders, maximizing rigor, and navigating uncertainty. By drawing lessons from their developmental processes, they provide valuable guidance for others who plan to do similar research.

Over the past two decades, technical communication researchers have performed many qualitative field studies, but comparatively few textual studies deployed techniques of statistical analysis. In "Statistical Genre Analysis: Toward Big Data Methodologies in Technical Communication," Graham, Kim, DeVasto, and Keith develop a statistical approach to perform a genre analysis on a data set whose size would be too large for the techniques typically used in rhetorical genre studies. In this analysis of deliberations conducted by the U.S. Food and Drug Administration's Oncologic Drugs Advisory Committee, the authors pilot a big data approach to genre analysis, one that allows them to systematically investigate effects of industry and stakeholder inclusion in science-policy deliberation. Through their hybrid methodological approach, the authors argue, genres can be defined with more precision—not based on individual cases but across the entire data set—and specific genre features can be correlated with specific outcomes.

These three articles represent and frame very different methodological developments in technical communication research. In "Getting to 'How Do You Know?' Rather than 'So What?' from 'What's New?'" Davida Charney puts these articles into context by discussing how they relate to various technical communication research trajectories. More important, she considers some fundamental moves in our work by asking: Where do we begin? How do we frame our research? Where are the failures, dysfunctions, and conflicts? And, ultimately, how do we know?

This issue also includes reviews of recent books that we see as key methodological resources for technical communication researchers. First, Hashimov reviews what he calls two "must-have" books for qualitative researchers: Miles, Huberman, and Saldaña's (2014) *Qualitative Data Analysis: A Methods Sourcebook* and Saldaña›s (2013) *The Coding Manual for Qualitative Researchers*. Hashimov discusses how readers will find useful each source's systematic approach to qualitative data collection, coding, analysis, and presentation. In her review of Johnson-Eilola and Selber's (2013) edited collection, *Solving Problems in Technical Communication*, Elizabeth Angeli argues for the value of this book's technical communication heuristics for undergraduate and graduate students, but she also invites readers to imagine an additional chapter that might have provided an overview of research methods technical communicators could use to solve problems (e.g., basic statistics, coding, eye-tracking). Last, Lambert reviews Potts' (2014) *Social Media in Disaster Response* as a model for the kind of methodological complexity contemporary technical communication researchers encounter, particularly when studying user-centered design and social media in the context of tragic events.

The 1998 *TCQ* special issue on research methodologies was a landmark issue that informed a generation of technical communication scholars as they defined their own objects of study, enacted their research ethics, and thought through their metrics. We hope that this special issue will similarly provide valuable grounding for technical communication researchers in the years to come.

## ACKNOWLEDGEMENTS

The authors extend thanks to everyone involved in this special issue. In particular, the authors thank *TCQ*'s previous editor Amy Koerber, who greenlighted this project, as well as the current editor, Donna Kain, who brought it to fruition. The authors also thank the *TCQ* editorial board for accepting their special issue proposal. The authors thank, too, the many reviewers who provided measured and thoughtful reviews. Most of all, the authors extend thanks to the authors in this special issue.

## REFERENCES

1. Artemeva, N. & Freedman, A. (Eds.). (2007). Rhetorical genre studies and beyond. Winnipeg, Manitoba: Inkshed Publications.
2. Barad, K. (2007). Meeting the universe halfway: Quantum physics and the entanglement of matter and meaning. Durham, NC: Duke University Press.
3. Bawarshi, A. & Reiff, M. J. (2010). Genre: An introduction to history, theory, research, and pedagogy. West Lafayette, IN: Parlor Press.
4. Bazerman, C. (1988). Shaping written knowledge: The genre and activity of the experimental article in science. Madison: University of Wisconsin Press.
5. Bazerman, C. (1994). Systems of genre and the enactment of social intentions. In A. Freedman & P. Medway (Eds.), Genre and the new rhetoric (pp. 79–99). Bristol, PA: Taylor & Francis.
6. Bazerman, C. (1997). Discursively structured activities. Mind, Culture, and Activity, 4, 296–308.
7. Bazerman, C. (2013). A rhetoric of literate action (Vols. 1–2). Fort Collins, CO: The WAC Clearinghouse and Parlor Press.
8. Bennett, J. (2010). Vibrant matter: A political ecology of things. Durham, NC: Duke University Press.

9. Berkenkotter, C. & Huckin, T. (1993). Rethinking genre from a sociocognitive perspective. Written Communication, 10, 475–509.
10. Blythe, S., Grabill, J. & Riley, K. (2008). Action research and wicked environmental problems: Exploring appropriate roles for researchers in professional communication. Journal of Business and Technical Communication, 22, 272–298.
11. Bogost, I. (2012). Alien phenomenology, or what it's like to be a thing. Minneapolis: University of Minnesota Press.
12. Brown, J. S., Collins, A. & Duguid, P. (1989). Situated cognition and the culture of learning. Educational Researcher, 18, 32–42.
13. Bryant, L. (2011). The democracy of objects. Ann Arbor: University of Michigan Press.
14. Cooke, L. (2003). Information acceleration and visual trends in print, television, and web news sources. Technical Communication Quarterly, 12, 155–181.
15. Coole, D. & Frost, S. (2010). New materialisms: Ontology, agency, and politics. Durham, NC: Duke University Press.
16. Cooper, M. (2011). Rhetorical agency as emergent and enacted. College Composition and Communication, 62, 420–449.
17. Corbin, J. & Strauss, A. (2008). Basics of qualitative research: Grounded theory procedures and techniques (3rd ed.). Newbury Park, CA: Sage.
18. Ding, H. (2008). The use of cognitive and social apprenticeship to teach a disciplinary genre: Initiation of graduate students into NIH grant writing. Written Communication, 25, 3–52.
19. Ding, H. & Savage, G. (2013). Guest editor's introduction: New directions in intercultural professional communication. Technical Communication Quarterly, 22, 1–9.
20. Dourish, P. & Bell, G. (2011). Divining a digital future: Mess and mythology in ubiquitous computing. Cambridge, MA: MIT Press.
21. Evia, C. & Patriarca, A. (2012). Beyond compliance: Participatory translation of safety communication for Latino construction workers. Journal of Business and Technical Communication, 26, 340–367. ,
22. Farkas, K. & Haas, C. (2012). A grounded theory approach for studying writing and literacy. In K. Powell & P. Takayoshi (Eds.), Practicing research in writing studies: Reflexive and ethically responsible research (pp. 81–96). New York, NY: Hampton Press.
23. Fischer, S. (2011). A history of writing. London, England: Reaktion Books.

24. Fleckenstein, K., Spinuzzi, C., Rickly, R. & Clarke Papper, C. (2008). The importance of harmony: An ecological metaphor for writing research. College Composition and Communication, 60, 388–419.
25. Fraiberg, S. (2013). Reassembling technical communication: A framework for studying multilingual and multimodal practices in global contexts. Technical Communication Quarterly, 22, 10–27.
26. Freedman, A. & Smart, G. (1997). Navigating the current of economic policy: Written genres and the distribution of cognitive work at a financial institution. Mind, Culture, and Activity, 4, 238–255.
27. Glaser, B. & Strauss, A. (2007). The discovery of grounded theory: Strategies for qualitative research. Piscataway, NJ: Aldine Transaction. (Original work published 1967)
28. Goubil-Gambrell, P. (1998). Guest editor's column. Technical Communication Quarterly, 7, 5–7.
29. Grabill, J. T. (2003). Community computing and citizen productivity. Computers and Composition, 20, 131–150.
30. Gries, L. (2013). Iconographic tracking: A digital research method for visual rhetoric and circulation studies. Computers and Composition, 30, 332–348.
31. Gygi, K. & Zachry, M. (2010). Productive tensions and the regulatory work of genres in the development of an engineering communication workshop in a transnational corporation. Journal of Business and Technical Communication, 24, 358–381.
32. Harman, G. (2002). Tool-being: Heidegger and the metaphysics of objects. Chicago, IL: Open Court.
33. Harman, G. (2005). Guerrilla metaphysics: Phenomenology and the carpentry of things. Chicago, IL: Open Court.
34. Harman, G. (2011). The quadruple object. Washington, DC: Zero Books.
35. Hawk, B. (2011). Vitalism, animality, and the material grounds of rhetoric. In J. Packer & S. Wiley (Eds.), Communication matters: Materialist approaches to media, mobility and networks (pp. 196–207). New York, NY: Routledge.
36. Hutchins, E. (1991). The social organization of distributed cognition. In L. Resnick J. Levine & S. Teasley (Eds.), Perspectives on socially shared cognition (pp. 283–307). Washington, DC: APA Press.
37. Hutchins, E. (1995). Cognition in the wild. Cambridge, MA: MIT Press.
38. Johnson-Eilola, J. (1997). Nostalgic angels: Rearticulating hypertext writing. Norwood, NJ: Ablex Press.

39. Kain, D. & Wardle, E. (2005). Building context: Using activity theory to teach about genre in multi-major professional communication courses. Technical Communication Quarterly, 14, 113–139.
40. Kimme Hea, A. (2014). Guest editor's introduction: Social media in technical communication. Technical Communication Quarterly, 23, 1–5.
41. Latour, B. (1988). The pasteurization of France. Cambridge, MA: Harvard University Press.
42. Latour, B. (1992). Where are the missing masses? The sociology of a few mundane artefacts. In W. Bijker & J. Law (Eds.), Shaping technology—Building society (pp. 225–259). Cambridge, MA: MIT Press.
43. Latour, B. (2013, November). Another way to compose the common world. An executive session of the *American Anthropological Association Annual Meeting*, Chicago, IL. In *HAU: Journal of Ethnographic Theory*, *4*, 301–307.
44. Lave, J. (1988). Cognition in practice: Mind, mathematics, and culture in everyday life. New York, NY: Cambridge University Press.
45. Mara, A. & Hawk, B. (2009). Posthuman rhetorics and technical communication. Technical Communication Quarterly, 19, 1–10.
46. McCarthy, J. E., Grabill, J. T., Hart-Davidson, W. & McLeod, M. (2011). Content management in the workplace: Community, context, and a new way to organize writing. Journal of Business and Technical Communication, 25, 367–395.
47. McNair, L. D. & Paretti, M. C. (2010). Activity theory, speech acts, and the "doctrine of infelicity": Connecting language and technology in globally networked learning environments. Journal of Business and Technical Communication, 24, 323–357.
48. McNely, B. (2009). Backchannel persistence and collaborative meaning-making. In *SIGDOC '09: Proceedings of the 27th annual international conference on design of communication* (pp. 297–304). New York, NY: ACM.
49. McNely, B. (2013). Visual research methods and communication design. In K. Gossett (Ed.), SIGDOC ‹13: Proceedings of the 31st Annual International Conference on Design of Communication (pp. 123–132). New York, NY: ACM.
50. McNely, B., Gestwicki, P., Gelms, B. & Burke, A. (2013). Spaces and surfaces of invention: A visual ethnography of game development. Enculturation, 15. Retrieved from http://enculturation.net/visual-ethnography

51. McNely, B. & Rivers, N. (2014). All of the things: Engaging complex assemblages in communication design. In D. L. Jones & B. McNely (Eds.), SIGDOC '14: Proceedings of the 32nd Annual International Conference on Design of Communication (pp. 1–10). New York, NY: ACM Press.

52. Miller, C. R. (1984). Genre as social action. Quarterly Journal of Speech, 70, 151–167.

53. Mirel, B. (1998). "Applied constructivism" for user documentation. Journal of Business and Technical Communication, 12, 7–49.

54. Mirel, B. (2004). Interaction design for complex problem solving: Developing useful and usable software. San Francisco, CA: Morgan Kaufmann.

55. Mirel, B., Barton, E. & Ackerman, M. S. (2008). Researching telemedicine: Capturing complex clinical interactions with a simple interface design. Technical Communication Quarterly, 17, 358–378.

56. Morton, T. (2007). Ecology without nature: Rethinking environmental aesthetics. Cambridge, MA: Harvard University Press.

57. Morton, T. (2013). Hyperobjects: Philosophy and ecology after the end of the world. Minneapolis: University of Minnesota Press.

58. Nardi, B. A. (1996). Studying context: A comparison of activity theory, situated action models, and distributed cognition. In B. Nardi (Ed.), Context and Consciousness: Activity theory and human-computer interaction (pp. 69–102). Cambridge, MA: MIT Press.

59. Nardi, B. (2005). Objects of desire: Power and passion in collaborative activity. Journal of Mind, Culture and Activity, 12, 37–51.

60. Norman, D. & Hutchins, E. (1988). Computation via direct manipulation. Final Report: ONR Contract N00014-85-C-0133. La Jolla: University of California, San Diego, Institute for Cognitive Science.

61. Potts, L. (2009). Using actor network theory to trace and improve multimodal communication design. Technical Communication Quarterly, 18, 281–301.

62. Potts, L. (2014). Social media in disaster response. London, England: Routledge.

63. Potts, L., Seitzinger, J., Jones, D. & Harrison, A. (2011). Tweeting disaster: Hashtag constructions and collisions. In C. J. Costa & C. Meghini (Eds.), SIGDOC '11: Proceedings of the 29th annual international conference on design of communication (pp. 235–240). New York, NY: ACM.

64. Prior, P. (1998). Writing/disciplinarity: A sociohistoric account of literate

activity in the academy. Mahwah, NJ: Erlbaum.
65. Prior, P. (2006). A sociocultural theory of writing. In C. MacArthur S. Graham & J. Fitzgerald (Eds.), Handbook of writing research (pp. 54–66). New York, NY: Guilford Press.
66. Prior, P. (2009). From speech genres to mediated multimodal genre systems: Bakhtin, Voloshinov, and the question of writing. In C. Bazerman A. Bonini & D. Figueiredo (Eds.), Genre in a changing world (pp. 17–34). Fort Collins, CO: The WAC Clearinghouse and Parlor Press.
67. Propen, A. D. & Schuster, M. L. (2010). Understanding genre through the lens of advocacy: The rhetorical work of the Victim Impact Statement. Written Communication, 27, 3–35.
68. Pullman, G. & Gu, B. (2007). Guest editor›s introduction: Rationalizing and rhetoricizing content management. Technical Communication Quarterly, 17, 1–9.
69. Rice, J. (2009). Networked exchanges, identity, writing. Journal of Business and Technical Communication, 23, 294–317.
70. Rice, J. [Jeff]. (2012). Digital Detroit: Rhetoric and space in the age of the network. Carbondale, IL: SIU Press.
71. Rice, J. [Jenny]. (2012). Distant publics: Development rhetoric and the subject of crisis. Pittsburgh, PA: Pittsburgh University Press.
72. Rickert, T. (2013). Ambient rhetoric: The attunements of rhetorical being. Pittsburgh, PA: University of Pittsburgh Press.
73. Russell, D. R. (1993). Vygotsky, Dewey, and externalism: Beyond the student/discipline dichotomy. Journal of Advanced Composition, 13, 173–197.
74. Russell, D. R. (1995). Activity theory and its implications for writing instruction. In J. Petraglia (Ed.), Reconceiving writing, rethinking writing instruction (pp. 51–76). Mahwah, NJ: Erlbaum.
75. Russell, D. R. (1997a). Rethinking genre in school and society: An activity theory analysis. Written Communication, 14, 504–54.
76. Russell, D. R. (1997b). Writing and genre in higher education and workplaces: A review of studies that use cultural-historical activity theory. Mind, Culture, and Activity, 4, 224–237.
77. Russell, D. R. (2009). Uses of activity theory in written communication research. In A. Sannino H. Daniels & K. D. Gutierrez (Eds.), Learning and expanding with activity theory (pp. 40–52). New York, NY: Cambridge University Press.
78. Russell, D. R. (2010). Writing in multiple contexts: Vygotskian CHAT

meets the phenomenology of genre. In C. Bazerman R. Krut K. Lunsford S. McLeod S. Null P. Rogers & A. Stansell (Eds.), Traditions of writing research (pp. 353–364). New York, NY: Routledge.

79. Schmandt-Besserat, D. (1986). The origins of writing: An archaeologist›s perspective. Written Communication, 3, 31–45.

80. Schuster, M. L., Russell, A. L. B., Bartels, D. M. & Kelly-Trombley, H. (2013). "Standing in Terri Shiavo›s shoes": The role of genre in end-of-life decision making. Technical Communication Quarterly, 22, 195–218.

81. Scott, J. B. (2008). The practice of usability: Teaching user engagement through service-learning. Technical Communication Quarterly, 17, 381–412.

82. Selfe, C. & Selfe, R. (1994). The politics of the interface: Power and its exercise in electronic contact zones. College Composition and Communication, 45, 480–504.

83. Sherlock, L. (2009). Genre, activity, and collaborative work and play in world of warcraft: Places and problems of open systems in online gaming. Journal of Business and Technical Communication, 23, 263–293.

84. Simmons, W. M. (2007). Participation and Power. Albany, NY: SUNY Press.

85. Slack, J., Miller, D. & Doak, J. (1993). The technical communicator as author: Meaning, power, authority. Journal of Business and Technical Communication, 7, 12–36.

86. Spafford, M. M., Schryer, C. F., Lingard, L. & Mian, M. (2010). Accessibility and order: Crossing borders in child abuse forensic reports. Technical Communication Quarterly, 19, 118–143.

87. Spinuzzi, C. (2003). Tracing genres through organizations: A sociocultural approach to information design. Cambridge, MA: MIT Press.

88. Spinuzzi, C. (2005). Lost in the translation: Shifting claims in the migration of a research technique. Technical Communication Quarterly, 14, 411–446.

89. Spinuzzi, C. (2007). Guest editor›s introduction: Technical communication in the age of distributed work. Technical Communication Quarterly, 16, 265–277.

90. Spinuzzi, C. (2008). Network: Theorizing knowledge work in telecommunications. New York, NY: Cambridge University Press.

91. Spinuzzi, C. (2010). Secret sauce and snake oil: Writing monthly reports in a highly contingent environment. Written Communication, 27, 363–409.

92. Spinuzzi, C. (2012). Working alone, together: Coworking as emergent collaborative activity. Journal of Business and Technical Communication, 26, 399–441.

93. Spinuzzi, C. (2013). Topsight: A guide to studying, diagnosing, and fixing information flow in organizations. Austin, TX: Amazon CreateSpace.

94. Spinuzzi, C., Hart-Davidson, W. & Zachry, M. (2006). Chains and ecologies: Methodological notes toward a communicative-mediational model of technologically mediated writing. In R. Pierce & J. Stamey (Eds.), SIGDOC ‹06: Proceedings of the 24th Annual International Conference on Design of Communication (pp. 43–50). New York, NY: ACM.

95. Strauss, A. & Corbin, J. (1990). Basics of qualitative research: Grounded theory procedures and techniques. Newbury Park, CA: Sage.

96. Suchman, L. A. (1987). Plans and situated actions: The problem of human-machine communication. New York, NY: Cambridge University Press.

97. Sun, H. (2012). Cross-cultural technology design: Crafting culture-sensitive technology for local users. New York, NY: Oxford University Press.

98. Swarts, J. (2009). Recycled writing: Assembling actor networks from reusable content. Journal of Business and Technical Communication, 24, 127–163.

99. Swarts, J. (2011). Technological literacy as network building. Technical Communication Quarterly, 20, 274–302.

100. Swarts, J. & Kim, L. (2007). Guest editor›s introduction: New technological spaces. Technical Communication Quarterly, 23, 211–223.

101. Teston, C. B. (2009). A grounded investigation of gendered guidelines in cancer care deliberations. Written Communication, 26, 320–348.

102. Teston, C. B. (2012). Moving from artifact to action: A grounded investigation of visual displays of evidence during medical deliberations. Technical Communication Quarterly, 21, 187–209.

103. L., Spafford, M. M., Schryer, C. F. & Lingard, L. (2007). Seeing and listening: A visual and social analysis of optometric record-keeping practices. Journal of Business and Technical Communication, 21, 343–375.

104. Whithaus, C. (2012). Claim-evidence structures in environmental science writing: Modifying Toulmin›s model to account for multimodal arguments. Technical Communication Quarterly, 21, 105–128.

105. Winsor, D. A. (1994). Invention and writing in technical work: Representing the object. Written Communication, 11, 227–250.
106. Winsor, D. A. (2001). Learning to do knowledge work in systems of distributed cognition. Journal of Business and Technical Communication, 15, 5–28.
107. Zachry, M. (2006). Interview with Bonnie A. Nardi. Technical Communication Quarterly, 15, 483–503.

# Chapter 4

## NEAR FIELD COMMUNICATION: TECHNOLOGY AND MARKET TRENDS

Gabriella Arcese, Giuseppe Campagna, Serena Flammini and Olimpia Martucci

Department of Business Studies, Roma Tre University, via Silvio D'Amico 77, 00145 Rome, Italy

## ABSTRACT

Among the different hi-tech content domains, the telecommunications industry is one of the most relevant, in particular for the Italian economy. Moreover, Near Field Communication (NFC) represents an example of innovative production and a technological introduction in the telecommunications context. It has a threefold function: *card emulator*, *peer-to-peer communication* and *digital content access*, and it could be pervasively integrated in many different domains, especially in the mobile payment one. The increasing attention on NFC technology from the academic community has improved an analysis on the changes and the development perspective about mobile payments. It has considered the work done by the GSMA (Global System for Mobile Communications Association) and the NFC Forum in recent years. This study starts from an analysis of the scientific contributions to Near Field Communication and how the main researches on this topic were conceived. Our focus is on the diffusion rates, the adoption rates and the technology life cycle. After that, we analyze the technical-economical elements of NFC. Finally, this work presents the state of art of the improvements to this technology with a deeper focus on NFC technologies applied to the tourism industry. In this way, we have done a case analysis that shows some of the NFC existent applications linked to each stage of the tourism value chain.

## INTRODUCTION

The telecommunication field is one of the most innovative sectors, of which

Near Field Communication (NFC) is one of the main examples. The NFC standard was issued in 2003 [1]. It is a data transmission technology that uses short-range radio waves at the specific frequency of 13.56 MHz, by which it is possible to read tags that are a kind of passive circuit [2]. This technology, among the different sectors in which it is applied, is also integrated in smartphones. It originates from the evolution of studies and researches in the RFID field, or Radio Frequency Identification [3]. It ranks among the technologies of automatic identification of people, animals and objects, proving to be very important in areas such as logistics, distribution and services [4].

The two technologies, NFC and RFID, have much in common, but one of the main differences between them is demonstrated by the antenna design [5]. Moreover, that the arrangement for the data exchange is no longer a card reader or a typical RFID but a smartphone, is another outstanding element.

The NFC Forum (a no-profit organization founded in 2004 by Philips, Nokia and Sony) developed a highly stable framework for the development of applications, interoperable seamless solutions and safe transactions. The NFC Forum has also coordinated the work of dozens of organizations through the creation of committees and working groups [6].

Near Field Communication has the core RFID technology, and it is able to leverage the existing ecosystem related to payments and contactless ticketing, which involves millions of users [1].

The aim of this work is to provide a comprehensive review oriented to the analysis of the scientific contributions related to NCFs technology, to deepen them through an analysis of its analyze the technical-economical elements. In addition, we show NFC applications in the tourism industry.

## LITERATURE REVIEW: TECHNOLOGY ANALYSIS

This literature review is the result of research of NFC related articles, reports and studies. It takes place from the research conducted using search engines Scopus, ISI Web Knowledge, Google Scholar and Google Chrome.

According to Haselsteiner and Breitfuß [7], Near Field Communication is an efficient technology for communications within short ranges, which offers an intuitive and simple way to transfer data between electronic devices. NFC is based on existing contactless technologies, it has an ecosystem that involves many stakeholders (Figure 1, [8]) and it is compatible with the RFID infrastructures around the world due to the standards mentioned above.

NFC devices can receive and transmit data at the same time [9]. Those NFC devices have many functions: they can operate, for example, as a smart contactless card, as a passive RFID tag and as a medium to exchange data between various devices. NFC devices can also be used to exchange data as text, images and URLs simply by holding the device near various smart tags. Hence, NFC has a wide applicability across a wide spectrum of enterprises.

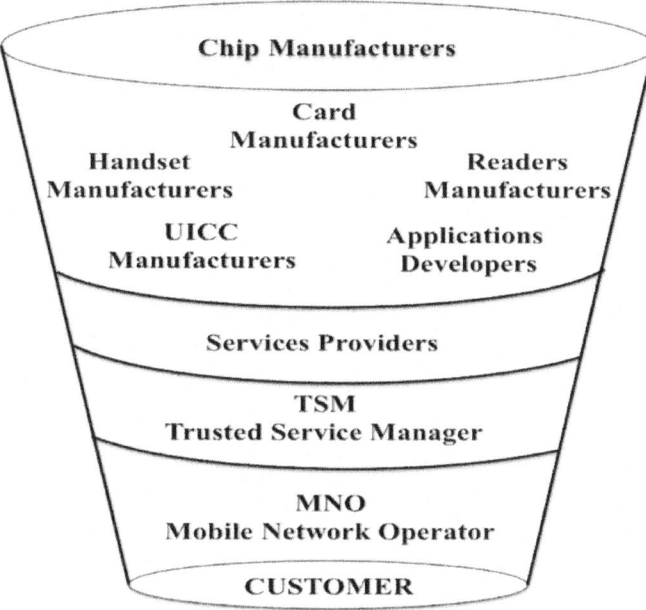

**Figure 1.** Near Field Communication stakeholder ecosystem (source: authors' elaboration based on [8].

Technology in the mobile industry has been moving towards the integration of NFC technology in mobile commerce [10]. The driving force behind NFC is the public increasing dependence on smartphones and the demand for their functionality. This trend opened up many mobile commerce channels that will allow businesses to conduct a huge variety of transactions using NFC technology integrated on mobile devices. In light of these considerations, the many benefits and the potential uses of NFC technology that will continue to push innovations in the field are evident.

To understand the NFC technology trend, the Gartner Hype Cycle model is often used. It provides a graphic representation of the maturity, the adoption rate and the technologies dissemination timing and their applications [11]. Among the examined variables, this model includes the influences generated by the advertising campaigns and the interest rate of consumers [12]. The Hype Cycle curve supplements the information provided by the known S-curve [13] and the diffusion of the technology curve, which respectively identify the trend of evolution and the trade-off between technological change and market growth [14,15]. Due to the Hype Cycle curve it is possible to understand the trend of future technologies by identifying economic activities, risks, opportunities and innovations that could be useful to CIOs (Chief Information Officer) in the business decision making process [16]. In particular, this curve allows for understanding which direction a technology is taking and how it is been seen by the market [17]. According to the Hype Cycle curve, Gartner, annually releases a report on the future technologies trends. The one released on August 2012 on the estimates for 2012 to 2013 places a greater focus on those technologies that can be used on a large scale. From the observations of the study, the state of Near Field Communication can be identified (Figure 2, [16]). It is now placed in the disillusionment phase, in which there is a decreasing rate of media interest. The plateau stage is expected to be reached in the next few years. As a matter of fact, the main infrastructure standards have been finalized and many mobile phone companies have also undertaken the market, by introducing improvements based on feedback collected following the trials carried out. Furthermore, a downward hype can be a sign of a delay to the diffusion of technology among users.

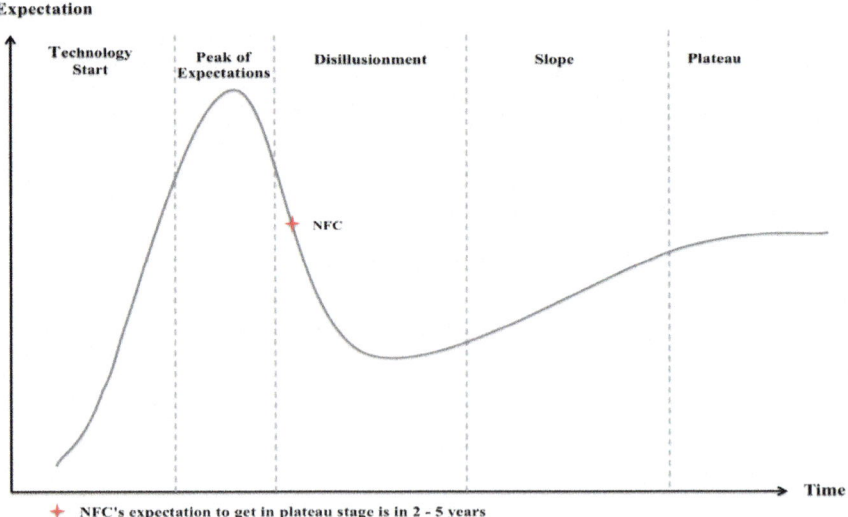

**Figure 2.** NFC technology in the Hype Cycle curve (source: authors' elaboration based on [16]).

Mobile payment service markets are currently under transition, with a history of numerous tried and failed solutions, and a future of promising but still uncertain possibilities with potential new technology innovations. The main problem is to define NFC business model concerning its application to the payment markets, because those are markets characterized by heterogeneity, and therefore are comprised of many interactions. In fact, it is well known that to define the business model of any emerging technology can be very complex [18]. In particular, the hardest choice for the service providers is "how to" cooperate with other stakeholders to get into the market (Table 1, [19]).

**Table 1.** Three models on how service providers can cooperate with other stakeholders to get into the market (source: authors' elaboration based on [19])

| Model | Explanation |
|---|---|
| *Collaborative* | In a given state, stakeholders, providers of secure element, the MCPA SP (Mobile Contactless Payment Application Service Provider) and other relevant parties all together define an environment that allows every person to participate. |
| *Bilateral* | Within certain territorial limits, a provider of secure element and a developer of contactless payment applications reach an agreement. |
| *Self-contained* | There is no collaboration. The application developer of the mobile contactless payment and NFC secure element supplier are the same subject. |

With reference to the model level, initially the NFC ecosystem was oriented more towards the self-contained model. With the feedback from trials and models adopted following some success stories, it has been decided to focus on the collaborative model, as this would facilitate the development of standards.

With the introduction of NFC technology, the potential contained in the smartphone has been exponentially growing due to its advantages, such as the simple and quick way of using this technology, the existence of compatible infrastructure around the world and the speed of connection establishment [20]. There are three main functions:

- *Card emulation.* allows the owner of the phone to use it as a tag for external readers, storing inside all the data related badges, payment cards, loyalty cards, access keys for the use of certain tools (e.g., printers), but also car keys, identity cards and health cards for public transport.
- *Reader/writer mode.* Is possible read or write external tags/smartcards such as those found on smart posters, download coupons directly on the device (ISO 14443)
- *Peer-to-peer* enables the exchange of data between devices (ISO 18092).

To highlight the main functions of NFC, Ok *et al.* [21] made an analysis, as shown in Table 2, which shows their benefits and future perspectives.

**Table 2.** Benefits and possible future perspectives NFC three main functions (source: authors' elaboration based on [20,21])

| | ISO | Strengths | Future Perspective |
|---|---|---|---|
| **Card Emulator Mode** | • 14443 | • Contactless Payments<br>• Data Storing<br>• Access Control | • Integration of personal ID-cards<br>• Storage of sensible data |
| **Reader/Writer Mode** | • 14443<br>• 15693 | • Applicability in many scenarios<br>• Marketing opportunity for brands | • Allow an higher customization<br>• Increase the number of possible scenarios |
| **Peer-to-Peer Mode** | • 18092<br>• 21481 | • Devices connection through physical proximity<br>• Quick sharing of data between devices | • Secure share of confidential/private information |

From the evidence, it appears that the spread of NFC technology has been rather slow, but the development time is needed to standardize the ecosystem and to make it interoperable [22].

The efforts of NFC ecosystem players in order to increase the rate of diffusion are driven by the idea that NFC could cover a significant role in the market of electronic payment systems, providing users with a wide range of benefits [2].

In order to have a clearer spectrum on Near Field Communication technologies, starting from the literature we made a SWOT Analysis to highlights strengths, opportunities, weaknesses and threats of NFC (Figure 3).

Elizabeth Buse, of Visa's Global Executive Solutions Inc., during the NFC Mobile Money Summit in New York in October 2013, states that: "[the] NFC market is no longer a zero-sum as was thought until 5 years ago, full of winners or losers. Today, cooperation is needed to expand the ecosystem. You can apply to NFC the four rules applied to the credit card system 30 years ago to replicate its success, which are: business model for all stakeholders of the ecosystem; open technology; agreements on standards and involvement of regulatory authorities" [23].

From the regulatory point of view, the European legislator, in implementing the European Digital Agenda, recognized the existing impact of the NFC technology payment system. In addition to activities at the national and community level, the actions undertaken by the EPC have further strengthened the influence of normative commitment at European level.

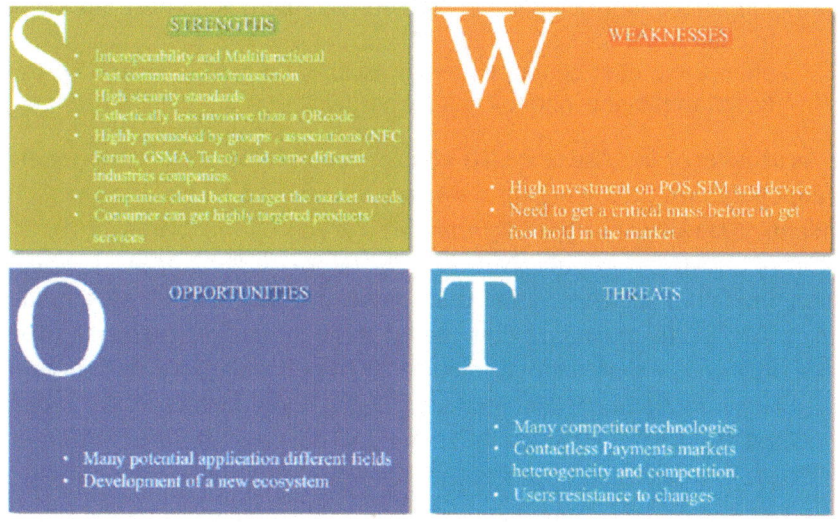

**Figure 3.** NFC Technology SWOT Analysis (source: authors' elaboration).

The guidelines for contactless transactions in the SEPA area (Single Euro Payments Area) are intended to accelerate the realization and the development of an NFC ecosystem [24]. In particular, the NFC main protocol is itemized by the ISO/IEC 18092 (ECMA 340) and some others important related standard are: ISO/IEC 21481 (ECMA 352); ISO/IEC 22536 (ECMA356); ISO/IEC 23917 (ECMA 362) and the ECMA 2005b (ECMA 373) [25].

"The new technologies and in particularly those related to the smartphones have been changing the telephony deeply. [...] The number of mobile phone in use far exceeds any other technical devices that could be used to market, sell, produce, or deliver products and services to consumers. These development open lucrative opportunities to merchants and service providers" [18].

Instead of the technologies that are already available in the market, NFC applied to payments introduces secure elements and stores the credentials for the payment on the device. There were several options potentially applicable before the GSMA (Group Special Mobile Association) opted for the adoption of NFC Subscriber Identity Module (SIM) [26]:

- *SIM card*: chip heart of all terminals GSM (Group Special Mobile) and is used as a security element for NFC payments.

- *Micro SD card*: likewise safe, it has been proposed by the banks, but the number of trials conducted on the feasibility there have shown some technical problems including incompatibility with certain phones, difficulties with others and, first of all, it would be the most expensive option among the three alternatives, and the most difficult one.

- *Embedded chip*: chip set in the terminal, there is no need for the user to change or move anything. In the event that you want to change your phone, the data contained in the secure element terminal are transferred to the new phone OTA (over the air).

As a matter of fact, the GSMA (Group Special Mobile Association) decided to adopt NFC SIM, allowing for the standardization of NFC technology. This standardization does not provide a model focused on the dominant role of a subject (e.g., MNO—Mobile Network Operator—or banks), but it suggests that the impact of standardization is accomplished thanks to all players in the market [27,28]. Its extending domination through vertical enablers (such as banks, operators and actors over the top "OTT") is able to drive bottom-line benefits for a range of vertical markets [29]. The key factors of this scenario are centered on the large standardization and on the uniformed adoption of NFC SIM. The basic conditions assumed for this scenario are:

- The complete standardization of NFC SIM, obtained with the adoption of infrastructures and protocols by all the actors in the ecosystem.

- The collaboration is focused only on the technological standard; it doesn't assume any collaboration on the go-to-market strategies, assets structure or joint investments.

- The MNO manages the secure element.

- The financial impact on the collaboration and standardization is limited to economies of scale.

- The main impact on the ecosystem is driven by the cost reduction and the effects of the network for key stakeholders in the private sector, as well as externalities and low barriers to entry.

- The consumer experience is defined interoperable inter-sector and inter-product.

The use of the SIM, otherwise known as the UICC (Universal Integrated Circuit Card), can be divided into security domains that allow service providers of third parts to manage and operate the services they provide, regardless of the mobile operators. The SIM card securely stores the identity of the holder and over the years has become more and more sophisticated, increasing the power of data processing, memory, and security management. This therefore provides an ideal environment in which to install an application, Pay-by-Mobile, which dematerialized a debit card or credit a card, and allows the user to use a phone as a wallet, counting on the SIM card as an element of security for transactions. In particular, the applications on the SIM card can be easily updated by mobile operators and be moved from one device to another [30].

The mobile network operators (MNO) and the Service Provider are equipping themselves with TSM platforms (Trusted Service Manager) [31], as the TSM is a neutral intermediary that controls the secure element and contact all relevant stakeholders (companies, banks, handset manufacturers and customers), enabling them to access remote data to a remote management application [32]. TSM was developed to overcome the issue of how to create an interoperable mobile NFC ecosystem that makes easier for Service Providers (SP) and MNOs to work together [29]. It acts as the link between the SPs and MNOs worlds from a technical perspective, ensuring also a level of trust and confidentiality between the actors:

- Providing the single point of contact for the Service Providers to access their customer base through the MNOs.

- Managing the secure download and life-cycle management of the Mobile NFC application on behalf of the Service Providers [33].

The role of TSM can be explained through three different models, as illustrated in Table 3, each of which enables different responsibilities among the parties according to the different modes of SP's applets management.

**Table 3.** Three management modes of service provider applets (source: authors' elaboration based on [29,34])

|  | **Simple Mode** | **Delegated Mode** | **Dual Mode** |
|---|---|---|---|
| **Applets Management** | SP delegates full management of its application to MNO. | SP can delegate card content management to TSM but each operation requires MNO's preauthorization (in the form of a token). | Performed by both MNO TSM and SP TSM. |
| **Card Content Management and Security Responsibilities** | MNO TSM performs the CCM and is responsible for both security domain management and secure element management. | MNO is still responsible for security domain management (allocating the space in the UICC). | Both have reserved domains allocated in the secure element. |
|  | SP TSM can monitor MNO TSM. | SP TSM is responsible for the secure element management. | The secure element must have at least two security domains. |
| **Data** | SP is responsible of the data personalization of its applet through MNO TSM. | SP TSM can install the secure element applet directly or through the MNO TSM, gaining access using the token. | The MNO is able to offer specific space for the SP's secure domain based on the rules to manage the memory allocated for a secure domain specified by GlobalPlatform. |

| Miscellaneous | For EMV (Europay, MasterCard, Visa) payment applet, the MNO TSM might be EMV certified. | | Card content management is fully delegated to a TSM for a sub area of the UICC. Several entities are authorized to perform CCM. |
|---|---|---|---|

These models cover application loading and personalization processes on UICC based SEs, which deploy NFC services [32].

Using over-the-air (OTA) channels and thanks to the connectivity provided by MNO, TSM can manage:

- Security domains' Life Cycle on the secure element in order to provide secured blocks of space for services.
- Applets' Life Cycle on the security domain of a secure element.
- The update of the secure element with to make it work on newer devices.
- The recovery mechanisms to the MNO and Service Provider utilizing the service in case of outages.
- The reporting to each service provider on the amount of space used and the number of services running.

Therefore, the TSM infrastructure can be defined as an OTA personalization system for secure element applets and a generic life-cycle manager of the provisioned applets [34].

Even manufacturers of mobile terminals and Point of Sale (hereinafter will be referred to by the acronym POS) are supporting the adoption and the deployment of NFC technology.

Recently, new form of POS emerged in the market, well responding to SMEs needs to deliver payment services. Equipping smartphones and/or tablets with a secure card reader, they can be turned into Mobile POS [25]. Some examples are Square, iZettle, Payleven and Jusp. The related business model is based on the same scheme for all the companies: low percentage fee per transaction and sometimes a set-up fee for the hardware, granting high flexibility to the merchant and new ways to engage the unserved small business segment customer [35].

The major device manufacturers such as Samsung, RIM and Microsoft Mobile Oyj (formerly Nokia) are launching a wide range of NFC phones that support the approach advocated by the GSMA. According to the estimates of the association, nearly 1.5 billion SIM—based NFC phones will be sold between 2010 and 2016, with a turnover estimated at about 50 billion dollars, according to predictions based on industry research conducted by firm Strategy Analytics. In addition, according to ABI Research, by 2016 the 85% of the terminal points of sale will be sent to NFC [25].

## NFC MOBILE PAYMENT

Together with the evolution of the devices, the habits of the users have also evolved. Thanks to smartphones, the "mobile payment" has spread this paradigm, which is changing the landscape of payments significantly, allowing users to run them anytime, anywhere (Figure 4). "The mobile payments are payments for goods, services, and bills with a mobile device by taking advantage of wireless and other communication technology". […] "The main players in the market for mobile payments are mobile payment service providers and their clients" [18].

There are two different kinds of mobile payment: remote mobile payment and mobile proximity payment. Remote mobile payment is when the dealer activates the payment remotely, allowing the customer to complete the purchase through different ways such as text message, website, by referring to a bar code scanned by the operator, reading QR codes, call to IVR (auto responder) and applications installed on the device. Mobile proximity payment consists in bringing the own device to an NFC- enabled POS to make the payment.

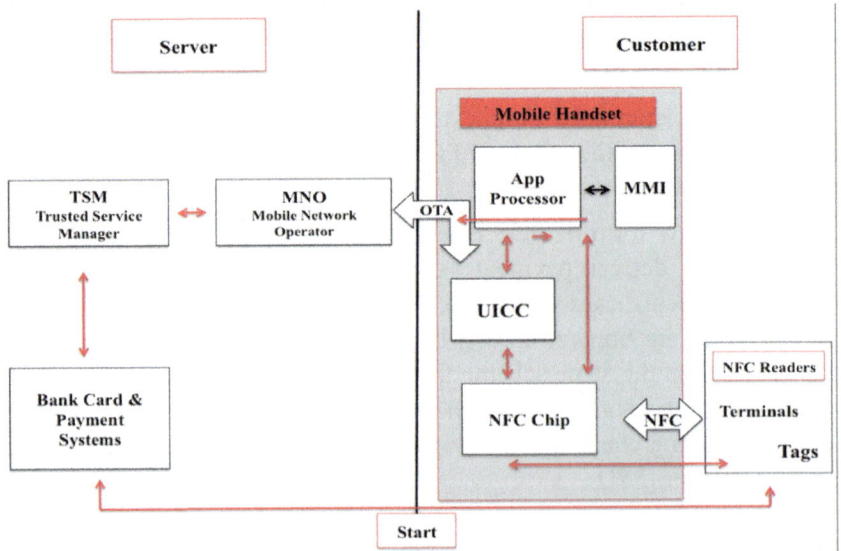

**Figure 4.** Payment process through NFC smartphones applets (source: authors' elaboration based on [36]).

Another division of the mobile payment concerns how it is possible to make the payment. In this case, there are "two categories: payments for daily purchases, and payments of bills. For purchases, and complement or compete with cash, credit cards, and debit cards. For bills, mobile payments typically provide access to account-based payment instruments such as money transfers, internet banking payments, direct debit assignments, or electronic invoice acceptance" [18].

With the increasing diffusion rate of smartphones, NFC and the expansion of NFC POS all over the world, the percentage of people that use NFC and mobile wallet services has been growing over time [37]. For example, in Italy this percentage is around 3% [38].

As we can observe in the Figure 5, in all markets the spread of NFC technology is driven by many factors.

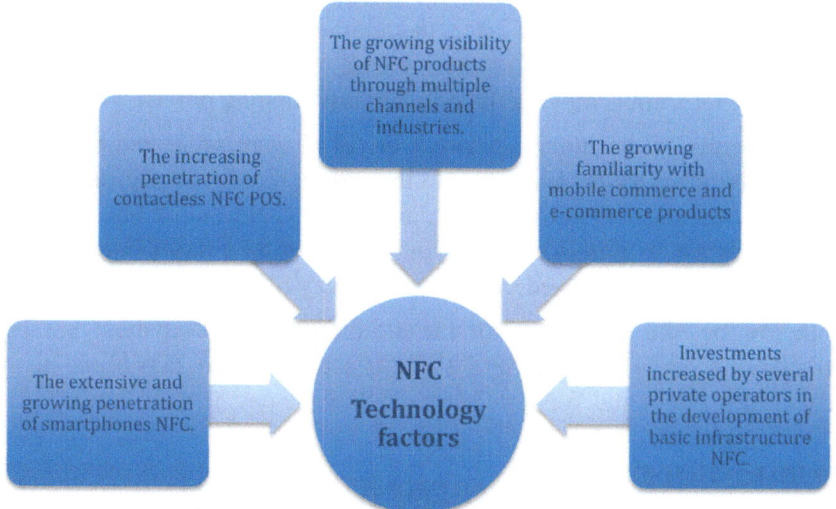

**Figure 5.** Example of some of the main NFC technology factors (authors' elaboration).

Linked to the volume of adoption there is technological standardization. From the general scenario it emerges that the greatest impact of technology standardization corresponds to an equal increase in transactions. This hypothesis is analyzed by the Working Group of the GSMA, and has defined the projections on market trends and on specific benchmarks of the industry [39].

According to this model, it is assumed that the replacement rate of infrastructure NFC-enabled in all vertical markets will be higher, thanks to the commercial benefits of the standardization [39]. These benefits affect the adoption rate of NFC terminals such as POS, turnstiles in public transport systems and ticket machines. In addition, the model predicts higher rates of diffusion and utilization, partly arisen by the acceleration in the implementation of the fundamental components of the ecosystem made by vertical enablers [40].

Despite the basis for the distribution of NFC are rising in all the markets; developments show that the adoption of this technology is directly related to the prevalence of compatible infrastructures and the degree of knowledge of the product in the market. Although several initiatives have been taken, the lack on the adoption of a high volume of infrastructures could inhibit the perceived usefulness of NFC products, limiting the awareness of them in the market.

According to data published by NFC and Mobile Payments at the Polytechnic University of Milan [41], in 2013 contactless NFC POS terminals should exceed 170,000 units, against the 30,000 at the end of 2012 and the 5000 of 2011. Whereas at the end of 2012, the number of NFC smartphones owned in Italy amounted to 2.5 million; the increase in adoption rates is noticeable, but it is still far from achieving the critical mass (tipping point).

The results of the mobile payment in 2013 were presented in a report published by the GSMA. According to the report, mobile devices enabled for tap-and-go, or payment through NFC technology, are beginning to achieve wide penetration, in fact, in 2012 one out of four of the smartphones that have been delivered were endowed of NFC technology [30].

In Europe, the technology of the mobile proximity payment has been available since early 2011 and by 2017, it is estimated that 25% of the phones in the United States and Western Europe will make payments in stores [42].

## The International Trend

The complexity of the ecosystem and the number of stakeholders involved leads to a discrete initial progress in the rollout of NFC technology. The pace of services for SIM-based NFC smartphones is growing rapidly thanks to the increasing number of mobile enabled. It is driven mainly by trial and experiments carried out by mobile operators and banks.

ABI Research estimates that in 2013 approximately 200 million NFC phones have been sold globally and NFC transaction value of mobile payments will increase, going from 4 billion dollars of 2012 to 191 billion dollars in 2017 [43].

Near Field Communication as a means of payment is becoming more and more known among consumers thanks to the success of the pilot tests. In May 2012, Juniper Research published a report according to which global NFC payments will exceed 180 billion dollars by 2017. Some of these trials have been launched on a small scale, focusing on cities that are considered strategic. This is the case of the joint venture ISIS, promoted by three mobile operators in the U.S. (AT&T, T-Mobile and Verizon Wireless), which have made experiments in the cities of Austin, Texas and Salt Lake City, Utah, providing a mobile wallet on which customers could upload their debit or credit card. They could choose among 40 compatible ISIS smartphone models. On 14 November 2013 instead of using the information collected during the trial, the commercial launch of mobile proximity payment service across the territory of the Member States took place, with the possibility to use also special offers and discounts in collaboration with partners such as American Express, Jamba Juice and Coca–Cola [44].

Following the trials carried out by Telco and banks, they are ready to begin the commercial launch. Some examples besides the above-mentioned ISIS in the U.S., there are LaCaixa (Spanish bank), ready to a national roll-out scheduled for February 2014 in collaboration with Telefónica, Vodafone and Orange, which together constitute 80% of the telecommunications market in Spain, and NTT DoCoMo ready for a worldwide service use. The Japanese Telco, following the agreement signed with MasterCard in October 2012, has been able to develop for its clients the chance to pay all over the world through a NFC smartphone to merchants who have MasterCard PayPass POS.

The market is characterized by several, potentially competing, technologies such as biometric authentication for validation of payments and the HCE (Hosting Card Emulator), that is, the ability to download data directly from the cloud of a payment card. These solutions are likely to increase consumer confidence in the use of mobile payment, because both can be integrated in smartphones. Besides of this, HCE also requires the NFC interface to communicate with the merchant's POS in order to close the transaction [45].

## Current and Future Trends

"NFC technology is considered the mainstream technology of the next generation for the mobile phone products" [25].

Several contactless services are already exploited by smartphones and soon new ones will be developed, such as: verifying the authenticity of a product, receiving detailed information on the composition and maturity of foodstuffs, buying tickets for matches or concerts directly from the smart poster, the spread of electronic meal vouchers, access to the hotel room lock through NFC. In addition, the car rental might be done through an online booking and confirmation through the smartphone containing the key [46]. Among other contactless services you can also find: visits to museums, parks and other places of interest, greater involvement in trade shows and events, as well as check-in at the airport, the exchange of business cards or the optimization of waste management.

## TOURISM VALUE CHAIN AND NFC

According to Buhalis and Law [47], among the ICT (Information and Communication Technologies), tourism is one of the most meaningful industries. Several ICT developments are not meant directly for tourism, but they are able to generate a strong impact on it. Travelers are using phones, tablets and the related apps before, during and after the trip [48]. Wang *et al.*[49] state that the tourist experience can be strongly affected by mobile phones. In support of this idea, Ricci also highlighted that smartphones are becoming important instruments to get information and therefore tourism mobile applications [50]. According to Pesonen and Horster [51], "NFC technology can be regarded as one of the recent ICT developments that has a huge potential for travel and tourism". As it is shown in the literature it is very important to be able to manage this topic which is developing continuously by making the topic significant in the tourism management perspective.

Even though the literature exploration of NFC application in the tourism industry is not that big yet [52], this technology has several uses within tourism value chain. Madlmayr and Scharinger, in 2010 [51,53] tried to gather these uses in three macro categories: information systems, workforce management and location-based services. Most recently, Egger [52] identified ten main functionalities of NFC applicable in tourism. They are: mobile payment, information supply, access authorization, network access, management of loyalty, bonus and membership cards, mobile ticketing, workforce management, identification and location of base services.

Starting from the evidence highlighted in the literature, in this part of our research work we focused the scientific exploration on NFC applications related to the macro areas of the tourism value chain (Figure 6). Therefore, the main objective was to see how NFC technologies could be related to the tourism value chain (TVC) prospect, published by DEVCO and UNWTO [54] in 2013, to improve the planned elements and/or those that have been developing, as it is shown in the figure below (Figure 6). To pursue this objective, we tried to map some selected examples of NFC applications linking each of them to a specific stage of the tourism value chain. In this way, it was possible both to get more concrete evidence on the opportunities offered by the applications of this technology in a managerial perspective and see the trend on which it has been orienting its development in the last few years.

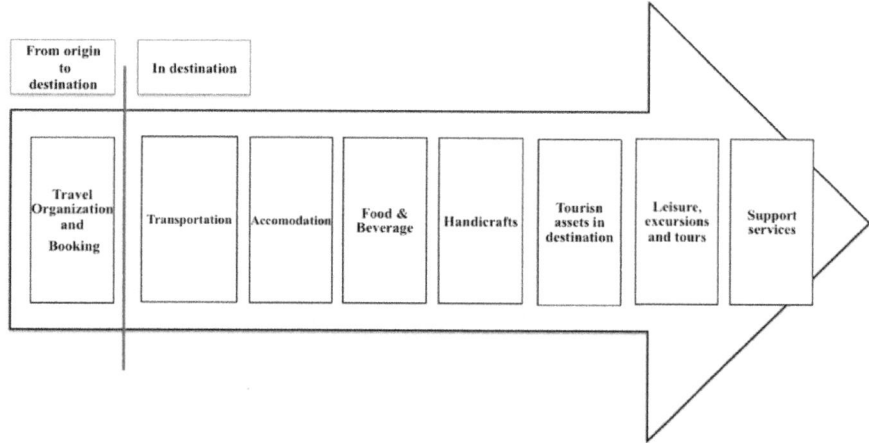

**Figure 6.** TVC -Tourism Value Chain (source: authors' elaboration based on [54]).

Looking at the NFC applications related to the TVC stages, we can find:

- *Travel organization and booking*:

The travel organization and booking stage includes all the steps of the trip settings, from the origins to the destination. One of the main NFC applications is related to the air-transport industry. In fact, in the White Paper done by GSMA and IATA "six different use cases have been defined where mobile NFC can bring great benefits to the airlines, airport authorities and the air-traveler, namely: Passenger check-in, Baggage check-in, Security check-point, Lounge access, Boarding, Post-flight" [55]. A direct example of that mentioned by Clark [52,56] concerns Scandinavian Airlines (SAS), which gives SmartPass stickers to Scandinavian Euro Bonus Gold frequent flyers in order to give them a check-in and boarding process that is easier and faster.

- *Transportation*:

The main highlighted NFC applications linked to the transportation stage are those related to bus and taxi services. For example, recently in London, the London's Radio Taxi operator built a huge marketing operation "by placing NFC and QR code stickers in its 2500 vehicles". In this way [...] "Scanning or tapping the stickers provides passengers with a direct link to the company's app, which they can then use to call the nearest Radio Taxi with one click as well as see the taxi's location in real time". According to Phil Coote, CEO of the company (RapidNFC) that had an important part in the creation of the Radio Taxi stickers, Radio Taxi have significantly increased the number of passengers, thanks to this marketing strategy [57].

Concerning bus service, in Rio de Janeiro 5000 NFC and QR code stickers have been placed to provide information on bus time and routes. Those five thousand stickers are part of a bigger project "Rio Smart City" that allow users to get information also to local tourist destination, events and point of interests [58].

- *Accommodation*:

In 2010, the **Clarion Hotel in Stockholm**, according to Clark [59], by using the RFID installed base locking systems infrastructure, offered the possibility for its customers to receive the room key on their NFC smartphone, skipping (or reducing the time for) the check-in and going directly to their room [60]. Most recently, the Aimia Hotel, part of the resort of Port de Soller, in Mallorca, has placed a panel with NFC tag d in the reception's area of the hotel, and guests, by tipping on it, can access different information, from those linked to the hotel like the restaurant menu or the hotel's WIFI password, to those related to local services like weather forecasts, places of interest and public transportation [61].

- *Food and beverage*:

Ho and Chen [62] explained nonetheless in their work how NFC may impact both the user experience and satisfaction, *i.e.*, in a **restaurant**, through NFC devices, customers could receive personalized menus, without foods they don't eat. In light of that, Argueta *et al.* developed a mobile application, NapkiNotes, that exploiting NFC technology "allows users to select dishes from a menu [...], filter food selection based on ingredient, submit the order, and be alerted when the food is ready". In fact, placing a sticker with NFC tag at each dining table the restaurant staff can easily find who made the order [63].

- *Handicrafts*:

Concerning some of the main NFC applications, more useful in TVC, linked to the handicrafts stage is it possible to associate: the shop in store, save offers and send money [64,65]. In this way, an example of a service that include all these features (and others) is the Google wallet. In fact, the 2.3 version include different features like:

1. **Shop in store:** Users with mobile phone NFC enabled devices can make contactless purchases in stores. This features makes the tourist's (and users in general) shopping more attractive by facilitating it.
2. **Save offers:** Users could be able to store a huge numbers of offers in Google Wallet, regardless where the users have found the offer. This feature cloud be useful for a tourist (or a user in general) who might have saved offers on some couponing websites (for example: Valpak).

3. **Send money:** With this service users can send money, by the app, to anyone in the United States who has an email account [64,65].

- *Tourism assets in destination*:

Another evidence of how to implement this technology in the tourism is reported by Clark [66], in the London Museum through NFC tags additional information has been provided about the objects and also there were tags for Facebook Check-Ins, and others to share contents on social network like Facebook or Twitter, to improve the customer's loyalty. A similar experience was set up in Wolfsoniana Museum in Genoa: according to Ceipidor *et al.* [67], they explained that through a mobile app which can use both NFC and QR technology, it was possible to enhance the visiting experience of the customers, delivering additional user-adjustable contents during the visit, like multimedia and interactive with innovative tools, transforming the Wolfsoniana in a Smart Museum.

- *Leisure, excursions and tours*:

An interesting example of NFC application in the TVC is the one reported by Clark [68] concerning an interactive walking tour exploiting NFC tags and QR codes In fact, the New South Wales Government has supported the development of an interactive walking tour of The Rocks, the oldest district of Sydney. Visitors by tipping or scanning the NFC tag and QR codes will have the access to an interactive self-guided tours.

- *Support services*:

According to Pesonen and Horster [51], Lindsey [69] presented the mobile application EpicMix, designed to be used in ski resorts. In fact, the application was launched in fall 2010, in Vail Resorts in Colorado; Resorts have been equipped with RFID scanners in order to offer to "the users the ability to track physical accomplishments and share the skiing experiences within social networks". Another interesting example of NFC application linked to support services is the "Shibuya Clickable Project" in Tokyo. In fact, Shibuya is one of Tokyo's busiest shopping districts. The firsts 300 streets of the area have been equipped NFC tag stickers, which allows users, by tapping the NFC tag, to get information and advertising services. For the future are planned some developments of the "Shibuya Clickable Project" like: emergency and civil disaster information, the chance to get involved in a treasure hunt game as well as an information service for international tourists [70].

As is it shown in the case analyses above, NFC technologies applied to the tourism industry can enrich and facilitate tourist travels experiences. In addition, companies can get more targeted information on the customers' behaviors in order to be able to release products and/or services that would answer to market needs.

## CONCLUSIONS

As we could see in the Hype Cycle curve, NFC technology is in the disillusionment stage. As we highlighted in this research work, there is the matter of fact that the main infrastructure standards have been finalized and many mobile phone companies have also undertaken the market. Furthermore, a downward hype can be a sign of a delay on the diffusion of technology among users.

As it is highlighted in the SWOT analysis, NFC technology has lots of strengths as well as some opportunities, but there are also some weakness and threats.

Mobile payment service markets are currently under transition, with a history of numerous tried and failed solutions, and a future of promising but still uncertain possibilities with potential new technology innovations. Even the acceptance of NFC is mostly dependent on payment systems. However, there are also new competitors coming up such as payment through fingerprints and facial recognition. In fact, it is well known that the payment markets are characterized by high heterogeneity and high competition. Finally, the customer's resistance to change could represent the main or at least one of the main threats for the diffusion of NFC technology.

Among the strengths of NFC technology we can highlight that companies can easily reach the consumers. Therefore, on one hand, companies can get from consumers behaviors, geo-localized and precise information about their habits, in order to provide more and more-targeted services and/or products based on the market demands; on the other hand, consumers can get targeted products and/or services that would answer their needs. A proof of that comes from what has emerged from the analysis of the tourism industry. In addition, especially from the findings related to the association of some example of NFC applications at each stage of the tourism value chain.

NFC technology has lots of strengths and opportunities that can facilitate and satisfy the user experience for customers in many other different industries beyond the tourism industry. One of the main challenges for the dissemination of NFC technology is to be able to overcome the potential consumer's resistance to change. However, this could be seen only with time and with future research [51].

## AUTHOR CONTRIBUTIONS

This review was conducted equally by all the authors, which have read and approved the final manuscript.

## REFERENCES

1. NFC Forum, www.nfc-forum.org. Available online: http://www.nfc-forum.org/resources/faqs#howwork (accessed on 29 April 2014).
2. Ortiz, S., Jr. Is near-field communication close to success? *Computer* **2006**, *39*, 18–20.
3. Yaqub-Undergraduate, M.U.; Shaikh-Undergraduate, U.A. Near Field Communication—Its Applications and Implementation in K.S.A. 2012. Available online: http://www4.kfupm.edu.sa/ssc/4845_MohammedUmair_Yaqub.pdf(accessed on 29 April 2014).
4. Talone, P.; Russo, G. *RFID. Fondamenti di una Tecnologia Silenziosamente Pervasiva*; Fondazione Ugo Bordoni: Rome, Italy, 2008.
5. Zimmerman, T.G. Personal area networks: Near-field intrabody communication. *IBM Syst. J.* **1996**, *35*, 609–617.
6. Want, R. Smartphone. *IEEE Pervasive Comput.* 2011, 10, pp. 4–7. Available online: http://www.sicherungssysteme.net/fileadmin/NFC_Pervasive_Computing_July-Sept2011.pdf (accessed on 29 April 2014).
7. Haselsteiner, E.; Breitfuß, K. Security in near field communication (NFC). In Proceedings of the Workshop on RFID Security, Graz, Austria, 12–14 July 2006; pp. 12–14.
8. Madlmayr, G.; Langer, J.; Scharinger, J. Managing an NFC ecosystem. In Proceedings of the 7th International Conference on Mobile Business, 2008 (ICMB '08), Barcelona, Spain, 7–8 July 2008; pp. 95–101.
9. Agrawal, P.; Bhuraria, S. Near Field Communication. *SETLabs Breifings* **2012**, *10*, 67–74.
10. Du, H. NFC technology: Today and tomorrow. *Int. J. Future Comput. Commun.* **2013**, *2*, 351–354.
11. Fenn, J. Hype Cycle for Emerging Technologies, 2010. Available online: http://www.chinnovate.com/wp-content/uploads/2011/09/Hype-Cycle-for-Emerging-Technologies-2010.pdf (accessed on 29 April 2014).
12. Linden, A.; Fenn, J. *Understanding Gartner's Hype Cycles*; Strategic Analysis Report N° R-20-1971; Gartner Inc.: Stamford, CT, USA, 2003.
13. Schilling, M.A.; Esmundo, M. Technology S-curves in renewable energy alternatives: Analysis and implications for industry and

government. *Energy Policy* **2009**, *37*, 1767–1781.

14. Lucchetti, M.C.; Arcese, G. Innovazione. In *Tecnologia & Produzione*, 2nd ed.; Chiacchierini, E., Ed.; CEDAM: Padua, Italy, 2012; pp. 99–152.

15. Arcese, G.; Flammini, S.; Martucci, O. *Dall'Innovazione alla Startup—L'esperienza d'imprenditori italiani in Italia e in California*, 1st ed.; McGraw-Hill: Milan, Italy, 2013.

16. Pettey, C.; van der Meulen, R. *Gartner's 2012. Hype Cycle for Emerging Technologies Identifies "Tipping Point" Technologies That Will Unlock Long-Awaited Technology Scenarios*; Gartner Inc.: Stamford, CT, USA, 2012.

17. Fenn, J.; Raskino, M. *Mastering the Hype Cycle: How to Choose the Right Innovation at the Right Time*; Harvard Business Press: Boston, MA, USA, 2008.

18. Dahlberg, T.; Mallat, N.; Ondrus, J.; Zmijewska, A. Past, present and future of mobile payments research: A literature review. *Electron. Commer. Res. Appl.* **2008**, *7*, 165–181.

19. Mobey Forum. White Paper Business Models for NFC Payments. 2011. Available online: http://www.sicherungssysteme.net/fileadmin/Mobey_Forum_White_Paper_Business_models_for_NFC_payments.pdf (accessed on 29 April 2014).

20. Falke, O.; Rukzio, E.; Dietz, U.; Holleis, P.; Schmidt, A. *Mobile Services for Near Field Communication*; Tech. Rep., LMU-MI-2007-1. University of Munich, Department of Computer Science, Media Informatics Group: Munich, Germany, 2007. Available online: http://www.mmi.ifi.lmu.de/pubdb/publications/pub/falke2007mobileServicesTR/falke2007mobileServicesTR.pdf (accessed on 29 April 2014).

21. Ok, K.; Coskun, V.; Aydin, M.N.; Ozdenizci, B. Current benefits and future directions of NFC services. In Proceedings of the 2010 International Conference on Education and Management Technology (ICEMT), Cairo, Egypt, 2–4 November 2010; pp. 334–338.

22. Moscoso, O.Z.; Lekse, D.; Smith, A.; Holstein, L. Understanding the current state of the NFC payment ecosystem: A graphbased analysis of market players and their relations. *Enfoque UTE* **2012**, *3*, 13–32.

23. NFC Mobile Money Summit. Visa Follow Four Rules Reproduce Age Plastic. 2013. Available online: http://www.mobileworldlive.com/visa-follow-four-rules-reproduce-age-plastic (accessed on 29 April 2014).

24. European Payments Council. Available online: http://www.europeanpaymentscouncil.eu/content.cfm?page=sepa_vision_and_

goals (accessed on 29 April 2014).
25. Wu, S.H.; Yang, C. A study on designing the new near field communication technology—NFC-micro SD Technology. *Inf. Technol. J.* **2013**, *13*, 1455–1458.
26. Edgar, Dunn & Company (EDC). Advanced Payments Report 2012. 2012. Available online: http://www.edgardunn.com/press/issues-and-opportunities/93-2012-advanced-payments-report (accessed on 29 April 2014).
27. Liu, Y.; Kostakos, V.; Deng, S. Risks of using NFC mobile payment: Investigating the moderating effect of demographic attributes. In Proceedings of the 15th International Conference on Electronic Commerce, Turku, Finland, 13–15 August 2013; pp. 125–134.
28. Mahajan, V.; Muller, E.; Bass, F.M. New product diffusion models in marketing: A review and directions for research. *J. Market.* **1990**, *54*, 1–26.
29. Global Platform. Global Platform's Proposition for NFC Mobile: Secure Element Management and Messaging, White Paper, 2009. Available online: http://www.globalplatform.org/documents/GlobalPlatform_NFC_Mobile_White_Paper.pdf (accessed on 29 April 2014).
30. GSMA. NFC—The Technology. 2013. Available online: http://www.gsma.com/mobilenfc/nfc-the-technology (accessed on 29 April 2014).
31. Easley, D.; Kleinberg, J. *Networks, Crowds, and Markets*; Cambridge University Press: Cambridge, UK, 2010; Volume 8.
32. EPC (European Payment Council)—GSMA. Trusted Service Manager, Service Management Requirements and Specifications. 2010. Available online: http://www.gsma.com/digitalcommerce/epc-gsma-trusted-service-manager-service-management-requirements-and-specifications-january-2010 (accessed on 29 April 2014).
33. Corda, A.; Bobo, L.; Azoulai, J. *U.S. Patent Application*, 2008. Available online: http://www.google.com/patents/US20100205432 (accessed on 20 June 2014).
34. GSMA. The Role of the Trusted Service Manager in Mobile Commerce. December 2013. Available online: http://www.gsma.com/digitalcommerce/wp-content/uploads/2013/12/GSMA-TSM-White-Paper-FINAL-DEC-2013.pdf (accessed on 22 June 2014).
35. Mobey Forum. The MPOS Impact: Shifting the Balance of Power. November 2013. Available online: http://www.mobeyforum.org/w/wp-content/uploads/Mobey-Forum-Whitepaper_The-MPOS-Impact.

pdf (accessed on 22 June 2014).

36. Warakagoda, N. Near Field Communication (NFC) Opportunities & Standards. Available online: http://www.umts.no/files/081028%20nfc_standards_payments%20Narada.pdf (accessed on 29 April 2014).

37. Mulliner, C. Vulnerability analysis and attacks on NFC-enabled mobile phones. In Proceedings of the International Conference on Availability, Reliability and Security (ARES '09), Fukuoka, Japan, 16–19 March 2009; pp. 695–700.

38. Neilsen Report. The Mobile Consumer—A Global Snapshot. 2013. Available online: http://www.nielseninsights.it/wpcontent/uploads/2013/03/03.global_mobile_report_02_25.pdf (accessed on 29 April 2014).

39. GSMA. Socio-Economic Benefits of SIM-Based NFC. 2011. Available online: http://www.booz.com/media/file/GSMA-Booz-Study_Socio-economic-benefits-of-SIM-based-NFC.pdf (accessed on 29 April 2014).

40. Acker, O.; Knott, M.; Marcelis, Y. Socio-Economic Benefits of SIM-Based NFC. GSMA, 2011. Available online: http://www.gsma.com/digitalcommerce/wp-content/uploads/2012/03/gsmaboozstudysocioeconomicbenefitsofsimbasednfc1.pdf (accessed on 29 April 2014).

41. Osservatorio NFC & Mobile Payment. Mobile Payment: l'Italia s'è desta! 2013. Available online: http://www.osservatori.net/c/document_library/get_file?folderId=1241114&name=DLFE-22128.pdf (accessed on 29 April 2014).

42. Juniper Research. NFC Mobile Payments & Retail Marketing—Business Models & Forecasts 2012–2017. 2012. Available online: http://www.juniperresearch.com/viewpressrelease.php?pr=315 (accessed on 29 April 2014).

43. ABI Research. *ABI: NFC Payments to Hit $100 bn*; ABI Research: New York, NY, USA, 2012.

44. Clark, S. Isis NFC Mobile Wallet Goes Live across the US. 2013. Available online: http://www.nfcworld.com/2013/11/14/326846/isis-nfc-mobile-wallet-goes-live-across-us/ (accessed on 29 April 2014).

45. Pyments.com. UL: HCE Can Speed NFC to Market, but Beware the Risks. 2014. Available online: http://www.pymnts.com/news/2014/ul-hce-can-speed-nfc-to-market-but-beware-the-risks/#.U2AJMa1_sa8 (accessed on 29 April 2014).

46. Telecom Italia. 2014. Available online: http://www.telecomitalia.com/

tit/it/innovation/hot-topics/mobile/NFC-auto.html (accessed on 29 April 2014).

47. Buhalis, D.; Law, R. Progress in information technology and tourism management: 20 years on and 10 years after the Internet—The state of eTourism research. *Tour. Manag.* **2008**, *29*, 609–623.

48. Guttenber, D. Virtual reality: Applications and implications for tourism. *Tour. Manag.* **2010**, *31*, 637–651.

49. Wang, D.; Park, S.; Fesenmaier, D.R. The role of smartphones in mediating the touristic experience. *J. Travel Res.* **2012**,*51*, 371–387.

50. Ricci, F. Mobile recommender systems. *Inf. Technol. Tour.* **2010**, *12*, 205–231.

51. Pesonen, J.; Horster, E. Near field communication technology in tourism. *Tour. Manag. Perspect.* **2012**, *4*, 11–18.

52. Egger, R. The impact of near field communication on tourism. *J. Hosp. Tour. Technol.* **2013**, *4*, 119–133.

53. Madlmayr, G.; Scharinger, J. Neue Dimensionen von Mobilen Tourismusanwendungen Durch Near Field Communication Technologie. In *mTourism. Mobile Dienste im Tourismus Wiesbaden*; Egger, R., Jooss, M., Eds.; Gabler Verlag: Wiesbaden, Germany, 2010; pp. 75–88.

54. DEVCO and UNWTO. Sustainable Tourism for Development. 2013. Available online: http://icr.unwto.org/content/guidebook-sustainable-tourism-development (accessed on 24 June 2014).

55. GSMA. The Benefits of Mobile NFC for Air Travel, White Paper Version 1.0—Non Confidential. 2011. Available online:http://www.iata.org/whatwedo/passenger/fast-travel/Documents/iata-public-whitepaper-issue1.pdf (accessed on 26 June 2014).

56. Clark, S. SAS to Introduce NFC to Airports. 2011. Available online: http://www.nfcworld.com/2011/06/15/38035/sas-to-introduce-nfc-to-airports (accessed on 26 June 2014).

57. Clark, S. London Taxi Firm Promotes App Downloads with NFC and QR Stickers. 2014. Available online: http://www.nfcworld.com/2014/05/20/329236/london-taxi-firm-promotes-app-downloads-nfc-qr-stickers/ (accessed on 26 June 2014).

58. Clark, S. Rio Gets 5,000 NFC Tags. 2014. Available online: http://www.nfcworld.com/2014/06/20/329851/rio-gets-5000-nfc-tags/ (accessed on 24 June 2014).

59. Clark, S. NFC Phones Replace Room Keys and Eliminate Check-In at Swedish Hotel. 2010. Available online: http://www.nfcworld.

com/2010/11/03/34886/nfc-keys-hotelsweden/ (accessed on 29 April 2014).
60. Clarion Hotel Stockholm, NFC Project. Available online: http://www.clarionstockholm.com/nfc-project (accessed on 29 April 2014).
61. Boden, R. Spanish Hotel Delivers Guest Information via NFC. 2013. Available online: http://www.nfcworld.com/2013/07/24/325127/spanish-hotel-delivers-guest-information-via-nfc/ (accessed on 24 June 2014).
62. Ho, T.; Chen, R. Leveraging NFC and LBS technologies to improve user experiences. In Proceedings of the 2011 International Joint Conference on Service Sciences, Taipei, Taiwan, 25–27 May 2011; pp. 17–21.
63. Argueta, D.; Lu, Y.T.; Ma, J.; Rodriguez, D.; Yang, Y.H.; Phan, T.; Jeon, W. Enhancing the restaurant dining experience with an NFC-enabled mobile user interface. In *Mobile Computing, Applications, and Services 5th International Conference, MobiCASE 2013, Paris, France, November 7–8, 2013, Revised Selected Papers*; Springer International Publishing Cham: Dordrecht, The Netherlands, 2014; pp. 314–321.
64. Clark, S. Google Confirms Commitment to NFC with New Google Wallet App. 2013. Available online: http://www.nfcworld.com/2013/09/17/325947/google-confirms-commitment-nfc-new-google-wallet-app/ (accessed on 26 June 2014).
65. Google Wallet. 2014. Available online: http://www.google.com/wallet/faq.html#tab=faq-general (accessed on 26 June 2014).
66. Clark, S. Museum of London Adds NFC. 2011. Available online: http://www.nfcworld.com/2011/08/16/39129/museum-of-london-adds-nfc/ (accessed on 29 April 2014).
67. Ceipidor, U.B.; Medaglia, C.M.; Volpi, V.; Moroni, A.; Sposato, S.; Carboni, M.; Caridi, A. NFC technology applied to touristic-cultural field: A case study on an Italian museum. In Proceedings of the 2013 5th International Workshop on Near Field Communication (NFC), Zürich, Switzerland, 5 February 2013; pp. 1–6.
68. Clark, S. Sydney Picks NFC and QR Codes to Guide Visitors around the Rocks. 2012. Available online: http://www.nfcworld.com/2012/07/02/316609/sydney-picks-nfc-and-qr-codes-to-guide-visitors-around-the-rocks/ (accessed on 24 June 2014).
69. Lindsey, J. Vail's EpicMix App Brings Location Tracking, Social Networking to Ski Slopes. 2010. Available online: http://www.wired.com/playbook/2010/09/vails-epicmix-app (accessed on 26 June 2014).
70. Boden, R. NFC Lamp Post Information Service to Launch in Tokyo.

2013. Available online: http://www.nfcworld.com/2013/05/24/324237/nfc-lamp-post-information-service-to-launch-in-tokyo/ (accessed on 24 June 2014).

# Chapter 5

# A SURVEY ON COMMUNICATION TECHNOLOGIES AND REQUIREMENTS FOR INTERNET OF ELECTRIC VEHICLES

Islam Safak Bayram[1] and Ioannis Papapanagiotou[2]

[1]Qatar Environment and Energy Research Institute, Qatar Foundation, Doha, Qatar
[2]Computer and Information Technology, Purdue University, West Lafayette, IN 47907, USA.

## ABSTRACT

Electric vehicles (EVs) are becoming a more attractive transportation option, as they offer great cost savings, decrease foreign oil dependency, and reduce carbon emissions. However, varying temporal and spatial demand patterns of EVs threatens power grid operations and its physical components. Thus, the ability of the power grid to handle the potential extra load has become a major factor in the mainstream success. In order for this integration to occur seamlessly, the power grid and the consumers need to be coordinated in harmony. In this paper, we address the critical challenges introduced by the penetration of EVs, systematically categorize the proposed frameworks for demand management, and the role of information and communication technologies in the solution process. We provide a comprehensive survey on the communication requirements, the standards and the candidate technologies towards the Internet of electric vehicles (IoEV). This survey summarizes the current state of research efforts in electric vehicle demand management and aims to shed light on the continued studies.

## REVIEW

### Introduction

As the dependence on a single energy source (crude oil) exposes economies to unstable global oil market and increases environmental concerns, there has been a growing interest to push electric vehicles into mainstream acceptance. The motivation for the electrification of transportation is multifaceted; electricity can be generated through diverse and domestic resources, electricity prices have been relatively stable in the last two decades, and electric miles are cheaper and cleaner [1, 2]. Therefore, internet of electric vehicles are expected to achieve a sizable market portion in the next decade. In fact, the study in [3] estimates that there will be around 50 million grid-enabled vehicles by year 2040.

Accordingly, there is a pressing need in the deployment of charging networks to accommodate the projected demand. For instance, [4] presents that there is an attempt to build a statewide charging station network in California. Similarly, Estonia is building the Europe's largest fast-charging station network with 200 nodes [5]. The number of EV charging stations is expected exceed four million in Europe and 11 million in the Globe by year 2020 [6].

However, as the power grid is becoming more congested due to the introduction of EVs, managing and controlling of corresponding demand should be carefully aligned with the available resources. Even though, the long term solution involves the upgrade of the power grid components, by considering the potential cost of such investments, the practical solution for the near term would be to develop intelligent control and scheduling techniques to aid the power grid operations. The realization of such frameworks requires appropriate communication architectures that will enable reliable interaction between the grid and the EV drivers to optimally control power flow under varying network conditions.

A handful of surveys have attempted to discuss general smart grid communication requirements, standards, and protocols for household demand management [7–10]. However, the case for the EVs is unique; electric vehicles can be mobile and a typical EV demand is large and, in fact, it can be more than the daily energy consumption of two households [11]. More importantly, the sustainability of the power grid operations is essential for human life. Therefore, careful attention is required to shed more light on the complex problems associated with electrictrification of transportation. Nonetheless, to the best of the authors' knowledge, this is the first study that focuses on the electric vehicle network communications for smart grid applications and, more specifically, to the IoEV challenges. Hence, in this work we

- comprehensively address the unique challenges introduced by the EV penetration specifically for each power grid components and identify opportunities to improve the grid operations and system reliability;
- systematically classify the mathematical frameworks for optimal control and management of EV demand; and

- survey the communication requirements, standards, and candidate technologies that could serve the IoEVs and smart grid applications.

The structure of this paper is as follows. In Section 2, we present the current status of the U.S. power grid, the projected EV roll-out, potential negative impacts on power generation, transmission network, and distribution grid. Next, in Section 3, we categorize the literature on control and coordination frameworks according to the objective function, employed model, and the scale of the problem. In Section 4, we classify published standards and communication technologies respect to each smart grid application. In Section 5, we discuss the communication requirements and performance metrics for the IoEV network communications.

# INTERNET OF ELECTRIC VEHICLES AND THE CURRENT POWER GRID

## Internet of Electric Vehicles

Over the last few years, the automotive industry has introduced a variety of new electric vehicle models that have drastically expanded the customer choices [11]. The main drivers that shape the EV adoption include the size of the battery packs (usually varies between 16 to 56 kWh) and the duration to recharge the vehicle. The battery pack determines the all-electric range of the vehicle and, hence, it is an important criterion to beat the range anxiety. On the other hand, the charging duration depends on the employed charger technology, and it becomes a critical element in order to be competitive against the gas-powered counterparts. For instance, during a charging period of 30 min, level II single, and three-phase, and DC fast charge can enable a Nissan Leaf model (Nissan Motor Co., Ltd., Yokohama, Japan) to drive 5.5, 11, and 83.4 miles, respectively [12]. The charging standards may vary from country to country, and we present an overview of the different charger standards in Table 1. Moreover, the popularity of each charging type will greatly be determined by the housing demographics [13]. For instance, in the early EV adopter cities, a substantial portion of the population lives in multi-unit dwellings and EVs in these locations will likely use public fast charging facilities. Furthermore, several studies are conducted by different organizations to forecast the EV penetration rates. Depending on the assumptions made, prediction results may diverge, but nevertheless there is a consensus that EVs will represent a sizable portion in the next decades. In Table 2, the projected EV roll-out is presented. In the rest of this section, we present the current status of the power grid, potential impacts of EV demand, and opportunities offered optimal management of EVs.

**Table 1:** Electric vehicle charger technologies[14]

| Type | Connection | Power (kW) | Max current |
|---|---|---|---|
| Europe | 1-Phase AC | 3.7 | 16 to 20 |
| Europe | 1 or 3 Phase AC | 3.7 to 22 | 16 to 32 |
| Europe | 3-Phase AC | >22 | >32 |
| Europe | DC Fast | >22 | >3.225 |
| USA | AC Level-1 | 1.44 | 12 |
| USA | AC Level-2 | 7.7 | 32 |
| USA | DC Fast | 240 | 400 |

**Table 2:** Electric vehicle penetration scenarios (approximate in millions) by different organizations

| Year | US EIA - USA | NRC (probable) - USA | IEA world |
|---|---|---|---|
| 2015 | 1 million | 1.5 million | 1.1 million |
| 2020 | 2.3 million | 3 million | 6.9 million |
| 2025 | 3.2 million | 7 million | 17.7 million |
| 2030 | 4 million | 14 million | 33.3 million |

US EIA: United States energy information administration [2, 15]; NRC: National Research Council [2, 15]; IEA: International Energy Agency [3].

## Power Generation and Electricity Prices

### *Current Status*

According to the US National Academy of Engineering, the power grid is 'the supreme engineering achievement of the twentieth century'. Currently, there are close to 3,200 utility companies serving more than 143 million customers in the United States. In order to serve the increasing customer demand, the required power supply is generated through diverse resources, including coal, nuclear, hydro, natural gas, and lately renewable sources, such as wind and solar [16]. Depending on the efficiency and the unit generation cost, power generation can be roughly divided into base load, intermediate load, and peak hour load. Factors that affect to dispatch a specific generation asset include variable operation and maintenance (O&M) costs, flexibility (fast vs. slow start generators), environmental 'head-room', and the distance to load and transmission. To meet the base load demand, utilities employ large scale (≥400 MW) and low cost generation assets (e.g., nuclear, hydro, coal). Moreover, base load generation is characterized by high load factor (the percentage of hours that a power plant runs at full capacity) [17]. For intermediate load generation (the difference between expected customer demand and base load generation), power plants with lower load factors (typically around 50%) such as combined cycle combustion turbine fueled by natural gas etc. are employed [2, 18]. Finally, utilities may need to employ additional generation assets to accommodate customer demand during peak hours. For this purpose, fast start, high cost, and usually environmentally unfriendly assets are employed. They are characterized by low load factor (5% to 10%), that leads to decreased utilization and hence and increased ratio of peak to average demand. Consequently, the use of such assets gradually increases the average kWh electricity price. A real-world scenario is illustrated in Figure 1a.

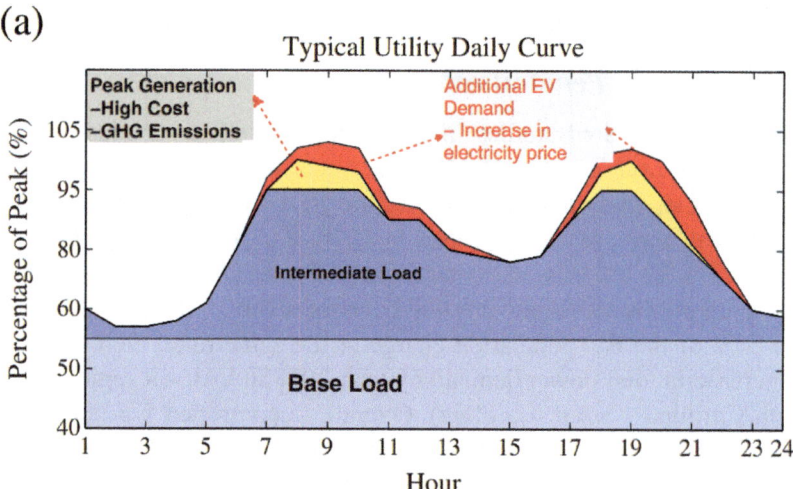

Impacts of electric vehicle penetration on power generation.

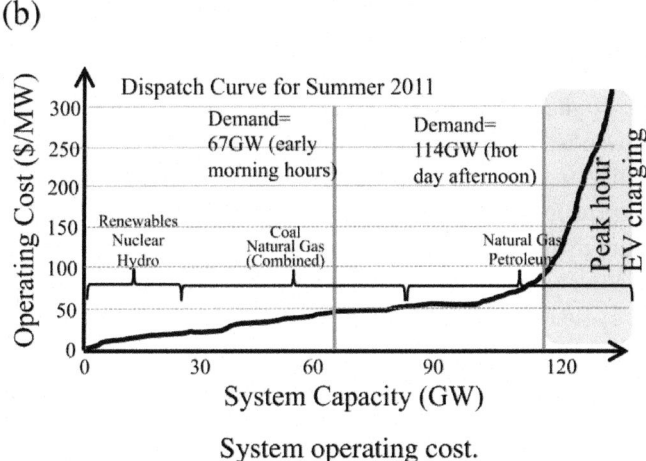

**Figure 1:** Impacts of EV charging on power generation and system operating cost. **(a)** Impacts of electric vehicle penetration on power generation. **(b)** System operating cost.

## Impact of the EV Penetration

There are a handful of studies investigating the impact of electric vehicle charging on power generation [19–23]. According to [21], plug-in hybrid electric vehicles (assuming all vehicles are PHEV20 with a battery pack of 7.2 kWh) can increase the total load by 2.7% and the peak load by 2.5% in Colorado. On the other hand, battery sizes of pure EVs range from 16 to 52 kWh, which means actual impacts will be more severe. Similarly, [24] presents that if 5 % of the EV population charge at the same time, there will be a 5 GW increase in total power demand by year 2018 in VACAR region (Virginia - North Carolina - South Carolina). Overall, uncontrolled EV charging will decrease the utilization of low cost generation assets, increase the peak to average load ratio, and increase the power generation cost. Potential impacts of EV demand on the cost of the power grid is presented in Figure 1b.

## Opportunities

The aforementioned effects can be mitigated with the deployment of necessary smart grid communication technologies which enable EV users to take advantage of low prices during off-peak hours. In such applications, known as valley filling, grid operators encourage customers to postpone their EV charging to low power demand periods aiming to increase the overall power grid efficiency. There are many opportunities to use valley filling applications.

The US power grid uses its maximum generation only around 5% of the time [25]. If optimal valley filling programs are employed, almost 73% of the vehicles in the US can be substituted by EVs [26]. Such an approach mandates EVs to be charged during the night when the aggregated power demand is low. For instance, the authors in [27] propose an EV charging framework for valley-filling applications in New York State with varying EV market penetrations of 5% to 40%. They show that the intelligent scheduling of EV chargings at off-peak hours increases the utilization of low cost generations, hence lowers the wholesale energy cost. In a similar study, authors of [23] argue that the savings gained due to intelligent charging of EVs could be reflected in charging tariffs and it promotes EV ownership. Furthermore, the work presented in [28] proposes a valley-filling algorithm and models the customer to grid interaction via pricing demand signals.

## Transmission Network

### Current Status

The transmission network ties the bulk power generation with the end users via high voltage lines. The US national grid includes three distinct geographic interconnections, namely the Eastern Interconnection, the Western Interconnection, and the Electric Reliability Council of Texas. The transmission network is composed of 170,000 miles of transmission lines rated at 200 (kV) and above, delivering the power generated at 5,000 (approximately) power plants [2]. Over the last two decades, the transmission network acts as an open highway which connects wholesale electricity markets to with end users. The primary goal of the network operators, on the other hand, is to make sure that transmission lines operate efficiently and reliably as it delivers the minimum cost generation to end users.

### Impact of the EV Penetration

According to a study conducted by the US Department of Energy [29], in the Western Interconnection network alone, one third of the lines experienced congestion at least once during the year of the study, and 17% of the lines are congested at least 10% of the times. This study also shows that the situation is even more severe in the Eastern Interconnection, as the infrastructure is older and the network is not designed for long distance delivery of power.

On the other hand, the growth in EV load along with the deployment of new generators requires a capacity expansion in the transmission network. However, due to economical and political reasons, the required investments may not be realized in the short term. Past experiences show that new transmission projects can cost up to billions of dollars and may be stalled if the cost allocation and the recovery of investments are not properly planned. To that end, uncontrolled EV demand will allow transmission bottlenecks to emerge. These bottlenecks will increase electricity costs and the risks of blackouts.

## *Opportunities*

The introduction of bidirectional chargers enables electric vehicles to transfer energy back to the grid (V2G) or to other electric vehicles (V2V) [30]. The utilization of such ancillary services can aid the transmission operations, mainly by reducing the congestion during peak hours. For example, group of vehicles can sell back part of their stored energy to other EVs who are in urgent need. This way, energy trading via V2V will eliminate the need to draw power from bulk power plants and hence the associated power losses in transmission will be minimized. For instance, studies in [31, 32] present mathematical framework to model the interaction of energy trading in a V2V scenario, where the groups of EVs determine the amount of energy to exchange and negotiate on unit price.

Moreover, EVs can transport their stored energy from one location to another which can support the grid via V2G applications. For example, [33] provides a transmission network based on the capability Internet of vehicles to transfer energy to the regions of high energy consumption. This way, the required upgrades will be deferred and occur gradually over time.

## Distribution Network

### *Current Status*

The distribution network is the final portion of the power grid which interfaces with the consumers. It is responsible for reducing the high voltage carried by transmission lines to appropriate levels for end users with the use of transformers typically rated between 2 to 40 kV. Over the last decade, the distribution network has been running up against its operating limits. In the US, national grid almost 7% of the electrical energy is lost (mostly in the form of heat) between generation units and end users and distribution network is mostly responsible for this. The distribution system is the most interruption-prone component of the power grid. According to [2], more than three-fourths of service interruptions originates in the distribution level.

## *Impact of the EV Penetration*

If charged at parking lots or customer premises, the distribution grid is the part where most electric vehicles will be attached to. Uncontrolled EV charging could stress the distribution grid and cause system failures such as transformer and line overloading deteriorate power quality (e.g., large voltage deviations, harmonics, etc.). Considering the fact that EV penetration is going to be geographically clustered, negative impacts will be more severe in certain regions [2, 34, 35]. For instance, the US distribution grid is designed to meet three to five houses [36] per transformer. Since charging of one EV doubles the daily load of a typical house, further challenges will be faced by the additional load introduced by EVs. A very typical scenario is illustrated in Figure 2 where five houses are served by a 37.5-kVA transformer. If just two level-2 chargers are used concurrently, local transformer is going to be overloaded. The frequent occurrence of such events will increase power loses and voltage deviations, and decreases transformer lifetime (high loading leads to high operating temperature) [3, 37, 38]. In [35], the authors presented a comprehensive study on the impacts of variety of EV charging scenarios on the required transformer upgrades and transformer efficiency.

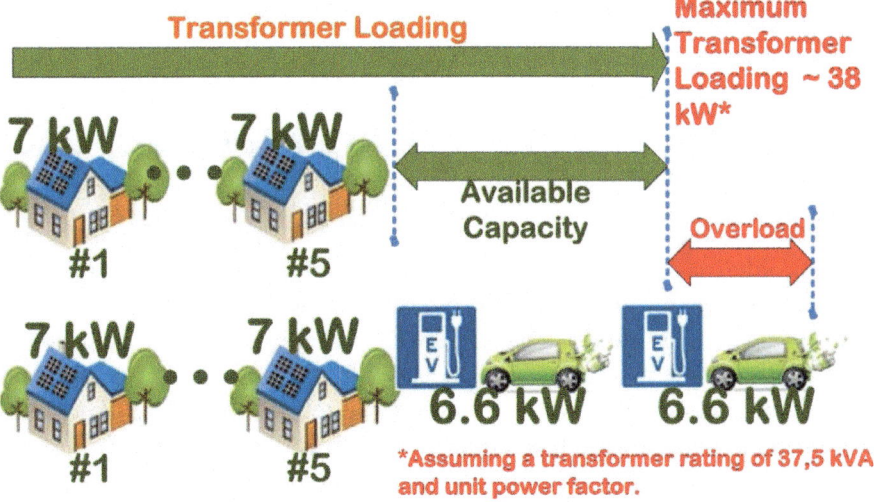

**Figure 2:** Potential distribution network overloading [39].

## *Opportunities*

Intelligent control mechanisms (presented in the next section) can mitigate the aforementioned effects. Such frameworks requires both parties (EVs and the grid) to communicate. According to [40], controlling EV charging can reduce the number of congested (overloaded) network components which need to be replaced, hence eliminate the need for costly upgrades. It is further shown that controlling EV charging can reduce the cost of energy losses by 20% when compared to uncontrolled charging. In addition, EVs can be seen as distributed-energy storage mediums which are very essential for ancillary smart grid applications like integration of renewable energy resources and frequency regulation applications [41]. We provide a summary of the negative impacts of uncontrolled EV charging in Figure 3.

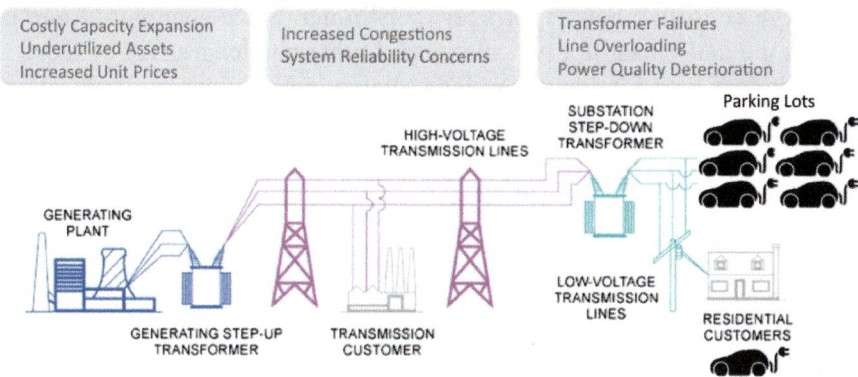

**Figure 3:** Impacts of uncontrolled EV charging.

# DEMAND MANAGEMENT FOR THE INTERNET OF ELECTRIC VEHICLES

In order to mitigate the negative impacts of EV demand, there has been a growing interest in developing coordination strategies. At the heart of such frameworks lies information and communication technologies to support, control, and manage energy transfer between vehicles and the power grid that varies both in time and space, known as the Internet of EVs. In this section, we provide a comprehensive overview on the related literature. We classify the demand management techniques with respect to the objective of the optimization problem, scale of the problem, and the employed mathematical techniques. We present an overview of the literature in Figure 4 and the benefits of demand side management of EVs is summarized in Figure 5.

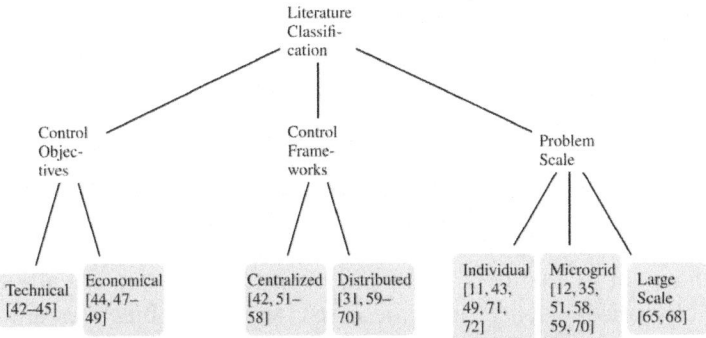

**Figure 4:** Literature classification of demand management techniques for IoEVs.

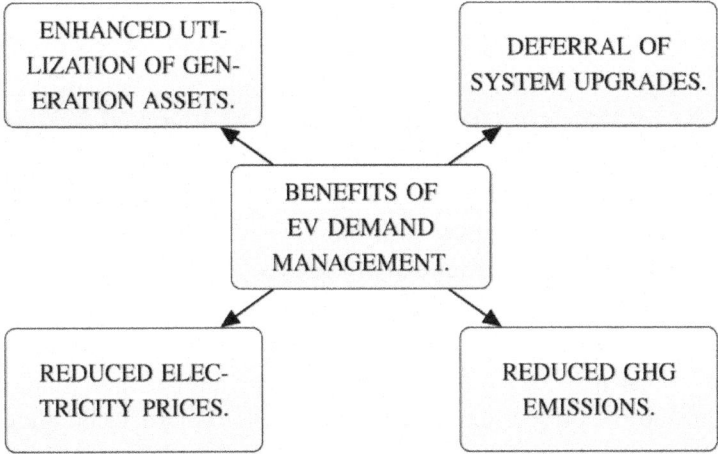

**Figure 5:** Benefits of electric vehicle management and control.

## Control Objectives

### *Technical Objectives*

The technical control objectives are usually related to the operating limits of the physical power grid assets. The most common objective functions are the minimization of energy losses, controlling voltage deviations, reducing peak-to-average load ratio, smoothing the consumer demand, and supporting renewable energy generation [42–45]. For vehicle-to-grid and vehicle-to-vehicle applications, the technical objectives include battery degradations and aging, thermal stability, etc. [46].

## *Economical Objectives*

The objective functions fall into this category are usually linked to energy market participants: consumers, producers, retailers, etc. The main objectives include minimization of electricity generation and consumption costs. In this case, the objective functions are usually modeled with utility functions and the goal is to develop a charging tariff such that the total cost of charging is minimized compared to uncontrolled case [44,47–49].

It is noteworthy that both of the objective functions are actually reflected in electricity prices. Hence, in some cases, technical objectives are coupled to economical objectives. Nodal pricing can be a good example [50], where the technical aspects (distance of generators, congestion of transmission lines, etc.) are translated into cost functions and the optimal pricing is solved with a more holistic approach.

## Control Frameworks

The aforementioned control objectives are used in the mathematical frameworks to manage the EV demand. The applied control techniques depends on the employed charger technology. As given in Table 1, level I and level II charging typically takes a few hours, hence for these types, it is assumed that EVs are located in the customer's premises or at large parking lots. The majority of the literature considers EVs as 'smart' loads as the carving current can be adjusted in order to maximize the control objectives given above.

On the other hand, for the fast charging case, the EVs are assumed to be mobile and due to short service duration, the common control techniques include admission control at individual stations and customer routing/assignment in a network of charging stations. Overall, for both cases, the related literature can be divided into two categories: centralized and distributed controls.

## *Centralized Control*

Centralized control employs a central authority (dispatcher) who up to a large extent controls and mandates EV charging rate, start time, etc. System level decisions, such as the desired state of charge, charging intervals, etc., are taken to finish all jobs by a certain deadline (e.g., by 7 am). Main advantages of centralized control include higher utilization of power grid resources and real-time monitoring of operation conditions across the network. On the other hand, to enable such functionalities, an advanced communication network is needed. Studies presented in [42, 51–56] are examples of centralized scheduling. These studies differ by the assumptions they make; interruptible vs. uninterruptible load, constant vs. varying charging rate, and preemptive vs. non-preemptive jobs. Management of EV fleets (e.g., school buses, postal service vehicles, etc.) can be a good example for centralized control. In this case, fleet owners can draw contracts with the utility operators and receive discounts. In return, utility can orchestrate EV demand according to network conditions to minimize his operating cost. Moreover, authors of [57] propose a deadline scheduling policy with admission control. They compare their algorithm with classic earliest deadline first and first come first serve scheduling. Similarly, the authors of [58] uses an admission control algorithm called Threshold Admission with Greedy Scheduling. In addition, their model incorporates renewable energy resources to charge electric vehicles.

## *Distributed Control*

Decentralized control allows customers to choose their individual charging pattern. Decisions can be based on the price of the electricity or time of the day. This method eliminates the need of third party controller (dispatcher) and complex monitoring techniques. Since decisions are taken individually, game theoretic models are extensively employed. The works presented in [31, 59, 60] use Stackelberg game to model interactions of system operator (*leader*), who sets the prices and have the first move advantage, with individual EVs (*followers*) who respond to price changes by adjusting their demand. Another popular method is the Nash equilibrium, in which optimal pricing is achieved through maximization of individual utility functions [61, 62]. Other employed models include mean field games, potential games, and network routing games [61–70]. In addition to scheduling of night time charging, there is an interest in large scale charging of group stationary EVs (park and charge). For instance, [71] uses swarm optimization to allocate power to EVs in a parking lot. Authors of [72] propose a combined pricing-scheduling quadratic integer programming model to determine optimal prices and schedules to manage EV demand in large scale parking lots.

## Scale of the Problem

The scale of the control framework can vary from individual level to entire transmission voltage level. We classify the scale of the problem into three categories.

- *EV scale:* This level of scale considers coordination of individual EVs according to the available information at the customer premises. Economical goals such as cost minimization and load profile smoothing are usually chosen [43, 49, 59, 73].
- *Microgrid scale:* This level of problem considers groups of vehicles

connected to LV/HV feeders. Typical examples include university campuses, parking lot (malls, airports, etc.), and microgrids. The control and coordination studies at this level include [12, 34, 58, 71].

- *Transmission scale:* At this scale transmission, system operators and wholesale energy markets operate. Corollary, the control techniques applied considers thousands of EVs located in large geographical regions. The primary goal of this scale is to develop pricing policies to achieve optimal valley-filling during night time [62, 69].

# AVAILABLE COMMUNICATION STANDARDS AND TECHNOLOGIES

The IoEV is based on the information and communication infrastructure to support the control and manage the energy transfer between vehicles and the power grid. In order to support such frameworks, we survey the related technologies and standards and the interdependency diagram which is presented in Figure 6. As this is a new area, some of the standards are either published or under development. We classify the communication standards and technologies into three groups:

1) the first group includes the technologies that are responsible for home charging applications and the message exchange between the EV and the charging equipment;

2) the second group includes the technologies for the mobile EV communication; and

3) the third group includes the standards for 'inter-control center' communication.

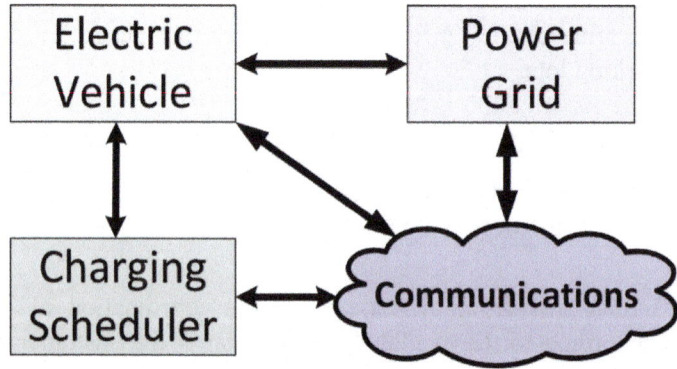

**Figure 6:** Interdependency of communications and EV demand management.

## Communication needs at Customer Premises

### EV-Electric Vehicle Supply Equipment

The communication at customer premises takes place in several places. First, group contains the standards and technologies between electric vehicle and electric vehicle supply equipment (EVSE) that is required for energy transfer monitoring and management, billing information, and authorization. The standardization is required for fast adoption of EVs and proper functioning of electric vehicle network components. The Society of Automotive Engineers (SAE) have defined the communication standards when an EV is being charged. We described these standards below [74, 75].

- *SAE J2293:* This standard covers the functionalities and architectures required for EV energy transfer system.

- *SAE J2836/1* and *J2847/1:* Define use cases and requirements for communications between EVs and the power grid, primarily for energy transfer. The central focus is on grid-optimized energy transfer for EVs to guarantee that drivers have enough energy while minimizing the reducing the stress on the grid.

- *SAE J2836/2* and *J2847/2:* Define the uses cases and requirements for the communications between electric vehicles and off-board DC charger.

- *SAE J2836/3* and *J2847/3:* Identify use cases and additional messages energy (DC) transfer from grid to electric vehicle. Also supports requirements for grid-to-vehicle energy transfer.

- *SAE J2931:* Defines digital communications requirements between EV and off-board device. SAE J2931/1 covers power line communications for EVs.

- *SAE J2931/2:* Defines the requirements for physical layer communications with in-band signaling between EV and EVSE.

In Figure 7, an overview of SAE communication standards is presented. For instance, J2836/1 use cases for utility programs may include time of use program, real-time pricing program, or critical peak pricing program [76]. Moreover, the International Electrotechnical Commission (IEC) is developing several standards under development for DC fast charging option. IEC 61851-23 presents the requirements for gird connections and communication architecture for fast charging. IEC 61851-24 defines the digital communications between EV and EVSE.

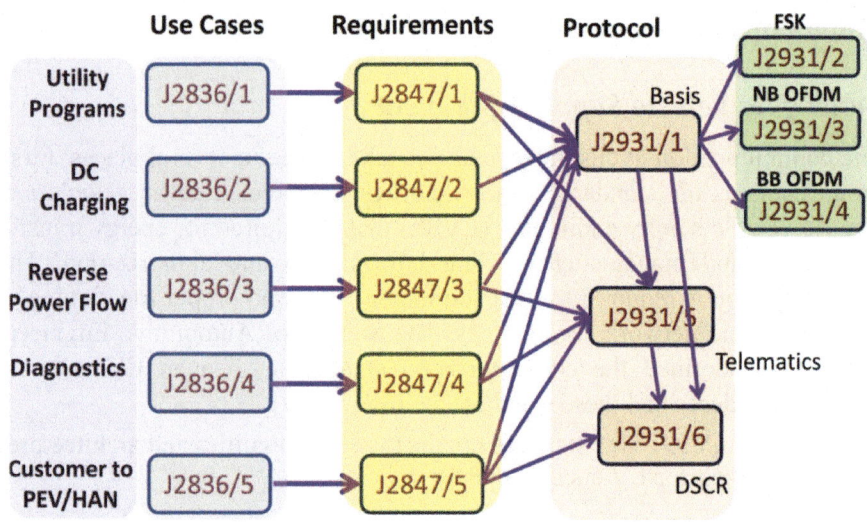

**Figure 7:** SAE communication standards.

## *Energy Management Unit to Power Grid*

Visualization of energy consumption clearly helps customers to understand the cost of their energy usage. However, optimal decisions can only be taken by automated management systems [77, 78]. Energy management units (EMU) enables customers to power grid interaction; customers can monitor, control, and optimize their energy consumption. Even though energy management systems have been in the market for a few decades, the widespread adoption has gained pace with the recent advances in smart grid. [77] presents recent advances in EMUs.

EVSE will connect to EMU via home area network (HAN). The most popular technologies for HAN are Zigbee [79, 80], 802.11-based wireless local area network (WLAN), and femtocells. Zigbee offers required coverage (30 to 40 m), data rate (256 Kbps), low power usage, and deployment cost. In fact, it has a considerable market share in utility world [7, 8]. The ubiquity of 802.11-capable devices makes WLAN a strong candidate for HAN. The details of WLAN technology is given in the next section. A comprehensive summary is presented in Table 3.

**Table 3:** Summary of candidate wireless technologies for IoEVs

|  | Latency | Throughput | Security | Scalability |
|---|---|---|---|---|
| WiFi |  |  |  |  |
| IEEE 802.11a | L | H | M | M |
| IEEE 802.11b | L | M | M | L |
| IEEE 802.11g | L | H | M | L |
| IEEE 802.11n | L | H | M | M |
| 3G |  |  |  |  |
| UMTS/HSPDA | M | M | H | H |
| EVDO | M | M | L | H |
| 4G |  |  |  |  |
| LTE/HSPA+ | L | H | H | H |
| IEEE 802.16e | L | H | H | H |

Wireless mesh network can be implemented with WiFi nodes. Low (L): latency (< 250 ms), throughput (< 500 Kbps), scalability (< 100 nodes/backhaul node). Medium (M): latency (250 ms to 1 s), throughput (500 to 1,500 Kbps), scalability (< 100 to 1,000 nodes/backhaul node). High (H): latency (> 1 s), throughput (> 1,500 Kbps), scalability (> 1,000 nodes/backhaul node).

Femtocells are usually employed as access points of cellular networks. This technology uses customer's broadband, DSL, etc. to connect to the wireless carrier's core network. This way, femtocells offer required indoor coverage and capacity for smart grid applications. Communication technologies with a special focus on security for home area networks is presented in [81].

For residential charging, the communications between EMU and the power grid is supported by the existing advanced metering infrastructure (AMI) network [82]. There are several candidates for this purpose.

*Power line communications (PLC):* PLC is a strong candidate for EMU to grid interaction. The main motivation for PLC is that already existing grid infrastructure reaches every EMU that wants to charge an EV. There are three different types of PLC technologies which are classified by the used frequency band and data rate. Broadband PLC uses 1.8 to 250 MHz frequency band and physical data rate varies between a few megabits to hundreds of megabits. Narrowband PLC operates in the 3 to 500 kHz band and provides lower data rates. Third type of PLC communications is ultra narrow band technology, which is also the oldest type of all three. It only provides data rate around hundred bits per second [83].

Several millions of PLC-based communications have already been deployed globally [84]. Moreover, for EV to EVSE communications, PLC supports an apparent physical association that cannot be achieved by its wireless alternatives. Another distinctive advantage is that the cost of PLC deployment is relatively low when compared to other wireline options and can be comparable to wireless technologies.

However, there are several disadvantages for PLC. First, the communication medium is harsh and noisy. Second, transformers cause high attenuation which limits the range of the communication. Repeaters can be employed to overcome this problem, but additional cost should be taken into account beforehand. The final disadvantage is that regulations in some countries limits the use of PLC. For instance, PLC is not allowed for indoor environments in Japan [85].

*White-space networking:* The long term assignment of wireless spectrum to parties like digital TV broadcasters has created inefficient use of ISM band. Fatemieh, 2010 [86] proposes to use TV white spaces to meet communication requirements between users and the grid. IEEE 802.22 is the wireless regional area network (WRAN) standard that uses white spaces in the spectrum. The use of this technology offers the following benefits. It allows high data rates in a cost-effective way. White space networking has deep penetration and long range transmission capabilities, which would eliminate the need for complex designs (for EMU to data aggregation units). Also, high coverage can easily be achieved using white spaces. IEEE 802.11af, also referred to as 'White-Fi' and 'Super Wi-Fi' is a recent proposal that allow WLAN operation in TV white space spectrum in the VHF and UHF bands [87, 88]. It uses cognitive radio technology to transmit on unused TV channels, with the standard taking measures to limit interference for primary users, such as analog TV, digital TV, and wireless microphones.

However, white-space networking is challenging. Available white spaces must be detected and interferences with the incumbents should be avoided. The underlying network should be able to run for varying bandwidths. Also, there are issues related to operation and management of the network [85, 86].

*Wired infrastructure:* Another option might be to build a wired infrastructure. Dedicated communication links give utilities full control over the network and reduce the reliance on the communication infrastructures operated by third parties. However, building such wired infrastructures is very costly. On the other hand, if the two-way communications is going to be a part of the power grid for the next century, it might be logical to build such an infrastructure gradually over time.

*Customer's broadband:* One school of thought suggests to use commodity broadband technologies, e.g., digital subscriber lines (DSL) or cable. The capital expenditures (CAPEX) for this case are lower, as the main communication infrastructure has already been deployed. Moreover, commodity broadband technologies uses Internet protocol (IP), so it can be easily connected to other ubiquitous IP-based communication networks. In a recent deployment, a DSL network was used as an underlying communication technology in Boulder, Colorado [89]. Nonetheless, there are several handicaps. The number of broadband connections is lower than the number of power meters. This is especially the case in developing countries. Moreover, the down times in some deployments is unacceptable for critical smart grid applications.

*Other technologies:* Mesh networks [85] have been proposed as alternative communication technology for AMI networks. Mesh networks tend to use different forms of wireless networks, i.e., IEEE 802.11, 3G/4G/5G, and mesh type of radio configuration. This choice is subject to technical, strategic, and even legal constraints. We present a detailed overview of such technologies in the next sections. In Table 4, we present an overview of candidate technologies and network technologies such as 3G/GSM, 4G/LTE (via smart apps such as [90, 91]).

**Table 4:** Candidate communication technologies customer-to-grid interaction for garage charging

| Technology | Pros | Cons |
| --- | --- | --- |
| Power line communications | Every EV owner has an access. Easy penetration | Indoor applications are not allowed in every country. Regulatory and technical issues |
| White-space networking | High penetration and coverage | Require technologies to operate at varying bandwidths |
| Utility-owned wired infrastructure | Full control over the network. No need for interoperability among various standards | Very high cost and cost of ownership is not clear |

| Fixed broadband | Low cost (customers already have it) | Level of broadband deployment can be problematic |
|---|---|---|
| Wireless cellular networks | Easy adoption with already existing structure | Coverage is limited in developing countries |
| WiFi mesh network | Low cost, unlicensed frequency band | May require complex designs |

An overview of the communication technologies for garage charging is presented in Figure 8 and summarized in Tables 5 and 6. Note that the communication requirements for the EV to EVSE is in the orders of milliseconds, while EVSE to EMU communication can occur in the order of seconds. Finally, the EMU can communicate with the grid in the order of minutes (typically every 15 min). In the next section, we will provide a comprehensive overview of such communication requirements.

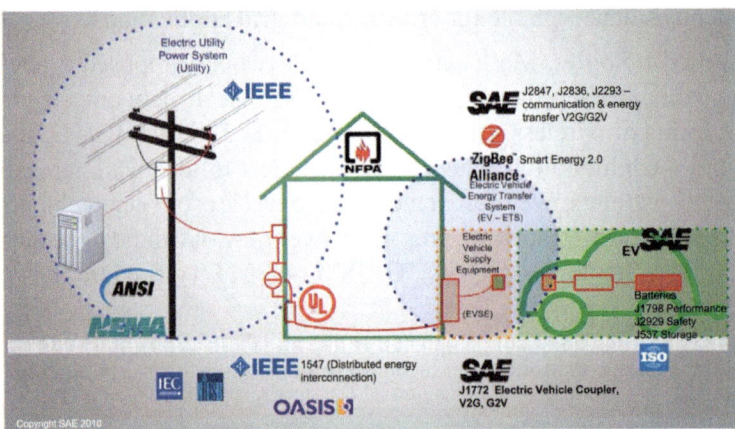

**Figure 8:** Overview of electric vehicle energy transfer standards (used with permission of SAE International [92]).

**Table 5:** Overview of communication standards for IoEVs

| End users | Application | Name of standards and technologies |
|---|---|---|
| EV-EVSE | Energy transfer - garage charging | SAE J2293, SAE J2836/1, J2847/1, SAE J2836/2, J2847/2, SAE J2836/3, SAE J2847/3, SAE J2836/4, J2847/4, SAE J2931, IEC 61851-23, IEC 61851-24 |

| EVSE - Energy Management Unit (EMU) | Home area network | Zigbee, 802.11, HomePlug |
|---|---|---|
| Customer (EMU) - grid | Garage charging, load shifting, valley filling, energy trading | PLC, 3G/4G/WiMAX/LTE/5G, WMN, TV white space, DSL, cable |
| Mobile EV - control center | Public charging | 3G/4G/WiMAX/LTE/5G, WMN |
| Inter-control center | Public charging | IEC 60870-6/TASE.2 |

Table 6: Summary of findings: communications needs and requirements for IoEVs

| Application | EV perspective | | Grid perspective | |
|---|---|---|---|---|
| | Communication needs | Communication requirements | Communication needs | Communication requirements |
| Public charging | Locate and reserve charging station | High availability, service differentiation may be required | Load balancing among neighboring stations | QoS requirements increases with EV population |
| Residential charging | Respond to price updates to minimize charging cost | Part of AMI network (see [85]) | Valley filling to better utilize power generation | Price updates sent every 15 min. Requirements for AMI hold |
| Energy trading via V2G | Sell part of stored energy to make profit or use stored energy during peak hours | High security and availability | Decrease the volume of storage medium needed by purchasing energy from EV fleets | The same as EV perspective |

## Mobile EV to Control Center Communications

Mobile EVs use public fast charging stations to fill up their batteries. Customer demand varies both spatially and temporally (e.g., downtown areas during rush hours) [37]. Also, the current status of the power grid limits grid operators to deploy the required number of charging stations. Hence, customer demand should be balanced among neighboring stations through the use of communication infrastructures. Thus, the ability to share data for mobile EVs becomes a necessity. In Figure 9, we present an overview of message exchange in electric vehicle networks.

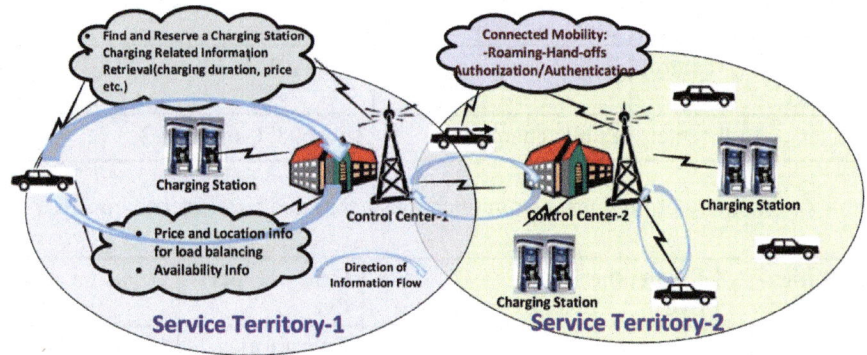

**Figure 9:** Internet of electric vehicles.

There are several wireless communication technologies that are projected to support 'electric mobility'. Two strong candidates are cellular network communications and wireless mesh networks.

## *Cellular Network Communications*

For the short term, ubiquitous public cellular networks can provide required communication coverage in a cost-effective way. Moreover, cellular operators offer service solutions for smart grid applications. Power meter manufacturers embed communication modules to enable use of cellular communications. For garage charging and vehicle-to-grid applications data (e.g., power usage, price, etc.) are exchanged periodically (typically around every 10 to 15 min). Most cellular networks have sufficient capabilities to support the required communication medium. Further, cellular networks have the following advantages:

1) cellular communication technology is mature enough to meet smart grid needs;

2) since all cellular networks operate on licensed spectrum, there is no need to pay for unlicensed bands; and

3) cellular networks are scalable enough to connect huge number of EVs.

Worldwide interoperability for microwave access (WiMAX) is another candidate. WiMAX offers high capacity, wide coverage, low latency, low per-bit cost, and required quality of service capabilities. For example, garage charging applications generate small amount of traffic, but the projected number of connections is very high. For mobile EVs, high data rate is needed to support location based applications. In most cases, in-vehicle application requires wide coverage, high throughput, and QoS support. WiMAX has required capabilities to handle the transmission of such data. In addition, mobile data service based on 4G long term evaluation (LTE) is becoming more popular as it can provides browsing experience comparable to wired connections. As of August 2013, there are more than 176 million LTE customers exist in the globe, and this number is expected to grow exponentially and exceed 1.3 billion by the end of 2018 [93]. Hence, 4G/LTE can provide a ubiquitous communication for EVs.

On the other hand, public charging applications require mobility support. As the mobile user moves faster, the supported data rate decreases. In Figure 10, we compare wireless communication networks according to mobility and throughput. 2.5G, 3G, 4G (WiMAX and LTE), and the upcoming 5G offer required connectivity for mobile EVs. IEEE P2030 standard [94] presents possible communication interfaces. The connection to central controller or telematics provider can be established by either equipment manufacturers OEMS or wide area communication.

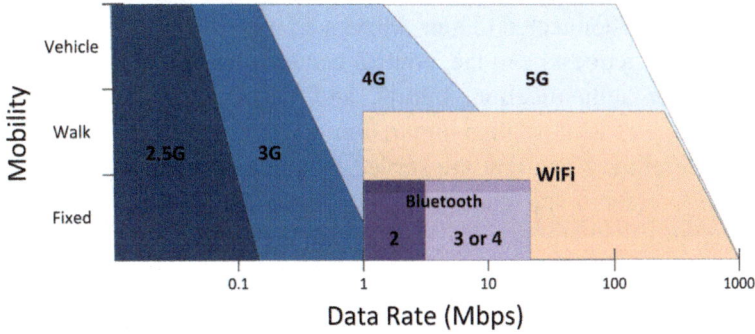

**Figure 10:** Data rate vs. mobility.

## *Wireless Mesh Networks*

Wireless mesh networks (WMNs) are qualified to deliver required connectivity to EV drivers and the power grid. Moreover, their low cost, high scalability, self-healing, and self-organizing nature along with mobility support makes WMNs a very strong candidate. WMNs can provide high bandwidth and seamless handover capabilities at high speeds (almost the same quality as third generation technologies) [95]. Also, WMNs are compatible with other networks: they can be integrated with other existing networks (e.g., IEEE 802.15, IEEE 802.16, cellular networks, etc.). Further advantages of WMNs include its higher physical layer transmission rate than most cellular networks and coverage can be extended without using extra channel capacity.

Several companies already deployed WMNs for smart grid applications [96, 97]. As EV population continue to grow fast, the need for a dedicated communication infrastructure will become more important. Especially in urban environments, where 'xG' networks are overloaded or not deployed yet, WMNs will become even more important. In [97], a medium city is successfully deployed with wireless mesh networks to support required connectivity to electric vehicles.

On the other hand, WMNs have several disadvantages. In urban environments, network coverage can be affected by interference and fading. Available bandwidth can reduce in the case of possible loop problems [8]. In order to enjoy benefits of WMNs, research efforts are being shown to solve complexity of these networks.

## Inter-Control Center Communications

As shown in Figure 9, different regions are served by different service providers. Each control center monitors and controls registered customer demand at each charging facilities connected to him. Moreover, when a customer from another service territory requests service, control centers should be able to exchange information for authentication, billing, and location. Currently, all-electric range of most EVs is more than hundred miles [2]. This range enables drivers to go to different regions that are served by some other utility (e.g., Central Europe etc.). Hence, the communication network should be able handle possible hand-off situations.

At the present time, utilities employ IEC 60870-6/TASE.2 (International Electrotechnical Commission Tele-control Application Service Element) communication standard for information exchange between control centers, utilities, and power pools [8]. However, additional communication features may be needed to keep track of mobile users.

## Further Communication Needs

Further, communication needs exist between EV and the charging equipment for the following periods: pre-charging, during the charging, and post-charging. In order to start the charging process, the EV and the charging equipment must be physically associated. Additional messages should be exchanged for identification and authorization purposes. During the charging, several parameters such as charging duration, direction of energy flow, available power and energy rate, vehicle status information (e.g., battery state of charge, usable battery energy, etc.) are needed to be exchanged between EV and EVSE. Precise measurement of transferred energy is also important for billing purposes [94].

# COMMUNICATION REQUIREMENTS AND PERFORMANCE METRICS

The end-to-end communication requirements for EV network applications require highly available, reliable, and secure communications. Different applications, such as V2G, load shedding, etc., may have different communication requirements. The use cases for EV applications serve as a starting point for communication requirements. A detailed use case analysis is presented in [98, 99]. Each use case scenario defines the end-users (e.g., customer, utility, EV, etc.), their types (e.g., individual, organization etc.), content, size, and the frequency of the required message exchange. In this section, we discuss communication system requirements and associated performance metrics.

## System Reliability and Availability

The successful management of EVs requires extensive use of reliable and (highly) available IoEV. The loss of availability is going to terminate the grid to customer interaction. During these isolation periods, customers will not be able to receive electricity prices, hence cannot optimally adjust and schedule their electricity usage. In fact, the cost of unavailability can be more severe. For instance, for garage charging scenarios, uncontrolled EV charging may lead to unwanted peaks and may overload some of the grid components, such as the distribution transformer.

Considering the aforementioned use cases, [100] explores the reliability requirements for home charging EV applications. The authors show that 11 different messages are used, and the minimum reliability requirement varies between 98.8% to 99.5%. This variety is attributed to some messages, such as vehicle identification number (VIN) information request, error messages related to EV charging rate, require high availability than other types.

The connectivity loss for mobile EVs is even more critical. Unavailability will refrain customers from locating and scheduling charging stations. Similarly, it may lead to suboptimal station selection both for customers (more expensive) and the grid operator (busy stations or long waiting lines may cause customer dissatisfaction) [101, 102]. There are a handful of studies that quantify the cost of bad communication system performance. For instance, garage charging applications use AMI network. In a related study, [103] presents a generic AMI communication network and performs availability analysis for each component (e.g., home area network, 3G network, etc.). Moreover, it quantifies the cost of unavailability due to suboptimal power allocation.

There exist quite a few studies that present the performance evaluation of related wireless communication technology (e.g., UMTS etc.) [104–106]. A similar approach can be applied to mobile EV networks to quantify the cost of suboptimal charging station selections. On the other hand, redundancy design may help to improve system reliability. Employing redundant communication links between critical nodes such as data aggregation units to utility or between control centers. We present the overall system in Figure 11.

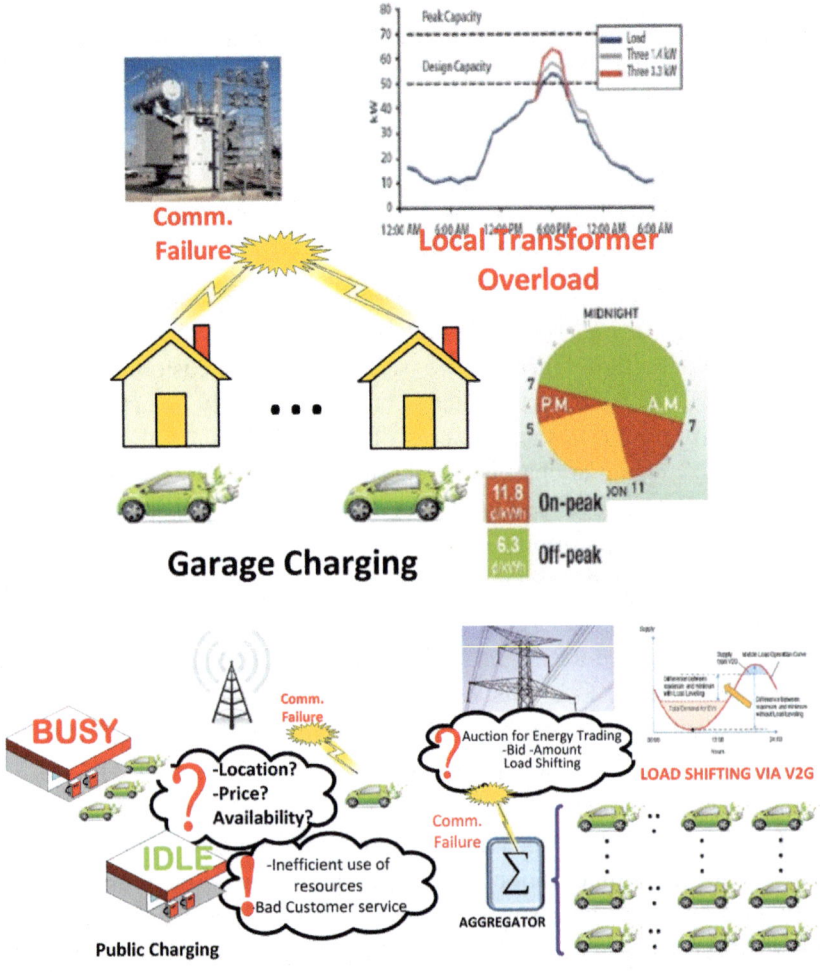

**Figure 11:** The negative effects of communication unavailability. Left panel:

uncontrolled charging [2], middle panel: suboptimal charging station selection, and right panel: unable to support required storage medium for load shifting [107].

## Quality-of-Service

The quality-of-service (QoS) needs are gradually increasing as the EVs gain widespread acceptance. Since centralized or decentralized control of EVs is done via price signals, degradation in communication system performance may cost. In [108], authors define QoS requirements for general smart grid communications using in terms of communication delays and outage probability.

The QoS requirements can be slightly different for mobile EVs and the grid operator. For instance, IEEE P2030 [94] states that an EV can afford to have a few seconds of latency to retrieve location, pricing, and availability information. However, in order to respond to the huge number of queries (approximate number depends on the EV penetration level) grid operator have to receive the information in a timely manner.

Even though today's mobile broadband technologies (e.g., 3G/HSPA/EV-DO etc.) promise high throughput and low latency communications, in some occasions, there can be a degradation in the user experience. This is attributed to the network capacity saturation in some areas. For instance, [109] shows that customer demand is going to exceed network capacity, for most metropolitan areas, in the next years. This will force time critical data transfer from EVs to compete with other bandwidth demanding applications such as video streaming and voice over IP.

On the other hand, the most recent mobile WiMAX/LTE technology can support necessary QoS requirements. More specifically, WiMAX offers four different QoS level, namely [110, 111]

1) unsolicited grant service (UGS);

2) real-time polling service (rtPS);

3) non-real time polling service (nrtPS); and

4) best effort (BE).

UGS can support low latency and low jitter and prioritize EV charging related data transfer. However, 4G technologies are not available everywhere and a limited but growing number of devices support 4G connectivity. Finally, some discussion is already undergoing about new 5G technologies [112].

In some areas, wireless mesh networks have been deployed using different versions of the IEEE 802.11 protocol. The cost of building such infrastructure is not expensive and does not require permission, since they function in the open 2.4 GHz or 5 GHz band. These networks can provide application access priority (starting from 802.11e and more recently with the 802.11ac), but they do not guarantee any strict QoS [113–116]. In addition, they have a limited range, which means that vehicles that want to communicate through them may be in a wireless blind spots.

## Cyber-Physical Security

The power grid is vital to human life and with the integration of information systems, the power grid becomes a huge cyber-physical system. The grid's unique nature poses new series of security challenges. The components of the power grid are vulnerable to a variety of new cyber-security threats that could affect national security, pubic safety, and revenues.

There has been an increasing interest in smart grid security aspect [117–126]. In [120], the authors present cyber-physical security overview of smart grid communication infrastructure. Su, 2012 [119] presents security threats for electric vehicle networks. They conclude that electric vehicle networks have the following security requirements:

1) availability (discussed in the previous section);
2) confidentiality (prevent attackers to obtain private information);
3) integrity (block unauthorized users from changing the data); and
4) authenticity.

If the security of the EV network communication is not provided at a high level, an adversary can impact the EV network in various ways. A hacker can route customers to a specific charging station to create chaos for drivers. Similar to a home appliance, the garage charging is also programmed to fill up EV battery when price is low. An adversary can launch an attack to inject negative prices to increase power usage (of automated appliances), which may result in a peak or spike in electricity usage. Similarly, price modification can cause instabilities in V2G energy trading.

In [126], the authors present the security threats in physical layer of wireless communications for smart grid applications. Moreover, [125] defines the attack types for smart grid communication networks. They introduce three different kinds of smart grid attacks:

- *Data injection:* The type of attacks in this category falsify the meter measurements (e.g., garage charging) to mislead the power grid operator. The main purpose of this type of attack is to create revenue loss.

- *Vulnerability:* This type of attack is caused by the failure of a communication channel or a device. Information on the feedback channel can be unsynchronized due to erroneous communication links.

- *Intentional:* In this type, the attacker has the full knowledge of network topology. It can be carried out by targeting the node with the highest degree with a denial-of-service attack.

Several organizations including IEEE (1402-2000, IEEE Guide for Power Substation Physical and Electronic Security), North American Electrical Reliability Corporation - Critical Infrastructure Protection (NERC-CIP), National Infrastructure Protection Plan (NIPP), and National Institute of Standards and Technology (NIST) [118]. In the second volume of NISTIR 7628 [122], NIST documents a comprehensive overview of guidelines for smart grid cyber-security. This documents contains several use cases concerning the security issues with EV charging. In [124], the authors evaluated the effectiveness of NISTIR framework for an electric vehicle charging infrastructure case. They claim that NISTIR 7628 framework is not strong enough in device authentication and protecting the protecting the location privacy of mobile EVs.

## Scalability

As the EV population is continuously going to increase for the next couple of decades, the underlying communication networks should be scalable enough to support required functionalities. Such scalability concerns can be alleviated by employing IP-based network designs. Considering the big smart grid picture on mind, it is very likely that that required communication networks will be based on IPv6. Moreover, IP-based solutions offer huge cost savings in deployment and maintenance [7].

## Capacity

Since EV applications generate data traffic, the underlying communication networks should be have enough capacity to meet minimum communication requirements. For mobile EVs, the required capacity can be measured in bits-per-second. However, for residential charging applications, the communication capacity is more likely to be measured in the maximum number of advanced meters (or smart meter) that it can support at a time (since most messages types/lengths are standard).

In a related study [127], researchers analyze the capacity of a linear chain network topology for an AMI network. They also compute the required network capacity for different amounts of nodes, varying message lengths, and meter reading periods (e.g., every 10 or 15 min). They also extend their study for larger networks with different communication infrastructures.

On the other hand, capacity comes at the expense of cost. Capacity planning is a critical step as it includes trade-offs that could affect the success of EV applications. Initial deployments may seem easy and does not require high capacity networks, since EV population will be low. This will allow utilities to have a good head start with low installation cost. However, short term solutions are likely to fail to scale. Hence, the expected exponential growth in EV population may force utilities to replace the entire communication network.

## Interoperability

The proper functioning of EV-related applications depends on different entities such as power system and communication system to work together. According to the US Independence and Security Act (2007), the NIST is appointed to be the main global coordination of such smart grid interoperability.

In its framework [128], NIST identifies the domains of the smart grid as: customers, markets, service providers, operations, bulk generation, transmission, and distribution. NIST's conceptual framework also provides the required information exchange between these domains. EV applications are unique in the sense that they bridge most of these domains. For instance, home charging deals with distribution network and the service provider, V2G deals with markets, and public fast charging is related to bulk transmission and customers.

IEEE P2030 Smart Grid Interoperability Series of Standards aims to establish an interoperability framework to develop IEEE-based standards on power system applications and control through the use of communication infrastructures. The first of this series IEEE Std 2030 (2011) presents communication and information networks interfaces for different domains of the smart grid. Moreover, this reference model presents the communication requirements for each interface (e.g., security, availability, latency etc.).

In addition, the IEEE P2030.1 Working Group [129] develops a draft guide for electric-sourced transportation infrastructures. Also, P2030 task force-3 defines communication requirements between devices in the smart grid. They are going to describe the network, transport, and session layers (from OSI reference model). Recently, IEEE has established a new technical advisory group (IEEE 802.24) which will work with multiple IEEE 802 working group standards of which are very essential for smart grid communications [130].

## Measurement-Based Studies

Previous paragraphs show that wide-area wireless communication technologies will be predominant role in EV network communications. On the other hand, since the number of mobile internet users has flourished, the user experience deviated significantly from theoretical results. Hence, there is a need for detailed measurement based studies to understand and predict the performance of the wireless technology and quantify the effects of performance degradation.

There are only a handful of measurement-based studies that focuses on the performance of the wireless network (WiFi, 3F (UMTS), EV-DO, and WiMAX) [131–133]. In [133], authors conducted a measurement study to evaluate the performance of the mobile Internet access with 3G (UMTS) and WiFi networks. The measurement was carried out in Seattle, San Francisco, and Amherst. Across all cities, the average availability of 3G and WiFi is 87% and 11%, respectively. The details of their findings is presented in Table 7. Then, they proposed a hybrid framework to improve the availability of 3G by augmenting it with WiFi.

**Table 7:** Availability performance of wide area wireless technologies [133]

|  | Amherst | | Seattle | | San Francisco |
|---|---|---|---|---|---|
|  | Average | Peak | Average | Peak | Average |
| 3G (UMTS) | 90% | 85.5% | 82% | 79% | 89% |
| WiFi | 12% | 10% | 10% | 8.5% | 11% |

Similarly, [132] presents an architecture to improve end user experience by exploiting (i) channel diversity, (ii) wireless network service provider diversity, and (iii) technology diversity (UMTS, CDMA, etc.). Their results shows that the proposed *Mobile Access Router* architecture decreases the blackout periods considerably and increases average throughput. In addition, [131] shows the results of a city-wide mobile Internet experimentation results. The mobile nodes in their test bed employs both EV-DO and WiFi interfaces. Their focus is on measuring the signal latency and TCP throughput performance. Their results indicate that average latencies varies between 150 to 400 ms and mobile TCP throughput is around 752 Kbps.

## CONCLUSIONS

In this paper, we provided a survey of the communication requirements and technologies for the Internet of electric vehicles. First, we presented the current status of the power grid. We specifically focused on the power generation and distribution networks. We identified the challenges introduced by the projected EV demand. Then, we showed that the EV demand may have disruptive effects in the current information and the IoEV infrastructures that are needed to support, control, and manage the energy transfer between vehicles and the power. Next, we grouped related smart grid applications and surveyed the communication requirements, standards, and candidate technologies for each group. We showed that in the absence of two-way communications, the proliferation of EVs will pose threats to the existing power grid and will not reach projected mainstream success.

In the future, we plan to expand our research in the following ways. The choice of communication technology and standards should consider the performance of the each candidate. It is also worth noting that the importance of performance evaluation will increase as the EVs gain widespread acceptance. For instance, if a central authority receives a few queries (location and pricing information for public charging stations) per minute, the cost of communication delays, unavailability, etc. will be negligible. On the other hand, as the query rate increases, underlying infrastructure should provide high availability and low latency. Thus, it is crucial to quantify the effects of the underlying communication technology.

## REFERENCES

1. Electrification roadmap: Revolutionizing transportation and achieving energy security *Technical report* 2009.
2. Kassakian JG, Schmalensee R: The future of the electric grid: an interdisciplinary MIT study. *Technical report, Technical report, Massachusetts Institute of Technology* 2011.
3. Technology roadmap: Electric and plug-in hybrid electric vehicles *Technical report, International Energy Agency* June 2011.
4. Tesla To Build National Electric Car Charging Network [Accessed: Aug 2014] http://www.forbes.com/sites/toddwoody/2012/09/25/tesla-to-build-national-electric-car-charging-network/
5. ABB Wins Tender for Europes Largest Electric Vehicle Fast-charging Network 125798000353578.aspx [Accessed: Aug 2014] http://www.abb.com/cawp/seitp202/d07e075541462e04c

6. Electric vehicles charging equipments *Technical report, Pike Research* 2011.
7. Yan Y, Qian Y, Sharif H, Tipper D: A survey on smart grid communication infrastructures: Motivations, requirements and challenges. *IEEE Commun. Surv. Tutor* 2012, 15(1):1-16.
8. Gungor V, Sahin D, Kocak T, Ergut S, Buccella C, Cecati C, Hancke G: A survey on smart grid potential applications and communication requirements. *IEEE Trans. Ind. Inform* 2012., 9(1):
9. Su W, Eichi H, Zeng W, Chow MY: A survey on the electrification of transportation in a smart grid environment. *IEEE Trans. Ind. Inform* 2012, 9(1):1-10.
10. Wang W, Xu Y, Khanna M: A survey on the communication architectures in smart grid. *Comput. Netw* 2011, 55(15):3604-3629. 10.1016/j.comnet.2011.07.010
11. Bayram IS, Michailidis G, Devetsikiotis M, Parkhideh B: Strategies for competing energy storage technologies for in dc fast charging stations. In *Proc. IEEE International Conference on Smart Grid Communications*. Tainan City, Taiwan; 2012:1-6.
12. Bayram IS, Michailidis G, Devetsikiotis M: Electric power resource provisioning for large scale public EV charging facilities. In *Proc. IEEE International Conference on Smart Grid Communications*. Vancouver, Canada; 2013.
13. Bloom E: Global building stock database: Commectical and residential building floor space by country and building type (2011-2012).*Technical report, Pike Research* 2012.
14. Falvo MC, Sbordone D, Devetsikiotis M, Bayram I S: EV charging stations and modes: international standards. In *Proc. IEEE International Symposium on Power Electronics, Electrical Drives, Automation and Motion*. Naples, Italy; 2014.
15. Transitions to Alternative Transportation Technologies–Plug-in Hybrid Electric Vehicles. The National Academies Press 2010.http://www.nap.edu/openbook.php?record_id=12826
16. Heydt GT, Ayyanar R, Hedman KW, Vittal V: Electric power and energy engineering: the first century. *Proc. IEEE* 2012, 100(Special Centennial Issue):1315-1328.
17. Arnold GW: Challenges and opportunities in smart grid: a position article. *Proc. IEEE* 2011, 99(6):922-927.
18. Wollenberg B, Wood A: *Power generation, operation and control*. John

Wiley&Sons, Inc; 1996.

19. Scott M, Meyer M, Elliot D, Warwick W: Impacts of plug-in hybrid vehicles on electric utilities and reginal US power grids. *Technical report, Pasific Northwest National Laboratory, Palo Alto, CA* 2007.

20. Denholm P, Short W: An evaluation of utility system impacts and benefits of optimally dispatched plug-in hybrid electric vehicles. *Technical report, National Renewable Energy Laboratory* 2006.

21. Parks K, Denholm P, Markel T: Costs and emissions associated with plug-in hybrid electric vehicle charging in the Excel energy colorado service territory. *Technical report, National Renewable Energy Laboratory* 2007.

22. Letendre SRW, Cross M: Plug-in hybrid vehicles the vermont grid: a scoping analysis. *Technical report, University of Vermont Transportation Center* 2008.

23. Shortt A, Malley OM: Quantifying the long-term impact of electric vehicles on the generation portfolio. *IEEE Trans. Smart Grid* 2014, 5(1):71-83.

24. Hadley WH: Impact of plug-in hybrid vehicles on the electric grid. *Technical report, Oak Ridge National Labs* October 2006.

25. Ipakchi A, Albuyeh F: Grid of the future. *IEEE Power Energy Mag* 2009, 7(2):52-62.

26. Shireen W, Patel S: Plug-in hybrid electric vehicles in the smart grid environment. In *Proc. IEEE PES Transmission and Distribution Conference and Exposition*. IEEE; 2010:1-4.

27. Valentine K, Temple WG, Zhang KM: Intelligent electric vehicle charging: rethinking the valley-fill. *J. Power Sources* 2011, 196(24):10717-10726. 10.1016/j.jpowsour.2011.08.076

28. Gan L, Topcu U, Low S: Optimal decentralized protocol for electric vehicle charging. *Proc. IEEE Conference on Decision and Control and European Control Conference* 2011, 5798-5804.

29. Abraham S: National transmission grid study. *Technical report* 2002.

30. Liu C, Chau KT, Wu D, Gao S: Opportunities and challenges of vehicle-to-home, vehicle-to-vehicle, and vehicle-to-grid technologies. *Proc. IEEE* 2013, 101(11):2409-2427.

31. Tushar W, Saad W, Poor HV, Smith DB: Economics of electric vehicle charging: a game theoretic approach. *IEEE Trans. Smart Grid* 2012, 3(4):1767-1778.

32. Wang Y, Saad W, Han Z, Poor HV, Basar T: A game-theoretic approach to energy trading in the smart grid. *IEEE Trans. Smart Grid* 2014,

5(3):1439-1450.
33. Yi P, Zhu T, Jiang B, Wang B, Towsley D: An energy transmission and distribution network using electric vehicles. *Proc. IEEE International Conference on Communications* 2012, 3335-3339.
34. Clement-Nyns K, Haesen E, Driesen J: The impact of charging plug-in hybrid electric vehicles on a residential distribution grid. *IEEE Trans. Power Syst* 2010, 25(1):371-380.
35. Shao S, Pipattanasomporn M, Rahman S: Challenges of PHEV penetration to the residential distribution network. *Proc. IEEE Power Energy Society General Meeting* 2009, 1-8.
36. Kwasinski A, Kwasinski A: Signal processing in the electrification of vehicular transportation: techniques for electric and plug-in hybrid electric vehicles on the smart grid. *IEEE Signal Process. Mag* 2012, 29(5):14-23.
37. Galus MD, Vayá MG, Krause T, Andersson G: The role of electric vehicles in smart grids. Wiley Interdiscip. *Rev. Energy Environ* 2013, 2(4):384-400.
38. Clement-Nyns K, Haesen E, Driesen J: The impact of charging plug-in hybrid electric vehicles on a residential distribution grid. *IEEE Trans. Power Syst* 2010, 25(1):371-380.
39. How the smart grid enables utilities to integrate electric vehicles (white paper) *Silver Spring Networks* 2012.
40. Verzijlbergh RA, Grond MO, Lukszo Z, Slootweg JG, Ilic MD: Network impacts and cost savings of controlled EV charging. *IEEE Trans. Smart Grid* 2012, 3(3):1203-1212.
41. Quinn C, Zimmerle D, Bradley TH: The effect of communication architecture on the availability, reliability, and economics of plug-in hybrid electric vehicle-to-grid ancillary services. *J. Power Sour* 2010, 195(5):1500-1509. 10.1016/j.jpowsour.2009.08.075
42. Sortomme E, Hindi MM, MacPherson SDJ, Venkata S: Coordinated charging of plug-in hybrid electric vehicles to minimize distribution system losses. *IEEE Trans. Smart Grid* 2011, 2(1):198-205.
43. Jian L, H Xue GXu, Zhu X, Zhao D, Shao ZY: Regulated charging of plug-in hybrid electric vehicles for minimizing load variance in household smart microgrid. *IEEE Trans. Ind. Electron* 2013, 60(8):3218-3226.
44. Rotering N, Ilic M: Optimal charge control of plug-in hybrid electric vehicles in deregulated electricity markets. *IEEE Trans. Power Syst* 2011, 26(3):1021-1029.

45. Wang J, Liu C, Ton D, Zhou Y, Kim J, Vyas A: Impact of plug-in hybrid electric vehicles on power systems with demand response and wind power. *Energy Policy* 2011, 39(7):4016-4021. 10.1016/j.enpol.2011.01.042
46. Yilmaz M, Krein PT: Review of the impact of vehicle-to-grid technologies on distribution systems and utility interfaces. *IEEE Trans. Power Electron* 2013, 28(12):5673-5689.
47. Xi X, Sioshansi R: Using price-based signals to control plug-in electric vehicle fleet charging. *IEEE Trans. Smart Grid* 2014, 5: 1-15.
48. Samadi P, Mohsenian-Rad A-H, Schober R, Wong VWS, Jatskevich J: Optimal real-time pricing algorithm based on utility maximization for smart grid. In *Proc. IEEE International Conference on Smart Grid Communications*. Washington D.C., USA; 2010:415-420.
49. Bayram IS, Abdallah M, Qaraqe K: Providing QoS guarantees to multiple classes of EVs under deterministic grid power. *Proc. IEEE International Energy Conference* 2014.
50. Chen L, Suzuki H, Wachi T, Shimura Y: Components of nodal prices for electric power systems. *IEEE Trans. Power Syst* 2002, 17(1):41-49. 10.1109/59.982191
51. Bayram IS, Michailidis G, Devetsikiotis M, Granelli F: Electric power allocation in a network of fast charging stations. *IEEE J. Selected Areas Commun* 2013, 31(7):1235-1246.
52. Alizadeh M, Scaglione A, Thomas RJ: From packet to power switching: digital direct load scheduling. *IEEE J. Selected Areas Commun* 2012, 30(6):1027-1036.
53. Saber AY, Venayagamoorthy GK: Efficient utilization of renewable energy sources by gridable vehicles in cyber-physical energy systems. *IEEE Syst. J* 2010, 4(3):285-294.
54. Lu H, Pang G, Kesidis G: IE, CS&E and EE Depts, Automated scheduling of deferrable PEV/PHEV load in the smart grid. Technical report. *Technical Report CSE-12-004, Pennsylvania State University, CSE Dept* 2012.
55. Waraich RA: 1 plug-in hybrid electric vehicles and smart grid: investigations based on a micro-simulation Transportation Res. *Part C: Emerging Technol* 2013, 28: 74-86.
56. Clement K, Haesen E, Driesen J: Coordinated charging of multiple plug-in hybrid electric vehicles in residential distribution grids. *Proc. IEEE Power Systems Conference and Exposition* 2009, 1-7.
57. Chen S, Ji Y, Tong L: Large scale charging of electric vehicles. *Proc.*

*IEEE Power and Energy Society General Meeting* 2012, 1-9.

58. Chen S, Ji Y, Tong L: Deadline scheduling for large scale charging of electric vehicles with renewable energy. *Proc. IEEE Sensor Array and Multichannel Signal Processing Workshop* 2012, 13-16.

59. Bayram I, Michailidis G, Papapanagiotou I, Devetsikiotis M: Decentralized control of electric vehicles in a network of fast charging stations. In *Proc. IEEE International Global Communication Conference.* Atlanta, GA; 2013.

60. Bayram IS, Michailidis G, Devetsikiotis M: Unsplittable load balancing in a network of charging stations under QoS guarantees. *IEEE Trans. Smart Grid* 2014, 6: 1-11.

61. Gan L, Topcu U, Low S: Optimal decentralized protocol for electric vehicle charging. *Proc. IEEE Conference on Decision and Control and European Control Conference* 2011, 5798-5804.

62. Callaway DS, Hiskens IA: Achieving controllability of electric loads. *Proc. IEEE* 2011., 99(1):

63. Ma Z, Callaway D, Hiskens I: Decentralized charging control for large populations of plug-in electric vehicles. In *Decision and Control (CDC), 2010 49th IEEE Conference On.* IEEE; 2010:206-212.

64. Rotering N, Ilic M: Optimal charge control of plug-in hybrid electric vehicles in deregulated electricity markets. *IEEE Trans. Power Syst* 2011, 26(3):1021-1029.

65. Galus MD, Andersson G: Demand management of grid connected plug-in hybrid electric vehicles (phev). *Proc. IEEE Energy 2030 Conference* 2008, 1-8.

66. Bayram IS, Ismail M, Abdallah M, Qaraqe K, Serpedin E: A pricing-based load shifting framework for EV fast charging stations. *IEEE International Conference on Smart Grid Communications* 2014.

67. Gan L, Topcu U, Low SH: Stochastic distributed protocol for electric vehicle charging with discrete charging rate. *Proc. IEEE Power and Energy Society General Meeting* 2012, 1-8.

68. Gan L, Topcu U, Low S: Optimal decentralized protocol for electric vehicle charging. *Proc. IEEE Decision and Control and European Control Conference* 2011, 5798-5804.

69. Ma Z, Callaway DS, Hiskens IA: Decentralized charging control of large populations of plug-in electric vehicles. *IEEE Trans. Control Syst. Technol* 2013, 21(1):67-78.

70. Fan Z: Distributed charging of PHEV in a smart grid. *Proc. IEEE*

*International Conference on Smart Grid Communications* 2011, 255-260.

71. Su W, M-Y Chow: Performance evaluation of a PHEV parking station using particle swarm optimization. *Proc. IEEE Power and Energy Society General Meeting* 2011, 1-6.
72. Deshpande A, Murali P: Pricing long-term permits and scheduling of electric vehicle charging in parking lots with shared resources. In*Control Conference (ECC), 2013 European*. IEEE; 2013:3584-3589.
73. Jian L, Xue H, Xu G, Zhu X, Zhao D, Shao ZY: Regulated charging of plug-in hybrid electric vehicles for minimizing load variance in household smart microgrid. *IEEE Trans. Ind. Electron* 2013, 60(8):3218-3226.
74. SAE Vehicle electrictification standards [Accessed: June 2014] http://www.sae.org/smartgrid/
75. Gowri K, Pratt RG, Tuffner FK, Kintner-Meyer MCW: Vehicle to grid communication standards development, testing and validation: status report. *Pacific Northwest National Laboratory, Technical report* 2011.
76. Bohn T, Chaudhry H: Overview of SAE standards for plug-in electric vehicle. *Proc. IEEE PES Innovative Smart Grid Technologies* 2012, 1-7.
77. Aman S, Simmhan Y, Prasanna VK: Energy management systems: state of the art and emerging trends. *IEEE Commun. Mag* 2013, 51(1):114-119.
78. Bartram L, Rodgers J, Muise K: Chasing the negawatt: visualization for sustainable living. *Proc. IEEE Comput. Graph. Appl. Conf* 2010, 30(3):8-14.
79. Zigbee Alliance [Accessed: Aug. 2014] http://www.zigbee.org/
80. Mu J: A minimum physical distance delivery protocol based on zigbee in smart grid. *EURASIP J. Wireless Commun. Netw* 2014, 2014(1):108. 10.1186/1687-1499-2014-108
81. Bou-Harb E, Fachkha C, Pourzandi M, Debbabi M, Assi C: Communication security for smart grid distribution networks. *IEEE Commun. Mag* 2013, 51(1):42-49.
82. Standardization roadmap for electric vehicles *Technical report, American National Standards Institute* April 2012.
83. Galli S, Scaglione A, Wang Z: Power line communications and the smart grid. *Proc. IEEE International Conference on Smart Grid Communications* 2010, 303-308.
84. Galli S, Scaglione A, Wang Z: For the grid and through the grid: the role of power line communications in the smart grid. *Proc. IEEE* 2011,

99(6):998-1027.
85. Kulkarni P, Gormus S, Fan Z, Motz B: A mesh-radio-based solution for smart metering networks. *IEEE Commun. Mag* 2012, 50(7):86-95.
86. Fatemieh O, Chandra R, Gunter CA: Low cost and secure smart meter communications using the tv white spaces. *Proc. IEEE International Symposium on Resilient Control Systems* 2010, 37-42.
87. Lekomtcev D, Maršálek R: Comparison of 802.11af and 802.22 standards - physical layer and cognitive functionality. *Elektro Revue* 2012, 3(2):12-18.
88. Flores AB, Guerra RE, Knightly EW, Ecclesine P, Pandey S: Ieee 802.11af: a standard for TV white space spectrum sharing. *IEEE Commun. Mag* 2013, 51(10):92-100.
89. Smart Grid DSL and QWEST Team Up [Accessed: Aug. 2014] http://gigaom.com/cleantech/smart-grid-dsl-current-and-qwest-team-up/
90. Plugshare- EV Charging Station Map [Accessed: Jan. 2014] http://www.plugshare.com
91. Electric Vehicle Charging [Accessed: Oct. 2013] http://www.chargepoint.com
92. Pkrzywa J: SAE ground vehicle standards smart grid. SAE Taipei. Available: http://sae-taipei.org.tw/image/1283265726.pdf
93. Bangerter B, Talwar S, Arefi R, Stewart K: Networks and devices for the 5G era. *IEEE Commun. Mag* 2014, 52(2):90-96.
94. IEEE draft guide for smart grid interoperability of energy technology and information technology operation with the electric power system (EPS), and end-use applications and loads *IEEE P2030/D5.0 February 2011* 2011, 1-126.
95. Sichitiu ML: Wireless mesh networks: opportunities and challenges. *Proceedings of World Wireless Congress* 2005.
96. Tropos Networks gridcom.tropos.com [Accessed: Aug. 2014]
97. Volkswagen Research [Accessed: July 2014] http://www.wireless-wolfsburg.de
98. Burns M: Interoperability knowledge base. http://collaborate.nist.gov/twiki-sggrid/bin/view/SmartGrid/InteroperabilityKnowledgeBase
99. Edison Smartconnect - Industry resource center: 2008-2009 smart grid use cases http://www.sce.com/CustomerService/smartconnect/industry-resource-center/smartgrid-usecase.htm
100. Hossain E, Han Z, Poor HV: *Smart Grid Communications and Networking*.

Cambridge Univ. Press, Cambridge, UK; 2012.

101. Bayram IS, Michailidis G, Devetsikiotis M, Bhattacharya S, Chakrabortty A, Granelli F: Local energy storage sizing in plug-in hybrid electric vehicle charging stations under blocking probability constraints. *Proc. IEEE International Conference on Smart Grid Communications* 2011, 78-83.

102. Bayram IS, Michailidis G, Devetsikiotis M, Granelli F, Bhattacharya S: Smart vehicles in the smart grid: challenges, trends, and application to the design of charging stations. In *Control and Optimization Methods for Electric Smart Grids. Power Electronics and Power Systems, vol. 3.* Edited by: Chakrabortty A, Ilic MD. Springer; 2012:133-145.

103. Niyato D, Wang P, Hossain E: Reliability analysis and redundancy design of smart grid wireless communications system for demand side management. *IEEE Wireless Commun.* 2012, 19(3):38-46.

104. Dharmaraja S, Jindal V, Varshney U: Reliability and survivability analysis for UMTS networks: an analytical approach. *IEEE Trans. Netw. Serv. Manag* 2008, 5(3):132-142.

105. Snow AP, Varshney U, Malloy AD: Reliability and survivability of wireless and mobile networks. *Computer* 2000, 33(7):49-55. 10.1109/2.869370

106. Bruce A: Reliability analysis of electric utility SCADA systems. *Proc. IEEE Power Industry Computer Applications* 1997, 200-205.

107. Inage S-I: Modeling load shifting using electric vehicles in a smart grid environment. *Technical report, OECD Publishing* 2010.

108. Li H, Zhang W: QoS routing in smart grid. *Proc. IEEE Global Telecommunications Conference* 2010, 1-6.

109. Mobile broadband capacity constraints the need for optimization *Technical report, RYSAVY Research* 2010.

110. Papapanagiotou I, Toumpakaris D, Lee J, Devetsikiotis M: A survey on next generation mobile WiMAX networks: objectives, features and technical challenges. *IEEE Commun. Surv. Tutor* 2009, 11(4):3-18.

111. Paschos GS, Papapanagiotou I, Argyropoulos CG, Kotsopoulos SA: A heuristic strategy for ieee 802.16 WiMAX scheduler for quality of service. *45th Congress FITCE* 2006.

112. Wang C-X, Haider F, Gao X, You X-H, Yang Y, Yuan D, Aggoune H, Haas H, Fletcher S, Hepsaydir E: Cellular architecture and key technologies for 5G wireless communication networks. *IEEE Commun. Mag* 2014, 52(2):122-130.

113. Papapanagiotou I, Paschos GS, Kotsopoulos SA, Devetsikiotis M: Proc.

IEEE Global Telecommunications Conference. 2007, 2530-2535.

114. Papapanagiotou I, Paschos GS, Devetsikiotis M: A comparison performance analysis of QoS WLANS: approaches with enhanced features.*Adv. Multimedia* 2007, 2007(1):1.

115. Paschos GS, Papapanagiotou I, Kotsopoulos SA, Karagiannidis GK: A new MAC protocol with pseudo-TDMA behavior for supporting quality of service in 802.11 wireless LANs. *EURASIP J. Wirel. Commun. Netw* 2006, 2006(3):8-189.

116. Papapanagiotou I, Vardakas JS, Paschos GS, Logothetis MD, Kotsopoulos SA: Performance evaluation of IEEE 802.11e based on ON-OFF traffic model. In *Proceedings of the 3rd International Conference on Mobile Multimedia Communications. MobiMedia '07*. ICST, Brussels, Belgium, Belgium; 2007:17-1176. http://dl.acm.org/citation.cfm?id=1385289.1385310

117. Yan Y, Qian Y, Sharif H, Tipper D: A survey on cyber security for smart grid communications. *IEEE Commun. Surv. Tutor* 2012, 14(4):998-1010.

118. Liu J, Xiao Y, Li S, Liang W, Chen CLP: Cyber security and privacy issues in smart grids. *IEEE Commun. Surv. Tutor* 2012, 14(4):981-997.

119. Su H, Qiu M, Wang H: Secure wireless communication system for smart grid with rechargeable electric vehicles. *IEEE Commun. Mag*2012, 50(8):62-68.

120. Mo Y, Kim TH-J, Brancik K, Dickinson D, Lee H, Perrig A, Sinopoli B: Cyber 2013; physical security of a smart grid infrastructure. *Proc. IEEE* 2012, 100(1):195-209.

121. Roadmap to achieve energy delivery systems cyber security *Technical report, The US Department of Energy* 2011.

122. NISTIR 7628: Guidelines for smart grid cyber security strategy, Architecture, and High-Level Requirements. Technical report, National Institute of Standards and Technology

123. Qiu M, Su H, Chen M, Ming Z, Yang LT: Balance of security strength and energy for a PMU monitoring system in smart grid. *IEEE Commun. Mag* 2012, 50(5):142-149.

124. Chan AC-F, Zhou Z: On smart grid cybersecurity standardization: issues of designing with NISTIR 7628. *IEEE Commun. Mag* 2013, 51(1):58-65.

125. Chen P-Y, Cheng S-M, Chen K-C: Smart attacks in smart grid communication networks. *IEEE Commun. Mag* 2012, 50(8):24-29.

126. Lee E-K, Gerla M, Oh SY: Physical layer security in wireless smart grid. *IEEE Commun. Mag* 2012, 50(8):46-52.

127. Karimi B, Namboodiri V: Capacity analysis of a wireless backhaul for metering in the smart grid. *Proc. IEEE Conference on Computer Communications Workshops* 2012, 61-66.
128. Framework N: Roadmap for smart grid interoperability standards. *National Institute of Standards and Technology* 2010.
129. IEEE P2030.1 Draft Guide for Electric-Sourced Transportation Infrastructure [Accessed: Aug. 2014] http://grouper.ieee.org/groups/scc21/2030.1/2030.1_index.html
130. IEEE 802.24 Smart Grid Technical Advisory Group http://standards.ieee.org/news/2012/802.24tag.html
131. Ormont J, Walker J, Banerjee S, Sridharan A, Seshadri M, Machiraju S: A city-wide vehicular infrastructure for wide-area wireless experimentation. In *Proceedings of the Third ACM International Workshop on Wireless Network Testbeds, Experimental Evaluation and Characterization.* ACM; 2008:3-10.
132. Ott J, Kutscher D: A disconnection-tolerant transport for drive-thru internet environments. *Proc. IEEE Computer and Communications Societies. Proceedings, vol. 3* 2005, 1849-1862.
133. Balasubramanian A, Mahajan R, Venkataramani A: Augmenting mobile 3G using WiFi. *Proceedings of the 8th International Conference on Mobile Systems, Applications, and Services* 2010, 209-222.

# CITATION

## CHAPTER 1
Dale-Marie Wilson, Aqueasha M. Martin and Juan E. Gilbert (2012). iTech: An Interactive Virtual Assistant for Technical Communication, Management of Technological Innovation in Developing and Developed Countries, Dr. HongYi Sun (Ed.), ISBN: 978-953-51-0365-3, InTech, DOI: 10.5772/37455.

## CHAPTER 2
Bridgeford, Tracy; Kitalong, Karla Saari; and Selfe, Richard, "Innovative Approaches to Teaching Technical Communication" (2004). All USU Press Publications. Book 147.

## CHAPTER 3
Brian McNely, Clay Spinuzzi & Christa Teston (2015) Contemporary Research Methodologies in Technical Communication, Technical Communication Quarterly, 24:1, 1-13, DOI: 10.1080/10572252.2015.975958.

## CHAPTER 4
Arcese, G.; Campagna, G.; Flammini, S.; Martucci, O. Near Field Communication: Technology and Market Trends. Technologies2014, 2, 143-163.

## CHAPTER 5
Islam Safak Bayram and Ioannis Papapanagiotou, "A survey on communication technologies and requirements for internet of electric vehicles," DOI: 10.1186/1687-1499-2014-223.

# INDEX

## A

advanced metering infrastructure (AMI) 293
automatic speech recognition (ASR) 4

## C

computer-supported cooperative work (CSCW) 231

## D

digital subscriber lines (DSL) 295
Disciplinarity 86

## E

electrictrification 278
Electric vehicles (EVs) 277
Energy management units (EMU) 292

## F

faculty activity report (FAR) 37
Fund for the Improvement of Post-Secondary Education (FIPSE) 64

## G

Geographic Information Systems (GIS) 99
graphical user interface (GUI) 6
grounded theory (GT) 232
GSMA (Group Special Mobile Association) 256
GSM (Group Special Mobile) 256

## H

home area network (HAN) 292
human–computer interaction (HCI) 231

## I

interactive television (ITV) 49
Interdisciplinarity 85
International Electrotechnical Commission (IEC) 291
Internet of electric vehicles (IoEV) 277
Internet protocol (IP) 295
iTech 1, 2, 3, 4, 5, 6, 7, 8, 9, 10, 11, 12, 13, 14, 15, 16, 17, 21, 22, 24, 25, 26, 319

## K

Knowledge Repository (KR) 5

## L